TEACHING HANDICAPPED STUDENTS

TEACHING HANDICAPPED STUDENTS

Colleen J. Mandell
Bowling Green State University

Veronica Gold
Bowling Green State University

WEST PUBLISHING COMPANY
St. Paul ■ New York ■ Los Angeles ■ San Francisco

Copy Editor: Barbara Paul
Cover Art: *The Parakeet and the Mermaid* by Henri Matisse.
Stedelijk Museum, Amsterdam
Design: Lucy Lesiak Design
Compositor: Carlisle Graphics

Photographs on pages 8, 34, 52, 139, 235 and 298 by Jeffrey Grosscup. All others by Norma A. Morris.

Printed in the United States of America

Library of Congress Cataloging in Publication Data

Mandell, Colleen J.
Teaching the educationally handicapped.

Includes bibliographies and index.
1. Slow learning children—Education. 2. Mentally handicapped children—Education. I. Gold, Veronica. II. Title.
LC4661.M28 1984 371.9 83-21837
ISBN 0-314-69665-2

To Steven and Paul

Contents

Preface

Before beginning the task of writing this book, we worked with many preservice and inservice level students who wanted to learn how to teach handicapped children and youth. Over time, we noticed that while there were many good texts available, they could be divided into two groups. One type focused on procedures for remediating specific defects within the handicapped learner while the other type tended to emphasize the teacher's roles and responsibilities in the teaching process. In truth, both perspectives are important. Successful teaching requires professionals to be aware of the general skills they need, as well as to consider the individual needs of each handicapped pupil in the classroom.

Teaching Handicapped Students recognizes both views. In fact, understanding the ecology of the learning environment in relationship to both teacher and pupil is the foundation for a successful educational experience for all involved persons. First, emphasis is given in the text to specific skills a teacher must have regardless of a student's, or group of students', learning deficits and strengths. Included is information on using appropriate assessment procedures and developing individualized instructional programs, as well as learning how to evaluate these programs. Also presented is an analysis of the many roles and responsibilities special educators must assume in order to best serve their handicapped students. After developing these comprehensive skills, the reader is exposed to specific types of learning problems as well as related remediation procedures.

ORGANIZATION

This text is organized into three sections. Section I, The Teaching Process, gives a philosophical orientation as well as instructional skills which will assist teachers in providing more effective educational programs to handicapped learners. Specifically this section presents a rationale for using an ecological model in terms of assessment, developing the instructional plan, and delivering instruction. Due to the unique needs of the exceptional adolescent and young adult, related assessment concepts and program selection options are covered in a separate chapter.

The last two sections focus on helping the handicapped student develop specific skills. Section II, Teaching Nonacademic Skills, identifies assessment and instructional strategies to be used to improve and maintain appropriate language, social, and thinking skills. The rationale for grouping these skill areas together is that regardless of the content area being remediated, a student's language development, thinking style, and social and behavorial needs must be taken into consideration when developing and delivering an intervention program.

Section III, Teaching Academic Skills, focuses on intervention approaches for improving handicapped students' reading, written expression, and arithmetic skills. Included within each of these chapters is a discussion of current remediation techniques, suggestions for realistic intervention in the regular classroom, and appropriate intervention strategies for use in the home.

PEDAGOGICAL AIDS

To assist students in mastering the concepts presented in the text, the following pedagogical aids are used:

- A *Critical Incident* introduces each chapter in Section I, The Teaching Process, to emphasize a current issue related to the chapter content. The purpose of these critical incidents is to highlight the impact of environmental and instructional variables on one's performance as opposed to viewing the handicapped student's disability as the source of school failure.
- Two *Case Studies* are presented at the beginning of chapters in Sections II and III. The purpose of the case studies is to illustrate the learning strengths and weaknesses of an elementary and a junior or senior high handicapped student in relationship to the specific skills being discussed in the chapter. For example, in the Written Expression chapter, the case studies discuss an elementary student's penmanship deficits and a junior high student's outlining and handwriting problems.
- *Applications* are given at the end of each chapter. For those chapters in Sections II and III, the applications illustrate instructional strategies appropriate for each of the two students discussed in the case studies. All of the other chapter applications relate a major chapter concept to a realistic classroom situation. For example, the application for Chapter 2 on noninstructional roles illustrates how one special educator copes with stress in relationship to working with other teachers in her school, while the application for Chapter 3, the assessment chapter, focuses on the special educator's involvement in each phase of the assessment process.
- *Summary Points* are used at the end of the chapters to reinforce major concepts covered within the chapter body.
- A list of *Suggested Readings* for each chapter is included to direct you to a more in-depth treatment of the concepts discussed throughout the chapter. Each list is current but should not be viewed as complete. There are many excellent texts written on each topic. However, the list should provide you with a starting point in your search to learn more information on teaching handicapped students.

ACKNOWLEDGMENTS

Writing a textbook is truly a major project requiring support of family, colleagues, and friends. We gratefully acknowledge the following reviewers for their valuable insights and contributions.

Robert Algozzine
University of Florida

Kenneth R. Beckman
Illinois State University

Austin W. Bunch
University of Mississippi

Anna Gajar
Pennsylvania State University

Alex B. Johnson
Winston-Salem State University

Jimmy D. Lindsey
Jacksonville State University (Alabama)

Linda Higbee Mandlebaum
Bowling Green State University (Ohio)

Barbara Wasson
Moorhead State University (Minnesota)

John W. Wilde
University of Missouri

In preparing and developing this text, we recognize Ruth Johnson, for her diligent efforts and fine work. Also special thanks to Tammy Schimoller Ummler for research, and Donna Pulschen, Norma Morris, Valerie Pocock, Denise Epke, and Donna Michel for manuscript preparation.

All of the staff at West Publishing Company were helpful and supportive of this project. We could not have asked for more. Thanks.

The development of this project was at times a challenge in terms of the life obstacles and events that intermittently showered our paths. Thank you, Clyde, for caring about us as people. Your constant acceptance was a motivating force.

Colleen J. Mandell
Veronica Gold

TEACHING HANDICAPPED STUDENTS

CHAPTER 1 An Ecological Perspective for Teachers

OUTLINE

I. Introduction
- A. Objectives

II. Critical Incident: The Source of Disturbance—A Matter of Choice
- A. Points for Consideration

III. Identifying Your Philosophy on Teaching the Handicapped
- A. The Child-Centered Pathology Model
- B. The Ecological Model

IV. Identifying the Educationally Handicapped
- A. Traditional Labels: Definitions and Characteristics
  1. *Behavior Disordered*
  2. *Learning Disabled*
  3. *Educable Mentally Retarded*
- B. Rationale for the Educationally Handicapped Concept

V. Summary Points

VI. Review Questions

VII. Application: Effective Teaching Requires Looking Beyond the Label
- A. William: Labeled Educable Mentally Retarded
- B. Carolyn: Labeled Learning Disabled
- C. Terry: Labeled Behavior Disordered
- D. Discussion Points

INTRODUCTION

Each year in the public schools there are students of all ages identified as not profiting from full-time regular classroom instruction. The least restrictive learning environment for many students with learning and behavior problems is the resource room or, for more severely impaired children and youth, a self-contained special education program. These students, representing many types of learners, often have problems not only in content areas, such as reading or math, but also in noncontent areas, such as social adjustment or study and organizational skills.

In order for these handicapped students to reach their potential, they need the instructional expertise of special educators. While each special educator may serve handicapped students in a variety of program models, his or her approach to planning, implementing, and evaluating instruction is systematic and thorough. In a study designed to identify characteristics associated with superior teachers, Westling, Koorland, and Rose (1981) concluded that superior teachers provided individual and small-group instructions, used postyear evaluation techniques, documented student progress, used informal testing procedures, kept records, and were involved with other professionals and parents. Thus, the effective learning environment requires an organized teacher who has an understanding of the importance of each phase of the instructional process and also is able to select the instructional approach and learning strategies that best meet each student's needs. In addition, the effective teacher accepts the wide range of roles and responsibilities he or she must assume in order to provide comprehensive services to handicapped children and youth.

Objectives

Upon completing this chapter, you should be able to

- identify limitations of a child-centered pathology model for teaching handicapped students;
- discuss major premises of ecological theory and their relationship to teaching the handicapped;
- define the term *educationally handicapped* and discuss advantages of its use as opposed to using categorical labels.

Critical Incident: The Source of Disturbance— A Matter of Choice

Midway through the school year, Mrs. Wick, a sixth grade teacher, referred one of her students, Cheryl Karnes, for multifactored assessment. According to Mrs. Wick, Cheryl's academic performance had slipped from low average at the beginning of the year to failing. Specifically, Cheryl's reading skills were noticeably poor. Further, within the past four weeks, Cheryl had completed only one out of seventeen homework assignments. Mrs. Wick concluded that Cheryl was unable to keep up with the rest of the class and would probably have her educational needs better met in a special education learning environment.

After reading the referral information, "Quiet student, shy, no friends, failing . . . ," Kathy Ross, the school psychologist, reviewed Cheryl's past school records. Even though Cheryl's previous classroom performance was not exceptional, it was adequate in all areas except reading. Her fourth and fifth grade teachers reported that although not a "leader," she had several close friends and was well liked by her peers. Reading appeared to be a consistent problem area for Cheryl. Ms. Ross also noted that, like many of the children in the school, Cheryl lived with her mother in a nearby neighborhood known for its poverty and crime.

After the fourth attempt to contact Mrs. Karnes, the school obtained parental permission for a multifactored assessment. Standardized test results indicated that Cheryl's abilities were within the average range of performance; however, she was functioning more than three years below grade level in reading. There was no definite pattern regarding Cheryl's learning style.

During several classroom observations, Ms. Ross noted that Cheryl fell asleep during independent work assignments. At best, she could be described as lethargic. Cheryl appeared timid, almost fragile. Upon questioning Mrs. Wick about Cheryl's behavior, Ms. Ross learned that dozing off in class was typical. Ms. Ross left the classroom wondering, "Why the sudden change in academic performance? Why is she sleeping every day in class?" The pieces just didn't seem to fit.

After spending time with Ms. Ross over a period of several weeks, Cheryl quietly confided that her mother was a prostitute and often took her along in the evenings. An investigation by the welfare department followed, and Cheryl was placed with her aunt.

In-depth multifactored assessment data indicated a significant discrepancy between Cheryl's potential and demonstrated classroom performance. This discrepancy indicated that Cheryl was eligible for special education services as outlined by Public Law 94–142. One of the major requirements of this law is the development and implementation of an **Individualized Educational Plan (IEP)** which outlines the special instructional services to be provided to an individual student with special needs. The Individualized Educational Plan requires a plan of instruction to be written by an educational team to include the following information: (1) statement of the child's current level of educational achievement; (2) annual goals; (3) short term objectives; (4) specific services required for the child to be educated; (5) dates when the services will begin; and (6) methods for evaluating the effectiveness of the planned services. At the committee meeting, it was recommended that Cheryl receive remedial assistance from the resource room teacher for seventy minutes each day. In addition, counseling services were recommended to help her to develop a more positive attitude about her own sexuality as well as deal with the separation from her mother.

Points for Consideration

- *How did Mrs. Wick and Ms. Ross differ in their perceptions of Cheryl?*

Mrs. Wick, focusing on Cheryl's poor academic performance, believed that Cheryl was incapable of doing better in school. She interpreted Cheryl's failure to complete homework assignments as evidence of below-average mental abilities. In addition, Cheryl's frequent sleeping in class was interpreted as an escape from doing difficult assignments. Mrs. Wick believed that Cheryl's problems were innate and that therefore a special education program would be best for her.

Ms. Ross, on the other hand, viewed Cheryl's academic behavior as only one facet of her life. Rather than just identifying learning strengths and weaknesses, Ms. Ross explored other aspects of Cheryl's life, such as the classroom and home environments, to assist her in presenting appropriate and complete educational information to other professionals involved in Cheryl's case. She recognized that Cheryl did indeed have learning problems that made it difficult for her to learn like her peers; however, the psychologist also realized that classroom behavior prompted by events occurring within the home magnified Cheryl's learning deficits.

From this perspective, Cheryl's learning strengths and weaknesses and the events in various facets of her life were given equal consideration. The emphasis was on the interaction between this student and her environment. The psychologist did not assume that low and erratic academic performance was to be expected because of Cheryl's poor socioeconomic background or her abusive home environment. Although these variables may have contributed to poor academic performance, appropriate assessment procedures indicated a significant discrepancy between Cheryl's learning potential and academic performance. This case study poignantly illustrates the impact that a professional's perspective on the cause and nature of learning and behavior problems has in identifying the most appropriate learning environment and individualized instructional program for handicapped students.

- *What professionals were involved in implementing Cheryl's program?*

Handicapped children and youth often have problems that extend beyond the classroom. In this case, Cheryl's emotional development was the responsibility of a psychologist, and her social adjustment was monitored by a caseworker from children's services within the welfare department. Although regular class and resource teachers cannot be expected to solve problems occurring outside the learning environment, they must be aware of them and their possible influence on school performance.

IDENTIFYING YOUR PHILOSOPHY ON TEACHING THE HANDICAPPED

By the time you have your own classroom, you will have a philosophy toward teaching that will have developed from your university experiences as well as experiences accumulated since childhood. Your attitudes on the etiology of learning and behavior problems and on the roles and responsibilities of the special educator will influence the following:

- which areas are to be investigated for collecting pertinent assessment data
- which assessment tools are to be used
- how assessment data are to be analyzed and interpreted
- which service delivery option is the most appropriate placement
- which instructional strategies and materials are to be used
- how the handicapped student's program is to be evaluated

Each of these variables will have a significant impact on the handicapped student's educational career.

The traditional perspective of identifying handicapped students tends to focus on the child as if he or she were being examined under a microscope, section by section. However, as indicated in the above critical incident, this child-centered pathology model does have its inherent weaknesses and dangers. An alternative approach to learning and behavior problems is the ecological perspective.

The Child-Centered Pathology Model

Traditionally, instructional programs for handicapped students have been developed using a **child-centered pathology** approach to identification, remedial assistance, and evaluation. From this perspective, learning and behavior problems are attributed to some type of pathological, behavioral, genetic, neurological, biophysical, or psychological dysfunction within the student. Each involved professional tends to focus only on those deficits related to his or her expertise.

The following case highlights the implementation of this approach. Ten-year-old Sam is placed in a special education program for instruction in all content areas; however, he is integrated into the regular art, music, and physical education classes. In addition, Sam attends two weekly speech therapy sessions and also participates in a weekly group therapy session designed to improve his social interaction skills. The last time Sam's parents, special education teacher, speech therapist, and psychologist met as a team was in May, when his IEP was developed. It is already December, and each team member continues to deliver his or her services without communicating with the others regarding Sam's progress.

In this example, the psychologist attended to Sam's social development; the speech therapist focused on his speech problems; and the special educator concentrated on Sam's academic deficits. This approach to delivering services to handicapped students reinforces the practice of adhering to defined role boundaries. When professionals work independently, with little awareness of or coordination with other specialists, the likelihood of implementing a program that will assist the student in reaching his or her potential is minimized.

The results of a longitudinal study (Ruben and Balow 1971) designed to investigate the prevalence of handicapped children in school indicate that the acceptance of traditional role boundaries and practices is widespread. On the basis of intelligence and readiness tests as well as socioeconomic and neurological data, 967 four-year-olds were identified as normal. At the time of the follow-up study, these children were enrolled in kindergarten through third grade. Their teachers, representing over two hundred school systems, were asked to indicate whether the students were (*a*) placed in special education, (*b*) retained a grade, (*c*) referred for special services, (*d*) a behavior problem, or (*e*) a combination of at least two of the above categories. The results were that 41.1 percent of the children (50.7 percent of the boys and 31.5 percent of the girls) were identified by their teachers as fitting into the above-stated categories. Almost 25 percent of the children were receiving special education or special services. The authors concluded that the "findings suggest that schools and teachers are oriented to a narrow band of expected pupil behaviors which are not consonant with typical behavior patterns . . . any pupil outside of that narrow range is treated as needing special attention" (p. 298).

This tendency for professionals to adhere to strict role boundaries when teaching handicapped pupils has also been reported by Speece and Mandell (1980). Designed to identify regular teachers' perceptions of resource teachers' responsibilities, this research project indicated that remedial assistance for learning and behavior problems associated with handicapped students was viewed to be the responsibility of special educators, not regular teachers. Yet, with an increasing number of handicapped students being placed in both regular and special education classrooms, it is critical that new role boundaries that are more flexible and broader in scope be established.

These results have serious implications for all professionals involved in teaching handicapped children and youth. It cannot be assumed with any degree of accuracy that the source of disturbance is within the child; rather, it is imperative that the school and classroom environments also be examined as possibly contributing to learning problems (Newcomer 1977). It is important to know how a pupil interacts with teachers and others in addition to knowing his or her learning strengths and weaknesses.

The Ecological Model

Ecological theory focuses on the relationship between student and environment, or ecosystem, to explain behavior and to identify intervention strategies. According to Thomas and Marshall (1977), an individual's **ecosystem** is a composite of a variety of physical and social habitats in which that person lives. Examples of social habitats would be student-teacher and student-student relationships. The playground and classroom settings are examples of physical habitats. Instead of viewing the source of disturbance as being within the student, educators with an ecological perspective view the relationships between the student and his or her ecosystem as being disturbed (Rhodes 1967).

Advocates of this approach are not negating that some handicapped students have deficits such as neurological or psychological disturbances. Rather, the point is that behaviors associated with such deficits are dependent upon the environment. Professionals who frequently observe students recognize that behaviors are indeed interrelated, and changes in one behavior will probably result in other behavioral changes (Williams 1977).

Also important to ecological theory is the premise that "the child is an inseparable part of a small social system, of an ecological unit made up of the child, his family, his school, his neighborhood, and community" (Hobbs 1966, 1108). In a discussion on current research practices in special education, Forness (1981) stated that "any single classroom transaction between a teacher and a child represents a minute-by-minute balancing of an array of social, attitudinal, temperamental, motivational, perceptual, linguistic, and cognitive variables" (p. 60). To ignore any of these components in the learning process minimizes success in school for handicapped learners. Because of its comprehensive perspective, the ecological model recognizes the critical role all these variables have in the teaching and learning environment.

Within this ecological framework, several implications regarding teaching practices are evident. First, events that occur in any one of these habitats will have an effect on the others. For example, Timothy, a nine-year-old student placed in a learning disabilities resource room, has a history of doing poorly on his weekly spelling quizzes. This week he earned an *A* on his quiz. The first thing he told his mother when he got home from school was that he got an *A*. She immediately smiled and hugged him. It is critical that teachers recognize the ripple effect that classroom experiences have on other facets of the student's life as well as seeing the importance that out-of-school experiences have within the classroom.

Successful intervention often requires professionals to observe a student's behavior in a variety of settings as well as in the classroom.

A second point to be made is that intervention strategies implemented almost exclusively within the educational habitat are inappropriate and probably will have minimal success (Rhodes 1970). For many handicapped students placed in both resource and regular classrooms, it is apparent that remedial efforts implemented solely in the special education environment will probably be less successful than those implemented in both settings.

Also, programming for the handicapped student requires active involvement by representatives of all the student's habitats, including vocational personnel, parents, regular and special educators, and auxiliary personnel.

According to Thomas and Marshall (1977), the handicapped student's ability to cope with or adapt to all of the demands placed on him or her by all the habitats within the ecosystem depends upon the following factors: the extent of the handicapping condition; recognition of the important role parents have in the adaptation process; the role medical data may have, for example, on educational or vocational decisions; a comprehensive training or educational program based upon specific needs; and finally, involvement of all aspects of the child's community, or ecosystem. From this perspective, success for the handicapped individual is dependent upon professionals and parents working cooperatively.

Another requirement for success is that all habitats be evaluated continually in order to determine if any program modifications are necessary. The dynamic nature of relationships between the student and corresponding habitats and their resulting impact on learning and behavioral development should not be overlooked. Changes in one habitat will often require or lead to changes in other habitats. As a result, the responsibility for helping handicapped students to develop viable skills shifts from the teacher to a team of which the teacher is a member. From an ecological perspective, the whole child, rather than just the disability, becomes the focus of the intervention team.

IDENTIFYING THE EDUCATIONALLY HANDICAPPED

When we talk about **educationally handicapped students**, we are referring to those children and youth who have consistently experienced failure in the traditional learning environment. Often these pupils are labeled as learning disabled (LD), behavior disordered (BD), or educable mentally retarded (EMR). It is interesting to note that each of these labels emphasizes the dysfunction within the student. For example, the terms *disabled, disordered,* and *retarded* all refer back to some aspect of the child.

One would expect these labels to identify or refer to three distinct populations. However, as indicated in the following discussion, there is considerable overlap of the three groups.

Traditional Labels: Definitions and Characteristics

Behavior disordered. The Joint Commission on the Mental Health of Children and Youth (as cited in Long, Morse, and Newman 1980) reported that an emotionally disturbed child is one who has an impairment of age-relevant capacity to perceive the external environment realistically, inadequate impulse control, a lack of rewarding interpersonal relationships, and a failure to achieve appropriate learning levels. Inability to learn, unsatisfactory interpersonal relationships, inappropriate behavior, unhappiness, and repetitive symptoms of illness after stress are characteristics associated with either the **emotionally disturbed** or **behavior disordered** population.

Seriously emotionally disturbed as defined in the Federal Register, is as follows:

(i) The term means a condition exhibiting one or more of the following characteristics over a long period of time and to a marked degree, which adversely affects educational performance:

(A) An inability to learn which cannot be explained by intellectual, sensory, and health factors;
(B) An inability to build or maintain satisfactory interpersonal relationships with peers and teachers;
(C) Inappropriate types of behavior or feelings under normal circumstances;
(D) A general pervasive mood of unhappiness or depression; or
(E) A tendency to develop physical symptoms or fears associated with personal or school problems.

(ii) The term includes children who are schizophrenic or autistic. The term does not include children who are socially maladjusted unless it is determined that they are seriously emotionally disturbed. (*Federal Register* August 23, 1977, p. 42478).

It should be noted that autism has since been removed from the category "seriously emotionally disturbed." Currently children identified as autistic are placed in the category of "other health impaired" (McDowell 1982).

Emphasizing the importance of using operational definitions, Algozzine, Schmid, and Conners (1978) developed the following definition for emotional disturbance:

> The emotionally disturbed child is the student who, after receiving supportive educational assistance and counseling services available to all students, still exhibits persistent and consistent severe to very severe behavioral disabilities which interfere with productive learning processes. This is the student whose inability to achieve adequate academic progress and/or satisfactory interpersonal relationships cannot be attributed primarily to physical, sensory or intellectual deficits (p. 49).

Regardless of the definition used, a set of inappropriate behaviors observed in children in the school setting is described.

Research has shown that the most frequently occurring of these behaviors fall into four major categories: conduct disorders, personality disorders, inadequacy-immaturity, and socialized delinquency (Von Isser, Quay, and Love 1980; Quay 1978). **Conduct disorders** consist of behaviors that differ from expectations set by the school or other social institutions and are "clearly aversive both to adults and other children" (Quay 1978, 9). Behaviors such as overt aggression (both verbal and physical), defiance of authority, disruptiveness, irresponsibility, and negativism are characteristics of this syndrome. **Personality disorders** involve such characteristics as social withdrawal, sensitivity, an inability to have fun, chronic sadness, and other behaviors having a negative impact on the child rather than his or her environment (Von Isser, Quay, and Love 1980). The third category, **inadequacy-immaturity**, consists of behaviors that are developmentally unexpected. Behaviors such as preoccupation, short attention span, excessive giggling, and clumsiness are included in this category. The fourth behavioral pattern, **socialized delinquency**, is associated with the behaviors found in delinquent subcultures. Characteristics of this dimension include involvement in gang activities, cooperative stealing, and truancy.

Learning disabled. Although definitions of learning disabilities are no more standardized than definitions of behavior disorders, psychologists and educators tend to agree that the label **learning disabled** refers to *(a)* children whose learning problems are not due to mental retardation or to environmental, cultural, or economic disadvantage; *(b)* children who have difficulty in understanding or using spoken or written language; and *(c)* children demonstrating a significant discrepancy between their learning potential and actual achievement (Harwell 1979; Glenn 1975). A comparison of one of the first definitions of learning disabilities (Kirk 1962) and the definition cited in Public Law 94–142 clearly illustrates the ambiguity associated with identifying this population. According to Kirk,

> A learning disability refers to a retardation disorder, or delayed development in one or more of the processes of speech, language, reading, spelling, writing or arithmetic resulting from a possible cerebral dysfunction and/or emotional or behavioral disturbance and not from mental retardation, sensory deprivation, or cultural or instructional factors (p. 263).

According to Public Law 94–142, **learning disabilities** refers to the following:

> Those children who have a disorder in one or more of the basic psychological processes involved in understanding or in using language, spoken or written, which may manifest itself in an imperfect ability to listen, think, speak, read, write, spell, or do mathematical calculations. Such disorders include such conditions as perceptual handicaps, brain injury, minimal brain dysfunction, dyslexia, and developmental aphasia. The term does not include children who have learning problems, which are primarily the result of visual, hearing, or motor handicaps, of mental retardation, of emotional disturbance, or environmental, cultural, or economic disadvantage (Public Law 94–142, 1975, Section 602, 4A).

It has been suggested that part of the difficulty in defining learning disabilities is that those trying to do so have assumed that there is homogeneity among this group of children (Reger 1979). In a study of more than five hundred learning disabled children, Klasen (1972) found that the problems that led to their being labeled learning disabled varied: 67 percent had visual perceptual difficulties; 65 percent suffered from anxiety; 44 percent had mixed laterality; 39 percent had poor concentration; 31 percent had low frustration tolerance; and 22 percent had speech disorders. Other problems that have been associated with learning disabled children include lack of motor control, poor memory, hyper- or hypoactivity, behavior problems, and disorders of language (Harwell 1979; Hayden et al. 1978).

Educable mentally retarded. The American Association of Mental Deficiency (AAMD) defines mental retardation as "significantly subaverage intellectual functioning existing concurrently with deficits in adaptive behavior, and manifested during the developmental period" (Grossman 1973, 11). Scores of two standard deviations below the mean on adaptive behavior scales and intelligence tests define deficits in adaptive behavior and subaverage intellectual functioning respectively. **Adaptive behavior** refers to a person's ability to perform in the areas of social responsibility and self-sufficiency relative to what is expected by his or her social, cultural, and age groups.

Most public school educators have come to recognize the fallibilities of intelligence assessment techniques and do accept the limitations of IQ scores. Relatively few, though, have had much experience with tests designed to measure adaptive behavior. In a sense, the use of adaptive behavior for determining eligibility for special education services for the mentally retarded is an idea whose time has come. Unfortunately, it yet lacks the technology to be implemented adequately.

The majority of children classified as mildly or **educable mentally retarded** (EMR) are usually normal in appearance, with no pathological signs of disease or injury. They may well be able to excel in nonacademic school activities but fail in learning activities. Like all children, they are individuals with unique characteristics. What they have in common is their inability to participate successfully in learning activities. Most struggle, are retained or considered for retention, and are finally referred for assessment and possible special education placement.

Many of these children exhibit emotional or behavioral disturbances due to constant frustration and failure to live up to the expectations of teachers, parents, and peers. Although the research evidence is mixed, there does seem to be a tendency for these children to harbor negative self-images (Robinson and Robinson 1976).

There is a wide diversity in the academic and behavioral performance of children classified as educable mentally retarded. Nonetheless, these children usually have a higher frequency of problems in certain areas of learning. In particular, they tend to have deficits in memory, ability to pay attention, verbal communication, motivation, ability to generalize, and understanding similarities and differences (Smith 1974; Neisworth and Smith 1978). In comparison with children with normal intelligence, EMR children have been characterized as exhibiting more speech problems, greater academic difficulties, shorter attention spans, poorer short-term memory, and a delay in development of sensory motor skills (Hutt and Gibby 1979; Becker 1978). Behavior problems and retarded language development have also been noted (Barksdale 1970).

Rationale for the Educationally Handicapped Concept

Upon examination of the definitions and related characteristics of these three populations, it becomes apparent that there is overlap among the groups. The variables that differentiate any one group from the others appear to be the particular subset of characteristics upon which emphasis has been placed and a definition developed. For example, IQ scores differentiate the EMR population from the LD and BD populations (Becker 1978). The LD population is distinguished from the BD and EMR populations in that deficits in academic skill areas are emphasized in the definition. Conduct and personality problems are the distinguishing factors that separate the BD population from the LD and EMR populations.

Too often diagnostic labels focus on characteristics or behaviors within the student with little or no regard for the many home, school, and community variables related to the learning process. Yet the previous discussion on ecological theory underscores the importance of viewing each child's behavior in relationship to all facets of his or her environment in order to plan effective individualized instructional programs. Although students with similar characteristics may be found within as well as across categories, educators cannot assume that these students' individualized educational programs will be similar in nature since each student enters the classroom with his or her own learning style, motivation level, needs, and goals.

SUMMARY POINTS

- How professionals attempt to meet the needs of educationally handicapped students depends, in part, upon where they perceive the sources or causes of the students' problems to be.
- Traditionally, many professionals involved with the educationally handicapped have assumed that learning and behavior problems were within the student. Therefore, intervention efforts focused on the handicapped child with little attention given to the possible influence of environmental variables.
- The ecological perspective in teaching educationally handicapped students views the teacher as one member of the team. Effective program planning and implementation require the participation of professionals from other disciplines as well as parental involvement.
- The ecological model focuses on the handicapped student's behavior in relationship to events occurring within all areas of his or her environment, not only those evident in the classroom.
- There is overlap of the characteristics commonly associated with the learning disabled, behavior disordered, and educable mentally retarded populations. Although each handicapped student may have different educational goals, the instructional methods used to achieve these goals may be similar regardless of the categorical labels.

REVIEW QUESTIONS

1. What definitions and guidelines does your state use to identify learning disabled, behavior disorderd, and educable mentally retarded students? Compare these definitions for similarities and differences.

2. Identify the advantages and disadvantages associated with using both categorical and noncategorical labels for instructional purposes.
3. Discuss the differences between the child-centered pathology model and the ecological model. How might each influence your professional roles and responsibilities?

Application: Effective Teaching Requires Looking Beyond the Label

Since the ecological perspective emphasizes the student and his or her behaviors in various settings, the value of labeling is minimal at best. In fact, the label provides the teacher with little insight into how best to teach any student. The trend toward noncategorical teacher certification, as indicated by Belch (1979), suggests that the actual teaching process is perceived to be similar for the learning disabled, behavior disordered, and educable mentally retarded.

The need for similar alternative teaching strategies, despite the use of three different labels, is apparent in the three cases of educationally handicapped students presented below. Background information and excerpts from each student's IEP are given.

William: Labeled Educable Mentally Retarded

Ten-year-old William Bell lives in inner-city Washington, D.C. The fifth of seven children, he shares a three-room apartment with his brothers, sisters, and parents. Both Mr. and Mrs. Bell have less than a fourth grade education and are considered illiterate. Employment for both parents on a full-time basis is difficult due to their lack of job skills.

Both parents are concerned about William. William was retained in the fourth grade this year in order that he might "learn the material this time around." However, according to his teacher, "he just doesn't seem to catch on."

Based on assessment data, the following strengths and weaknesses were noted:

Strengths:

- Attempts most tasks presented
- Responds to social reinforcement
- Well liked by peers
- Cooperates in both small- and large-group instruction
- Understands basic addition and subtraction concepts
- Spelling is at 3.2 grade level
- Understands sound-symbol relationship for all consonants

Weaknesses:

- Limited verbal expression
- Written expression, especially manuscript writing, is poor
- Limited understanding of following math concepts: time, money, measurement, and fractions
- Unable to discriminate short vowel sounds
- Reading comprehension is three years below grade level
- Lacks motivation to do academic work

Recommendations:

- Special education placement for reading, math, and social studies
- Regular class placement for spelling, art, physical education, and music

Suggested instructional approaches:

- Allow William to spell words orally because of poor handwriting.
- Use concrete or manipulative materials to develop math concepts.

- Use phonetic approach to reading instruction.
- Initial instructional periods should be limited to fifteen minutes.

Carolyn: Labeled Learning Disabled

Mr. and Mrs. Jacobs, both accountants, are perplexed by Carolyn's learning difficulties. According to her fifth grade teacher, "Carolyn really tries her best, but for some reason she has problems keeping up with the other children, especially in language arts and reading. Her written work is barely legible."

The following is a summary of the assessment team's findings and recommendations:

Strengths:
- At grade level in math
- Shy but well liked by peers
- Responds appropriately to teacher's requests
- Good verbal expression; frequently shares travel experiences

Weaknesses:
- Has difficulty expressing thoughts in writing
- Cursive writing is poorly executed
- Word recognition level is at the 2.8 grade level
- Reading comprehension is three years below grade level
- Spelling and reading performance indicates confusion of short vowel sounds
- Unable to copy board work accurately
- Appears frustrated after fifteen- to twenty-minute instruction periods

Recommendations:
- Special education placement for reading, handwriting, and spelling
- Regular class placement for math, gym, music, art, and social studies

Suggested instructional approaches:
- Tests should be administered orally, and Carolyn should respond orally. Avoid written tests.
- Carolyn seems to learn best via the auditory channel; therefore, reading instruction should be phonetic.
- Limit instruction to no more than twenty minutes.
- Instructional settings should be in small-group or one-to-one settings.

Terry: Labeled Behavior Disorderd

Although eleven-year-old Terry Hansen's parents agree that he has always been a "problem" child, they admit that his behavior problems seem to have escalated this year. His fifth grade teacher, Mr. Lytle, agrees. Specifically, he comments, "Terry refuses to participate in group projects and routine classroom activities and even to answer questions in class. He is definitely a loner. He has no friends. It's like he doesn't exist in the classroom. At first I thought Terry was shy and that he would become more involved in the class. Unfortunately, just the opposite has occurred. He's withdrawing more and more. Academically, Terry can do the work, I think, when he's not daydreaming."

Based upon a multifactored assessment, the following information was presented to the IEP committee:

Strengths:
- Reading comprehension and spelling are one year above grade level
- At grade level in math
- Usually cooperates in one-to-one setting
- Responds to tangible reinforcers

Weaknesses:
- Has difficulty in large or small-group activities
- Demonstrates limited verbal expression
- Has difficulty with cursive writing

- Has difficulty focusing on a task for more than ten to fifteen minutes
- Social relationships with peers and adults are poor

Recommendations:

- Full-time special education placement with emphasis on written and verbal expression skills and the development of interpersonal skills

Suggested instructional approaches:

- Begin with a one-to-one instructional setting.
- Use concrete manipulative aids to help Terry focus on tasks.
- Plan instruction that requires Terry to attend for ten minutes, and gradually increase the time.
- Use a token system that reinforces attending behavior in group settings.
- Assist Terry in gradually assuming a verbal participatory role in small-group settings.
- Use a multisensory approach for developing written expression skills.

An analysis of the selected information presented above illustrates that although these three students have been given different labels, they have common instructional needs. While similar teaching approaches and techniques could be implemented, it is important to point out that the rate of learning, management procedures, and establishment of goals may be different for each student. Often out of zeal to serve handicapped students, special educators assume that the needs of individuals within a group are similar. It should be remembered that both within and across categories, there will be similarities and differences in learning strengths, weaknesses, and needs.

Discussion Points

1. Identify which instructional needs these three students have in common.
2. Do the identified strengths and weaknesses provide you with enough information for program planning? If not, what additional information do you need?

CHAPTER 2 Identifying Noninstructional Responsibilities

OUTLINE

INTRODUCTION

In addition to meeting the daily demands of teaching in the classroom, today's special educator must also assume professional roles and responsibilities that extend beyond the classroom learning environment. Unlike special educators in the past, today's special educator is required to work with parents, regular teachers, school psychologists, language therapists, administrators, as well as with any other persons involved in the handicapped student's educational program. The outcome of special education services is more likely to be successful if specialists are able to function skillfully in a variety of ecosystems.

Objectives

After reading this chapter, you should be able to

- recognize the debilitating effect of stress on today's special educator and state strategies for reducing stress;
- identify role changes associated with today's special educator serving educationally handicapped students;
- state the differences between the resource model and consultant model and cite specific professional duties associated with each of these support service paradigms;
- discuss the importance of noninstructional responsibilities in effectively serving educationally handicapped students;
- identify the basic components of consultation and teaming;
- recognize the important role that special educators have in involving and educating parents in their child's educational program;
- identify specific professional services that should be provided to parents;
- recognize the impact of the regular classroom teacher on the handicapped student's educational well-being;
- state techniques for building positive interaction with regular teachers;
- identify barriers that inhibit professional and parent teams from functioning successfully.

Critical Incident: Stress and the Professional

Stress is one of those interesting words that have several meanings. One way to define stress is to view it as a build-up of internal pressure between body parts caused by external events in the environment. Stress is also synonymous with significance; that is, there are certain issues we give more attention to because of their importance. Unfortunately, teacher education programs may ignore the impact of stress on teachers and neglect identifying procedures for effectively dealing with it.

Some of the comparatively minor symptoms of stress are fatigue, irritability, and difficulty in relaxing. However, continued stress and anxiety can lead to more serious consequences, such as hypertension, heart disease, ulcers, or insomnia (Gray 1979). Within the classroom, stress can lead to an impaired ability to teach since survival concerns take precedence over concerns for students and quality teaching. Fuller (1969, cited in Youngs 1978) reported that teachers under stress ranked their needs as follows: (1) survival training, (2) survival training and performance skills, (3) methods for making an impact on students, and (4) skills for increasing what students learn.

One reason teachers suffer from anxiety or stress-related illnesses is that they are often overloaded with responsibilities. They are responsible for students' safety, psychological well-being, values, behavior, and learning needs. In addition, they must interact, often in a crisis situation, with regular class teachers, parents, administrators, supervisors, and other auxiliary persons.

Other causes of stress include poor interpersonal relations among staff members, faulty organizational structure, and poor leadership. Also, within the classroom, fear of students' physical and verbal abuse can be stressful to teachers of the educationally handicapped (Johnson, Gold, and Vickers 1982).

The multiplicity of responsibilities and role expectations takes its toll in terms of stress and anxiety and can lead to professional apathy. It is therefore imperative that beginning teachers be aware of symptoms associated with stress and know how to cope with it before they develop potentially serious mental and physical illnesses.

The increased likelihood of stress and anxiety for special educators is highlighted by the following list of tasks that one *beginning* teacher was asked to perform:

1. Given a budget figure, I was to order materials and equipment I would need;
2. Develop job descriptions and interview applicants for other positions in the program, including teachers and teacher aides;
3. Provide inservice training to regular education staff on student reading problems;
4. Help evaluate an existing program at another site;
5. Identify, schedule, and begin working with appropriate students with minimal

disruptions to the rest of their individual schedules (Bell 1979, 169).

Four or five years of university training can be rendered useless if teachers find themselves unable to perform professional responsibilities that extend outside the classroom. Teaching is a difficult job, and the attrition rate is alarming.

Points for Consideration

- *College programs preparing students to become special educators must clearly address the very real problem of teacher burnout.*

As Silberman (1970) has pointed out, the teacher's personal needs are the most often overlooked aspect of teacher education programs. Teachers must be aware of environmental situations that promote stress and develop appropriate strategies for dealing with these problems. In our efforts to become effective teachers, we cannot lose sight of our own personal and professional needs.

- *Due to the multifaceted nature of special education programming, it is imperative that administrators identify role boundaries and required professional responsibilities.*

The beginning teacher should know the limits, if any, associated with a position before he or she begins the job. Often discussions with special educators already in the school system will provide insight regarding role boundaries.

- *Although the beginning teacher should utilize information gathered from all ecosystems in a student's life when planning an individualized program, it is important to point out that the special educator often needs help in sorting out this information and in making sound programmatic decisions.*

To minimize errors in judgment, it is recommended that the beginning teacher solicit advice from veteran teachers, the building principal, the supervisor, or university personnel. Often these professionals are able to look at problems from a different perspective and thus offer viable alternatives for solving them.

ROLE CHANGES

In the past, a teacher's concerns centered primarily on students in the classroom. Today's teacher shares skills, students, and plans with a variety of adults. This is a major departure from traditional instructional duties; teachers must now be as skilled in working with adults as they are in working with children. School psychologists, reading teachers, principals, speech therapists, and other professionals are no longer people to send children to; they are colleagues to work with to implement individual programs for handicapped children.

In order to work effectively with others, special educators should be skilled in public relations (Reger 1972; Wiederholt 1974), well versed in interpersonal skills (Heller 1972), and able to relate with empathy, understanding, and patience to teachers (Bauer 1975; Lott, Hudak, and Scheetz 1975). In fact, establishing excellent working relationships is probably one of the most difficult tasks for resource teachers (Morse 1977) and is equal in importance to diagnostic, remedial, and planning skills (Hawisher and Calhoun 1978).

Support Service Models

The majority of educationally handicapped students spend at least part of their school day in the regular classroom. In such cases, the special educator assumes a support service position to the regular teacher and handicapped students. Both the resource model and the consultant model are increasingly being used to provide special education services to educationally handicapped students.

Resource model. The **resource model** evolved from two needs: (1) to serve more handicapped children directly and (2) to provide support services to regular teachers who were instructing exceptional students. Resource teachers serve students whose behavior and learning deficits inhibit success in a regular classroom on a full-time basis. The resource room can be viewed as a transitional placement between self-contained, special placement and full-time placement in a regular classroom. Here, the handicapped student receives remedial instruction or tutorial assistance from the resource teacher, while the remainder of the student's instructional needs are met in the regular class.

It is not uncommon for resource teachers to have their professional roles and responsibilities poorly delineated by the administration. In fact, Bensky, Shaw, Gouse, Bates, Dixon, and Beane (1980) reported that this lack of role clarification results in greater stress for resource teachers than for teachers in regular classrooms or in self-contained placement situations. It is therefore important that administrators identify changing responsibilities for both regular and special teachers. Otherwise confusion and failure to meet some of the needs of handicapped students are more likely to occur.

Consultant model. Within the **consultant model,** the special educator has few, if any, direct teaching responsibilities. Possible consultant roles include being a "diagnostician, remedial teacher, materials specialist, an advocate, and administrator of varied services that impinge on the entire school building's education program" (Hawisher and Calhoun 1978, 141). For example, a consultant may work directly with regular classroom teachers to establish instructional goals and

Providing individualized instruction in a small group setting is just one classroom responsibility for this resource teacher.

teaching strategies as well as to make classroom accommodations to mainstream handicapped pupils.

An advantage of the consultant model is that many handicapped learners can be served indirectly. The regular educator takes an active role in the student's learning by using skills developed through consultation with the special educator. Also, professional skills of the regular educator are enhanced through interaction with the consulting teacher. As a result, all students in the classroom benefit from the teacher's increased skill. Figure 2–1 compares the interaction between special and regular teachers in the resource and consultant models. It is apparent that the consultant model places greater instructional responsibility on the regular teacher.

In the above discussion comparing resource and consultant models, differences in job responsibilities are obvious. However, in practice, responsibilities are not always clearly outlined and are not necessarily within the boundaries associated with a specific model. For example, some resource teachers may provide only direct services to handicapped students, whereas others might also be required to provide consultation services to regular teachers.

Support Service Roles

The noninstructional responsibilities of special educators in support service roles have expanded due to federal and state rules and regulations and the resulting increased practice of mainstreaming. As a result, special educators need to work with regular teachers; yet, as indicated by Kass and Johnson (1972), barriers to effective professional interaction exist.

☐ **FIGURE 2–1**
Comparison of Resource and Consultant Interaction with Regular Teachers

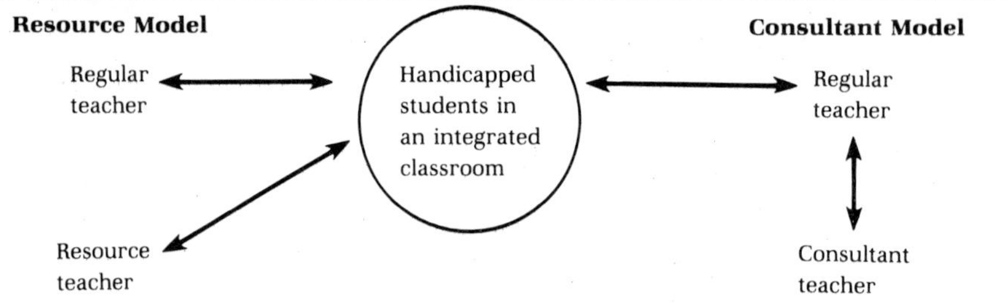

From C. Mandell and E. Fiscus, *Understanding Exceptional People* (St. Paul, Minn.: West Publishing, 1981), p. 176.

> Communication and teamwork are the most important considerations for successfully integrating learning disabled children into the regular classrooms. . . . In practice, the defense mechanisms of both special and regular teachers may be triggered by the dynamics of the situation. Too often, regular teachers view a consultant as patronizing in manner and threatening in action; too often, the special teacher views the regular teacher as either overprotective or rejecting toward the child. Communication problems make it difficult to have successful teamwork for the good of the child (pp. 17-18).

It is apparent that successful mainstreaming is dependent not only upon the handicapped student's readiness for integration but also upon all involved professionals' willingness to work cooperatively.

It is not uncommon for special educators to be expected to assume a leadership role in the special education process. This is a difficult job, especially when a beginning teacher is required to interact with veteran professionals. However, an understanding of the dynamics associated with teaming and consultation should help minimize barriers to productive interaction between professionals and between professionals and parents.

Teaming. Effective teamwork is a cooperative undertaking in which all members participate and interact. Such interaction is dependent upon members who are prepared; distributed leadership functions; adequate and efficient coverage of the agenda; an accepting, nonthreatening climate; and an ongoing group evaluation process (Hill 1977). In light of these considerations, it is apparent that group behavior is dependent upon many factors, including leadership style, administrative structure, and role identification. As a result, each teacher's first experience as a team member will be different. However, the beginning special educator is more likely to be an effective team member if he or she is able to recognize the individuality among group team members and identify barriers to effective teaming.

Team members' roles. The individual functioning of each team member affects the success of the group. Ideally, all team members both contribute and ask for information. In practice, team members do not always participate or share in the decision-making process on an equal basis. When it is apparent that the group is having difficulty functioning, there are specific roles team members can assume in order to enhance communication and the group process. These roles can be categorized as group task roles and group interactive roles. Group task roles help the team to complete the various tasks required in the decision-making process. They include the following:

- Initiator—proposes goals, defines problems, or suggests solutions
- Information giver and seeker—provides and seeks relevant information, ideas, and suggestions
- Clarifier/interpreter—gives examples and clears up confusion
- Summarizer—combines related ideas
- Surveyor for concensus—attempts to get each team member's opinion on issues

When problems occur among team members, individuals within the group can assume interactive roles. Whereas task roles help the team focus on more factual issues, interactive roles serve to keep the team communicating and working together cohesively. They include the following:

- Encourager—encourages and accepts the contributions of others
- Harmonizer—explores and reconciles differences
- Gatekeeper—attempts to keep communication open and facilitates the participation of others
- Compromiser—disciplines oneself in order to maintain team cohesion
- Standard setter—expresses and applies standards of team functioning
- Expresser—senses and expresses the feelings and moods of the team members

All of the group task and interactive roles identified above are not likely to exist at any given team meeting; yet, by observing different teams, teachers will see many of these roles emerge. It is important to realize that a team member's roles are not necessarily consistent. Team composition, leadership style, and the issues being discussed all influence an individual's behavior within the group.

Barriers to teaming. There are two sets of barriers that prevent a team from functioning effectively: nonfunctional group roles and organizational problems. A **nonfunctional group role** is a style or posture a group member assumes, either consciously or subconsciously, that prevents the team from meeting its objectives. Often these barriers can be eliminated or minimized if team members purposefully assume appropriate group task or interactive roles discussed previously. Nonfunctional group roles include the following:

- Blocker—argues about everything and goes off on tangents
- Competitor—constantly competes with the ideas of others; uses the "yes, but . . ." technique
- Aggressor—develops own status by criticizing others' ideas
- Withdrawer—refuses to participate in the group

- Special pleader—constantly brings up a few pet ideas regardless of the purpose of the group
- Joker—diverts the focus of the group by clowning and joking to gain attention
- Monopolizer—talks all of the time

Organizational problems occur when careful consideration has not been given to the planning, implementation, and evolution phases of the team process. Organizational problems include the following (Holland 1980; Fenton et al. 1979; Fenton 1977):

- Lack of effective communication among school personnel and parents
- Inadequate support for the team by building principal
- Inadequate staff to carry out the total IEP process
- Insufficient program alternatives from which to choose
- Lack of guidelines for avoiding waste of time and money
- Loose organization of each step in the process (screening, assessment, placement, monitoring)
- Insufficient in-service training to clarify roles and responsibilities of regular teachers as well as special educators (Regular teachers need to develop sensitivity to and understanding of handicapped children; special educators need assistance in developing their new roles as consultants)
- Lack of adequate time to carry out professional responsibilities appropriately
- Failure to establish roles and responsibilities for each team member

Consultation. Many educators are convinced that if the concept of educating handicapped students in the least restrictive environment is to be implemented appropriately, consultation, a relatively new method of special education service delivery, will have to be utilized more fully. As handicapped pupils are educated more and more within regular classrooms, regular teachers and other educational personnel will need the cooperative support and assistance that special educators and other professionals can provide.

Consultants' roles. Special educators can expect to provide consultation services to many diversified groups. Hawisher and Calhoun (1978) describe five of the roles consultants may take as follows:

1. As a consultant to teachers, the professional frequently works with concerns such as classroom management, scheduling conflicts, grading procedures, and instructional adaptations to meet the individual pupil's needs.
2. As a consultant to students, the team member works with problems and concerns related to students' academic progress, social skills, peer relationships, and self-concept development.
3. As a consultant to the school district, the professional must be concerned about and become involved in staff development needs and the provision of in-service training to enhance the IEP process.

4. As a consultant to parents, the team member becomes involved in communicating with parents about their child's educational progress. The consultant might also assist parents in obtaining their rights and carrying out their responsibilities in the IEP process. The consultant may also organize parent groups in order to facilitate communication and enhance the development of the parents' role.
5. As a consultant to volunteers and paraprofessionals, the professional helps to identify roles and responsibilities for these groups, communicates ongoing organizational management issues, and helps to provide appropriate recognition for their role in the educational effort.

Consultation is a service delivery method that has been utilized in the helping professions for many years. Although many models of consultative services have been developed, the model most likely to succeed in implementing special education mandates is one that emphasizes the collaborative and problem-solving nature of consultation. Collaborative, or conjoint, consultation, as described by Morse (1976), focuses on "mutual problem solving on the theory that the vast majority of teachers do want the best for their charges and will have creative solutions if they can see the total problem clearly" (p. 6). A consultative relationship characterized by an expert giving advice to a nonexpert is not likely to be as effective as a collaborative relationship that stresses equal status among all involved persons (Dinkmeyer and Carlson 1975).

Consultation skills. Since consultation is an indirect method of serving handicapped students, it can frustrate special educators accustomed to working directly with handicapped children. Parker (1975) has identified four major skills that consultants should possess: (1) the ability to assess the child's strengths and weaknesses, (2) the ability to negotiate goals, (3) the ability to develop a treatment plan, and (4) the ability to teach skills to the regular teacher. These competencies differentiate the task of teaching children from that of interacting with adults.

Assessing the child's strengths and weaknesses is done in conjunction with the classroom teacher. To get a complete assessment, the consultant must also be able to evaluate the teacher's strengths and weaknesses and understand any teacher biases. This information may come from classroom observation or from an interest survey completed by the teacher. For example, Ms. Lynden, a seventh grade English teacher, requires all her students to write a weekly in-class theme. The weekly topic is given to the students at the beginning of the period in which the theme is to be written. Mark Andrews, a handicapped student in Ms. Lynden's class, failed the first two themes. As a result, Mr. Stephens, the resource teacher, observed the English class. On the basis of his observation and a discussion with Mark, he concluded that Mark knew the material; however, it took him a long time to outline his thoughts and then put them in writing. Mr. Stephens shared his concern for Mark with Ms. Lynden, who was also distressed about Mark's failure. Mr. Stephens suggested that Mark be given the theme topic one period before the English class. Under the supervision of Mr. Stephens in the resource room, Mark would use this time to outline his ideas in writing. English class time would be used for the actual writing of the theme. Ms. Lynden agreed, and the following two theme grades were a *B* and a *C+*.

After the assessment, the consultant must decide which goals have priority, often through negotiation with other involved professionals and parents. For example, Ms. Trude sees increasing hand-raising behavior as the critical goal for one of her third graders, while the consultant believes increasing the student's time at his desk should be the priority. Consultants are more likely to be effective if they focus on the needs of those they are advising rather than on the task or goal itself. In the above example, the consultant worked with Ms. Trude to develop a plan to increase hand-raising behavior. After this intervention program was implemented successfully, the next priority was identified--to increase the student's time at his desk. The consultant must be willing to compromise as well as be able to set priorities.

A treatment plan involves determining a method for accomplishing the stated goals. For example, if the goal for one student is to reduce the difficulty level of tasks, the plan might include using different materials, assigning a peer tutor, or restructuring lessons. To develop the treatment plan, the consultant may need to teach the regular educator the necessary skills. Role playing, modeling, and team-teaching could be employed. In order to help mainstream handicapped students, one special education teacher taught reading to first and second graders in small groups as part of the regular team. The specialist helped devise plans for the handicapped readers within the context of these reading groups. By not singling out the poorer readers, this approach avoided stigmatizing them.

Barriers to consultation. Acceptance by others is critical to the consultation process. However, special educators may have more difficulty than regular classroom teachers in becoming accepted by coworkers since there usually are not many other specialists employed in any given school. For example, in some schools the various departmental members at the secondary level congregate in separate teacher lounges to socialize, relax, and plan lessons. The special education teacher may feel like an outsider in many of these group situations and, as a result, floats from group to group and thus does not really become an accepted member of any of them. This is a difficult problem for a new teacher to resolve. Also, the resource teacher's professional responsibilities are often supervisory in nature. Thus, the professional responsibilities of the special educator may force him or her into a role that is difficult for new teachers to assume and for veteran regular teachers to accept.

Gaining the respect and acceptance of others is difficult and does not occur during the first week or even first semester of the school year. However, special educators can facilitate their acceptance by deliberately getting involved with other teachers. Elman and Ginsberg (1981) suggest that special educators:

- perform regular duties, such as lunch room, rest room, and bus;
- spend time eating and socializing with other teachers and avoid eating alone in the classroom;
- volunteer to help on school committees;
- volunteer to help with school functions, such as plays, special programs, and sports events;
- attend evening programs--even ones that are not required;
- participate in extracurricular programs with the other teachers.

When specialists become actively involved in school functions not related specifically to handicapped students, they develop a professional association with other teachers that emphasizes what they have in common rather than their differences. As a result, when it is time to focus on programmatic planning or issues related to handicapped students, professional interaction is more likely to be positive.

IMPLEMENTING NONINSTRUCTIONAL RESPONSIBILITIES

Common noninstructional responsibilities that may be difficult for beginning special educators include interacting with parents and developing positive relationships with regular teachers. These responsibilities are discussed below, along with suggestions for implementing them.

Interacting with Parents

In order to effectively educate and involve parents in their child's educational program, teachers must be aware of parents' attitudes toward the school as well as their expectations of the program. Rather than turning to family services agencies, social workers, or other support services, parents tend to seek their child's teacher's opinion or advice when confronted with problems (Croft 1979); yet too often parents feel alienated by the school and believe that the school or teacher does not really understand their child's unique needs. Professionals themselves have been guilty of holding one set of expectations for parents of handicapped children and another for parents of normal children. Too often parents of exceptional children are expected to perform with unrealistically high levels of skill (Cansler, Martin, and Voland 1975).

Research has demonstrated that training programs for children where parents work with professionals often produce positive results (Barth 1979). Professionals can train parents in behavioral principles. They can also help parents construct and apply a therapeutic program for their children or conduct group therapy themselves. When professionals have done this, they have been able to effect changes in children's speech dysfunctions, self-injurious behaviors, oppositional behaviors (such as tantrums and disobedience), and other antisocial, immature types of behavior (Johnson and Katz 1973). Parents, teachers, and other professionals must work together. Each group can learn something from the others about working with the child, for each sees the child functioning in different ecosystems.

Teachers can promote positive interaction with parents by recognizing the multiple roles that parents of handicapped students have, by being aware of the handicapped student's impact on siblings, and by identifying distinct services they should provide to parents.

Parental roles. While several of the parental roles discussed below are relevant to all parents, the responsibilities are intensified in the case of parents with exceptional children. These roles, described by Heward, Dardig, and Rossett (1979), are as follows:

- *Teacher*: Without systematic plans, children with learning handicaps do not learn as readily as their nonhandicapped peers. The extension of teaching methods used in the school into the home is often essential for consistent, efficient learning.
- *Counselor*: Exceptional children have the same anxieties and joys as other children. In addition, parents of these children are concerned about others' perceptions of and possible rejection of their child, their child's future, and his or her inability to participate in tasks in which many of their peers are engaged.
- *Behavior Manager*: Some exceptional children exhibit a wide range of inappropriate behaviors. Parents often find themselves in the challenging position of helping their children develop appropriate behavioral patterns to replace the aggressive, self-injurious, or inappropriate self-stimulating behaviors.
- *Parents of Nonhandicapped Siblings*: The relationship between parents and the handicapped child's siblings is often strained. Parents must help brothers and sisters (*a*) to understand the exceptional child, (*b*) to assist in cooperative instruction in the home, and (*c*) to respond appropriately to the jeers and queries of their peers.
- *Spouse*: Exceptional children often place a real strain on the marriage relationship. If cooperative efforts of the school and family are to be successful, both parents must agree with the plans. This means that parents must cement their own relationship to prevent it from being pulled apart by the critical issues involved in raising exceptional children.
- *Educator of Significant Others*: In addition to immediate family members, there are many others with whom the handicapped child comes into contact. These significant others (e.g., neighbors, relatives, storekeepers) have an influence on the child's development too critical to leave to chance. Parents often assume the responsibility for educating these persons so that their child's progress is not inadvertently impaired by some random, inappropriate behavior on the part of others.
- *School and Community Relations Person*: Parents of exceptional children have certain rights and responsibilities under the law. It is important for them to understand these rights and responsibilities and to act accordingly. In doing so, they are quite likely to develop close relationships with the schools as well as with agencies and institutions within the larger community.

Sibling reactions. Gath (1974) found that older brothers and sisters are more affected by the presence of an exceptional child than younger siblings are. Sisters appear to be more affected than brothers because they are the ones expected to deal with the burdens of actual care for the handicapped child. Also, studies have shown that the exceptional child's feelings about his or her family are typically less positive than those of the brothers and sisters.

In some families, normal siblings may attempt to avoid intimacy with the handicapped child by participating excessively in extracurricular activities outside of the home (Van der Veen and Novak 1974). Of course, there are also families in which brothers and sisters of exceptional children assist with any treatment that might be required, play with the child, and protect him or her from the abuses and cruelty of others. However, these siblings also may have special feelings concerning their family. It is useful for parents and professionals to be sensitive to the feelings of siblings in order to assist them in their own efforts at judgment. Cansler, Martin, and Voland (1975) list the following concerns and feelings of siblings:

- Siblings wonder what caused their brother's or sister's handicap and sometimes fear that something may be wrong with themselves.
- Siblings sometimes feel that having to help take care of the handicapped child interferes with their own activities.
- Siblings may want to talk with their parents about the handicapped child's problems but may not know how to bring up the subject.
- Siblings may feel upset and angry that parents have to spend a lot of time with the handicapped child. Sometimes siblings try to get attention from the parents by acting like the handicapped child.
- Some siblings feel that they have to work extra hard (in school, sports, etc.) to make up to parents for the handicapped child's deficiencies.
- Siblings worry about how to tell their friends that they have a handicapped brother or sister and wonder whether their friends will make fun of them or the family for being different.
- Siblings wonder whether they will be able to marry and have children.
- Siblings may worry about whether they will eventually have to take care of the handicapped child; they may wonder whether they will be able to care for the child if anything happens to their parents.

In planning comprehensive programs for handicapped students, the feelings and attitudes of all involved family members should be considered. When professionals are aware of all relationships within a given family, they are likely to make more realistic decisions both in the classroom and in the home environment.

Services to parents. Just as parents of handicapped children often assume additional responsibilities, so does the special educator.

Information sharing. Parents most often rely on the teacher to provide them with relevant information concerning their child's education. Professionals therefore have a responsibility to keep abreast of current trends and issues in order to best serve their students. If they don't know or are unsure of what a parent is asking, they should find out.

The following example highlights the trust parents have in teachers. Mrs. Hulchins, whose nine-year-old son had been diagnosed as hyperactive and having severe learning problems, read a magazine article about a new diet that supposedly cured hyperactivity. She explained the diet to her son's teacher and asked if she should try it. The teacher responded, "I don't know if it works, but it sounds harmless. Why not give it a try?" This type of advice, based on lack of knowledge, is dangerous. As it turned out, this diet had not been studied under rigorous research conditions and required a great deal of preparation as well as changes in eating patterns for the whole family. A more appropriate response from the teacher would have been, "I'm not familiar with the diet; however, I'll see what I can find out."

Teachers who take time to keep parents informed and who involve them in their child's program build a more cooperative relationship between home and school. Also, the child will probably benefit by knowing that his or her parents really care enough to become involved and may be more responsive in the classroom. Finally, through effective parent-training sessions, the parents and the school become allies instead of enemies.

Too often the schools have not been responsive enough to parents. Consider the following commentary by Helsel (1978) on the schools: "Educators have been arrogant, viewing parents as serving only two purposes for the schools: (1) production of the clientele, and (2) paying for the system" (p. 33). Like Helsel, there are many parents of handicapped children who would echo similar sentiments. It is the responsibility of the schools to change these feelings. The sooner they are able to do so, the sooner they will enjoy better reputations among parents of the children they are seeking to educate. "Working with parents may be one of the most important and significant activities that educators can engage in. Not only is the activity mandated by law, but the development of consistency between school and home may make it possible for children to grow enough to function in society" (Kroth 1978, 90).

Parent advocacy at the IEP meeting. Administrators and teachers alike frequently accuse parents of being difficult to work with and often perceive a visit from a parent as an adversary situation. Middle-class parents are described as being too eager to push their children too far, while lower-class parents are accused of being lazy, neglectful, and apathetic about their children's education (Roper 1977). Helsel (1978) points out that these preconceptions on the part of professional educators are often erroneous. Many parents simply are not motivated by the school to participate in a positive manner, and many parents of the lower socioeconomic groups do not participate in planning for their children simply because they are too exhausted from a long day of work or are intimidated by the large bureaucratic system of the school. Also, many parents may feel that they are too uneducated or unsophisticated to be able to help their children. Many parents may have had negative school experiences themselves and may be manifesting avoidance behaviors. Parents in general, regardless of their socioeconomic status, are not well informed about how to deal with the school or about what their exact rights are. As a result, their involvement in the IEP meeting may be minimal.

The following are some suggestions offered by Morgan and Bray (1978) for motivating parents to participate in the IEP planning meeting for their child:

1. Be senstitive to the day-to-day problems inherent in the average family's schedule. Have the parents come in at their convenience, insofar as it is possible. Consider problems such as transportation, employment, and child care for other siblings.
2. Make an effort to get to know the parent or parents prior to the visit to the school. This can be accomplished by a telephone call or in person, through a prearranged home visit. With this initial contact, it is crucial that the team

member establish a supportive and positive relationship with the parents. Then, when the parents do come to the school, they will know someone and can feel more relaxed about a stressful situation. Let the parents feel that you are interested in them and their child.

3. Parents should be met at the door of the school building by a familiar person and led to the meeting room. The other team members should avoid appearing as though they have all been waiting for the parents to arrive at a meeting that is already in progress. This makes the parent feel less like an outsider who is trespassing into an alien group.
4. Some informal time should be spent before the meeting starts in order to introduce everyone and to let the parents orient themselves.
5. Allow the parents to have frequent input throughout the meeting. Parents can provide valuable insights and information about their child. They know the child more intimately than the school can, and without parental support and permission, no program can be legally implemented.

Holding conferences. The purpose of parent-teacher conferences is to share information regarding the student's educational performance. In planning and implementing these conferences, it is recommended that the teacher follow the general guidelines suggested by Cramer (1978) and Elman and Ginsberg (1981):

1. Preparing for the Conference

   If you have had little or no experience with parent conferences, role play a conference with a colleague or a friend to upgrade your confidence.

   Be sure that your communications, written or verbal, are friendly.

   Indicate in your invitation how much time is available for the conference. Be realistic on time lines. Too often conferences are consecutively scheduled to last fifteen to twenty minutes. This limited time is barely enough for introductions or summaries. A minimum of thirty minutes is recommended.

   Prepare a folder that includes examples of the child's work and current accomplishments. This folder may be taken home by the parents and should serve as a reminder to the parents and the child of the positive relationship between home and school.

   Prepare notes on particular concerns and recommendations you wish to share with the parents.

   Outline your goals and objectives for the conference to assist you in keeping on target. However, recognize that parents certainly may raise issues not related to your agenda.

   Make sure that parents who arrive early have a comfortable place to wait.

2. Conducting the Conference

   Greet the parents warmly and begin the conference with an encouraging note about the child's progress.

   Arrange the seating so that no desk is between you and the parents. Otherwise parents may perceive you as an authority figure and feel inhibited in expressing their opinions or sharing their concerns.

   Listen carefully to the parents, accepting their feelings, ideas, and attitudes. This sincere interest does not mean that you approve or disapprove but that you do respect the parents and desire to form a partnership.

Avoid educational jargon. If you cannot find a synonym for a specific educational term, be sure to explain it.

Avoid comparing the child with other children in school or with older brothers and sisters.

Have a copy of the child's IEP and state how goals and objectives are being met.

Offer the IEP to parents and specifically ask them to critique it. You might say, for example, "These are the skills I have planned for Timothy this year. I would like your opinion. Are there other skills you would like me to add? What do you think is important for Tim?"

If a discussion of the child's problem behavior develops, use problem-solving skills. State the behavior, why it is inappropriate, and strategies that might help to change it. Refer to skill deficits positively; for example, you could say, "John needs to learn to tell time to the hour, half hour, and quarter hour." Never identify problems without offering a solution or stating that you are trying to find the best way to remedy the problem.

Listen to parents. Avoid responding off the top of your head or lecturing. If you don't have an answer to one of their questions, say so.

Ask the parents questions and give them time to respond.

At the conclusion of the conference, summarize the discussion and any steps for action that have been agreed upon. Make sure that your summary communicates your appreciation of the parents' ideas.

Parents are more likely to become involved in their child's program if the professional recognizes the important role parents have in the educational process.

Be sure the parents know when you are planning to meet again and that you are available to meet with them at times other than regularly scheduled conferences.

3. Follow-Up and Evaluation

Devise plans for evaluation of each conference. List goals and objectives for planning strategies or plans of action over a period of time. This will help you to identify progress.

Inform appropriate teachers of the plans resulting from the conference and of any decisions reached.

Carry out the plans agreed upon. Provide feedback to the parents before the next personal conference. Make firm arrangements to communicate with parents between conference sessions.

Even our most sincere efforts can be misinterpreted. One way to develop appropriate skills for conferences is to tape several conferences and then critique them using the above guidelines. One resource teacher who prided herself as being a good listener was shocked after using this technique. She taped three conferences and discovered that she talked 72 percent of the time!

Another consideration for teachers is dealing with parents' anger. Angry parents care about their child; otherwise they wouldn't be upset. Too often teachers become defensive when parents are angry. Remember, parents may be experiencing an array of feelings related to the diagnosis of their child's handicapping condition, attempts to obtain services for the child, and the behavior of their child (Honig 1979). Any of these factors, which form the basis of the emotional reaction, is yet another justification for parental involvement. Special teachers must consider the feelings and turmoil that many parents have experienced when communicating with them about their child's educational program (Kroth and Scholl 1978).

Rather than trying to get your point of view across, *listen* to the parents. Then let them know you want to work together planning and implementing their child's program. For example, one parent angrily accused the resource teacher with the following statement: "You are not doing your job! Smitty has been in your class for three months, and he still can't read!" The resource teacher, also concerned about Smitty's lack of progress, responded with, "I too am concerned about Smitty's reading skills. I have some alternative instructional suggestions I'd like to share with you." This statement reflects the teacher's acceptance of the parents' anger as well as the need to change the instructional program. Parents of handicapped children can assist the teacher to focus on their child's most critical needs, identify areas of interest observed in the child, and support the teacher's efforts with the child (Losen and Diament 1978).

Counseling. At times teachers working closely with parents find themselves in the role of helper or counselor. While teachers are not expected to perform the duties of a professional counselor, they are often the first professional with whom a parent is able to establish a trusting relationship. Parents frequently request referral to a professional counselor following the establishment of such a relationship.

Teachers should be aware of the characteristics of a good counselor so that they can incorporate them into their own helping style as they work with parents. Stewart (1978) has suggested that a good counselor is one who (1) is interested in people, (2) is accepting, trusting, and respectful, (3) is empathetic, (4) is able to establish rapport readily, (5) is honest and genuine, (6) is attentive, (7) behaves ethically, and (8) understands human behavior. Teachers who desire to establish positive relationships should seek opportunities to develop these qualities.

Often family dynamics are so complex that there are no simple solutions to problems presented by the handicapped child. However, parents are more likely to confide problem situations to a professional who is open and accepting. When problems require counseling or therapeutic intervention beyond the teacher's skill level, he or she should refer the parent to the appropriate professional.

Interacting with Regular Teachers

The sharing of responsibility for a handicapped student's program by special and regular teachers has caused role changes for both professional groups. Formerly special educators often spent much of the day serving exceptional students with little opportunity or need for interacting with other professionals in their school. Now all professionals in the school must work cooperatively on a daily basis.

Presenting the regular teachers' perspectives on Public Law 94-142, John Ryor (1978), then president of the National Education Association, stated that the integration of handicapped students into regular classes had prompted feelings of anxiety in some regular educators. Specifically, concerns focused on feeling unprepared to teach these students. In addition, teachers believed they were spending too much time with handicapped students. Another problem was the relationship between regular and special educators. Ryor stated that the "potential for conflict is clearly present during this time of changing professional roles and relationships. However, there has never been a time when we needed each other more. The problems of educating handicapped students no longer fall within the exclusive domain of the special educator. Making the goal of a free appropriate public education a reality for our handicapped students is going to take our combined thoughts and energies" (13). Regular teachers expect special educators to help them in meeting this challenge.

Establishing role boundaries. Effective interaction between special and regular teachers depends upon clearly specified responsibilities for each professional group. Although policies among schools may differ, the responsibility for establishing and monitoring the role boundaries of regular and special educators ideally belongs to the school administration. This reponsibility should be executed in conjunction with input from all involved teachers. Also, such policies should be made available, in writing, to all involved professionals.

Unfortunately, many policies evolve on a trial and error basis, with little or no planning. Thus, it is not surprising for teachers to be unsure of their responsibilities or for unilateral decision making to occur.

The establishment and implementation of realistic role boundaries are more likely to occur if policies are developed by a group consisting of administrators, regular teachers, and special educators. The following process would help such a committee develop realistic role boundaries:

1. Make a list of all possible reponsibilities associated with the special education process, beginning with screening and referral and ending with program evaluation.

2. From this list, identify those responsibilities that require the involvement of both the regular teacher and the special educator. For example, if an educationally handicapped student is placed in both a regular classroom and a special education unit, then it is appropriate that both teachers attend the parent-teacher conference.
3. Identify those responsibilities on the list specific to each professional. It is not uncommon for teachers to disagree on some practices, such as grading procedures or scheduling arrangements. Whenever several professionals are involved in a student's program, it is imperative that the responsibilities of each be established.
4. Identify guidelines and procedures for handling special cases. No matter how thorough the establishment of roles might be, there are always exceptions to every rule.
5. Develop a written policy statement outlining both joint and individual role boundaries. Since parents are sometimes not sure which professionals are responsible for their child's program, it might be helpful to provide them with a summary statement of joint and individual professional responsibilities.
6. Provide periodic opportunities to evaluate the effectiveness of the established policies.

Although using a group to determine role boundaries is time consuming, decisions made by a group are more likely to be acted upon than those made unilaterally.

Services to teachers. Depending upon each school's guidelines, the services special educators provide to regular teachers will vary. In some schools, interaction may be limited to informal consultation, whereas other schools might schedule daily consultation services on a formal basis. In addition, special educators are often required to keep regular teachers up-to-date on topics related to serving handicapped students.

Consultation. Just as each handicapped student's needs are different, each teacher's style of teaching is different and is reflected in the way his or her classroom is organized. This variability prevents the special education consultant from providing standardized or set consultation services. However, there are several general procedures that consultants should adhere to regardless of whom they are advising. Parker (1975) suggests that consultants can minimize problems in communicating with regular teachers by recognizing the following:

- *Differences in Expertise:* The consultant has been trained to work with exceptional children; therefore, he or she feels more comfortable with special programs than does the regular teacher. For example, professional terminology may lack concrete meaning for the teacher. By translating technical concepts into understandable ideas, the consultant can help to overcome differences in training and background, which ultimately benefits the student.
- *Class Size:* The consultant and regular teacher focus on one child during a consultation; but in the daily situation, the classroom teacher is responsible for 25 to 30 students, or for 100 to 150 students at the secondary level. This variability emphasizes the necessity of considering each classroom as a

separate ecosystem. A consultant may recommend, for example, that a chapter in a social studies text be taped so that a child with inadequate reading skills can more readily grasp the content. This recommendation should then include plans for having the story taped (perhaps by an older student), identification of those students who could benefit from this experience, and suggestions on how this technique can fit into the teacher's overall lesson plan.

- *Status:* Classroom teachers traditionally have taken primary responsibility for all classroom activities. For some teachers the addition of a consultant may be a welcome relief; yet for others the consultant may be viewed as a threat to the teacher's authority and expertise. To ensure a good working relationship, the consultant must not only be sensitive to defensive attitudes but also expect them. If a teacher is unprepared to teach handicapped students, frustration and anger should be anticipated. Usually the teacher is not angry *with* you, even if his or her anger is directed *at* you. For example, Mrs. Talbot approaches the high school resource teacher in the hallway with, "I don't think Mark should have been placed in my eleventh grade general science class. He doesn't belong, and I think it might be better for him to spend this time in your class. He doesn't do his in-class work and is constantly talking to other students." The resource teacher, who works with Mark for two periods daily, is surprised by this statement since Mark is cooperative in the resource class. In this instance, the resource teacher is faced with a choice. He could state that Mark is doing well in his class. Although such a comment is factual, it serves to underscore the science teacher's feelings of incompetency and will tend to be a roadblock for further interaction. A more appropriate remark might be, "Mark often says he enjoys your class. Maybe we can get together and see what we can do," or "Mark sometimes has problems doing work in my class too. Why don't we get together to try to come up with some alternative strategies." Such statements provide a more accepting climate for the regular teacher's feelings and yet encourage consultation. A consultant must also prove that he or she has something of value to offer and be willing to explore any hostile feelings. If consultation is viewed as burdensome rather than as a process for problem solving, the handicapped student benefits little and professionals are less likely to interact on a frequent basis.
- *Coordination:* Professionals other than regular teachers interact with the child. In order to establish a consistent approach with the child, communication among these people must be smooth. For example, if a student is receiving help from the school counselor to control disruptive behavior, the consultant needs to translate goals established by the counselor into workable classroom activities. Meetings need to be arranged so that all involved can share information, evaluate progress, and, if necessary, change plans.

All of the above factors should be considered by the special educator when suggesting modifications in the regular classroom. Rather than having a predetermined list of changes, the special educator must be aware of the dynamics within each classroom before making suggestions for change.

Due to the increasing practice of placing handicapped students in the mainstream, special educators are often required to provide services and training to regular classroom teachers.

Heron and Catera (1980) have described a functional consultation process based upon the following assumptions: *(a)* all students can learn; *(b)* all teachers can learn, including how to effect change in their students; *(c)* to evaluate teacher effectiveness, the teacher's ability to effect change in the learner is evaluated on the basis of measurable change; and *(d)* the most promising method of helping teachers change instructional strategies or alter student social progress is derived from behavioral analysis.

The process for functional consultation is as follows:

1. The special and regular educators define the problem. To do so, they maintain oral and written communication.
2. An appropriate design is established to measure the problem behavior. The special or regular teacher records the frequency of behavior targeted for intervention.
3. The special and regular educators define an intervention strategy. At this stage, the special educator does not volunteer an intervention strategy unless the regular educator specifically asks for one. The special educator prompts the regular educator to volunteer a strategy by asking such questions as, "What has worked for you in similar situations?" or "What would you like to try to solve this problem?"
4. The special and regular educators specify an appropriate measurement procedure for assessment of the intervention strategy. Either the special or regular educator then charts the student's behavior to monitor the direction of change.

5. If the intervention strategy is observed as unsuccessful, the special educator should revert to step three but is free to offer suggestions by using such statements as, "Here's an idea that might work," or "Why don't we try this for a while to test it?" or "This has worked for me. Let's try it with this student."
6. Again, a measurement procedure is designed to evaluate the new intervention strategy. Either the regular or special educator can chart student behavior to monitor the direction of student change.
7. The final step in this functional consultation process is to establish a method of ongoing evaluation. At this stage, the successful intervention may be withdrawn for a short period of time and later reinstated to document its effectiveness. Either the special or regular educator charts student behavior at this stage. It is also a good idea to congratulate the regular educator for his or her efforts and establish a time for review of the method or discussion of strategies for other students.

Utilization of functional consultation is dependent upon the special educator's ability to analyze the classroom environment, the regular teacher's willingness to attempt a cooperative endeavor, the ability of the special educator to allow the regular teacher to play an active role in the joint decisions, and the ability of the educators to reach a consensus and give each intervention a reasonable trial period.

In order to identify realistic modifications to be made in the classroom or the student's behavior, it is important that the consultation be a collaborative effort. Decision making must be a joint responsibility, shared equally by the two professionals. Consultation cannot be carried out successfully after simply reading about it. It takes practice and flexibility to become an expert consultant. An attitude of understanding and tolerance is crucial. If the consultant is too task oriented without due regard for the feelings of the classroom teacher, parents, and other professionals, little will be accomplished.

Problem solving. No matter how prepared a special educator is to assume the role of consultant, controversies among professionals do occur. In fact, consultants should anticipate problem situations and be prepared to deal with them in order to better serve handicapped students.

When planning and implementing individualized instructional plans with other professionals, special educators can use specific communication strategies to clarify and reduce interpersonal problems. One set of communication techniques originally developed by Smith (1975) for use by psychologists with their clients, is appropriate for use by special educators. A synopsis of these communication strategies and their application in the consultation process follows. As indicated in the related examples, these techniques can be used with other professionals and parents as well as with regular teachers.

- **Broken record** is a technique designed to assist professionals in establishing a goal. It simply involves stating and restating a goal as many times as necessary without tones of anger or frustration. For example, if a secondary teacher is talking with the principal about a student who she feels needs a change in placement from a work-study program to a tutorial model, the teacher might make repeated statements during the conference such as, "I know the timing for an annual review is awkward, but Mike's test scores indicate a need for a change of placement." In this example, since the teacher's goal is to schedule an annual review, statements indicating the need would be made repeatedly.

- **Workable compromise** is used when individuals have a difference of opinion. Resolution should not infringe upon the self-respect of either professional. For example, if the special educator is talking with a vocational teacher who is unwilling to provide study guides for a handicapped student, the special teacher, using workable compromise, might say something like, "Perhaps we could make arrangements for the school's parent volunteers to prepare study guides for this student and others who may need them." In this example, each professional feels it is the other's responsibility to prepare the material. The workable compromise statement solves the student's problem without infringing on either professional.

It should be noted that broken record and workable compromise are usually used in combination with each other. In the last example, the special educator could have used both broken record and workable compromise by saying, "Mike needs this study guide" (broken record). "Perhaps we could make arrangements for parent volunteers to prepare it" (workable compromise).

- **Free information** was originally designed to encourage social conversation but can be used in professional communications as well. For example, when talking with a student who has expressed interest in a career for which he has not acquired the sufficient skills, the special teacher, using free information, may say, "Mark, you're telling me that you want to become an electrician. I think that is a realistic goal, but you'll probably have to change your approach to studying."
- **Self-disclosure** is simply offering an opinion. For example, when a special educator talks with a regular educator about a student he or she perceives as easily distracted, the special educator may say, "Mary raises her hand more often during the early part of a lesson. Perhaps if you call on her to respond, she may attend for longer periods."
- **Fogging** is the ability to agree in principle with some truth or logical criticism, while still maintaining a seemingly contradictory position. For example, if the vocational director tells a secondary special educator that "those slow learners don't belong at the vocational high school," the teacher may respond by saying, "You're right. Many slow learners can't be successful here; but one of my students, Judy, can, and I would like her to be admitted to your program."
- **Negative inquiry** is a process whereby one inquires about implied or direct criticism. For example, when Tim failed his history test a second time, Ms. Reed, the special educator, contacted his teacher for an appointment and perceived some nonverbal cues that she interpreted as resentment. Rather than attempt to discuss Tim's failure in such an atmosphere, she used negative inquiry and said, "I'm getting the impression that you resent discussing Tim's failure with me now. Am I correct?" While using this technique requires risk taking on the part of the special educator, it can be

beneficial because it often leads to open, honest communication, free of barriers and hidden agenda.

For many special educators, these techniques will prove useful in developing effective communication with diverse groups. For these techniques to be used effectively, it is suggested that special teachers practice them in low-anxiety situations before using them in professional conversations with professionals and parents. Further, additional training in assertiveness and other communication strategies should be investigated in depth and acquired as an integral component of the professional's training program.

Teacher advocacy at the IEP meeting. Too often the handicapped child's regular classroom teacher is ignored or slighted at team meetings. One research project on the perceived roles of regular classroom teachers on child study teams found that most of the fourteen hundred regular teachers responding to a questionnaire did not feel like important members of such teams; furthermore, other team members shared this perception (Rucker and Vautour 1978). The study also revealed that the regular teachers did not attend meetings very often, were passive when they did attend, did not understand clearly the duties and the goals of the team, and tended to be dissatisfied with decisions reached by the team.

A person's commitment to a decision is directly related to his or her participation in reaching that decision. If the regular teacher is not satisfied with a decision about a particular student, then it is not likely that the teacher will be eager to see that it is implemented. This lack of enthusiasm and support can mean that the educational goal will not be met. The educational planning meeting then fails to achieve its purpose (Rucker and Vautour 1978).

Since regular teachers may feel inadequate at IEP meetings or be unfamiliar with the IEP process, the special educator should assume responsibility for helping them to achieve equal status at the meetings and to be prepared to participate in team discussions.

Before entering the IEP meeting, each team member should assess biases or issues concerning fellow professionals. As noted earlier, professionals may sense that they are not living up to others' expectations or may encounter role conflicts with other personnel (Bensky et al. 1980; Butler and Maher 1981). While a delineation of role responsibilities and a group evaluation effort will help to fend off feelings of inadequacy and competition, resolution is not necessarily immediate. Recognizing the source of uneasy feelings is the first step. It is highly recommended that when the professional cannot resolve these issues alone, he or she discuss them, preferably with the perceived source of conflict, or the IEP committee's chairperson. Only when the special educator recognizes that biases exist is he or she able to take action to minimize them before the meeting begins.

The special educator is often in an excellent position to help teachers prepare to participate in team discussions and decisions. Often teachers fail to become actively involved because they have not been included in any events prior to the meeting. To help them become more knowledgeable, special educators should provide teachers with a meeting agenda indicating the expected contributions of each participant and also with a written summary of assessment findings and recommendations made by other team members. One reason for providing written materials is that it allows teachers to formulate questions, consider alternatives, and reevaluate their perspectives prior to the meeting. Also, when regular educators are included in the assessment process, they will have some concrete information to share with the group.

Although such responsibilities may not be required, special educators who recognize the needs of regular teachers and the important role they have in serving handicapped students realize that cooperation is likely to better serve the student.

SUMMARY POINTS

- Although stress is a problem for all professionals, the demands placed on special educators, especially resource teachers, contribute to increased burnout.
- Since the educational needs of educationally handicapped students are often met by more than one professional, it is imperative that special educators be trained to work with adults.
- Both the resource and consultant models cast the special educator in the role of providing support services to other professionals and parents.
- The roles of regular classroom teachers have also changed. Through appropriate consultation procedures, the special educator can help to meet their needs, thus increasing the likelihood of better serving handicapped students.
- Parents should play an active role in developing and implementing their child's educational program. By providing comprehensive professional services (information sharing, parent advocacy, conferences, and counseling), the special educator is more likely to have positive relationships with parents.
- Teams are more likely to be effective when each participant is valued and everyone's input encouraged. Special educators should play an active role in preparing regular teachers to participate in team meetings.
- Consultation between special and regular educators is more likely to be effective when it is viewed as a collaborative effort. There are no set consultation services; rather consultation services depend upon the needs of each teacher and each handicapped student.

REVIEW QUESTIONS

1. Maintaining communication channels with regular classroom teachers and parents is critical to implementing a student's educational program. Identify five specific activities you could employ to keep parents aware of their child's school progress.
2. Contact at least two school districts and ask them if they have a written description of a resource (or consultant) teacher's roles and responsibilities

and also a written description of a regular teacher's responsibilities for teaching handicapped students. If available, obtain a copy of these guidelines. Are there any noninstructional roles listed? Are each professional's responsibilities clearly outlined?

3. Based on the critical nature of noninstructional roles in serving handicapped students, develop a list of related questions regarding role boundaries that you might ask a potential employer during an interview.

SUGGESTED READINGS

Cansler, D. P.; Martin, G. H.; and Voland, M. C. 1975. *Working with families.* Winston-Salem, N.C.: Kaplan.

Croft, D. J. 1979. *Parents and teachers: A resource book for home, school, and community relations.* Belmont, Calif.: Wadsworth.

Elman, N. M., and Ginsberg, J. 1981. *The resource room primer.* Englewood Cliffs, N.J.: Prentice-Hall.

Hawisher, M. F., and Calhoun, M. L. 1978. *The resource room: An educational asset for children with special needs.* Columbus, Ohio: Charles E. Merrill.

Fiscus, E. D., & Mandell, C. J. 1983. *Developing individualized education programs.* St. Paul, Minn.: West.

Parker, C. A., ed. 1975. *Psychological consultation: Helping teachers meet special needs.* Reston, Va.: Council for Exceptional Children.

Stewart, J. C. 1978. *Counseling parents of exceptional children.* Columbus, Ohio: Charles E. Merrill.

Wiederholt, J. L.; Hammill, D. D.; and Brown, V. 1978. *The resource teacher: A guide to effective practices.* Boston: Allyn & Bacon.

Application: The First Year

Ms. Sally Ortiz's first teaching assignment was an intermediate-level resource unit. Previously there had been only one self-contained special education unit in her building. The decision to move the self-contained unit to another school and replace it with a resource unit was made on August 12. School began September 3.

Ms. Ortiz's professional responsibilities included providing remedial programs to students identified as educationally handicapped (EH) and presenting monthly in-service programs to regular classroom teachers in the school. The following are excerpts of anecdotal records Sally recorded that year:

Tuesday, September 20. Almost one month into the school year, I feel comfortable with my kids--some are really doing well in my class. I guess my reward system is working. One of the most popular items is "eating lunch with teacher." I can't believe how much time I spend preparing for class and trying to be organized. Yesterday one of the third grade teachers told me on the way out of school that none of the three handicapped kids mainstreamed in her class belonged there. If only they knew how to teach these kids. Individualizing instruction is going to be the topic of my October in-service program.

Friday, October 24. Well, the in-service was today--Friday, after school. On a scale of one to ten, it was about a zero. Five out of twenty teachers came. No one asked questions. No one took notes. One person said that I did a nice job, as she was putting her coat on. I just stood in front of them and talked. I see teaming going on--the team of them against me.

Friday, November 21. Parent-teacher conferences came and went. Parents showed up; however, the majority of the regular teachers sent prior notice that there was no need for them to attend these conferences since I was the "expert" on handicapped kids. I felt foolish trying to feebly answer parents' questions about their children's regular class performance--I've never been in any classroom long enough to know what's going on.

Friday, November 28. Despite the turkey and other goodies, I've lost ten pounds since September. I can't wait until Christmas vacation. At times I feel like I'm on the firing squad every time I enter school. Yesterday I actually forgot one student's name.

Either things have to change or I'm going to look for a job with the telephone company.

Monday, December 29. I have spent much of my vacation talking to experts--the regular teachers' supervisor, my supervisor, and my principal. I think two major problems exist. First, I'm hired to do two jobs--remediate the kids and work with the teachers; yet I'm scheduled to work all day with the kids and provide one hour of in-service per month after school. The second problem is that the other teachers and I aren't doing a very good job working together. They expect me to solve all these kids' problems. I can't.

I hope the New Year's entries are less pessimistic than November's depressing prose. I hope the ideas I have work. I hope . . . .

Friday, January 16. Upon returning to school, I talked with Jake (the principal) about rearranging the monthly torture sessions, frequently referred to as "in-service." He agreed, on a trial basis, that I could rearrange my schedule so that Wednesday mornings and Friday afternoons would be available for regular teachers to visit with me or vice versa. I started eating lunch with them--no more 100 percent time for kids only. Also, I started sending weekly notes to my students' teachers. For example:

> *Jason Walker* *Mrs. Simon*
>
> *Weekly Summary:* Jason told me his favorite "school time" this week was being selected to read his poem in front of the class. He said, "My teacher thought it was funny, too!"
>
> Apparently Jason really likes poetry. I'd like to stop by and read his poem. He's really proud of it. Maybe I could use poetry to motivate him in other areas. I'd like your suggestions.
>
> Thanks, Sally Ortiz

I hope these notes will help me be more accepted by the teachers.

Wednesday, February 18. I think things are improving. For the last two Wednesday mornings, I have been meeting with several of the teachers. Rather than talking, I've been trying to listen. Rather than trying to provide all the answers, I'm trying to use questioning techniques (suggested by a psychologist friend) that promote group problem solving. It seems that many of their concerns are related to classroom management problems. I never realized how frustrated they were. And angry, too. I don't think they resent the kids. Rather, they resent not knowing what to do with them.

A major breakthrough in education occurred this week--I was invited to observe handicapped students in two classrooms.

Wednesday, March 25. This month I invited any interested teachers to attend a regional workshop sponsored by our state Council for Learning Disabilities. The sessions were filled with practical ideas applicable to the regular classroom. After the workshop the four teachers and I went out for dinner and talked about how the ideas would work in *our* building.

On the drive home, I knew I was accepted, at least by this small group, when they asked me to join the baseball team.

Friday, April 24. Everything seems to be at a plateau. No additional teachers are using the Wednesday and Friday consultation sessions. However, I haven't lost the eight who have been meeting with me.

Our baseball team is on a winning streak!

Friday, May 29. Nobody ever prepared me for annual reviews. I don't think I could have made it without the cooperation and support of the other teachers. For eleven of my fifteen parent-teacher conferences, all involved teachers were present. We really were a team.

The baseball team lost the pennant . . . .

Monday, June 8. School is out! But not for long. Several of the teachers and I are planning to meet three times throughout the summer. The purpose of the meetings is to identify alternative strategies for mainstreaming handicapped students in our school.

Discussion Points

1. Why do you think Sally had a difficult time interacting with the other teachers?
2. Discuss how the building principal and school administration could have helped prepare both Sally and the other teachers for the transition from the self-contained unit to the resource room unit.
3. What other strategies could Sally have used to promote equal status between herself and the regular classroom teachers?

CHAPTER 3 Assessing for Instruction

OUTLINE

INTRODUCTION

Each handicapped student's involvement in the learning environment is related to many factors. Past as well as current out-of-school experiences, motivational needs, and unique learning strengths and weaknesses all contribute to an individual's classroom performance. Developing an effective instructional plan for each student requires special educators to identify the influence that these variables have on learning.

Salvia and Ysseldyke define **assessment** as "the process of understanding the performance of students *in the current ecology*" (1981, 4, italics in original). Since special educators are the most knowledgeable professional group regarding learning and behavior problems, and are most directly involved with handicapped students, their skill in identifying variables affecting performance is necessary for successfully implementing the special education process.

The whole area of assessment could never be addressed in one chapter. Due to its significant role in teaching handicapped students, the topic merits broader coverage. Refer to the suggested readings at the end of this chapter for current assessment references.

The purpose of this chapter is to highlight the important role special educators have in assessment. Special educators' assessments affect not only placement, but instructional and evaluation decisions, all of which are part of the special education process. The second purpose of the chapter is to identify assessment procedures that will assist you in identifying your students' instructional needs. The procedures discussed here can be used effectively in content areas as well as noncontent instructional areas.

Objectives

After reading this chapter, you should be able to

- discuss assessment issues relevant to the special educator;
- identify the four phases of the assessment and program-planning cycle and discuss the special educator's responsibilities within each phase;
- define assessment from an ecological perspective;
- list the purposes and limitations associated with informal and formal assessment procedures;
- identify specific informal assessment procedures and discuss the type of information each might provide in order to develop an individualized instructional plan.

Critical Incident: The Special Educator's Role in the Assessment Process

All phases of the special education assessment process are related, and their successful implementation is dependent upon the special educator's assessment expertise.

As indicated in Figure 3-1, during the initial phase of the assessment process, the specialist is often asked to assist regular teachers in selecting appropriate screening instruments, or may actually be required to administer such tools. During the multifactored assessment phase, special educators may be required to administer and interpret various assessment tools. Effective planning and implementation of an IEP demands further assessment expertise. During the IEP meeting the special educator is involved in explaining assessment findings and their implications for instruction to professionals and parents.

Once a handicapped student is placed in a special education program, the special teacher usually is solely responsible for the next two phases of the special education process––program implementation and evaluation. Diagnostic data collected thus far frequently reflect the use of standardized procedures, which are not usually helpful in identifying a student's instructional needs. As a result, the special educator must be knowledgeable about additional assessment techniques designed to pinpoint precise instructional needs. Also, program evaluation is the responsibility of the special educator, who often is required to assume a leadership role on the team.

Active involvement in the assessment process may be viewed as an awesome burden by teachers. Some special educators naively assume that their primary role is that of providing instruction. Certainly their goal is to teach; however, the complexity of each student requires teachers to be able to uncover variables related to effective instruction. In essence, the special educator must expect that he or she will first implement a comprehensive assessment program in order to determine a student's instructional needs.

An important component of such a program is the selection of assessment procedures. Too often teachers rely on standardized tests to make programmatic decisions. Although formal medical, psychological, and educational tests may be appropriate for placement decisions, such standardized tests are not necessarily beneficial for instructional planning. Effective teachers use a variety of assessment procedures, depending upon each student's needs. The goal is to learn as much as possible about a student's behaviors in various habitats--a task too complex for standardized tests alone.

Points for Consideration

- *The classroom teacher should not be expected to have the same assessment expertise as professionals such as school psychologists or psychometrists.*

However, teachers should know how to interpret tests administered by other team members. In addition, they should have a positive working relationship with professionals from other disciplines since the development of appropriate individualized instructional programs requires continuous interaction among all involved professionals.

- *For assessment to be considered comprehensive, it must look beyond the student's innate learning strengths and weaknesses.*

Pertinent variables in the classroom, home, and community must also be identified prior to program development. By considering the information gathered from these habitats, often by informal assessment procedures, the special educator is likely to produce a more realistic instructional plan.

☐ **FIGURE 3–1**
Educational Assessment/Program-Planning Cycle

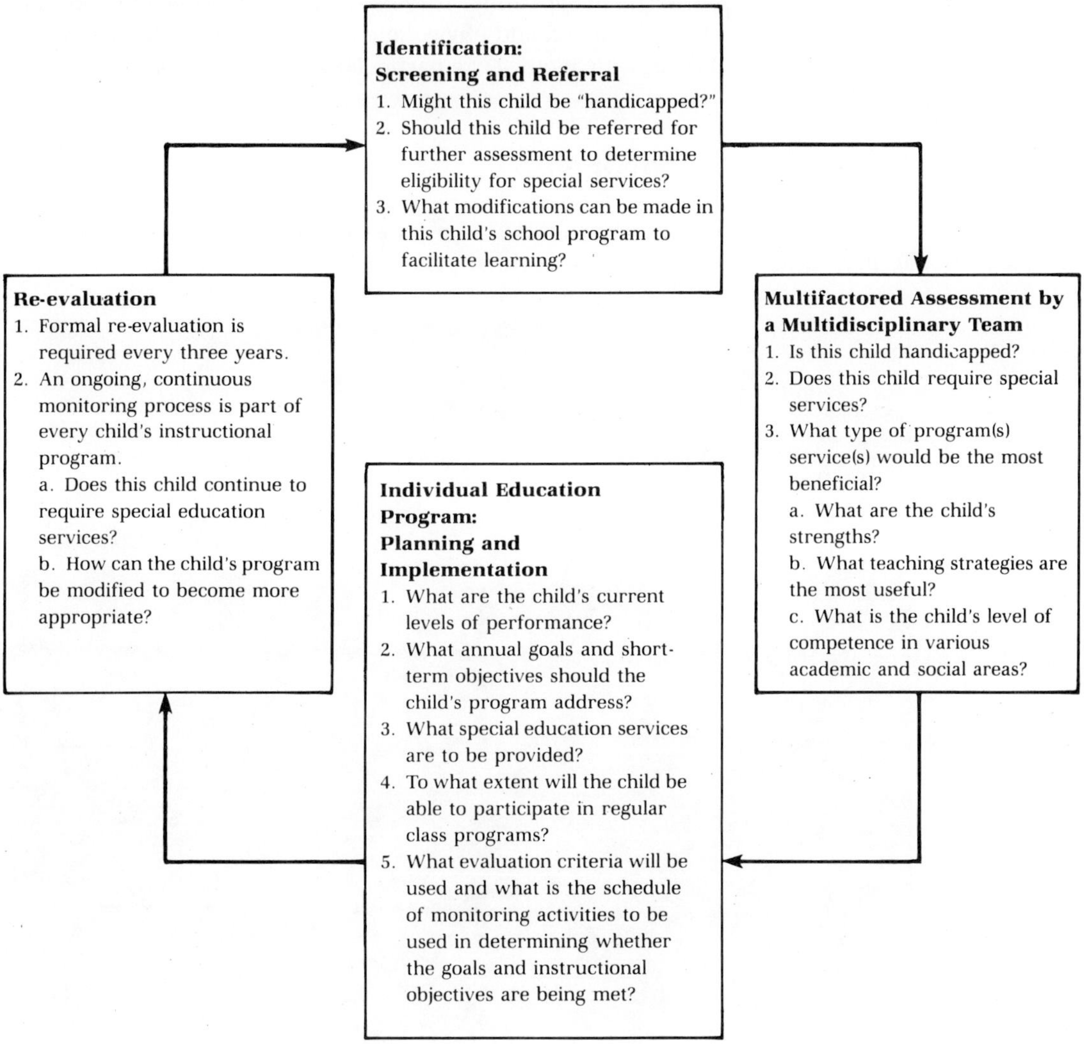

Identification:
Screening and Referral
1. Might this child be "handicapped?"
2. Should this child be referred for further assessment to determine eligibility for special services?
3. What modifications can be made in this child's school program to facilitate learning?
Multifactored Assessment by a Multidisciplinary Team
1. Is this child handicapped?
2. Does this child require special services?
3. What type of program(s) service(s) would be the most beneficial?
a. What are the child's strengths?
b. What teaching strategies are the most useful?
c. What is the child's level of competence in various academic and social areas?
Individual Education Program:
Planning and Implementation
1. What are the child's current levels of performance?
2. What annual goals and short-term objectives should the child's program address?
3. What special education services are to be provided?
4. To what extent will the child be able to participate in regular class programs?
5. What evaluation criteria will be used and what is the schedule of monitoring activities to be used in determining whether the goals and instructional objectives are being met?
Re-evaluation
1. Formal re-evaluation is required every three years.
2. An ongoing, continuous monitoring process is part of every child's instructional program.
a. Does this child continue to require special education services?
b. How can the child's program be modified to become more appropriate?

From Mandell, C., and Fiscus, E. *Understanding Exceptional People* (St. Paul, Minn.: West Publishing, 1981), p. 52.

COMMON ASSESSMENT MISCONCEPTIONS

There are specific intervention strategies associated with each handicapping condition. It is an error in professional judgment to use the same instructional procedures to teach all learning disabled students. Instead, the classroom teacher must provide individualized assessment to identify each student's instructional needs. Each group of handicapped students is indeed a heterogeneous population, requiring divergent assessment and teaching procedures.

Assessment data are prophetic in nature. Since assessment information represents a student's performance at any given point in time, scores or test performance should not be used to predict future behavior. Individual needs change, as do a student's ability to attend, interact, and recall. For example, instructional needs that are appropriate in September may be outmoded in November. By continuing to evaluate develomental and environmental variables, professionals are likely to have a more accurate picture of a particular student's needs.

ECOLOGICAL ASSESSMENT

From an ecological perspective, "the goal of assessment is to obtain sufficient information for determining intervention priorities for each child" (Hardin 1978,

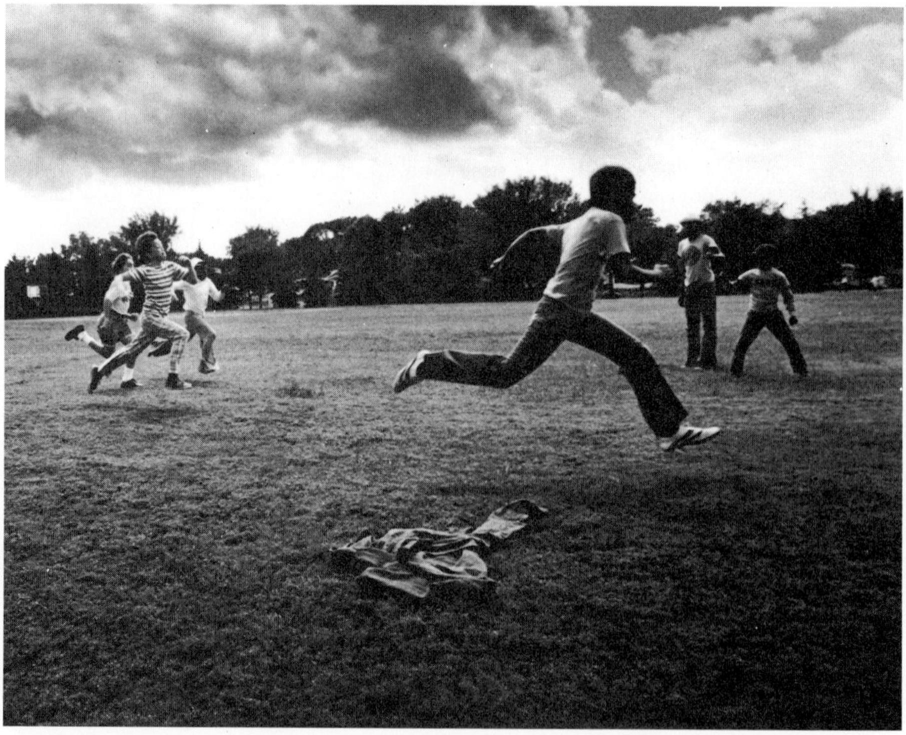

Behavioral observations, which focus on a student's performance in a variety of settings can give the special educator assessment information critical to program development.

16). Since the needs as well as the strengths and weaknesses of each student vary, it is critical that professionals examine a variety of factors that may be contributing to the educationally handicapped student's learning and/or behavior problems.

Ecological assessment evaluates the educationally handicapped child in relation to the various environments in which he or she functions (Thomas and Marshall 1977; Newcomer 1977; Carroll 1974). This may include examining the way in which the child and teacher interact, the appropriateness of the child's curriculum, relationships with peers, and situational factors outside the school setting. All of this information is necessary to reveal factors precipitating or maintaining a student's learning and behavior problems. As Newcomer (1977) states:

> [t]he focus on learning problems as strictly child-centered disorders ignores or at least de-emphasizes the fact that learning is an interactive phenomenon and that failure to learn is often intricately associated with breakdowns in a child's relationship with teachers and peers. More succinctly, diagnosing and remediating a child's academic difficulties in settings removed from the classroom may not be sufficient if the problems interfering with learning relate primarily to the types of experiences the child has within the classroom (p. 85).

Although a handicapped student may have specific learning and behavior problems attributed to psychoeducational deficits, performance is influenced by the demands of various habitats. For example, seventeen-year-old Mitchell spends half of his school day in a self-contained special education program designed to develop realistic vocational skills through academic instruction. In the afternoon Mitchell is placed in a work setting, where he is periodically supervised by the school's work-study coordinator. Although Mitchell is experiencing success in the classroom, he is failing on the job despite the fact that he is required to do similar tasks in both the work and school settings. He is now talking about quitting school. Observations of Mitchell in each setting and discussions with his teacher and boss yielded the following information:

- In the classroom Mitchell gets his assignments in writing, whereas at work he is told what to do by his boss, with little or no opportunity to ask for further explanations. Even though he realizes that he is unsure of what he is supposed to be doing, Mitchell is hesitant to ask for clarification. As a result, he often performs the wrong task.
- Mitchell's mother telephones him on the average of twice a day to "make sure he's still at work or to ask him what time he is coming home." His boss is annoyed with these disruptions.

Mitchell's case not only exemplifies how various environments (in this case the home, school, and work settings) influence a student's performance, but also highlights why assessment must be comprehensive and continuous if a student is to succeed. Frequently the focus of instruction is on content areas, such as reading, arithmetic, and writing; therefore, these areas are targeted for assessment. Yet problems in these areas are often caused or magnified by noncontent variables, such as deficits in social, behavioral, thinking, or language skills or changes in the classroom, home, or community ecosystems.

In some situations, such as Mitchell's, it is relatively easy to pinpoint a student's learning or behavior problem and then plan or modify an instructional program. However, often it is not readily apparent to the professional what factors are related to poor performance. As a result, the professional may be at a loss as to where to begin assessment. Guerin and Maier (1983, pp.54-55) suggest that professionals routinely examine performance information associated with the specific domains listed below:

> *Achievement areas:* Basic skill and subject areas such as reading, math, language, history, physical education, music, and science
> *Behavior areas:* Those areas of personal behavior that include emotions, self-control, responsibility, motivation, humor, attitudes, values, empathy, and interests
> *Perceptual-motor development:* A group of sensory-related skills including auditory-visual-tactile-haptic perception, sensory integration, and perceptual-motor integration
> *Social interaction:* The student's ability to relate effectively with others in one-to-one and group experiences and including skills such as cooperation, leadership, and support
> *Language development:* The comprehensive ability to receive, understand, and express language in an oral or manual communication mode
> *Adaptive behavior:* The student's ability and skill to manage needs, interactions, responsibility, and self-care in a variety of settings outside the school
> *Vocational/careers:* Those interests, aptitudes, and skills that make success and satisfaction likely in current and future work and recreation
> *Ability measure:* A varied group of indices that suggest the general growth rate in cognitive and behavioral areas and speculate as to potential for growth in specific areas
> *Learning style:* The student's preferred sensory mode, interest areas, priorities, choice of teaching methods, and organizing processes

Given the myriad of factors related to each student's performance, it is imperative that these domains not only be assessed prior to implementing an individualized program but also be monitored continually to ensure success.

SELECTING APPROPRIATE ASSESSMENT PROCEDURES

One of the more difficult decisions special educators must make is the selection of appropriate assessment procedures. Selection can be simplified by identifying what area or domain is to be assessed (for example, reading or language skills) and by determining the purpose of the assessment.

Before discussing various types of assessment tools, it is critical to point out that a teacher should investigate any test's purpose, normative population (if any), and reliability and validity data to determine if the selection is appropriate. Since professional journals continually report such data on various assessment tools and procedures, they should be a part of every special educator's professional library.

Formal Procedures

Assessment procedures can be categorized as either informal or formal. Formal assessment procedures usually refer to standardized tests, which have a long history in special education. **Standardized tests,** also known as norm-referenced tests, are designed to compare a student's performance with that of a group of individuals with similar characteristics. Such tests focus on a particular student's standing within a group rather than his or her mastery of content. If the purpose of assessment is to compare a student's performance with a norm group, then selecting a norm-referenced test is appropriate. In fact, decisions regarding a student's eligibility for special education services are usually made on the basis of standardized test scores.

There is an overwhelming tendency for special education professionals to rely on specific tests. Ysseldyke, Regan, Thurlow, and Schwartz (1981) reported that "regardless of the professional conducting the assessment, regardless of the decision to be made, and regardless of the type of student being assessed, certain devices are likely to be used"(p. 23). The most frequently used test, according to their study, was the *Wechsler Intelligence Scale for Children--Revised,* with the *Bender Visual-Motor Gestalt Test* and then the *Wide Range Achievement Test* following in frequency of use. Jenkins and Pany (1978) also pointed out that standardized achievement tests are widely used in special education. These authors have added that "despite growing suspicion of conventional achievement tests in some circles, the educational community continues to place enormous confidence in them; when achievement test results run counter to teachers' perceptions of children's progress, the achievement test score is usually accepted as the more valid assessment" (Jenkins and Pany 1978, 448). Such standardized diagnostic tests do not assist special educators in planning individualized instructional programs; their use should therefore be minimized (Gallagher 1979).

Rather than relying on standardized tests for program development, special educators must identify procedures that assess a variety of behaviors in the handicapped student's natural setting and are directly related to intervention (Stainback and Stainback 1980). "Although the use of norm-referenced tests is not excluded when needed for various purposes, the assessment is not, generally speaking, norm referenced but is based on the individual functioning of the child in various curricular areas" (Stainback and Stainback 1980, 244). Teachers skilled in the selection and development of informal assessment procedures are more likely to implement and evaluate appropriate instructional programs than teachers who rely on formal assessment procedures in program development.

Informal Procedures

Unlike formal procedures, which compare a student's performance with that of a normative group, informal assessment procedures are designed to "focus on student performance in relation to the demands of the student's environment" (McLoughlin and Lewis 1981, 164). Since informal procedures tend to be continuous in nature and are not necessarily test oriented, they are often more beneficial sources of data than formal procedures for instructional planning and program evaluation. Affleck, Lowenbaum, and Archer (1980) have pointed out that such ongoing assessment procedures enable teachers not only to make better program-

Standardized tests are often used to get an overall picture of a student's performance in relationship to established norms.

matic decisions but also to improve communication with professionals and parents since the information is data based rather than opinion oriented.

Although informal assessment is preferable for program planning and evaluation, there are several drawbacks to its use. The major disadvantage focuses on technical construction. Since informal procedures, either commercial or teacher made, are not concerned with a student's standing in a group, the reliability and validity of the measures may not be addressed. Professionals must make certain that the informal assessment tools they use are indeed measuring what they are intended to measure on a consistent basis. Another disadvantage of informal procedures is that they are initially time consuming to make as well as administer. As a result, teachers often avoid using them despite the valuable instructional information they can provide. The irony is that quickly administered standardized tests frequently provide little, if any, direction to special educators on where to begin instruction. When planning programs for educationally handicapped students, teachers must therefore be skilled in using an array of informal assessment procedures in addition to formal assessment tools.

Criterion-referenced tests. When planning a curriculum for a handicapped student, it is imperative that the special educator know not only what skills are needed for mastery of the content area and in what sequence they are needed but also the student's current skill level in relationship to the content area (Samuels 1979).

Criterion-referenced tests (CRTs) are designed to compare a student's performance or skill level with material to be mastered. An example of a criterion-referenced test is the *Criterion Test of Basic Skills* (Lundell, Evans, and Brown 1976). The related test protocol is presented in Table 3-1. Note how this test provides special educators with more valuable information for program development than a standardized diagnostic reading test, which reports only a student's grade equivalent as a percentile score.

In a discussion of CRTs, Gronlund (1973) points out that "strictly speaking, criterion-referenced measurement refers only to the method of interpreting the results and, thus, could be applied to any classroom or standardized test. This would simply involve analyzing the test, item by item, and describing each student's achievement in terms of some expected level of performance for each area of the test" (p. 2). However, the majority of norm-referenced tests do not lend themselves to criterion-referenced interpretation procedures for the following reasons (Gronlund 1973, 3):

1. The conglomerate of learning tasks would provide a poor frame of reference for describing individual achievement.
2. Since test items that all students answer correctly tend to be omitted from norm-referenced tests, the learning tasks mastered by the entire group would not be included in the description of an individual's achievement.
3. If multiple-choice items (or other selection-type items) were used, some of the correct answers could be due to chance and the description of an individual's achievement would be distorted to an unknown degree. This is especially serious with those norm-referenced tests that use just a few test items to represent each area of achievement.

The first step in developing a CRT involves identifying the skill or area of knowledge to be tested. Next, instructional objectives related to the skill area are written. Remember that the student's behavior, the task itself, and the acceptable level of performance must be stated for each objective. The final step is to construct the CRT based upon the performance objectives already identified (Howell, Kaplan, and O'Connell 1979). For example, ten-year-old Mark is unable to decode consonant-vowel-consonant-vowel (CVCV) patterns correctly. His teacher, Ms. Michaels, goes through the following process in developing a CRT:

- *Objective:* When presented with a list of twenty CVCV words, the student will say the words with 95 percent accuracy within three minutes.
- *Criterion-Referenced Test:* Decode twenty CVCV words written on a word list—*made, game, mope, cape, cube, wipe, bite, tape, fake, rite, hope, site, time, dime, fine, make, same, lake, daze,* and *cake.*

Note the similarity between the stated objective and the CRT. Many teachers develop their CRT pretests on the basis of stated instructional objectives.

CRTs are a valuable assessment procedure at the mastery instructional level since basic skills are relatively sequential in nature and the skills to be learned are limited in scope. Therefore, percentage-correct scores tend to be a valid indicator of the student's progress. However, using CRTs to assess a student's knowledge at the development level of learning is more difficult because it extends beyond the basic skill areas. At this point, the student is required to use higher thinking skills

☐ **TABLE 3–1**
Reading Assessment Record Protocol for the *Criterion Test of Basic Skills*

	Skill Areas & Objectives	Directions & Materials	Responses (Circle Correct Responses)	Number of Correct Items: Frustration Level 0–49%	Instructional Level 50–89%	Mastery Level 90–100%
I. Letter Recognition	A. LOWER-CASE LETTERS The student will identify the names of the lower-case letters.	DIRECTIONS: "Say the names of these letters." Materials: Stimulus Card 1	t n h a g m o b j p i f k s r l z d e w q c v y u x	0 1 2 3 4 5 6 7 8 9 10 11 12	13 14 15 16 17 18 19 20 21 22 23	24 25 26
	B. CAPITAL LETTERS The student will identify the names of the capital letters.	DIRECTIONS: "Say the names of these letters." Materials: Stimulus Card 2	T N H A G M O B J P I F K S R L Z D E W Q C V Y U X	0 1 2 3 4 5 6 7 8 9 10 11 12	13 14 15 16 17 18 19 20 21 22 23	24 25 26
	C. LETTER DISCRIMINATION The student will identify correctly formed letters.	DIRECTIONS: "When I say the name of a letter, you show me that letter in the box to which I point." Materials: Stimulus Cards 3–5	a s m d y p w b c g u q	0 1 2 3 4 5	6 7 8 9 10	11 12
II. Letter Sounding	A. VOWELS (visual-vocal) The student will say the short vowel sounds.	DIRECTIONS: "Say the sounds of these letters." (If the student gives the long vowel sound, ask for another) Materials: Stimulus Card 6	o e i a u	0 1 2	3 4	5
	B. CONSONANTS (visual-vocal) The student will say the consonant sounds.	DIRECTIONS: "Say the sounds of these letters." Materials: Stimulus Card 7	t n h g m b j p f k s r l z d w q c v y x	0 1 2 3 4 5 6 7 8 9 10	11 12 13 14 15 16 17 18	19 20 21
	C. VOWELS (auditory-vocal) The student will give the names of the short vowels when the sounds are given.	DIRECTIONS: "When I say a sound, you tell me the name of the letter."	o e i a u	0 1 2	3 4	5
	D. CONSONANTS (auditory-vocal) The student will give the names of the consonants when the sounds are given.	DIRECTIONS: "When I say a sound, you tell me the name of the letter." (Accept "C" and "K" interchangeably)	t n h g m b j p f k s r l z d w q c v y x	0 1 2 3 4 5 6 7 8 9 10	11 12 13 14 15 16 17 18	19 20 21
III. Blending & Sequencing	A. TWO-LETTER BLENDING The student will blend two-letter sounds together.	DIRECTIONS: "Here you see two letters. Put them together into one sound like this." (Example) (Accept long or short vowel sounds) Materials: Stimulus Cards 8–9	m-a r-e s-i n-u z-o o-p i-k u-t i-d e-b	0 1 2 3 4	5 6 7 8	9 10
	B. THREE-LETTER BLENDING The student will blend three-letter sounds together	DIRECTIONS: "Here you see three letters. Put them together into one sound like this." (Example) (Accept long or short vowel sound) Materials: Stimulus Cards 10–11	m-a-t p-e-g s-i-p n-u-t l-o-t p-a-n b-e-d f-i-t r-u-n l-o-g	0 1 2 3 4	5 6 7 8	9 10
	C. LETTER SEQUENCING The student will identify correctly sequenced words.	DIRECTIONS: "When I say a word, you point to the right one." Materials: Stimulus Cards 12–14	saw top mit let mop rug	0 1 2	3 4 5	6

TABLE 3–1 (continued)
Reading Assessment Record Protocol for the *Criterion Test of Basic Skills*

IV. Special Sounds	A. CONSONANT BLENDS The student will read words containing consonant blends.	DIRECTIONS: "Read these words as I point to them." Materials: Stimulus Cards 15–18	bl cl fl gl pl sl sc sm sn sp st sw br cr dr fr gr pr tr tw	0 1 2 3 4 5 6 7 8 9	10 11 12 13 14 15 16 17	18 19 20
	B. CONSONANT DIGRAPHS The student will read words containing the following consonant digraphs: th, ch, wh, sh, ph.	DIRECTIONS: "Read these words as I point to them." Materials: Stimulus Card 19	th ch wh ph sh th	0 1 2	3 4 5	6
	C. VOWEL DIGRAPHS The student will read words containing the following vowel diagraphs: ay, ee, ai, oa, ea.	DIRECTIONS: "Read these words as I point to them." Materials: Stimulus Card 20	ay ee si oa ea	0 1 2	3 4	5
	D. CONTROLLING *R* The student will read words in which the "r" controls the vowel sound.	DIRECTIONS: "Read these words as I point to them." Materials: Stimulus Card 21	fur pork par dirt per	0 1 2	3 4	5
	E. FINAL *E* The student will read words in which the final "e" makes the vowel sound "long."	DIRECTIONS: "Read these words as I point to them." Materials: Stimulus Card 22	o e i a u	0 1 2	3 4	5
	F. DIPHTHONGS The student will read words containing the following diphthongs: ow, oy, ou, oi.	DIRECTIONS: "Read these words as I point to them." Materials: Stimulus Card 23	ow oy ou oi	0 1	2 3	4
V. Sight Words	SIGHT WORD READING The student will read the basic 220 sight words.	DIRECTIONS: "Read these words to me as I show them to you." Materials: Use your own sight word cards or list.	Keep lists of words that are correctly and incorrectly read.	0–108	109–196	197–220
VI. Letter Writing (Optional)	A. LOWER-CASE LETTERS The student will write the lower-case letters.	DIRECTIONS: "Write these letters when I say them to you."	t n h a g m o b j p i f k s r l z d e w q c v y u x	0 1 2 3 4 5 6 7 8 9 10 11 12	13 14 15 16 17 18 19 20 21 22 23	24 25 26
	B. CAPITAL LETTERS The student will write the capital letters.	DIRECTIONS: "Write these letters when I say them to you."	T N H A G M O B J P I F K S R L Z D E W Q C V Y U X	0 1 2 3 4 5 6 7 8 9 10 11 12	13 14 15 16 17 18 19 20 21 22 23	24 25 26

From *Criterion Test of Basic Skills: Reading*. K. Lundell, J. Evans, and W. Brown (Novato, Calif.: Academic Therapy Publications, Inc., 1976).

to learn complex material, which does not lend itself to scope-and-sequence charts common at the basic skill level (Gronlund 1973). Refer to Table 3-2, which compares testing procedures at the mastery and developmental levels.

Like all informal procedures, CRTs also have limitations. For example, the reliability and validity of CRTs may not be established (Harris and Wolf 1979). In addition, Anastasi (1976) cautions special educators not to assume mastery has been achieved on the basis of CRTs only. The fact that a student has demonstrated success in the resource room, for example, does not ensure success in the regular classroom. Since academic performance is in part determined by the social and emotional climate of the learning environment, the special educator must consider variables related to performance in other environments. For example, the regular teacher's attitude toward the educationally handicapped student will either help or hinder performance.

Task analysis. When confronted with a student who is having difficulty understanding a concept or completing an activity successfully, it is sometimes helpful for the special educator first to identify all the parts of the activity and then observe which parts the student is able to do and which parts are creating difficulties. This process of identifying subtasks or components of an instructional task is called **task analysis.** It is often used for both assessment and instructional purposes. By breaking down an instructional goal into subskills and evaluating the learner's performance at each level, the teacher is able to locate where the instructional problem is.

We analyze tasks continually on a daily basis. Suppose you are looking for an apartment to rent. Your plan of action may include (1) determining the maximum amount of money you can pay; (2) checking newspapers, realtors, and community bulletin boards for vacancies; (3) making appointments to see prospective apartments; (4) listing each apartment's advantages and disadvantages; and (5) deciding which apartment best suits your needs, based on your analysis. The sequence of action is important. It would be illogical to look at rentals first and then decide how much you could affort since you would be wasting a good deal of time looking at $500 apartments when you can spend only $250. Task analysis, whether applied to our personal lives or to instructional programs, provides a concrete, sequential method of thinking about how to reach goals.

To analyze a task, first identify the desired objective in behavioral terms. Next, identify the sequential skills one must learn to accomplish the objective. The following is a sample task analysis for learning to tell time based on an article by Hofmeister and LeFever (1977):

Terminal Objective: Given a clock face, the student will read the time to the nearest five-minute interval with 100 percent accuracy.

Task Analysis:

1. Given a clock face with no hands and with circles in place of numerals, the student will write in the correct numerals.
2. Given a clock face with numerals and hour hand only, the student will read the hour as ________ o'clock by stating the numeral that is immediately before the hour hand.

☐ **TABLE 3–2**
Summary Comparison of Criterion-Referenced Mastery Testing and Testing at the Developmental Level

	Criterion-Referenced Mastery Testing	**Testing at the Developmental Level**
Purpose	Measure mastery of minimum essentials.	Measure degree of achievement beyond the mastery of minimum essentials.
Types of Learning Tasks	Basic skills and simple knowledge outcomes that are prerequisite to further learning. Minimum skills needed to perform some important task safely and effectively.	Complex types of achievement that depend on an intergrated response pattern that typically must be measured as a total functioning unit (understanding, application, thinking skills).
Nature of the Learning	Learning is frequently sequential. Specific tasks can be learned separately and in a clearly defined sequence.	Learning is seldom sequential. Complex learning outcomes depend on the cumulative effect of many diverse learning experiences that can be organized and integrated in many different ways.
Nature of the Instructional Objectives	Objectives are limited to instuctional outcomes that can be fully mastered.	Objectives provide direction toward goals that can never be fully achieved.
Specifying the Specific Learning Outcomes	Limited domain of behavior makes it possible to clearly define the domain. A relatively large proportion of the specific learning outcomes can be identified for each objective.	Unlimited domain of behavior makes complete definition impossible. Only a relatively small proportion of the specific learning outcomes can be identified for each objective.
Building the Table of Specifications	Confine to a unit of instruction and include all, or nearly all, learning outcomes and content areas to be measured.	Confine to some clearly defined area of instruction and include a representative sample of the learning outcomes and content areas to be measured.
Setting Performance Standards	Arbitrarily set level of mastery at 85% correct and adjust up or down as experience dictates.	Use norm-referenced interpretation and develop approximate nonmastery standards from experience in teaching and testing.
Constructing Test Items	Match item difficulty to the difficulty of the learning task to be measured and follow standard rules of item construction.	Obtain range of item difficulty for each objective and follow standard rules of item construction.
Reporting Test Results	Indicate degree of mastery of each objective, or unit of instruction, by using percentage-correct score, and classify performances as mastery or nonmastery.	Indicate relative degree of progress toward each objective by describing performance (or using percentage-correct score), and indicate relative level of performance by indicating position in some clearly defined group.

3. Given a complete clock face (numerals, hour and minute hands), the student will identify the hour and minute hands by drawing a circle around the hand asked for by the teacher.
4. Given a complete clock face with minute hand held constant, the student will correctly read the hour when asked.
5. Given a clock face with numerals and minute hand only, the student will count by fives starting at the top of the clock to the minute-hand position and state the number of minutes indicated.
6. Given a clock face with either a minute or an hour hand, the student will state which hand is on the clock and then read the appropriate minutes or hour.
7. Given a complete clock face with the minute hand positioned only at five-minute intervals, the student will read the time by stating the hour first and then the minutes.

The true test of any task analysis is how it works in the actual teaching situation. You may find that your task analysis does not have enough detail. For example, item 5 in the above task analysis assumes that the student knows how to count by fives. If the student does not possess this skill, you must teach it before developing an instructional plan for task 5.

Task analysis identifies a student's performance for any given skill; however, it does not provide information on how to teach––only on what needs to be taught. Therefore, it is important for the teacher to understand the student's individual learning style in order to select appropriate instructional strategies and materials. In the example used earlier, a teacher may accomplish the different steps in a variety of ways. If a pupil has trouble differentiating between hour and minute hands, it may be necessary to color code the hands (e.g., black for hour, red for minute) until the student becomes more discriminating. If junior high school students are being taught, it may be more meaningful to use a factory time clock to emphasize the correlation between telling time and maintaining a job.

There are several benefits to using task analysis: instruction is organized; learning is simplified because only one concept is presented at a time; learning builds upon previous knowledge because tasks are sequential in nature; and weak areas in a student's skills can be identified.

Task analysis also has certain limitations. While it is relatively easy to analyze simple tasks, more complex learning skills do not lend themselves to task analysis. In many skill areas, there is a lack of agreement on the exact sequence of tasks. (McLoughlin and Lewis 1981).

Work-sample analysis. Whereas task analysis identifies components of a skill, **work-sample analysis** is an informal assessment technique that attempts to expose a student's procedural errors when attempting a task. According to Easley and Zwoyer (1975), teachers are more likely to be successful if they focus on a student's thinking process rather than on the outcome. Applicable to any domain, work-sample analysis can provide teachers with valuable information necessary for planning instruction (Bachor 1979) since the process for deriving an answer, rather than the answer itself, is more valuable for determining a student's performance level.

Bachor (1979) has developed guidelines for teachers using work samples as diagnostic tools. For example, assignments should be designed so that they are able to expose procedural errors. Unlike standardized tests, work-sample analysis should enable teachers to go beyond finding an error to pinpointing its origin. For example, if a student computes that $8-5=6$, all that can be concluded is that a mistake has been made. However, if a student computes that $7-3=4$, $10-8=2$, and $2-1=4$, the teacher can conclude that the student knows the operation of subtraction. The source of error becomes apparent when, asked to read the problem $8-5$, the student responds with, "eight minus two equals six." Even though he or she has interchanged the *5* and the *2*, that answer is correct. Remedial instruction should focus on discriminating between the digits *5* and *2* rather than on further subtraction facts. Probing students to explain their work often provides valuable instructional information.

McLoughlin and Lewis (1981) have outlined the following steps to be used in **error analysis**:

1. Score the student's assignments.
2. Categorize the errors.
3. Search for an error pattern.
4. Summarize the types of errors made.
5. Hypothesize why the student made errors.

Probably the most difficult step is the last one––hypothesizing why the student performed the task inaccurately. It is helpful to look at the student's process of thinking in attempting to classify errors. Bachor (1979) suggests that professionals classify errors as input, elaboration, or output errors.

Input errors occur when a student does not scan or attend to all the critical details of the content or when a student is receiving too much information at a time. The following two incidents are examples of input errors:

- Nine-year-old Steven was told by his teacher to complete three pages of math for homework and to have his parents sign each page. The next morning he gave his teacher the homework, which was done correctly; however, he had failed to have the work signed. His teacher, recalling the hectic end-of-school events of the previous day, concluded that Steven had been frantically looking for his misplaced hat and mittens rather than attending to her directions.
- Twelve-year-old Mark was asked to read three paragraphs and then identify all the nouns, verbs, and adjectives. In addition, he was to provide appropriate punctuation. Mark's work indicated that he was unable to do either task correctly. Suspecting that he was receiving too much information, his teacher changed the task so that he had to identify the parts of speech in one paragraph and write in the correct punctuation for another paragraph. He completed this revised task with 80 percent accuracy for parts of speech and 90 percent accuracy for punctuation.

Output errors occur when a student is expressing an answer; they are often the result of fatigue or anxiety. Output errors can occur even though appropriate attending and thinking (input level) skills have been used. It is not uncommon for students to realize their mistakes when reviewing their work. For example, Lisa is now in the fourth grade and has consistently failed at spelling. Before her weekly Friday spelling tests, she actually breaks out in a cold sweat. Over a five-week period, Lisa's average spelling test score has been 65 percent. This reinforces her negative perceptions of her spelling skills despite her ability to identify and then correctly spell the misspelled words on Monday.

Elaboration errors are the kinds of mistake a student might make while working through a problem. There are three types of elaboration error: simplification, omission, and inappropriate rule (Bachor 1979). Simplification error is a strategy a student might use when the task is too complex. In essence, he or she applies knowledge already acquired to solve a problem. For example, eleven-year-old Tina spelled *kitchen* as *kichun;* that is, she applied the phonics rules she knew to solve the spelling problem. In simplification error students reduce the complexity of a task to a level that they are able to solve. Omission errors occur when part of a task is left out or ignored. Obvious examples of omission errors occur during oral reading; some students omit words or phrases, thus distorting passage comprehension. Inappropriate rule errors occur when a student uses an incorrect strategy to complete a task. The student who uses periods rather than question marks at the end of an interrogative statement exemplifies this type of error. Another example is the student who writes and says *childs* and *goed* instead of *children* and *went.* Here the student does not understand irregular plurals and past tenses.

By analyzing a student's behaviors throughout task performance, (that is, input, elaboration, and output), a teacher will be better able to specify where and why an error is occurring. This information provides more insight into the learning process than merely analyzing output, or responses, and thus increases the likelihood of developing appropriate instructional approaches.

Observation. **Observation** procedures allow professionals to analyze a student's academic and social behaviors to determine not only the frequency of a problem behavior but also a possible pattern or cause for the behavior. Observation techniques are classified as either nonsystematic or systematic (Salvia and Ysseldyke 1981). In nonsystematic observation the teacher simply observes and notes the student's interactions and behaviors. Because of their subjective nature, nonsystematic observations tend to provide professionals with little reliable data. For example, Mr. Stucky, a fourth grade teacher, requested that the school psychologist observe Katie, whom he labeled as "a child who bothers her classmates when they are working." During the one-hour observation, the psychologist saw Katie demonstrate only one aggressive behavior; thus, he concluded that she was not aggressive. After he left Katie had five "acting-out" episodes within thirty minutes.

Perhaps if the observation had been systematic, a more accurate impression of Katie's behavior would have been conveyed. In order to implement systematic observation, the following steps are taken:

1. First, an objective is formulated that defines specifically the behavior to be observed. In the example above, it is not enough to define the objective as observing whether or not Katie is aggressive. Katie's talking during independent seat work, however, is a behavior that is specific enough to be observable.
2. The next step is to determine how to measure the behavior. It is impossible to watch a student every second of the school day. Therefore, it is important to

limit observations in terms of time or location. In the case of Katie, simply counting the times she verbally interrupted her peers would be appropriate since independent seat work lasts only thirty minutes and the teacher would be able to monitor each occurrence. There are a variety of procedures a professional can use to measure behavior. Selection of the best method for collecting data depends upon the behavior being observed. Regarding the observation of verbal behavior, Howell and Kaplan (1980) caution professionals to be "prepared to score the behavior as it occurs or to store it for later. There is a tendency when scoring any assessment to simply count the number of mistakes and report the sum. Such information is nearly always useless" (p. 56). An alternative to merely reporting a numerical score is to analyze the behavior in terms of antecedent events and the consequences that follow the behavior each time it occurs. Any observation form used to measure or count behavior should provide space for such notations.

☐ **FIGURE 3–2**
Observation Recording Form

Behavior: Number of times Katie's talking interrupts peers during independent seatwork

Frequency:	9	11	5	4	5	10	12	7	5	6
Days:	1	2	3	4	5	6	7	8	9	10

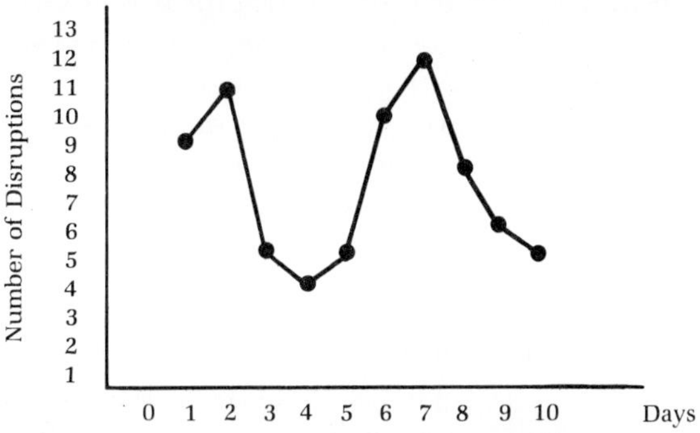

Comments:

On Mondays and Tuesdays (days 1, 2, 6 + 7 on graph) independent seatwork precedes reading. Katie, a poor reader, does not like to read. Often she begins reading with comments such as, "I'm not good at this."

Most of Katie's interruptions are questions directed to her peers, e.g., "What page?" or "How many questions?" or "Where's my book? Pencil?"

Conclusions:

Be sure Katie has all necessary materials and understands her assignments prior to beginning seatwork

Reduce anxiety regarding oral reading group lesson by either reviewing reading assignment before seatwork or have Katie read her lesson on a one-to-one basis with the teacher.

3. After observing the behavior, it is important to record the findings. It is also important to collect a representative sample of the behavior to ensure accuracy. Figure 3-2 illustrates an observation chart designed to analyze Katie's behavior over a two-week period. She appeared to interrupt her classmates more frequently on Mondays and Tuesdays. A visual presentation such as a chart or graph provides an overview of the student's performance and assists in analyzing the data. Finally, an interpretation of the data permits professionals to conclude whether or not there is a problem and, if so, to determine a possible starting point for intervention.

It is comparatively easy to determine an acceptable level of performance for academic behaviors. Defining acceptable performance for social behaviors is more difficult. By using the ecological approach, however, the professional will be better able to establish criteria for acceptable nonacademic behaviors (Prieto and Rutherford 1977). Specifically, a teacher should expect a student to have those skills that are "(*a*) available in his or her environment; (*b*) acceptable to others in the environment; and/or (*c*) commonly occurring in the environment" (Howell and Kaplan 1980, 9). Rather than evaluating a behavior according to personal attitudes and values, the focus shifts to expectations of the environment. This perspective permits professionals to evaluate social behavior with greater objectivity.

Although systematic observations permit professionals to analyze classroom interaction, among students as well as between teacher and student, they do have limitations (Salvia and Ysseldyke 1981). Effective observation procedures take time to plan and implement. Also, there are times when an observer's presence in the classroom distorts or distrupts the behaviors being observed. Therefore, observation should be considered only as part of the total information-gathering process. By continually crosschecking their own observations with information from other sources (such as formal and informal tests) and by comparing their views with the perceptions of others, teachers can control the influence of personal bias.

Check lists and rating scales. Professionals do not always have the opportunity to observe students directly in various settings. In such instances, check lists and rating scales are used to gather otherwise unobtainable assessment data. Both procedures require either an informant to render his or her perceptions of a student's behavior or the student to give a self-report of his or her own behavior.

Check lists usually require the informant to indicate whether a child does or does not have a specific skill or behavior. In contrast, rating scales permit the informant to identify the intensity or frequency of a behavior. For example, the self-reporting *Tennessee Self-Concept Scale* (Fitts 1965) asks students to respond to each item on a five-point scale ranging from "completely false" to "completely true." Scales such as the *Behavior Rating Profile* (Brown and Hammill 1978) provide a more comprehensive indication of a student's behavior since input from peers, teachers, and parents is required in addition to the student's own perceptions. Due to the potential significance of check lists and rating scales in making educational decisions, the informant's exposure to the student as well as objectivity is necessary.

Check lists and rating scales are commonly used in screening programs to identify areas where further in-depth assessment may be appropriate. Because of reporting bias and inaccuracy, intervention or placement decisions should not be made on the basis of this type of information alone. However, rating scales and check lists can assist professionals in pinpointing areas that need to be further evaluated.

Check lists and rating scales can also be extremely helpful in collecting information on what instruction procedures, methods, and materials are most likely to be motivating or appropriate for individual students. While testing procedures usually provide the necessary information on *what* to teach, other more informal assessment techniques, such as check lists and rating scales, provide important clues as to *how* to teach (Zigmond, Vallecorsa, and Silverman 1983).

Special educators can develop their own check lists or rating scales for a variety of purposes. One secondary resource teacher was working on developing independent work skills in the regular classroom with five of her students. Specifically, she wanted to know if these students were completing in-class and homework assignments in their regular classrooms. Since she could not directly observe these students' progress, she designed the check list presented in Figure 3-3 to be completed by the regular teachers for each handicapped student in their classes.

□ **FIGURE 3–3**
Teacher's Check List

Teacher ______________________________ Date __________
Student's Name ______________________________

To help me follow this student's progress, indicate with a check mark those tasks this student did not satisfactorily complete on a daily basis. Please put this form in my mailbox on Friday.

Thank you.

Zoe Austin, Resource Teacher

	M	T	W	Th	F
1. Completed in-class assignments on time					
2. Attempted but did not complete in-class assignments					
3. Followed all directions for in-class assignments					
4. Used appropriate media (pencil, pen, etc.) to do in-class assignments					
5. Written in-class assignments are legible and neat					
6. Wrote homework assignments in "homework notebook"					
7. Completed homework assignment					
8. Attempted but did not complete homework assignment					
9. Followed all directions for homework assignments					
10. Used appropriate media to do homework					
11. Written homework is legible and neat					

Comments:

The resource teacher also provided consultation services to the regular teachers. Consultation focused on how they could modify their instruction to increase the handicapped students' in-class and homework productivity. To determine if her suggestions were being used, she asked her students to complete on a weekly basis the check list presented in Figure 3–4.

It is important to note that prior to making any instructional or consultation changes, the resource teacher needed two kinds of information—the regular teacher's perceptions about each handicapped student's performance and the student's perceptions about his or her teacher's use of alternative instructional strategies for increasing the number of completed assignments. By analyzing responses to both check lists, she could ascertain where she needed to focus more of her professional time.

Interviews. One other procedure often utilized to collect relevant assessment data is the structured interview. Like check lists and rating scales, its use is generally limited to gathering information that is not readily accessible. Interviews require communication between two persons, often the professional and the parent. It is important that professionals practice the interview process before actually conducting an interview. The degree to which teachers feel comfortable asking for personal information and their ability to ask for such information in a nonevaluative manner will influence the success of their interviews.

Interviews can be either haphazard or structured. The more thought a specialist puts into planning an interview, the more likely it will provide the desired information. The following are suggestions for conducting effective interviews with either parents or other professionals:

☐ **FIGURE 3–4**
Student's Check List

Name ______________________________ Date __________
Teacher's Name ______________________________

Check those items that your teacher did not do. On Friday, put this form in your work folder.

	M	T	W	Th	F
1. Asked to see your homework notebook and checked to see if you wrote down the assignment					
2. Wrote the homework assignment on the board					
3. Said when the homework was due					
4. Used suggestions agreed upon at our conference to help you complete homework assignments					
5. Write directions for in-class assignments on the board					
6. Used suggestions agreed upon at our conference to help you complete in-class work					

Comments:

- Begin the interview with introductions and ask the person being interviewed if he or she has anything to share with you.
- Next, explain the purpose of the interview and tell the person being interviewed that you would like to keep notes about the meeting. Be sure that copies of written work, assessment data, etc., are available for review.
- Allow the person being interviewed enough time to respond to each of your questions or concerns.
- At the end of the interview, ask if there is any other pertinent information that you should know.
- End the interview with a restatement of the purpose of the interview. If necessary, schedule a follow-up conference and give all involved persons an appointment card with the next meeting date, time, and place on it.

Like rating scales and check lists, interviews should be interpreted cautiously since they, too, rely on someone's perceptions of the student. It is not uncommon for informants to report information inaccurately.

ADMINISTERING ASSESSMENT TOOLS

Since assessment results are used to make important decisions, it is critical that all instructions for administering tests be followed carefully. When the examiner deviates from established time limitations or procedures for recording responses or inappropriately prompts a student, the results cannot be interpreted accurately. Instructions for test administration are usually given in the test manual. Under no circumstances should a test be administered unless the examiner thoroughly understands the test manual and has practiced giving the test. There is no set rule regarding how many times to practice giving the test. This depends on the complexity of the test as well as the examiner's background in testing. The following are guidelines for developing proficiency in both formal and informal test administration:

- Read the test manual carefully. It might be helpful to use a highlighter for underlining the examiner's oral directions; thus, when actually giving the test, you will know the sequence of structured responses you are required to give the student.
- Familiarize yourself with both acceptable and unacceptable student responses. Also, some standardized tests allow the examiner to prompt a student in order to give additional information or to clarify a response. Each test is different.
- Begin practice testing by administering the test to adults. This will assist you in getting to know the test. After you feel comfortable with the test process, begin practice testing on children of different ages. By testing developmentally different students, you will be exposed to a greater proportion of the test items. Be sure to have an experienced test examiner review your scoring procedures and interpretation of results.

- Finally, have an experienced examiner observe you administering the test. If he or she identifies a problem in your administering, scoring, or interpreting skills, then return to one of the above steps and work through the process until your testing procedures are without error.

Probably one of the worst mistakes a professional can make is to administer a test without adequate training. It is critical to note that test scores, along with other data, assist the professional team in making placement and programmatic decisions for a student. Misuse of tests can be frustrating to teachers as well as damaging to students. However, when properly used, tests can provide assessment information that is invaluable to effective instructional planning, implementation, and evaluation.

SUMMARY POINTS

- The assessment process includes screening, diagnosis, program planning, and evaluation.
- Comprehensive assessment investigations include not only identifying a student's needs but also examining the contributions that environmental variables have on performance.
- The four interrelated phases of the special education cycle are identification, multifactored assessment, planning and implementing the IEP, and program reevaluation.
- In order to best understand a student's present performance and behaviors, it is important to recognize the role that current life circumstances, developmental history, and interpersonal factors have in programmatic and instructional decisions.
- Formal standardized testing procedures are most commonly used to diagnose educationally handicapped students; however, they usually are not appropriate for instructional planning.
- By utilizing various informal assessment procedures, professionals are better able to develop, implement, and evaluate appropriate individualized programs. Professionals responsible for developing individualized programs must be concerned with gathering information on both what to teach and how to teach.
- Because of the unique needs of each student, special educators should have expertise using a variety of assessment procedures. There is no single test battery that will meet the needs of all students.
- Informal procedures include task analysis, work-sample analysis, criterion-referenced tests, observation, check lists and rating scales, and interviews.

REVIEW QUESTIONS

1. What guidelines, if any, does your state mandate for special and regular class teachers' participation in the diagnostic and IEP planning phases of the special education cycle?
2. Identify the advantages and disadvantages associated with formal and informal assessment procedures. State what kind of assessment information each type of informal procedure might provide a special educator about a student's performance.

SUGGESTED READINGS

Guerin, G. R., and Maier, A. S. 1983. *Informal assessment in education.* Palo Alto, Calif.: Mayfield.

McLoughlin, J. A., and Lewis, R. B. 1981. *Assessing special students.* Columbus, Ohio: Charles E. Merrill.

Salvia, J., and Ysseldyke, J. E. 1981. *Assessment in special and remedial education.* 2d ed. Boston: Houghton Mifflin.

Wallace, G., and Larsen, S. C. 1979. *Educational assessment of learning problems: Testing for teaching.* Boston: Allyn & Bacon.

Zigmond, N.; Vallecorsa, A.; and Silverman, R. 1983. *Assessment for instructional planning in special education.* Englewood Cliffs, N.J.: Prentice-Hall.

Application: Assessing for Program Development

The following is a step-by-step analysis of one special educator's involvement in the assessment process for a student suspected of being educationally handicapped:

Phase I: Referral

Nine-year-old Andrea Testone's third grade teacher, Mrs. Wyatt, first became concerned about Andrea in October. At that time, she asked the school psychologist and resource teacher to help her modify Andrea's program. Mr. Watkins, the resource teacher, suggested that the amount of work be reduced for each assignment and that Andrea receive additional phonics instruction. He provided Mrs. Wyatt with supplementary reading activities to be used in the regular class.

Phase II: Diagnosis

By December, little improvement was noted. After obtaining parental permission to begin the assessment process, the following assessment tools were used to collect diagnostic data: *WISC-R, Woodcock Reading Mastery Tests, Key Math.* The instruments used in this case were selected specifically for this child; a different set of instruments might be chosen in another child's case.

Based upon these assessment procedures, the following conclusions were drawn:

General ability level: Andrea functions within the average range of intellectual ability, although her true potential may have been somewhat disguised by her apparent level of anxiety during the test administration. Her relatively high scores on vocabulary and block design (subtests of the WISC-R) indicate a potential for "above-average" intellectual functioning.

Relative strengths:

1. Performance in math is somewhat hindered by her difficulties with story problems, which often require reading skills beyond her current level of functioning
2. General understanding of concepts expected of her age group through listening and awareness
3. Cooperative and friendly with peers and adults

Relative weaknesses:

1. Attending to tasks that approach her instructional frustration level
2. Word attack skills and use of phonetic rules
3. High level of anxiety related to some academic tasks, particularly reading

Phase III: IEP Meeting

After collecting the multifactored assessment data, the IEP committee met to write Andrea's IEP. Andrea was identified as educationally handicapped, and the service delivery model recommended by the committee was regular class placement for all areas except reading. The resource teacher would be responsible for developing Andrea's reading skills. In addition, he would provide consultation services to Andrea's regular classroom teacher on an as-needed basis. The focus of these consultation services would be identifying specific instructional strategies and materials designed to meet Andrea's needs. In addition, the school psychologist and counselor would work with the classroom teacher, parents, and Andrea where appropriate. It was apparent that the success of Andrea's program was dependent upon the educational team, not just one professional.

Phase IV: Individualized Instructional Planning

The next step of the special education cycle, program development, was the responsibility of Mr. Watkins, the resource teacher. Although diagnostic data confirmed that Andrea had a reading problem, the data did not provide directions for instruction.

Using a problem-solving approach recommended by Guerin and Maier (1983), Mr. Watkins posed the following questions to assist him in planning Andrea's reading instructional program:

1. What is the problem?
2. What additional information is needed?
3. What assessment procedures are appropriate for collecting this needed information?

The answers to these three questions served as a plan of action for Mr. Watkins in his attempt to identify and meet Andrea's special instructional needs. First, Mr. Watkins determined that Andrea's learning problems were primarily in the reading domain; although some deficits in social interaction were also identified. Next, Mr. Watkins realized that in order to plan an appropriate instructional program, further assessment was needed in all reading areas and in various social grouping patterns. Finally, to identify Andrea's reading instructional needs, Mr. Watkins decided to administer the *Gray Oral Reading Test—Form A.* In addition, he decided to make an informal inventory of Andrea's reading skills by using task analysis to look specifically at subskills such as phonics, word attack, analysis, and comprehension. To evaluate Andrea's performance in these reading processes, he would use error analysis.

For identifying Andrea's social interaction skills, Mr. Watkins decided to use structured observation to determine her performance in various grouping patterns and under different learning situations. In addition, he conducted a home interview and administered the *Adaptive Behavior Inventory for Children* (ABIC).

The *Gray Oral Reading Test* and the informal reading inventory indicated the following levels of performance and discrepancies:

1. Andrea's independent reading is at the early first grade level, and she is at a late first to early second grade instructional level.
2. Andrea's reading comprehension and her listening capacity are above the level of expectation, considering her weak word attack skills. Even when she is not able to pronounce the words, she can understand enough of the story from contextual clues to respond to questions of fact. Her overall scores on tests of oral reading ability are influenced by the great amount of time she requires.
3. Andrea's word attack skills are on the second grade level. She demonstrates difficulty in pronouncing consonants and consonant blends in both the initial position (e.g., *sh*ut) and final position (e.g., ba*th*). She has much difficulty with three-letter initial blends (e.g., *spr*ing), although she can correctly pronounce all the short and long vowels in isolation. She has much difficulty applying phonetic rules (e.g., a single *e* at the end of the word makes the preceding vowel long). Andrea demonstrates difficulty in pronouncing vowels in the medial position (e.g., she says "clumb" for "climb").
4. Andrea's level of sight-word recognition is below the third grade level. She tends to rely on phonetic rules to decode irregular words.

In social interaction, the following information was obtained:

1. On the *Adaptive Behavior Inventory for Children* (ABIC), Andrea scored in the at-

risk category for nonacademic school roles, but not for the remaining five areas—family, community, peer relations, self-maintenance, and earner/consumer.

2. The interview with Mrs. Testone revealed that at home Andrea was often impatient, especially when asked to attempt new tasks difficult for her to accomplish readily.
3. The structured observations indicated that Andrea often failed to complete assignments, stated that she couldn't do her work, made negative statements to her peers, and avoided eye contact with peers and adults.

Mr. Watkins was then ready to identify Andrea's specific instructional needs. Based on the assessment information he had collected, he wrote the following instructional objectives and related evaluation procedures:

1. When given a list of ten words selected from her reading vocabulary list, each of which begins with a single consonant, Andrea will pronounce each correctly in two seconds or less. (Teacher-made test)
2. When given a list of ten words from levels two and three of the Dolch word list, each of which begins with a double consonant blend, Andrea will pronounce each correctly in two seconds or less. (Teacher-made test)
3. When given a list of ten words from levels two and three in the Dolch word list, each of which ends in a double consonant blend, Andrea will pronounce each correctly in two seconds or less. (Teacher-made test)
4. When given a list of thirty words from levels two and three of the Dolch list, each of which contains a CVC pattern, Andrea will pronounce each correctly in three to five seconds. (Teacher-made test)
5. When given a list of thirty words from levels two and three of the Dolch list, each of which contains a CVCV pattern, Andrea will pronounce each correctly in three to five seconds. (Teacher-made test)
6. When given a list of thirty words from levels two and three of the Dolch list, each of which contains a CVVC pattern, Andrea will pronounce each correctly in three to five seconds. (Teacher-made test)
7. When given a list of fifty words that include five trials for each vowel in long and short form, Andrea will isolate the vowel sound and state its symbol name as the teacher pronounces each for her. (Teacher-made test)
8. Andrea will pronounce every word in the Dolch word list through level three in ten seconds. (Teacher-made test)
9. Andrea will pronounce content vocabulary in arithmetic, social studies, and science as developed by the teacher with 100 percent accuracy. (Teacher-made test)
10. Andrea will complete all appropriate assignments independently with 100 percent accuracy. (Teacher observation)
11. When asked by the teacher, Andrea will make two positive statements regarding a mastery task she has completed. (Teacher observation)
12. Andrea will look at the teacher during structured lessons 90 percent of the time. (Teacher observation)
13. Andrea will identify and write her feelings about self and school in a journal on a daily basis. (Journal entries)

Discussion Points

1. From this application, it is apparent that the special educator had the primary responsibility to plan and monitor the individualized instructional plan. What other assessment procedures could Mr. Watkins have used to evaluate and monitor Andrea's social interaction performance?
2. The assessment team tended to rely on standardized tests, whereas the resource teacher placed greater emphasis on the use of informal procedures to determine instructional needs. Why do you think this difference existed?

CHAPTER 4 Planning the Learning Environment

OUTLINE

INTRODUCTION

There are many considerations that special educators must be aware of in order to preserve an ecological balance that promotes learning for handicapped students. These important factors include scheduling, arranging the physical environment, and grouping for instruction. In addition, the importance of understanding interactions that occur in instructional ecosystems, such as the regular and special classrooms, should not be overlooked.

Objectives

This chapter will help you to

- state criteria for successfully arranging the physical environment;
- develop appropriate grouping arrangements for instruction;
- identify procedures for developing effective resource room and self-contained program schedules;
- identify procedures for developing a student's daily schedule.

Critical Incident: Scheduling Demands—A Dilemma for Teachers

Ann Jacobson walked out of the county superintendent's office in late August, having signed a contract as a special education teacher at Liberty High School. She was scheduled to meet with the principal to begin organizing for the new school year, which was just four days away. When Ms. Jacobson arrived at the principal's office, the secretary told her that the principal was in a meeting and would meet with her later that morning. In the meantime, the secretary gave Ms. Jacobson the keys and directions to her classroom.

The room had previously been assigned to a speech therapist and was approximately two-thirds the size of the other classrooms. Inside, Ms. Jacobson found a portable storage closet, a teacher's desk and chair, and one round table with four student chairs. No audio-visual or educational materials were provided.

While Ms. Jacobson was making a list of needed equipment, the secretary paged her to return to the principal's office. When she arrived, she was introduced to the principal, Mrs. Krause, and the guidance counselor, Ms. Dixon. Mrs. Krause explained that there were twenty-five students enrolled in the resource class and that while the IEPs for these students were completed last spring, none of the twenty-five students had yet been scheduled into classes. Ms. Jacobson, with Ms. Dixon's assistance, was to select and schedule the appropriate regular classes for each of these students.

Ms. Jacobson showed Mrs. Krause the list of furniture and equipment she needed and asked how she could obtain it. Mrs. Krause called the maintenance engineer and asked him to help her obtain needed furniture. She also told Ms. Jacobson to talk with the media specialist about audio-visual equipment and to obtain purchase requisitions for materials from the school secretary. Before she left the office with the maintenance engineer to look at furniture for her classroom, Ms. Jacobson arranged to meet with Ms. Dixon the following morning to begin the scheduling process.

As she reviewed her list of tasks during lunch, Ms. Jacobson realized that it had grown considerably. She needed to schedule students into regular classes; obtain materials, furniture, and media equipment; arrange the classroom; and plan the resource room schedules for her students.

Points for Consideration

- *Ms. Jacobson was not familiar with the educational and social needs of her students yet by necessity was responsible for selecting appropriate regular classes for them.*

Scheduling decisions should be based on each student's academic, social, and behavioral skills. Further, the instructional style of each regular teacher and the course requirements should also be considered in the decision-making process. When both the handicapped student's needs and regular classroom environments are recognized as critical to effective scheduling, the student is more likely to experience success.

- *Ms. Jacobson was responsible for creating the physical environment for students served in her program.*

The ability to arrange the physical environment successfully is an important professional competency because, like the strategies and materials selected for use, the physical environment has an impact on students' rate of learning. Special educators must therefore be familiar with all variables contributing to an effective physical environment as well as sources for materials needed within the environment. Often state education offices publish guidelines that can assist special educators in this endeavor.

COMMON INSTRUCTIONAL MISCONCEPTIONS

The special teacher serves a small number of handicapped students. The number of students served by a special teacher is often governed by state regulations. Typically these regulations are based on the nature and severity of the student's handicapping condition. Special educators trained to work with severely handicapped students usually serve fewer students than those who provide instruction for mildly handicapped students. In the latter case, student enrollment can be close to that of regular classes.

It is the administrator's responsibility to arrange and maintain the learning environment for all classes in a school. While administrators are legally responsible for activities, personnel, equipment, and materials in a school building, they typically have limited training or experience regarding handicapped students. As a result, building administrators often rely on the knowledge and expertise of the special educator to plan and implement special education programs. However, administrators should play a supportive role by promoting a positive climate for special education programs within the school.

FACTORS RELATED TO DELIVERING INSTRUCTION

When handicapped students are placed in special education programs, the first step in scheduling is to identify how much time each student needs in every program in which he or she is served. Specifying instructional time seems like a simple task. However, since most handicapped students usually spend some time in the regular classroom, such decisions are often quite complex. Therefore, after a special program has been selected for a student, general and special educators must make time-sharing decisions.

Guidelines for developing an effective schedule are dependent upon the type of service delivery model being used. The following discussion focuses on scheduling procedures for self-contained and resource room programs which are the most common service delivery options for students with learning and behavior deficits.

Self-Contained Schedule

The self-contained service delivery model is the most restrictive of the programming options typically available to handicapped students. This is due to the limited contact with nonimpaired peers provided in such a program. Typically the daily schedule for students in a self-contained classroom is similar to that in a regular classroom since the special educator is providing most, if not all, instruction for these students. Figure 4–1 provides an example of how one special educator schedules instruction.

The groups referred to in this figure are formed on the basis of common instructional needs. However, even when assessment results identify similar instructional needs among students, each student's learning style may require the use of a different instructional approach from that used for other students. Therefore, the special educator must consider both the skill needs and learning style of

FIGURE 4–1
Self-Contained Schedule

8:30– 8:45	General Business: Attendance, Lunch Money, Announcements
8:45–10:00	Reading: Groups A, B, C, D
10:00–10:20	Recess
10:20–10:30	Organizational Time
10:30–11:45	Arithmetic: Groups A, B, C, D
11:45–12:00	Organizational Time
12:00–12:30	Lunch
12:30– 1:00	Monday, Wednesday, Friday: Physical Education Tuesday and Thursday: Music
1:00– 2:00	Written Expression: Groups A, B, C
2:00– 2:15	Recess
2:15– 2:30	Organizational Time
2:30– 3:15	Monday and Wednesday: Science Tuesday and Thursday: Social Studies Friday: Art
3:15– 3:20	Dismissal

Comparison of resource and consultant interaction with regular teachers. From C. Mandell and E. Fiscus, *Understanding Exceptional People* (St. Paul, Minn.: West Publishing, 1981), p. 176.

each student when making group decisions. As a result, one or several students could make up a group for scheduling purposes.

The daily schedule illustrated in Figure 4–1 allows a total of forty minutes a day for organizational time. Organizational time is interspersed throughout the school day to allow the teacher to monitor and evaluate student activity. While forty minutes may appear excessive, Gallagher (1979) indicates that organizational time is essential because it allows the teacher to perform such activities as explaining directions or checking student work on independent tasks. Further, this time gives students the flexibility to finish independent tasks and prepare for the next lesson or activity.

The schedule in Figure 4–1 also represents an attempt by the teacher to alternate preferred activities with those that are less preferred by students. In this example, neither reading nor arithmetic was preferred by students; so the teacher arranged for nonacademic activities to follow each of these subjects.

Resource Room Schedule

A staggered master schedule (Wiederholt, Hammill, and Brown 1978) for the resource room is designed to provide the special educator with flexibility to arrange for time sharing with regular educators. Each student may spend from fifteen to forty-five consecutive minutes in the resource room, leaving and returning to the regular class throughout the day at various times. An example of a staggered resource room schedule appears in Figure 4–2.

The assignment of a student to a group in the resource room depends upon several variables related to the student's learning style, such as attention span, ability to interact with others, rate of learning, communication skills, emotional needs, and social skills. For example, a withdrawn student may not attempt to participate in group instruction, and an easily distracted student may be inattentive during small-group lessons. Typically the special educator's goal for these students should be to teach them to communicate and to attend to instruction in a group setting.

The time scheduled for daily evaluation and record keeping is often used by the teacher to analyze students' progress toward stated objectives and goals. The special educator may, for example, prompt communication in the withdrawn child by having that student take responsibility for checking work or having each student praise the others' work. The easily distracted student can be taught attending skills at nonacademic, clerical tasks, such as record keeping, before he or she is expected to attend to academic instruction in a group.

As indicated in the figure, time for evaluation and record keeping is allocated so that the special educator may analyze student performance in order to identify future lessons and mastery tasks. Record keeping should be designed to motivate students by providing them with a visual representation of their progress, thus building into the schedule routine opportunities for the teacher to praise students' efforts and accomplishments.

Instructional events illustrated in Figure 4–2 change every fifteen minutes. Justification for the fifteen-minute interval is related to basic principles of instruction. The difficulty of a task depends more on the size of the task than on the concept under study (Blake 1976). For this reason, the special educator arranges for students to learn over an extended period of time rather than in concentrated periods of time. Furthermore, in this way handicapped students' involvement in regular class activities is not impeded by lengthy vists to the resource room for instruction. Students may visit the resource room once during a typical school day or for forty-five minutes at two different times in a school day, depending on their unique instructional needs.

The planning time and lunch period are arranged so that the special educator has the flexibility to consult with parents or professionals with different schedules. When time blocks for consultation and lunch periods are scheduled sequentially, the special educator has the ability to adapt to the different schedules of other professionals in the building and may find it easier to reach these professionals for consultation.

The time reserved at the end of the day is devoted to supplemental assistance. Generally, special educators use this time to assist students with nonroutine tasks, such as helping them take tests orally, write reports for general education classes, or review certain concepts. The last half-hour of the day is devoted to this type of activity because it is a time when many students are not receiving academic instruction in the regular classroom.

Problems develop in time-sharing practices between general and special educators if the special educator begins to support the student in the general education class by supplementing the instruction received there. If this occurs, then the

☐ FIGURE 4–2
A Staggered Master Schedule for a Resource Room

Time	*Activity*
8:30– 9:00	Organization: Arrange materials, distribute student work, ready learning centers
9:00– 9:15	Instruction: Group A
9:15– 9:30	Instruction: Group B; Mastery Task: Group A
9:30– 9:45	Instruction: Group C; Mastery Task: Group B; Skill Reinforcement: Group A
9:45–10:05	Evaluation & Record Keeping: Groups A and B; Mastery Task: Group C
10:05–10:30	Instruction: Group D; Skill Reinforcement: Group C
10:30–11:30	Planning and Consultation
11:30–12:10	Lunch
12:10–12:30	Evaluation & Record Keeping: Groups C and D
12:30–12:45	Instruction: Group E
12:45– 1:00	Instruction: Group F; Mastery Task: Group E
1:00– 1:15	Instruction: Group G; Mastery Task: Group F; Skill Reinforcement: Group E
1:15– 1:35	Evaluation & Record Keeping: Groups E and F; Mastery Task: Group G
1:35– 2:00	Instruction: Group H; Skill Reinforcement: Group G
2:00– 2:15	Instruction: Group I; Mastery Task; Group H
2:15– 2:30	Evaluation & Record Keeping: Groups G and H; Mastery Task: Group I
2:30– 2:45	Evaluation & Record Keeping: Group I
2:45– 3:15	Supplemental Assistance on Individual Basis

student may not develop in the resource room the basic skills in communication, reading, or mathematics needed for self-sufficiency. Some limited time at the end of a school day for supplemental support is acceptable, but it should not interfere with instructional time allocated for development of basic skills. If the handicapped student cannot cope in the general education class with minimal instructional support, then he or she has been inappropriately placed.

Scheduling Individual Students

In addition to developing a master daily schedule, special educators in both self-contained and resource programs must develop a daily schedule for each handicapped student. The special educator must be aware of other professionals who are also responsible for some portion of the handicapped student's daily education. For example, both grade-level teachers and specialists in subjects such as art, music, and physical education must be involved in scheduling discussions. In addition, the availability of auxiliary personnel, such as speech therapists and psychologists, must be determined. The amount of communication that must occur makes this task formidable, but it can be accomplished smoothly and quickly if approached in an organized fashion.

The first task in developing a daily schedule is to learn the times of daily or regularly occurring events, such as lunch periods, recesses, library visits, and physical education, music, and art classes. Second, each regular teacher's schedule should be obtained to identify when subjects such as reading, math, or spelling are taught. The special teacher then should review the IEP to note what related services each student needs and also which instructional needs are to be met in the special education program. All of this information is collected on a form designed for organizational purposes (See Figure 4–3). Finally, the special educator in a resource program attempts to schedule the student into a special class for instruction in an academic subject at the same time that similar instruction is provided within the regular class. If the special educator is operating a self-contained program, he or she tries to schedule the student into a regular class at the same time similar instruction is provided in the special class.

The Student's Daily Schedule

To maintain purposeful activity in the classroom, the special educator must also plan for a flow of students within the special class from the time they enter until they leave. For example, when students enter the classroom, they may stop at a

☐ **FIGURE 4–3**
Individual Scheduling Plan

Child: Jim Kelly
General Teacher: Miss Chamberlain
Special Teacher: Miss Youther

Routine Activities:			*General Instruction:*		*Special Education Instruction:*
M	Gym	9:00–9:50	Reading:	10:00–10:30	Reading
T	Art	9:00–9:50	Recess:	10:30–10:45	Handwriting
W	Gym	9:00–9:50	Reading:	10:45–11:30	
Th	Art	9:00–9:50	Lunch	11:30–12:10	
	Library	2:30–3:00			
F	Music	9:00–9:50	Group Activity:	12:10–12:30	
			Penmanship:	12:30– 1:00	
			Math:	1:00– 1:45	
			Recess:	1:45– 2:00	
			Social Studies:	2:00– 2:30	
			Science:	2:30– 3:00 M T W F	
			Dismissal:	3:00– 3:15	

Resource Room Schedule: 10:00–10:30 Reading
12:30– 1:00 Handwriting & Evaluation

designated area to pick up their work folders. Next, they may proceed to a language arts or math and science area and prepare for a lesson from the teacher. Those who have just finished a lesson with the teacher return to their seats to complete a mastery task. The group that has completed their mastery task may spend ten to fifteen minutes at a learning center. The sequence of activities is communicated to the student through a weekly schedule stored in his or her folder or may be written on the blackboard by the teacher at the beginning of each day. Figure 4–4 is an illustration of such a schedule.

Teachers who develop student schedules find that many practical benefits are derived. Students become self-sufficient and independent. Teachers are less likely to be interrupted. Most important, students are not kept uninformed; they are told exactly what they will focus on during lessons and independent work.

Arranging the Physical Environment

Each handicapped student comes to the special class with unique learning needs. For example, some students need group instruction, while others cannot profit from it; some learn more quickly than others; also communication styles vary among students. Within each special education classroom microenvironments should exist to accommodate the learning and behavioral characteristics of each handicapped student.

Accordingly, there must be space for individual and group instruction, individual seating for students, space where distractions are reduced, storage space, audio-visual centers, and academic instructional areas. In addition, the classroom must be arranged to accommodate simultaneous student use of a variety of skill reinforcement activities, such as peer tutoring or games. A typical room arrangement incorporating all of the above areas is depicted in Figure 4–5.

As illustrated, areas for academic instruction or skill reinforcement are in the corners of the room near the blackboards, bookcases, and bulletin boards. Each of these areas contains a large table for individual or small-group instruction. Often

☐ **FIGURE 4–4**
Daily Schedule of Activities

Student: Brian Smith

Lesson		*Mastery Task*	*Skill Review*
M	Multiples of 3	Activity Sheet #1	Learning Center: Let's Travel Activity #1
T	Review of Multiples of 2 & 3	Skill Builder #2	Learning Center: Let's Travel Activity #2
W	Multiples of 4	Activity Sheet #3	Learning Center: Let's Travel Activity #3
Th	Multiples of 4	Activity Sheet #4	Learning Center: Let's Travel Activity #4
F	Review of Multiples of 2, 3, & 4	Skill Builder #3	Learning Center: Let's Travel Activity #5

☐ **FIGURE 4–5**
Diagram of a Special Education Classroom

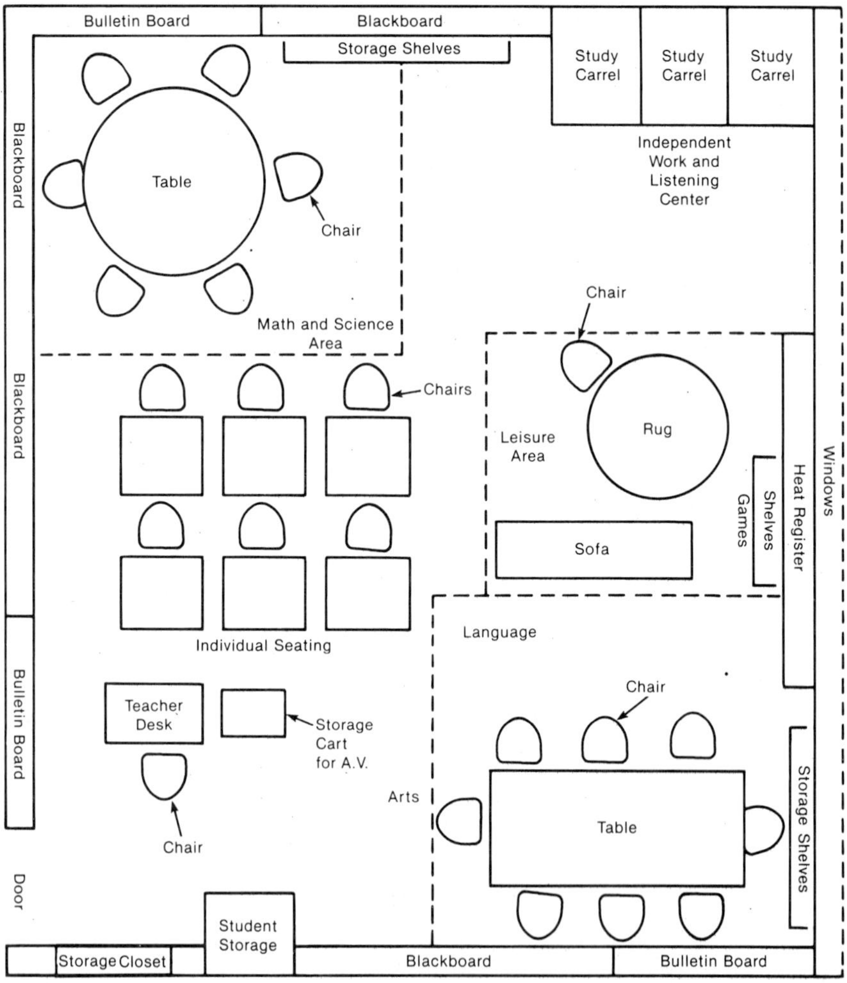

related learning center activities are arranged on shelves or bulletin boards in these academic areas.

The teacher's desk is near the entrance and toward the center of the classroom for easy accessibility to all areas. Each student has an assigned seat for completion of mastery tasks or skill reinforcement activities, and study carrels are in a corner of the room for students who need such an environment from time to time.

A storage cart for audio-visual equipment is near the center of the room for easy access to any area. File cabinets are out of traffic areas since they are not used during the school day. Students have individual storage areas near the classroom door so that they can get organized quickly as they enter or depart. Finally, there is a leisure area for reinforcing activities or learning games.

Grouping for Instruction

When grouping students for instruction, the special educator has three options from which to choose: large-group instruction, small-group instruction, or one-to-one instruction. All grouping decisions should be based on the individual needs of each student. Since most students are involved in all three types of grouping patterns throughout the day, the physical environment should be arranged to allow the groups to operate simultaneously.

Large-group instruction. Large-group instruction can be used effectively for general learning activities, such as class meetings, movies, games, or sharing times. However, large-group instruction does not lend itself to skill acquisition because of the variation in students' behavioral skills and academic needs. When multiple learning levels exist, it is difficult for teachers to provide individualized instruction in a large group.

Small-group instruction. In small-group settings, there is more likely to be greater interaction between the student and teacher as well as among students. Carnine and Silbert (1979) have reported that students tend to participate in small-group instruction when the group consists of approximately five students in a semicircle and when those students who are easily distracted are seated in the center.

Small-group instruction is commonly used by teachers to teach academic skills. Membership in the group is based on common learning styles and academic needs. For example, if three students in an intermediate class need to learn to make change for one dollar, then they are grouped together until each reaches mastery. As each student reaches mastery, he or she is placed in a new group.

One-to-one instruction. One-to-one instruction may be used by the teacher when a student requires intensive instruction in a specific skill or is unable to profit from group instruction. For example, a student receiving small-group instruction on making change may need more guided trials at the task than others in

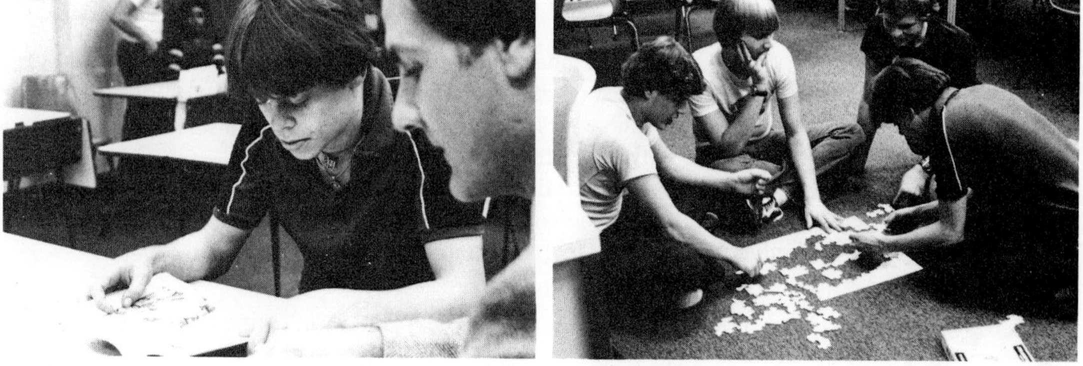

Like the student above, it is not uncommon for handicapped students to be placed in various grouping arrangements, depending upon their individualized instructional needs.

the group. The teacher can replace or supplement this student's small-group learning sessions with one-to-one instructional time.

There are also social, emotional, and behavioral factors that must be considered when making grouping decisions. For example, the withdrawn student may not be comfortable learning sound-symbol associations in a group because such a skill requires vocalization. In this case, a more effective approach would be brief instructional time with the teacher on a one-to-one basis. Then, when the student reached mastery and had more confidence in his or her ability, the teacher would change the instructional setting to a small group.

SUMMARY POINTS

- Special educators must be familiar with scheduling procedures common to the resource and self-contained special education models since they often assume major responsibility for scheduling tasks.
- Scheduling procedures require the special educator to communicate with a variety of regular and auxiliary personnel in order to provide a comprehensive program for handicapped students.
- The unique needs of each handicapped student can best be met when all professionals responsible for meeting the student's instructional needs are included in the planning process.
- Special educators should be able to arrange a physical learning environment that addresses each student's unique learning needs and permits simultaneous occurrence of a variety of skill reinforcement activities.
- The physical environment of the special classroom should be arranged to accommodate large, small, and one-to-one grouping practices. The student's learning style should guide the teacher in the selection of an appropriate grouping pattern.

REVIEW QUESTIONS

1. You are a special educator charged with the responsibility of organizing a resource room. Provide a detailed outline of all the tasks you would have to accomplish to meet this goal. In your outline, include a description of the types of assistance other professionals could provide you.
2. What guidelines, if any, does your state have regarding the implementation of self-contained and resource room programs? Include information on room size, number of students, instructional time, materials, and budgets.

SUGGESTED READINGS

Elman, N. M., and Ginsberg, J. 1981. *The resource room primer.* Englewood Cliffs, N. J.: Prentice-Hall.

Pasanella, A. L., and Volkmor, C. B. 1981. *Teaching handicapped students in the mainstream: Coming back or never leaving.* 2d ed. Columbus, Ohio: Charles E. Merrill.

Application: Individualizing Classroom and Students' Schedules

On Wednesday, August 31, Ann Jacobson reviewed the list of tasks to prepare for her students to begin the new school year. She needed to accomplish the following tasks:

- Meet with Ms. Dixon, the guidance counselor, to arrange for regular class placement for her students
- Obtain furniture and equipment for the classroom
- Arrange the classroom
- Select and order materials for the class
- Borrow materials to use until permanent materials are obtained

To arrange all the necessary schedules for her students, Ms. Jacobson used the following procedures:

1. She read the students' IEPs and made notes on which subjects would be taught in regular classes and which would be taught in the resource room. For example, a list of freshmen assigned to the program is shown in Figure 4–6.
2. Next, Ms. Jacobson designed a master schedule for the resource room. After reviewing the times when each regular content area was offered, she assigned either a content area or noninstructional responsibility to each time period as shown in Figure 4–7.
3. Ms. Dixon met with Ms. Jacobson to determine which classes were best suited for each student. Together they plotted each student's daily schedule on a master schedule. The master schedule for freshmen is illustrated in Figure 4-8. A similar schedule for sophomores, juniors and seniors was also developed.
4. When Ms. Jacobson knew which regular educators would be responsible for her students, she visited each of their classrooms to introduce herself in order to begin to establish a pattern of regular communication. During her conversation with each of these regular teachers, Ms. Jacobson gathered the following information:
   - The times each teacher would be available for consultation
   - Copies of texts and other materials used for instruction
   - A list of instructional units taught in the class
   - The teacher's policy on homework (how often it was assigned and whether any class time was allowed for it)
   - The teacher's knowledge of students in the class who could function as peer tutors
   - The teacher's grading practices

5. Ms. Jacobson also distributed the form shown in Figure 4–9 to the regular teachers to monitor her students' progress in their classes. She asked each teacher to complete the form weekly for each of the handicapped students and leave it in her mailbox.

By the first day of school, Ms. Jacobson had spent much time preparing for her students. However, she realized that continual communication with regular teachers throughout the year would probably result in scheduling and program changes.

Discussion Points

1. Assume that one of Ms. Jacobson's students was placed in a regular class in which the teacher resented the presence of handicapped students. Discuss consultation strategies Ms. Jacobson might employ with such a teacher as well as how she might prepare the student to achieve success in that class.
2. Ms. Jacobson had to schedule students into classes even though she was not familiar with her students or the regular teachers in the school. When she schedules her students into regular classes in the future, what criteria might she use to make effective scheduling decisions?

☐ **FIGURE 4–6**
Freshmen Assigned to Program

Freshmen	*Regular Class*	*Resource Room*
Jack Blair	Math, Science, P.E., Ind. Arts	English, Reading, Social Studies
Tim Alcorn	English, Social Studies, P.E., Ind. Arts	Math, Science
Judy Beech	Ind. Arts, English, Social Studies, Science, P.E.	Math, Supplemental Assistance
Mike Thorn	Math, Science, P.E., Ind. Arts	English, Reading, Social Studies
Alicia Sims	Math, Science, P.E., Ind. Arts	English, Reading, Social Studies
Becky Logan	Math, Science, P.E., Ind. Arts	English, Reading, Social Studies

☐ **FIGURE 4–7**
Resource Room Schedule

Period	Subject	Student
1	Language Arts	Jack Blair, Mike Thorn, Alicia Sims, Kate Creeger
2	Social Studies	Jack Blair, Mike Thorn, James Smith, Alicia Sims, Becky Logan
3	Language Arts	Becky Logan, Curt Szilinski, Lowell Washington, Tory Williams
4	Math/Science	Tim Alcorn, Judy Beech, Steve Ruben
5	Lunch	
6	Consultation	
7	Math/Science	Mark Bishop, Don Johnstone, Celeste Jones, Mark Goldberg
8	Supplemental Assistance	Judy Beech, Steven Hayes

☐ **FIGURE 4–8**
Master Schedule of Freshmen Students

Student	*PE*	*Math*	*Science*	*Social Studies*	*English*	*Reading*	*Ind. Art/ Home Ec.*	*Study Hall*
Jack Blair	6—Mr. Thomas	3—Ms. Allison	5—Mr. Craig	2—R.R. *	2—R.R. *	1—R.R. *	8—Mr. Blake (1st sem.) Ms. Zennia (2nd sem.)	7
Tim Alcorn	8—Mr. Jones	4—R.R. *	4—R.R. *	1—Ms. Jacoby	2—Mr. Myles	3—Study Hall	6—Mr. Blake (1st sem.) Ms. Zennia (2nd sem.)	7
Judy Beech	7—Ms. Hazel	4—R.R. *	3—Mr. Craig	5—Ms. Jacoby	1—Mr. Myles	2—Reading Lab—Mr. Leu	6—Ms. Zennia (1st sem.) Mr. Blake (2nd sem.)	8—R.R. *
Mike Thorn	3—Mr. Jones	5—Ms. Allison	6—Ms. Schmidt	1—R.R. *	2—R.R. *	7—Reading Lab—Mr. Leu	4—Mr. Blake (1st sem.) Ms. Zennia (2nd sem.)	8
Alicia Sims	3—Ms. Hazel	4—Ms. Allison	7—Ms. Schmidt	2—R.R. *	2—R.R. *	1—R.R. *	6—Mr. Blake (1st sem.) Ms. Zennia (2nd sem.)	8
Becky Logan	6—Ms. Hazel	3—Ms. Allison	7—Mr. Craig	2—R.R. *	2—R.R. *	1—R.R. *	4—Mr. Blake (1st sem.) Ms. Zennia (2nd sem.)	8

☐ **FIGURE 4–9**
Student Progress Form

Student ______________________ Class ________ Period ________ Week of ________

Was homework turned in? yes no On time? yes no Complete? yes no

Does this student require help on any skill? yes no
Specify ____

Was student on time to class? yes no No. of days? _____

Did student participate appropriate? yes no Percent of time _____

CHAPTER 5 Preparing for Instruction

OUTLINE

INTRODUCTION

Thorough instructional planning is one of the hallmarks of effective teachers. Although time consuming, comprehensive planning permits teachers to focus on a student's learning and behavioral needs, strengths, and weaknesses. The development of realistic instructional strategies requires teachers to use assessment data on the student's school performance as well as evaluative information on events occurring outside the school environment. The impact that home and community variables might have on a student's school success should not be minimized. This ecological orientation to planning and delivering instruction motivates teachers to consider their students' long-term social and survival needs (Carlson 1980) in addition to current academic needs.

Objectives

This chapter will allow you to

- discuss the purposes of instruction;
- define strategies and methods for skill reinforcement;
- develop an Individualized Educational Plan (IEP);
- write instructional objectives appropriate to the learner's needs;
- select, adapt, and create materials that compliment a student's learning and behavioral needs;
- write and implement a lesson plan appropriate to the student's instructional needs;
- develop a system of record keeping to monitor the learner's educational progress;
- evaluate the impact of the lesson on the student;
- alter instructional practices when evaluation results so indicate.

Critical Incident: Evaluation of Instruction

An important component of effective instruction is evaluation. An ecological orientation to instruction demands an evaluation of vairables related to instruction, such as materials, grouping practices, instructional procedures, and communication techniques selected by the special educator. As indicated in the following dialogue, evaluation requires special educators to monitor not only the student's performance during a lesson but also his or her behaviors.

Mrs. Gifford, a master teacher with ten years of special education experience, sat talking with Carrie Jacobson, a student teacher.

Mrs. Gifford: Carrie, I thought the questions you asked the class following your lesson on the digestive system were excellent. The questions were related to your instructional objectives and required more than memorization from your students.

Carrie: Thanks, Mrs. Gifford. I took your advice and wrote out the questions I wanted to ask. This helped me to pay more attention to the quality of my questions.

Mrs. Gifford: I'm worried about Ruthann though. Did you notice how she avoided eye contact with you and couldn't respond to the question you asked her? What do you think we should do?

Carrie: As much as I hate to admit this, I don't think that Ruthann learned much during this lesson. She is inattentive much of the time. When she does attend, she doesn't seem to retain information.

Mrs. Gifford: Carrie, as conscientious teachers, it's hard to admit that we're unsuccessful with students, but I believe that the skill of critical self-evaluation is an important first step toward learning to help students. Let's talk about some things we can do to help Ruthann. She is more likely to focus on the lesson if she sits near you and if you discuss the major purposes of the lesson before the group meets. Why don't you review her assessment report to see if there is any information that might help you develop some different strategies for her? Then we can discuss Ruthann's needs more thoroughly.

Carrie: Those are good ideas. I'd also like to observe you teach Ruthann to get a few more ideas.

Points for Consideration

- *Teachers have a responsibility to change the instructional setting when a student experiences failure.*

Rather than place the blame for failure solely on the student, Mrs. Gifford also analyzed the failure relative to the student teacher's skill in planning and delivering instruction. Critical self-evaluation is a competency that all teachers must develop if they are going to expand their instructional skills to help students. Self-evaluation permits the special educator to ask, "Where did the instruction break down?" and "How could I have changed this lesson to make it better?" With an ecological orientation to instruction, teachers consider themselves critical components of the teaching process.

- *Teachers can use unsuccessful lessons to improve their teaching skills.*

The special educator has control over every variable in the student's learning environment. The teacher determines everything from where the student sits to how much time will be provided for responses to questions. With that power goes the responsibility of correcting variables that contribute to a failure experience for the student. In Ruthann's case, Ms. Jacobson may change grouping patterns and provide individual instruction to prompt attending behavior. In addition, she may limit the number of concepts in the lesson to encourage retention. When self-evaluation is part of the evaluation process, the teacher is able to explore a wider range of instructional options.

COMMON INSTRUCTIONAL MISCONCEPTIONS

When failure occurs, the problem is rooted within the student. It is true that failure is reflected in a student's behavior. This is different from saying that the student is the source of failure. The former statement enables one to critique variables within the failure pattern, such as the instructional environment, the teacher, and the instructional methods.

Parents should assume a passive role in their handicapped child's program. Although some parents may not care about their children, most do. There are many reasons why parents may seem uncaring, such as anger or disbelief that their child is handicapped, poor verbal skills, or a belief that professionals know best. Parents often know their child better than the teacher. Productive interaction between parents and professionals will assist handicapped children in meeting their educational goals.

Teachers should limit their responsibility to academic rather than psychological or social needs of students. There is evidence that suggests that students who are educationally handicapped and labeled for funding purposes experience problems in areas of social adjustment, social perception, motivation, and self-concept (Algozzine 1979). Also, repeated school failures prompt many social and emotional problems that complicate the student's learning experience. When instructional planning focuses on helping students develop self-management skills, their potential for learning academic, survival, and social skills increases. As students learn to determine some criteria for behavior in a variety of situations, they free themselves from restrictions that limit their acceptance and capabilities (Wehman et al. 1978)

PURPOSES OF INSTRUCTION

The purpose of instruction is threefold: to help students learn new skills, to help them retain learned skills, and to help them apply these skills to problems that arise throughout life. From the teacher's perspective, instruction should provide skill development, skill reinforcement, or skill application opportunities. When the purpose of a lesson is identified, the likelihood that learning will occur increases.

Skill Development

In skill development, the teacher's task is to identify those academic, social, and vocational skills, concepts, or behaviors that the student needs to develop. A skill development approach to instruction has also been called direct or systematic teaching (Carnine and Silbert 1979; Stephens 1977). Regardless of the term used to describe purposeful skill development, its major focus is to help the student achieve skill mastery.

Mastery learning occurs when a student has achieved specified performance criteria determined acceptable by the teacher. This level of performance is numerically defined and is often expressed in terms of a percentage. For example, the teacher could specify that John accurately compute the sum of four addition problems when given five problems whose sums are less that ten. Here, the criteron is four-fifths, or 80 percent.

Skill Reinforcement

Once a student reaches mastery, the purpose of instruction changes. The emphasis is then on instructional experiences that encourage the student to retain skill proficiency (Haring 1978). Instructional experiences for skill reinforcement do not necessarily occur within the context of a formal lesson between teacher and student. Rather, the teacher might assign independent mastery tasks using strategies such as peer tutoring, learning games, learning centers, or skill sheets, all of which provide opportunities for skill reinforcement.

Peer tutoring. Peer tutoring is a strategy teachers use to provide practice experiences for students. Usually one student with proficiency in a skill assumes the role of teacher and teaches the skill to another student who lacks proficiency. Older students commonly act as tutors for younger students, although "same age" tutors have been effective in teaching a variety of skills to classmates (Parson and Heward 1979).

To implement the peer tutor model, the teacher selects tutors and trains them in the skill they will be teaching (Howell and Kaplan 1978). Next, the teacher demonstrates instructional, reinforcement, and evaluation procedures to the tutors. The teacher then observes several practice sessions to safeguard against student error or improper skill development. Initially the time investment for this model is intensive, but results are often increased student learning, fewer demands on the

Peer tutoring sessions can be an effective instructional strategy if all students are equally involved in the learning activity.

teacher's time, and at least two students available to teach the same skill to others who need it.

Games. Handicapped students are often poorly motivated to complete traditional skill reinforcement strategies, such as work sheets, because of numerous failure experiences with such materials. At the same time, many of these students profit from repeated practice of a skill. The dilemma confronting the special educator is to provide such drills while avoiding student resistance to drill activities. Instructional games have been used increasingly by teachers because they provide practice experience but do not resemble traditional reinforcement activities, which students often associate with failure.

Games can be purchased or made by the teacher. The teacher should have a well-defined purpose for the game and a knowledge of student skills that it requires. By considering the students' interests and developmental needs, games can be constructed for independent use by students.

Commercial reference books or game boards may be used to provide teachers with ideas for a variety of learning games. Examples of these references are *100 Individualized Activities for Reading* (Criscuolo 1974) and *Mathematics Their Way* (Baratta-Lorton 1976).

Learning centers. Learning centers should be designed to provide students with a review of concepts learned in either a small-group or a one-to-one instructional setting. A **learning center** is a set of activities or games that allows students to explore a particular skill area and, in some cases, its application in real life. For example, a learning center focusing on travel might include academic skills needed for travel by car, such as reference skills to identify locations and map symbols and addition and simple division skills to compute distances and time requirements.

To construct a learning center, the following guidelines should be observed:

- Select an instructional skill or concept as the focus of the center. The selected skill should appeal to students' interests, and activities should be constructed in an attractive manner.
- Assemble materials needed for construction. Use materials that are durable and can be used frequently.
- Write directions for each activity in a simple and clear manner. For nonreaders, directions could be given using symbols or pictures. Further, the teacher may explain how to complete the activity before allowing nonreading students to use it.
- Organize the center for ease of storage and retrieval of materials. Empty food-storage containers can be number or color coded to help to organize center activities. If audio-visual materials are needed, locate them near the learning center.
- Consider space requirements for the center. Some activities can be completed individually at the student's desk, while others may require a group work area if two or more students participate in the activity. Directions for each activity should include the location for completing it.

- Provide a record-keeping system to monitor student progress through center activities. This can be accomplished with a learning contract and monitored daily during time scheduled for evaluation and record keeping.
- Include pre- and posttests based on instructional objectives. Use test results to assign appropriate learning center activities.
- Provide several learning centers throughout the classroom and change or add activities within each center on a regular basis.

Teachers can use the resource handbooks on today's market to obtain ideas and directions for constructing learning centers. In addition, examination of scope-and-sequence charts of basic skills or curriculum guides can provide inspiration for themes of learning centers. After a theme for a learning center has been identified, one to three activities should be constructed and the center should immediately be put to use. The center can be expanded as the teacher has time to develop new activities. Examples of resource references for center activities are *Kids' Stuff, Reading and Language Experiences Intermediate-Junior High* (Forte, Frank, and MacKenzie, 1973) and *Center Stuff for Nooks, Crannies, and Corners* (Forte, Pangle, and Tupa 1973).

Traditional tasks. Student work sheets are the most common of the traditional skill reinforcement materials. Teachers use these because they provide needed practice for the student while allowing the teacher time for instruction. Archer and Edgar (1976) note that skill work sheets provide practice that leads to student mastery. However, students who spend a great deal of time using this skill reinforcement method may experience feelings of anger, frustration, or failure. By observing the following guidelines, teachers can minimize the negative side effects associated with traditional skill reinforcement activities:

- Minimize the number of problems on work sheets. It is not only the skill or concept that makes the task difficult but also the number of problems on the work sheet (Blake 1976).
- Provide immediate feedback to students. This allows the teacher to monitor procedures used by the student so that errors do not become habits. It also provides the teacher with frequent opportunities to praise student effort and success.
- Give students sufficient time to complete assignments. If students are provided with a realistic time frame, they are more likely to respond accurately and experience a sense of accomplishment.
- Combine the use of traditional methods for skill reinforcement with other strategies. Students who have opportunities to play instructional games or to complete activities in learning centers are less likely to become bored or frustrated with traditional reinforcement tasks.

Skill Application

Of importance to students and teachers are the daily life applications of academic skills. Carlson (1980) suggests that one factor related to student motivation is how a "particular experience will affect the learner now and in the future" (p. 60). Therefore, it is important that teachers explain the significance of learning a skill and help students to apply that skill later in solving problems in their daily lives.

After a student reaches mastery, the teacher arranges for instruction opportunities that encourage the student to generalize the behavior or skill and apply it to real situations. Depending on the student's age and needs, instruction that focuses on skill application can occur in a variety of environments. For example, junior and senior high teachers might provide initial instruction on work behaviors in their classrooms, but the application of the work-related skill would occur at work stations in the school building or vocational settings in the community.

DEVELOPING THE INDIVIDUALIZED EDUCATIONAL PLAN

Many components of the IEP are developed by the special education teacher on the basis of information gathered through the multifactored assessment process. The IEP concisely presents a student's educational needs and can be conceptualized as the master plan for instruction for a student in a special education program. IEPs that include the following: *(a)* instructional goals, *(b)* skills the student needs to learn, written in an objective format, *(c)* instructional strategies and materials, and *(d)* evaluation of student performance often are the basis for developing effective lesson plans. Figure 5–1 is a portion of one student's IEP and is followed by a discussion of each component.

Writing Objectives

Instructional objectives are precise statements, reflective of goals, that describe expected student behaviors following instruction (Mager 1962). Instructional objectives should be stated in sequence to assist the handicapped student to master broad skills stated in the goals for that student. Since instructional objectives are critical aspects of individualization, the following five criteria outlined by Blake (1974) should guide the teacher in writing objectives:

1. Objectives should be culturally relevant, appropriate to the student, and sequential within the specific content area.
2. Any material to be used to help the student meet the objective should be stated in the objective.
3. Objectives should be neither too precise nor too broad. They should reflect the student's general level of functioning.
4. Objectives should be clear so that any person reading them can ascertain the instructional methods, evaluation techniques, and the criteria for student mastery.
5. Objectives should be complete. They should contain three components—content, behavior, and level of mastery.

The behavioral component of an objective describes the skill that the student is required to demonstrate. The content of the objective describes the conditions that will prompt the behavior. The level of mastery of an objective reflects the time limitations, testing procedures, and other evaluation criteria the student must

□ **FIGURE 5-1**
Individualized Educational Plan

Student's Name: *Benjamin Layne*
Goal: Benjamin will add and subtract digits one through ten

Instructional Objective	Instructional Methods	Materials	Date Begun	Date Completed	Retention Check
When shown a group of one to ten objects, Benjamin will state the numerical value in one second with 100 percent accuracy.	Use blocks in consistent arrangement. Benjamin selects corresponding digit card and writes corresponding digit. Number Digit Writes □□ \[2\] □ □□ \[3\]	blocks, laminated digit cards	9/15/80	9/26/80	10/7/80
When shown a group of one to ten objects that represent a sum and given an addend, Benjamin will write a number sentence providing the missing addend with 100 percent accuracy.	Use number configuration cards. Benjamin selects addend card that completes sentence and writes number sentence based on grid. $2 + _ = 5$ $_ + 3 = 5$ $1 + _ = 5$	laminated configuration cards, math grid taped on table in learning center	9/26/80	10/7/80	11/1/80
When shown a group of one to ten objects that represent the minuend and given the subtrahend or difference, Benjamin will write a number sentence providing the missing subtrahend or difference with 100 percent accuracy.	Use number configuration cards. Benjamin supplies missing subtrahend or difference and writes number sentence based on grid. $3 - 2 = _$ $3 - _ = 1$	laminated configuration cards, math grid	10/7/80	11/1/80	11/15/80

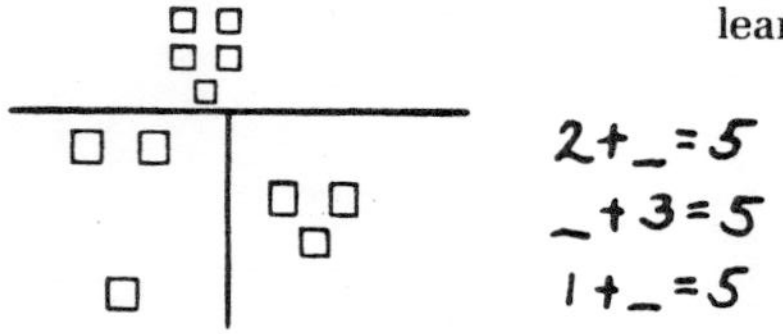

meet to assure that the behavior occurred as a result of learning rather than by chance. The following is an example of an instructional objective written for a second grade student in a resource room program:

> Instructional Objective: Following instruction on blends and given the *Criterion Test of Basic Skills in Reading,* John will pronounce each word containing a blend with 100 percent accuracy in two seconds or less.

The verbs used in an instructional objective should allow the teacher to observe a specific behavior in the student. Archer and Edgar (1976) note that using a specific question as a guide in the observation process improves the observation. Table 5–1 is a list of verbs teachers may find useful when writing objectives for students. While this list is not comprehensive, it does provide the beginning teacher with some examples of verbs which, when used in instructional objectives, permit measurement of student behavior.

Identifying Instructional Procedures

After the instructional objectives for a student have been written, the teacher uses assesment data to identify appropriate instrucitonal methods to help the student achieve the objectives. Instructional principles suggest the use of various methods, techniques, materials, and environmental and time factors to help students master skills. A teacher's familiarity with and use of these principles are just as critical to a student's success as are the formal methods for teaching specific mate-

☐ **TABLE 5–1**
Verbs for Objectives

adjust	cite	choose
align	copy	classify
apply	define	compare
close	describe	contrast
construct	explain	decide
(dis)assemble	letter	detect
(dis)connect	list	differentiate
draw	name	discern
duplicate	quote	distinguish
insert	recite	divide
load	record	identify
manipulate	repeat	isolate
measure	reproduce	judge
open	(re)state	match
operate	transcribe	pick
remove	write	select
replace		associate
stencil		
tune		
turn off (on)		
type		
practice		
recognize		

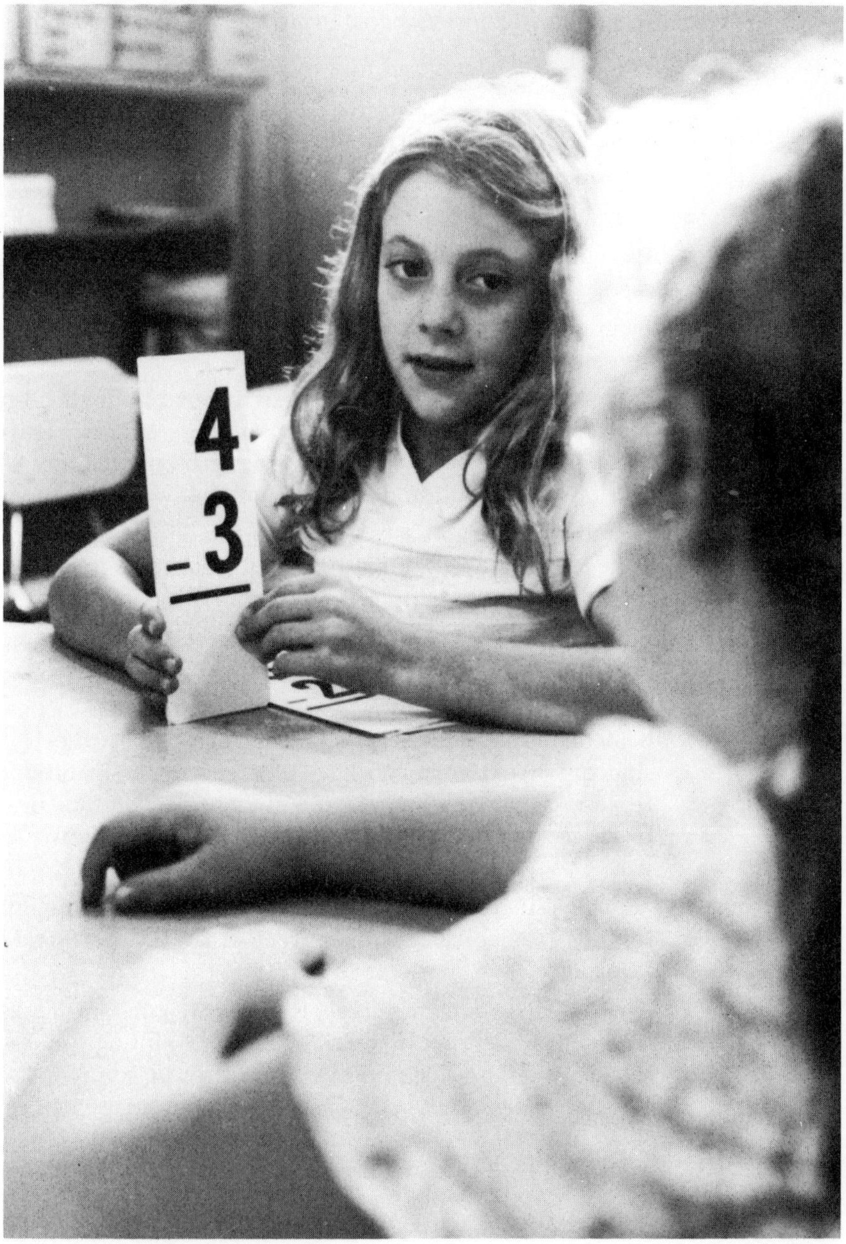

Teacher-made materials, like the one above, should be durable and related to the students' instructional needs.

rial. The following instructional principles are based on motivation and learning theory research (Wehman and McLaughlin 1980; Ausubel 1978; Blake 1976, 1975, 1974):

- Prior to instruction, tell the student what is about to be studied, how it will be studied, and how he or she will be evaluated.
- Provide immediate performance and evaluation feedback to the student.
- Use questioning techniques, prompts, and modeling procedures that allow the student to respond correctly to questions.
- Limit drill techniques to concepts that require drilling, such as basic operations in arithmetic.
- Relate the unknown to the familiar through both concrete and symbolic representation. Concrete representation uses manipulatives with which students are familiar, while symbolic representation uses two-dimensional or visual imagery to promote understanding.
- Limit the number of tasks to be completed in an independent study session. Blake (1975) has found that the number of tasks to be completed is directly related to the difficulty of the assignment.
- Provide frequent practice sessions over time to assist a student in acquiring a new skill.
- To facilitate retention of new skills, have students practice skills beyond the point of mastery. This is commonly referred to as **overlearning.** Generally, students should practice skills 50 percent more than the time they took to reach mastery. For example, if a student needed four practice sessions to reach mastery on multiples of three, then probably two additional sessions would be needed for the student to retain this skill.
- Allow the student to rest or get involved in another activity after the practice session. This increases the accuracy of student performance on the skill being developed.
- Use simulation activities to achieve transfer of learning. For example, a teacher may first provide instruction on counting change in the classroom, then in a simulated store environment set up in the hall outside of the classroom, then in the school cafeteria, and finally in a community store. If skill generalization is to occur, students must realize that procedures associated with the skill are the same regardless of envirnomental changes.

An application of these instructional principles is presented in the following example. Mr. Wing planned to teach Sarah the relationship between digits and numbers by relating the unknown to the familiar. He planned ten lessons. Five lessons used concrete representation (blocks), and five lessons used symbolic representation (pictures of blocks).

Since Sarah was six years old, building blocks were familiar objects within her environment. Other objects, such as matchbox cars or jacks, could be used depending on the specific student's likes or interests. Another principle apparent in the instructional procedures Mr. Wing planned for Sarah was the repetition of the same visual imagery. The arrangement of the blocks in concrete or symbolic form never varied. This simple principle made it more likely that Sarah would retain what she learned.

The number of lessons planned for Sarah was speculative and based on Mr. Wing's observation of Sarah's rate of learning during previous trial lessons with him. If Sarah had progressed more quickly than planned in acquiring this skill, Mr. Wing would have moved to the next objective on her IEP. If Sarah had not progressed as planned, he would have adjusted his instructional strategies and continued to teach this skill.

The instructional method section of an IEP is optional but should be included to enable the special educator to use the document for daily lessons. Therefore, it should be written to provide a detailed reminder of the approach to instruction tailored to the student's age, interests, rate of learning, attention span, and grouping and developmental needs.

Selecting Materials

After identifying the most appropriate instructional procedures for a student, the next step is selecting instructional materials. Teachers have a choice of selecting commercial materials, adapting existing materials, or making their own materials. Regardless of the type of material used, it is important that teachers not lose sight of the purpose of the instructional materials. It is the teacher who is responsible for instruction. The teacher should not abdicate this role by relying on the materials to provide step-by-step instructional procedures, activities, and objectives. Teachers who understand the purpose of materials use them for what they are—a resource—rather than as a basis for a student's instructional program.

Commercial materials. Since many special educators are faced with limited funds for purchasing materials, it is critical that they be familiar with and apply selection criteria when deciding which materials to buy. These same criteria can also be of help to the teacher when creating or adapting materials.

Teachers should begin a selection process by asking themselves some general questions in order to identify which subject areas require materials (Cohen, Alberto, and Troutman 1979). They should also ask themselves which skills are most difficult for students to understand and thus require more varied instructional activities. Also, if a teacher does not feel qualified to make instructional materials to provide different learning experiences, then it may be necessary to purchase them.

After teachers have identified skill areas in which additional materials are needed, the next step is to develop a list that ranks materials critical to instruction. At this time, some teachers make a supplemental "wish list" of materials given less priority. Often civic groups, parents, or the school may later volunteer to purchase one of these items for the classroom.

Prior to purchasing needed materials, teachers should make arrangements to preview them to determine if they are in fact appropriate for their students' use. Teachers may borrow such materials from area media centers, such as county or district educational offices or special education regional resource centers. Sometimes publishers will allow materials to be previewed for a limited time. When previewing materials, it is a good idea to use a materials evaluation form to record information since it is difficult to recall the strengths and weaknesses of materials after they have been returned. Table 5–2 illustrates such a form.

The following is a list of questions professionals should ask themselves before purchasing a material:

Is the cost justifiable?

Whether or not the cost of a material is justifiable depends on the amount of money available, the need for the material, and the effectiveness of the material. For example, regardless of how great a need there is for a material or how extensively it has been developed and field tested, if the cost exhausts all or a major portion of the materials budget, it might be realistic to postpone ordering it or to select a similar, less expensive item. Cost is also related to durability and development. If the material has been field tested and modified, it may cost consid-

☐ TABLE 5–2
Materials Evaluation Form

Skill Area: ______	Material Name: ______			
Publisher & Address: ______	Cost: ______			
Student Age Range:				
Material Development Process:				
Sequence of Skills comments:	poor	fair	good	excellent
Objectives/Learning Activities: comments:	poor	fair	good	excellent
Format Arrangement: comments:	poor	fair	good	excellent
Repetition of Skills/Vocabulary:	poor	fair	good	excellent
Student/Teacher Directions: comments:	poor	fair	good	excellent
Application to Life Skills: comments:	poor	fair	good	excellent
Evaluation of Skills: comments:	poor	fair	good	excellent
Reinforcement comments:	poor	fair	good	excellent
Durability: comments:	poor	fair	good	excellent
Record Keeping: student, teacher comments:	poor	fair	good	excellent
Student Language Requirements: writing, reading; readability level				
Student Time Expenditures: 10 15 20 30 minutes/lesson comments:				
Teacher Involvement: minimal moderate major comments:				
Storage Requirements:				

erably more than other materials. Also, the durability of a product may increase its cost. The teacher should consider all of these factors when weighing costs. If possible, durability and field testing of the material should be given priority over cost. It is important to know that the material will last and that it has been found to be generally successful with handicapped students.

For what age group or developmental level is the material designed?

The age range of students for whom the material is designed should be considered when evaluating the material. Materials developed for primary students should contain manipulatives or models. Materials designed for older students should address topics that are of general interest as well as provide opportunities for the application of academic skills to day-to-day problems.

Does the format promote mastery learning?

The format of a material should be related to student retention. For example, a material that provides seventy-five trials or practices on a single page violates an instructional principle: the large number of trials increases the difficulty of the task. On the other hand, if the material exposes the student to a concept only once or twice, it may not provide sufficient trials for learning and skill retention to occur.

Is the material biased?

When evaluating a material, the illustrations and focus of its content should also be examined for cultural, racial, and sexual biases. For example, are black and female individuals portrayed equally in leadership roles with white males? Does the material describe life of an adolescent in urban areas when the student population comes from rural backgrounds? If biases are discovered, similar unbiased materials should be examined.

Is there a correspondence between mastery activities provided by a material and instructional objectives?

A correspondence between the teacher's instructional objectives and the learning activities provided by the material is needed for sequential instruction. Some commercial materials are organized illogically, thus confusing both students and teachers. The objectives of a material should be stated in order of importance. There should be a correspondence between the importance of an objective and the number of activities designed to help students meet that objective, with most activities addressing primary objectives. Learning activities and objectives should be relevant and practical.

Are directions clearly stated?

Directions for the materials should be clear enough for the student to read and follow independently, if necessary. The format of the material should be arranged so that the directions are in front of the student at all times. Components of the activity should also be arranged so that they are easily available to the student. In other words, a student should not be required to flip pages back and forth to complete an activity or reread the directions. The material should not interrupt the teacher's or student's train of thought. Rather, it should be designed to facilitate concentration or attention to the task.

What kinds of student response are required?

The response requirements posed by a material are critical to learning and motivation. For example, does the material consistently require a written response? Are schematics of illustrations used to convey concepts? Is written material the only option open to the student for learning? Are audio and visual tapes included? Does the material regularly present the information through at least two different learning modalities within any phase of instruction, whether it is introduction to a concept or evaluation of student mastery? This last question is particularly important since many handicapped students display expressive and receptive communication deficits (Wiig and Semel 1980). Instructional lessons should provide these students with opportunities to express themselves in a variety of ways.

How much time is needed to use the material?

The time required to complete a learning activity or mastery task is related to student age and attention span. A primary student might be expected to attend to a task for five to fifteen minutes, while an adolescent would be expected to have an attention span of twenty to thirty minutes. Generally, the time required for task completion should be minimal.

Is the material motivating for students?

The material should also reflect motivational learning principles in its evaluation and reinforcement strategies. For example, are materials self-correcting so that students are provided with immediate feedback on their performance? Are students able to chart their own progress? Is the material color keyed by level so that progress is visually apparent to students? Some materials contain certificates of completion, student record books, stickers, or other devices that provide tangible evidence to students that they have mastered some skill. This component of a material is very important to handicapped students, who typically have experienced frequent failure in school.

Who is to use the material?

Some materials are designed to be used by teachers for instruction. Others are made to be used independently by students. For example, materials in many basal reading series are coordinated by the teacher, who directs students in their use, whereas Language Master (a self-instructing teaching machine available through Bell & Howell, Co., Chicago, Ill.) may be used exclusively by students. Attention to who the user will be can assist in determining practicability.

Are special storage requirements needed?

Another practical aspect of material selection is storage. The amount of space required for an item is an obvious consideration. Less obvious are the number of components of a material that must be maintained and the environmental conditions that must be present to preserve the material. Transparencies, records, and filmstrips can be damaged by heat. Paper materials can be warped or destroyed by water and humidity. Dust can scratch records and audio and visual tapes. Therefore, physical space is not the only variable to be considered. Proper storage of equipment can increase the life of expensive materials and equipment. If the material includes numerous components, a logical question is, Are these components going to become lost and, if so, how will the loss affect the overall use of the material? Experienced teachers can testify to the frustration of having one component of a material lost or permanently damaged.

Adapting materials. Since educational materials are designed for students with a wide range of interests, abilities, and rates of learning, it is not likely that any commercial material can meet all of the evaluation criteria discussed above.

Goodman (1978) suggests that "further adaptations or modifications are often necessary to bring mastery of the content to within the child's grasp" (p. 93).

The following are some general guidelines for modifying materials:

- Rewrite material so that it may be read independently by a student.
- Provide study guides that include vocabulary terms, definitions, and a general outline of the concept being studied.
- Allow students to respond to questions orally or through audio tapes.
- Obtain old texts or workbooks and use them to build a skill reinforcement file. Such a file can be color coded for independent use by students.
- Offer limited drill activities and arrange the format of these activities so that they are balanced on a standard page.
- Develop supplemental kits for various concepts or skills. Such kits could include concrete materials and a list of pictures, films, filmstrips, library reference texts, and speakers.
- Tape directions of written material and allow the student to listen for increased comprehension.
- Have students paraphrase written directions to insure understanding.
- Change the directions on old workbook pages to use the material to teach a new or different skill.
- Teach as sight words those terms commonly found in written directions, such as *match, choose, write,* and *complete.* Have students underline key terms in the set of directions before completing the task.

These suggestions for adaptation of learning materials are relatively easy to implement. The special teacher may want to offer these guidelines to regular educators who have handicapped students in their classes. In addition, student or parent volunteers are often happy to adapt materials.

Teacher-made materials. The third alternative for planning instructional materials is to make them. Teacher-made items often address students' skill needs far better than commercial materials because special educators are acutely aware of their students' skill needs and learning styles and thus are in the optimal position to create excellent instructional materials.

Teacher-made materials should be geared to the student's interests, communication abilities, attention span, and reading level. Further, they should be self-correcting, because they provide immediate feedback of learning progress to the student, enable the student to avoid practicing mistakes, and confine knowledge of errors to the student.

Keeping Records

The final section of the IEP is for record keeping. It is the only section of the IEP that is completed after instruction has begun. Record keeping is a process of gathering information on students' academic and behavior progress. It permits the teacher to monitor a student's progress in relationship to written instructional objectives. Further, students may be motivated by charting their progress. Teachers also achieve satisfaction from documenting student growth (Haring and Schiefelbusch 1976). Finally, record keeping directs the teacher to alter the instructional approach when necessary and forms the basis for annual program planning.

It is recommended that a record-keeping system be implemented on two levels. First, a system should be devised to monitor student progress on instructional objectives contained in the IEP (Poplin 1979). Second, a more comprehensive system of record keeping should be designed for daily use. Table 5–3 illustrates a record-keeping system used to monitor student attainment of objectives in the IEP.

The instructional objectives in Table 5–3 are listed in order of difficulty. Proper ordering of objectives is important so that students will not be confronted with skills for which they may not have the appropriate background learning. Beginning teachers may not feel confident about establishing an appropriate sequence for instructional objectives; however, published scope-and-sequence check lists in various content areas are available.

A record-keeping system designed to record daily progress of students should be clear and simple to use. Many teachers find it convenient to construct record-keeping charts for various subject areas and tasks on manila folders, which students can also use to store work sheets related to those tasks. Objectives contained on daily record-keeping charts are related to instructional objectives contained in the IEP. Figure 5–2 illustrates an example of a record-keeping chart designed to monitor daily progress.

The score recorded on the instructional record-keeping forms is based on the evaluation activities conducted at the end of a lesson. Usually a student demonstrates the skill on which the lesson focused a number of times so that the teacher can observe the degree of progress and ultimately the impact of instructional methods and materials on student learning. For example, if the teacher were evaluating whether Susan could pronounce consonant sounds in isolation, she might present ten letter symbols and say, "Tell me the sound for each symbol." When Su-

☐ **TABLE 5–3**
A Record-Keeping System for Instructional Objectives Listed on the IEP

	In Process	*Mastery*	*Accuracy Check*
When shown a list of nonsense words based on the CVC pattern, Susan will pronounce correctly nine of ten words in two minutes or less.	9/1	9/15	10/1; 10/15
When shown a list of words based on the CVCV pattern, Susan will pronounce correctly nine of ten of those words in two minutes or less.	9/24	10/15	11/1; 12/1
When shown a list of words based on the CVVC pattern, Susan will pronounce correctly nine of ten of those words in two minutes or less.	10/15	10/30	11/15; 12/15

☐ **FIGURE 5–2**
Daily Recording Chart

1. When shown consonants with a visual cue, Susan will pronounce each consonant sound with 100 percent accuracy.

	8/25	8/26	8/27	8/28	8/29
correct	16	18	18	17	19
error	5	3	3	4	2
correct	18	19	20	19	20
error	3	2	1	2	1
correct	19	20	21	21	21
error	2	1	0	0	0

2. When shown upper- and lower-case consonant symbols in isolation, Susan will pronounce each with 100 percent accuracy.

	9/1	9/2	9/3	9/4	9/5
correct					
error					
correct					
error					
correct					
error					

3. When shown vowels with a visual cue for short-vowel sound, Susan will pronounce each short-vowel sound correctly.

	9/8	9/9	9/10	9/11	9/12
correct					
error					
correct					
error					
correct					
error					

4. When shown lower-case vowel symbols in isolation, Susan will pronounce each sound correctly with 100 percent accuracy.

	9/15	9/16	9/17	9/18	9/19
correct					
error					
correct					
error					
correct					
error					

5. When shown ten lower-case short vowels and consonants paired in a VC pattern, Susan will blend each of these sounds into a unit with 100 percent accuracy.

	9/22	9/23	9/24	9/25	9/26
correct					
error					
correct					
error					
correct					
error					

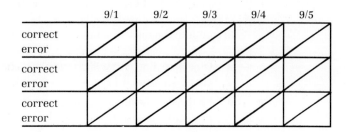

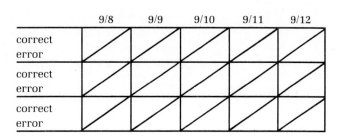

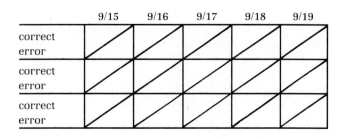

san finished the evaluation, the number of correct and incorrect responses would be recorded by Susan or the teacher in her presence.

Some instructional objectives on the student's IEP are related to social behaviors. These behaviors, too, can be recorded in order to promote student motivation and to ascertain the effectiveness of strategies used to teach or change behaviors. However, the form of these records or charts varies from that of academic charts. Refer to Figure 5–3, which depicts the frequency of foul language used by a twelve-year-old girl over three weeks of school.

Evaluating Instruction

Typically evaluation of instruction is based on the student's performance on a mastery task following instruction. For example, Mrs. Cook was teaching Barbara to compute the balance of a checkbook, as outlined below.

- Objective: Barbara will compute the balance of a checkbook when given four check amounts to be deducted with 75 percent accuracy.
- Materials: Vocabulary cards, transparency of check and check stub, overhead projector, grease pencil, work sheet, completed checks, and check stubs
- Procedure:

  1. Review basic terms (vocabulary cards).
  2. Demonstrate computation of balance once (transparency of check and check stub, overhead projector, grease pencil).
  3. Guide Barbara in the process three times (teacher-made work sheet).
  4. Give a mastery assignment (four complete checks and check stubs).
  5. Grade mastery assignment with Barbara.

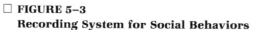

☐ **FIGURE 5–3**
Recording System for Social Behaviors

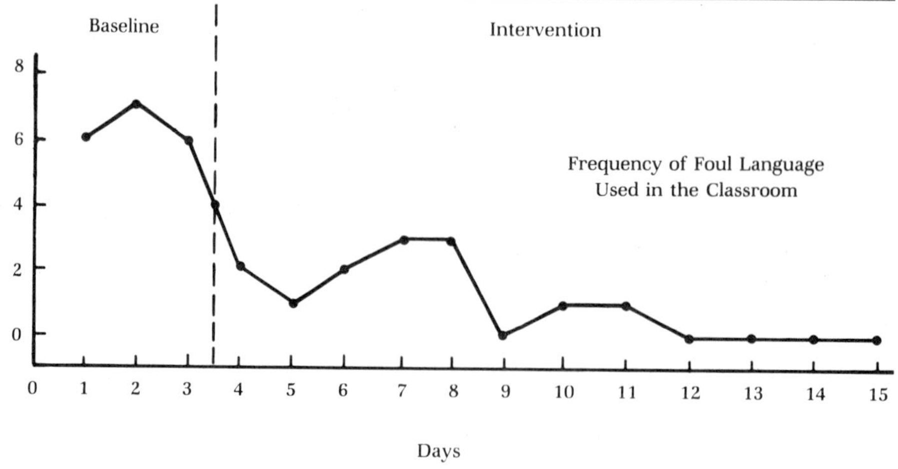

As Mrs. Cook observed Barbara complete this task, she noted that although Barbara could compute the correct checkbook balance, she could not borrow when two minuends in the cents column were zeros. Even though Barbara achieved a 75 percent accuracy rate on the objective as state, the teacher made a written note to review the borrowing process at the next lesson and to provide Barbara with a review work sheet to reinforce this skill.

Evaluation data assist teachers in determining the focus of future lessons as well as provide them with opportunities to determine if instructional objectives have been met. Evaluation of student performance also provides feedback to teachers so that they can identify whether alternative instructional procedures might be needed to teach a skill. For example, if Barbara required further instruction in this skill but exhibited low tolerance for self-made errors, Mrs. Cook could demonstrate the procedure three times, guide Barbara three times through the process, and then have Barbara compute the balance using two checks and check stubs rather than the four given during the previous lesson. The general sequence of a lesson remains constant, but the procedures used to teach new material to the student vary according to learning style and need.

The ecological orientation allows the teacher to ask, "How can I alter procedures I'm using to help this student achieve success on a mastery task?" In essence, this orientation helps teachers avoid conflict and failure typically associated with teachers who do not perceive the need to examine their own behaviors. The teacher is the prime instructional variable in the ecology of the learning environment. Evaluation permits teachers to look at all variables, including themselves, when analyzing a student's success or failure.

SUMMARY POINTS

- Student failure is a function of planning and instructional error. Special educators who possess the skill of critical self-evaluation can minimize errors in planning and instruction, thereby increasing the likelihood of student success.
- The IEP is the master plan for instruction. It is mandated by Public Law 94-142 (*Federal Register* 1977) and used by many teachers as a daily lesson plan.
- When used as a lesson plan, the IEP should contain a description of materials, instructional procedures, and a record-keeping system as well as goals and objectives that address the student's skill needs.
- The purposes of instruction are skill acquisition, retention, and application. To that end, the special educator uses a direct, systematic instructional approach in order to meet students' needs.
- In addition to special methods for teaching specific content material to educationally handicapped students, there are basic instructional principles that teachers should follow. Use of these principles during daily instruction will increase students' learning.
- A key component of instruction is evaluation. Analysis of student performance on evaluation activities directs the teacher to focus on new skills, modify instructional procedures, or both.

- Instructional objectives are formulated based upon data gathered during the assessment process. They are related to a student's skill needs and written in measurable terms.
- Materials may be purchased, adapted, or constructed by teachers. Regardless of the nature of materials, it is critical for teachers to remember that materials should supplement, rather than form, the basis for instruction.
- Record-keeping systems are designed to monitor student progress toward instructional objectives. In addition, use of record-keeping systems can be motivating to both students and teachers.
- In addition to planning for direct instruction with students, special educators must also plan for skill reinforcement. Often skill reinforcement can be accomplished independently by students through such strategies as games, learning centers, peer tutoring, and traditional tasks.

REVIEW QUESTIONS

1. How might materials differ for primary and secondary students requiring instruction on basic addition of numbers zero through twenty? Discuss those considerations upon which your selection of materials would be based.
2. Evaluate the performance of students in the following three examples. What conclusions could a teacher make regarding the effectiveness of instruction for each student?

Student A:

Correct	3	3	2	2	1
Incorrect	5	5	6	6	5

Student B:

Correct	3	4	5	5	5
Incorrect	2	1	0	0	0

Student C:

Correct	2	3	2	4	2
Incorrect	3	2	3	1	3

SUGGESTED READINGS

Blake, K. A. 1976. *The mentally retarded: An educational psychology.* Englewood Cliffs, N.J.: Prentice-Hall.

Gallagher, P. A. 1979. *Teaching students with behavior disorders: Techniques for classroom instruction.* Denver: Love.

White, O. R., & Haring, N. G. 1980. *Exceptional teaching.* 2d ed. Columbus, Ohio: Charles E. Merrill.

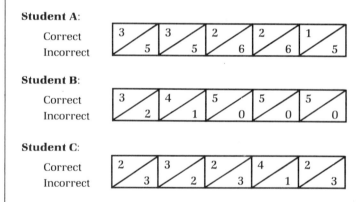

Application: Delivering Instruction— An Evaluation Process

Jeff, at six years of age, is repeating kindergarten. He is aware of his lack of progress in school, telling everyone that he "flunked." Jeff's teacher, Ms. Brooks, referred him for possible special education placement due to significant learning deficits. Her assessment of Jeff's readiness skills revealed that he could not reproduce basic geometric designs or identify primary colors, his name, or body parts. When given a model of his name, Jeff typically reproduced it backwards and reversed (ﬀɘL). Ms. Brooks also noted that Jeff was beginning to dominate and bully his classmates.

Following assessment, the placement team recommended special education services through a modified self-contained program. Jeff was to be mainstreamed with first grade peers for physical education, music, and art. The special education teacher, Mrs. Myles, would be responsible for instruction in language arts, arithmetic, social studies, and science. She reviewed the report of the assessment team as a basis for development of instructional strategies. Mrs. Myles then arranged for several trial lessons as part of the planning process. During these lessons she noticed that Jeff was not consistently focusing attention on her or any of the concrete experiences introduced during the lessons. Based on these observations, Mrs. Myles recommended to the committee that three additional goals be added to Jeff's IEP:

- Jeff will attend to tasks for ten-minute intervals.
- Jeff will complete mastery tasks independently.
- Jeff will verbalize self-directive and self-reinforcing statements to build and maintain attending skills.

In addition the team established the following annual goals for Jeff:

- Jeff will learn arithmetic skills commensurate with those identified for first grade students in the curriculum handbook.
- Jeff will develop reading skills identified in the curriculum guide for first grade students.
- Jeff's self-concept will show improvement.
- Jeff will learn science and social studies concepts identified as appropriate for first grade students.
- Jeff will develop social skills necessary for positive peer interaction.

During trial lessons, Mrs. Myles's observational skills helped her to identify strategies that would help Jeff be more successful with academic and social tasks. Based on her observations, Mrs. Myles used manipulatives for the concrete experiences they provided. She also used record-keeping and token systems to reinforce Jeff for attending to instruction and mastery tasks. Simultaneously she taught Jeff to subvocalize self-directive and self-reinforcing statements.

As Jeff began to initiate self-directive statements without a verbal prompt, Mrs. Myles changed from individual to small-group instruction to help Jeff generalize his newly acquired behavioral skills. After Jeff had been receiving writing instruction in a small-group setting for about one week, she noticed that he was not responding quickly to her hand on his shoulder, a nonverbal cue used to prompt the self-directive statement. She began to record the time lapse between the cue and Jeff's response as shown on the chart shown below.

The data recorded on the chart confirmed Mrs. Myles's observation that Jeff was not learning to direct himself in an appropriate manner. She knew that the longer it took Jeff to direct himself following the prompt, the more likely his attention would focus on irrelevant variables in the environment. To prompt an immediate self-directive statement by Jeff, Mrs. Myles readjusted her instructional procedures. She included individual instruction as well as small-group instruction, arranged for Jeff to sit near a student who modeled on-task behavior, and increased the number of practice sessions for the self-directive statement.

Mrs. Myles's efforts to make Jeff aware of and proficient in behaviors critical to success in a variety of academic tasks produced gains beyond those stated on the IEP. Not only did Jeff meet goals related to academic and social development, but he also began to generalize these self-directing skills to other situations. As Jeff became more assured of his capabilities, provocations with classmates decreased. Rather than bully classmates, Jeff began to use the self-corrective and reinforcement statements he had learned to help him. Other teachers reported hearing Jeff tell his peers, "Let's concentrate and get this done," or "If you keep trying, you'll get it right." Mrs. Myles's assessment of the effects of Jeff's self-directive behaviors on academic tasks proved to be a major factor in identifying instructional strategies critical to his success as a student and the development of positive social skills.

Discussion Points

1. If Mrs. Myles had been attempting to teach Jeff to take responsibility for the quality of his independent work, what type of self-directive statements and instructional strategies might have been used?
2. Write two complete instructional objectives for each of the three annual goals Mrs. Myles added to Jeff's IEP.

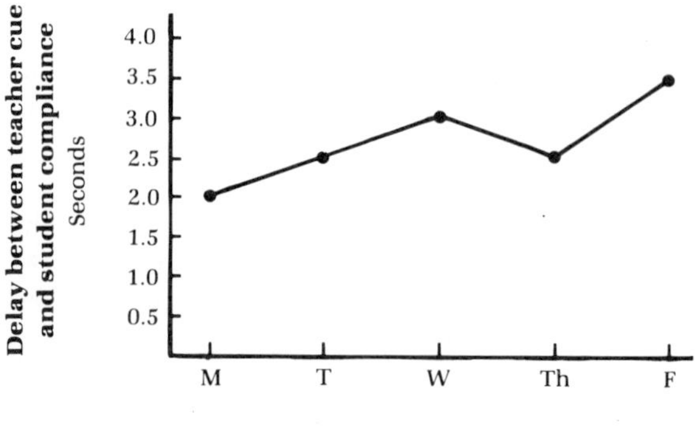

CHAPTER 6 Educational Alternatives for Handicapped Adolescents

OUTLINE

INTRODUCTION

Until recently the focus of educational programming for the handicapped has been on children between the ages of six and twelve. This emphasis has been attributed to factors such as pressure from parents seeking help for their young children who could not master basic skills, a lack of teacher education programs for professionals planning to work at the secondary level (Mercer 1979), and an overall neglect of special education programs at the secondary level (Heller 1981).

Too often professionals have assumed that special education intervention during the elementary years would remedy or minimize later learning and behavior problems. Although early remedial intervention has been effective for some handicapped students, others have continued to require special education assistance at the secondary level. Due to the varying needs of handicapped adolescents, a variety of secondary options should be available to them.

Objectives

After reading this chapter, you should be able to

- discuss program options for the secondary handicapped student;
- describe career competencies that secondary handicapped students should develop;
- describe tools and practices for assessing handicapped students' career needs;
- describe competencies needed by special educators at the secondary level;
- list community resources with which handicapped students should be familiar;
- describe the special educator's role in postsecondary programs for the handicapped;
- discriminate between career and vocational competencies.

Critical Incident: Expanding Secondary Program Options

In a survey of service delivery models at the secondary level, Deshler, Lowrey, and Alley (1979) reported that 45 percent of the programs were devoted to basic skills, 24 percent to content subjects, 17 percent to functional and life skills, 5 percent to work-study, and 4 percent to study skills. The majority of service delivery options emphasize remedial intervention or assistance with content subjects, while fewer programs offer instruction related to the development of future vocational or career skills.

Increasingly, special education professionals are rejecting the traditional secondary curriculum as inappropriate for many handicapped youth (Laurie et al. 1978; Malouf and Halpern 1976). Their belief is that the irrelevancy of subject content and secondary instructional practices, grouping arrangements, materials, and testing methods pose unnecessary burdens for many handicapped students and are actually counterproductive to meeting their needs. Even though continued emphasis on remedial and tutorial efforts to maintain handicapped students in the regular secondary class may serve some handicapped students effectively, there are many handicapped students who need alternative programs in order to succeed as adults within the mainstream of society.

While remedial or tutorial assistance is not an inherently poor instructional practice, programs stemming from a broader ecological perspective might better benefit secondary handicapped students. Such a perspective can help special educators see beyond the immediate academic needs of handicapped students in one ecosystem, the school, to their needs in other ecosystems, such as the home, leisure, and vocational environments. When special educators begin to perceive both the immediate and future needs of their students, more comprehensive program models will be developed and stronger career education components will be added to service delivery models for these students.

Points for Consideration

- *Elementary service models such as the resource model are not always appropriate for secondary handicapped students, yet many students who have not acquired the academic and social skills to meet the expectations of secondary teachers are placed in secondary classes with supplemental assistance through a resource room model (Kokozka and Drye 1981).*

In order to avoid inappropriate placement for these students, the special educator trained to work at the secondary level must be aware of alternative service models. Keogh and Levitt (1976) suggest that special educators serve as student rather than program advocates.

- *Secondary teachers should consider the immediate and long-term curricular needs of handicapped adolescents.*

According to Doyle (1979), special educators with an ecological perspective will question the "functional value or adaptive significance of behaviors in an environment" (p. 189). From this perspective effective teachers incorporate career competencies in the curriculum because of their potential to prepare students to live independently as adults.

COMMON INSTRUCTIONAL MISCONCEPTIONS

The resource model is appropriate for most handicapped students at the secondary level. For those students who require continued support during the secondary phase of their educational experience, service delivery options should include noneducational services, residential schools, full-time special classes, part-time special classes, resource models, and consultative services to regular educators (Wiederholt 1978). Secondary special education programs will be effective only if a variety of options are available to handicapped adolescents.

Graduation from high school marks the end of educational training for handicapped students. Typically this is true in secondary programs that do not plan for a transition from high school to independent living. Special educators should recognize that some secondary school graduates will need continuous community support services while others will matriculate to higher education.

PROGRAM OPTIONS

The handicapped student's needs, skills, and future goals all play a role in identifying the most appropriate service delivery option. Those adolescents with mild handicapping conditions may best be served in the mainstream of the secondary school with supplemental assistance from the teacher consultant, tutor, or resource room models. Other handicapped students may be served through a combination of regular secondary and vocational education with supplemental special education support in both the traditional and vocational settings. Appropriate program options for adolescents with more severe learning and behavior problems may be self-contained special classes or special vocational training centers. These program options and suggested guidelines for professionals making placement decisions for handicapped adolescents are described below.

Resource Model

The resource model at the secondary level is an extension of the model used at the elementary level. The special educator provides remedial instruction in areas of skill deficits in a resource room, and the student spends the remainder of the school day in the regular high school or vocational program. An abusive practice associated with the resource model occurs when adolescents are placed in regular secondary classes for which they do not have the prerequisite skills for success. In an attempt to minimize failure for these adolescents, the special educator mistakenly attempts to provide additional tutorial services using time allocated for remedial assistance. Regarding this issue, MacMillan, Jones, and Meyers (1978) point out, "[S]ome decisions must be made if the attempts at implementation (of mainstreaming) continue to fail to show desired results in order that the children in question are not harmed" (p. 156).

For appropriate placement in a resouce model, the adolescent should have the prerequisite skills for success in regular secondary classes. He or she should be able to succeed in these classes with little, if any, assistance from the special educator. In this model, the special educator's primary roles are to use the limited instructional time to: (*a*) provide remedial instruction in weak academic areas; (*b*) provide career education; and (*c*) to consult with general and vocational educators as an advocate for handicapped adolescents.

Tutorial Model

Some high school programs provide tutorial programs for handicapped adolescents. This model is commonly observed in schools providing a transition service for handicapped students moving from resource room programs to regular secondary educational programs. To profit from a tutorial model, adolescents should have the prerequisite academic skills required for classes in the regular secondary program. The special educator's role is to help the student make this transition by developing study, organizational, and attending skills needed to survive in the mainstream.

Teacher Consultant Model

The major function of the teacher consultant is to work with regular educators who have handicapped students in their classes. Like the special educator in the tutorial model, the teacher consultant works to help the handicapped student succeed in a regular secondary setting. However, the focus is on assisting regular teachers rather than working directly with handicapped students. Often special educators in both resource and self-contained models perform the functions of teacher consultants.

The success of this program model is contingent on the ability of the handicapped student and the attitudes and perceptions of regular secondary teachers about the handicapped (Gickling and Theobald 1975). While students placed in this service delivery model should have the basic academic and social skills to meet the demands of the regular curriculum, special educators must have consultation skills necessary for effectively working with other adult professionals on topics such as behavioral principles, evaluation, assessment, and alternative instructional styles.

Work-Study Programs

The purpose of **work-study programs** is to provide students with both on-the-job training in the community and classroom instruction that emphasizes basic academic skill development. Students in a work-study program spend a portion of each school day learning a vocational skill in the community and another portion receiving remedial instruction in the special class. As students progress through such a program, more time is spent in the community placement and less in the special class.

One advantage of this model is that students learn a vocational skill in the community while continuing to receive remedial instruction. However, too often work-study participants are given training in low-status occupations with little opportunity for advancement (Razeghi and Davis 1979). Further, this program model offers little opportunity for handicapped students to interact with nonhandicapped peers and does not always emphasize career competencies as an important instructional component.

This option should be considered only if handicapped students cannot succeed academically in content subjects, even with special educational support, or if their behavior seriously interferes with learning in the regular class. Those special educators functioning within work-study programs should include career competencies as a vehicle for teaching basic skills within their instructional program.

Many school systems employ work-study coordinators to teach and supervise students in aspects of career education related to vocational competencies. In such cases, the special educator and work-study coordinator should function as a team to provide comprehensive career education, the former focusing on daily living and personal social skills and the latter focusing on occupational guidance and preparation.

Vocational Programs

An additional source for vocational training is the vocational high school sponsored by one or more school districts. In some communities, the vocational school serves both handicapped and nonhandicapped adolescents. Other communities have vocational high schools exclusively for handicapped students. Training received in a vocational center can provide handicapped students with specific, marketable skills necessary for future employment.

Too often this program option is not available to handicapped students. While 10 percent of vocational funds must be spent on vocational training for the handicapped (Razeghi and Davis 1979), only about 2 percent of handicapped students actually receive service in the vocational setting (Brolin and D'Alonzo 1979). Vocational educators have been hesitant to work with handicapped students for a variety of reasons, such as student immaturity (Bingham 1978).

To increase the availability of this program option for handicapped secondary students, special educators need to assume a more active role in placement decisions and arrange for collaboration with vocational educators during the assessment and instructional phases of vocational training (Phelps 1978; Weisenstein 1977). When a vocational placement is selected for a handicapped student, the special educator must take action to assure that such a placement does not result in less attention to other, equally important curricular needs, such as basic skill development. One method for meeting this need is to locate special education resource units in those vocational centers that do not include basic academic skills and career competencies as a part of their formal vocational program.

SECONDARY TEACHER COMPETENCIES

Frith (1981) points out that

> the mandates of PL 94-142, such as related services, individualized education programs (IEP's), free appropriate public education, and due process, while emphasizing the child's welfare, have forced special educators into a position where they must frequently serve "two masters" (p. 487).

Special educators at the secondary level must not only provide direct teaching services but also coordinate services for the handicapped with counselors, administrators, work-study coordinators, students, parents, and regular vocational teachers from a variety of disciplines, trades, and technical backgrounds.

Zigmond, Silverman, and Laurie (1978), recognizing the advocacy dilemmas of special educators, have outlined competencies that special educators should have in order to be both successful employees of a school system and advocates for handicapped adolescents. Those competencies are:

1. interpreting psychological reports and identifying findings that can assist in educational planning;
2. using a variety of formal and informal assessment strategies with secondary students;
3. conducting interviews and observing secondary students in a variety of settings to gather information relative to their interests and motivation;
4. developing individual programs based on assessment data;
5. teaching basic skills such as reading, arithmetic, and written expression;
6. selecting or creating appropriate educational materials that meet the learning and interest needs of adolescents;
7. using classroom management techniques that are motivational and that minimize maladaptive behavior;
8. providing adolescents with activities and programs that promote acquisition of career competencies;

Regardless of the service delivery model used, it is important that secondary special educators understand the growth and developmental needs of adolescents and be prepared to work with other professionals.

9. providing activities that allow the adolescent to explore attitudes and build a positive self-image;
10. providing assistance to regular educators in adapting the curriculum, instructional practices, and classroom management techniques;
11. analyzing the system for direct service options for students.

Many secondary special educators believe that their personal knowledge base in subjects such as government, the sciences, mathematics, English, and computer science is helpful to handicapped adolescents. Nevertheless, the competencies listed above cluster around four major areas: (1) assessment and evaluation, (2) instruction, (3) social skills, and (4) consultation. Strategies that secondary special educators can use to increase their effectiveness within each of these areas are discussed below.

Career Education

Handicapped students have in the past received and continue to receive vocational training (Sitlington 1979). Hoyt (1977) suggests that **vocational training** provides students with an employment skill, while **career training** includes developing skills for job exploration, decision making, job seeking, and good work habits as well as vocational training. The concept of career training affords the special educator a broader scope from which to plan career-related experiences for students.

Working from this broader perspective, Brolin and Kokaska (cited in Brolin 1982) developed a Life Centered Career Education Matrix (See Table 6–1). Over one hundred competencies are grouped into three global areas—daily living skills, personal social skills, and occupational guidance and preparation. The first 42 competencies prepare the individual to practice daily living skills; competencies 43 through 75 emphasize personal and social skills; the remaining competencies, 76 through 102, are related to traditional vocational preparation. Only about 25 percent of the 102 competencies are related to vocational preparation. It may be that vocational programs which focus only on this limited aspect of career education are neglecting many other skills students need to maintain an adult lifestyle and promote a sense of well-being. Since vocational teachers typically address the majority of those competencies related to occupational guidance and preparation, it is the special educator's responsibility to provide instruction emphasizing the other two career curricular areas—daily living skills and personal social skills.

Assessment and Evaluation

As indicated in the chapter on assessment, the special educator is a member of a team that assesses results in order to make decisions regarding program options and instruction. At the secondary level, a major component of assessment influencing these decisions is career and vocational assessment. Since career assessment has the effect of channeling handicapped students into specific vocational directions, assessment should focus on three distinct areas—student aptitude, interest, and attitude (Wallace and Larsen 1979).

A variety of approaches to career assessment should be used by the assessment team to insure that a comprehensive profile of the student is obtained. Often the assessment process begins with formal assessment procedures, some of which are described below.

The *Social and Prevocational Information Battery* (Halpern et al. 1975) is designed to assess skills in purchasing, budgeting, banking, job-related behavior, job search skills, home management, health care, hygiene and grooming, and functional signs. Appropriate for junior and senior high handicapped students, this test requires only survival reading skills. It uses a forced-choice response format, and students' scores on each subscale can be compared to norms. An example of test items to which students respond is illustrated in Figure 6-1. In this example, the student is to read each sign correctly. Based on assessment results, the teacher ranks those career areas for which each student has the greatest instructional need, then groups students according to areas of common instructional need.

An example of a formal assessment tool that probes student interest is the *Strong-Campbell Interest Inventory* (Campbell 1974). This assessment tool provides the student, parents, and special educator with information regarding the student's interest in school subjects and activities, leisure activities, and types of people; occupational preferences; and personal characteristics. The inventory requires approximately thirty minutes to complete and yields profiles related to career clusters, interests, and occupational scales. Such profiles of individual students can assist the teacher in planning lessons that engage students in the learning process.

An assessment tool that measures student aptitude is the *USES Nonreading Aptitude Test Battery* (U.S. Department of Labor 1970). Developed for use with disadvantaged individuals and persons with low reading ability, the battery includes ten subtests: (1) picture-word matching, (2) oral vocabulary, (3) coin matching, (4) design completion, (5) tool matching, (6) three-dimensional space, (7) form matching, (8) coin series, (9) name comparison, and (10) assembling and disassembling. The battery can be administered to six students at a time. Test items are arranged in eight test booklets, in which students record their responses. Responses can be machine scored and yield an aptitude score and general occupational aptitude patterns.

Formal assessment tools such as the ones described above have an important place in the assessment process. They provide professionals with a starting point regarding a student's interests, aptitude, and attitude. However, the information provided by formal assessment alone is insufficient for career planning and programming.

After the career assessment team has gathered formal test data, the next step is to arrange simulated experiences in vocational areas for which assessment has identified student interest and aptitude. These opportunities provide students with firsthand exposure to variables associated with different careers. For example, if a formal test indicates that a student has an interest in and aptitude for a medical career, then a work sample simulating medical experiences should be arranged. During the simulation the student is taught to perform certain medical and office functions, such as taking blood pressure and heart rate, filing, and performing billing procedures. During the simulation, the student's ability and atti-

☐ TABLE 6–1
Brolin and Kokaska's Life Centered Career Education Matrix

Curriculum Area	*Competency*		
DAILY LIVING SKILLS	1. Managing Family Finances	1. Identify money and make correct change	2. Make wise expenditures
	2. Selecting, Managing, and Maintaining a Home	6. Select adequate housing	7. Maintain a home
	3. Caring for Personal Needs	10. Dress appropriately	11. Exhibit proper grooming and hygiene
	4. Raising Children, Family Living	14. Prepare for adjustment to marriage	15. Prepare for raising children (physical care)
	5. Buying and Preparing Food	18. Demonstrate appropriate eating skills	19. Plan balanced meals
	6. Buying and Caring for Clothing	24. Wash clothing	25. Iron and store clothing
	7. Engaging in Civic Activities	28. Generally understand local laws & government	29. Generally understand Federal Government
	8. Utilizing Recreation and Leisure	34. Participate actively in group activities	35. Know activities and available community resources
	9. Getting Around the Community (Mobility)	40. Demonstrate knowledge of traffic rules & safety practices	41. Demonstrate knowledge & use of various means of transportation
PERSONAL SOCIAL SKILLS	10. Achieving Self-Awareness	43. Attain a sense of body	44. Identify interests and abilities
	11. Acquiring Self-Confidence	48. Express feelings of worth	49. Tell how others see him/her
	12. Achieving Socially Responsible Behavior	53. Know character traits needed for acceptance	54. Know proper behavior in public places
	13. Maintaining Good Interpersonal Skills	58. Know how to listen and respond	59. Know how to make & maintain friendships
	14. Achieving Independence	62. Understand impact of behaviors upon others	63. Understand self-organization
	15. Achieving Problem-Solving Skills	66. Differentiate bipolar concepts	67. Understand the need for goals
	16. Communicating Adequately with Others	71. Recognize emergency situations	72. Read at level needed for future goals
OCCUPATIONAL GUIDANCE & PREPARATION	17. Knowing & Exploring Occupational Possibilities	76. Identify the personal values met through work	77. Identify the societal values met through work
	18. Selecting & Planning Occupational Choices	82. Identify major occupational needs	83. Identify major occupational interests
	19. Exhibiting Appropriate Work Habits & Behaviors	87. Follow directions	88. Work with others
	20. Exhibiting Sufficient Physical-Manual Skills	94. Demonstrate satisfactory balance and coordination	95. Demonstrate satisfactory manual dexterity
	21. Obtaining a Specific Occupational Skill		
	22. Seeking, Securing, & Maintaining Employment	98. Search for a job	99. Apply for a job

☐ TABLE 6–1—continued
Career Education Curriculum Competencies

Subcompetencies

3. Obtain and use bank and credit facilities	4. Keep basic financial records	5. Calculate and pay taxes		
8. Use basic appliances and tools	9. Maintain home exterior			
12. Demonstrate knowledge of physical fitness, nutrition & weight control	13. Demonstrate knowledge of common illness prevention and treatment			
16. Prepare for raising children (psychological care)	17. Practice family safety in the home			
20. Purchase food	21. Prepare meals	22. Clean food preparation areas	23. Store food	
26. Perform simple mending	27. Purchase clothing			
30. Understand citizenship rights and responsibilities	31. Understand registration and voting procedure	32. Understand Selective Service procedures	33. Understand civil rights & responsibilities when questioned by the law	
36. Understand recreational values	37. Use recreational facilities in the community	38. Plan and choose activities wisely	39. Plan vacations	
42. Drive a car				
45. Identify emotions	46. Identify needs	47. Understand the physical self		
50. Accept praise	51. Accept critcism	52. Develop confidence in self		
55. Develop respect for the rights and properties of others	56. Recognize authority and follow instructions	57. Recognize personal roles		
60. Establish appropriate heterosexual relationships	61. Know how to establish close relationships			
64. Develop goal-seeking behavior	65. Strive toward self-actualization			
68. Look at alternatives	69. Anticipate consequences	70. Know where to find good advice		
73. Write at the level needed for future goals	74. Speak adequately for understanding	75. Understand the subtleties of communication		
78. Identify the remunerative aspects of work	79. Understand classification jobs into different occupational systems	80. Identify occupational opportunities available locally	81. Identify sources of occupational information	
84. Identify occupational aptitudes	85. Identify requirements of appropriate and available jobs	86. Make realistic occupational choices		
89. Work at a satisfactory rate	90. Accept supervision	91. Recognize the importance of attendance and punctuality	92. Meet demands for quality work	93. Demonstrate occupational safety
96. Demonstrate satisfactory stamina and endurance	97. Demonstrate satisfactory sensory discrimination			
100. Interview for a job	101. Adjust to competitive standards	102. Maintain post-school occupational adjustment		

☐ **FIGURE 6–1**
Test Items Related to Purchase Habits in the *Social and Prevocational Information Battery.*

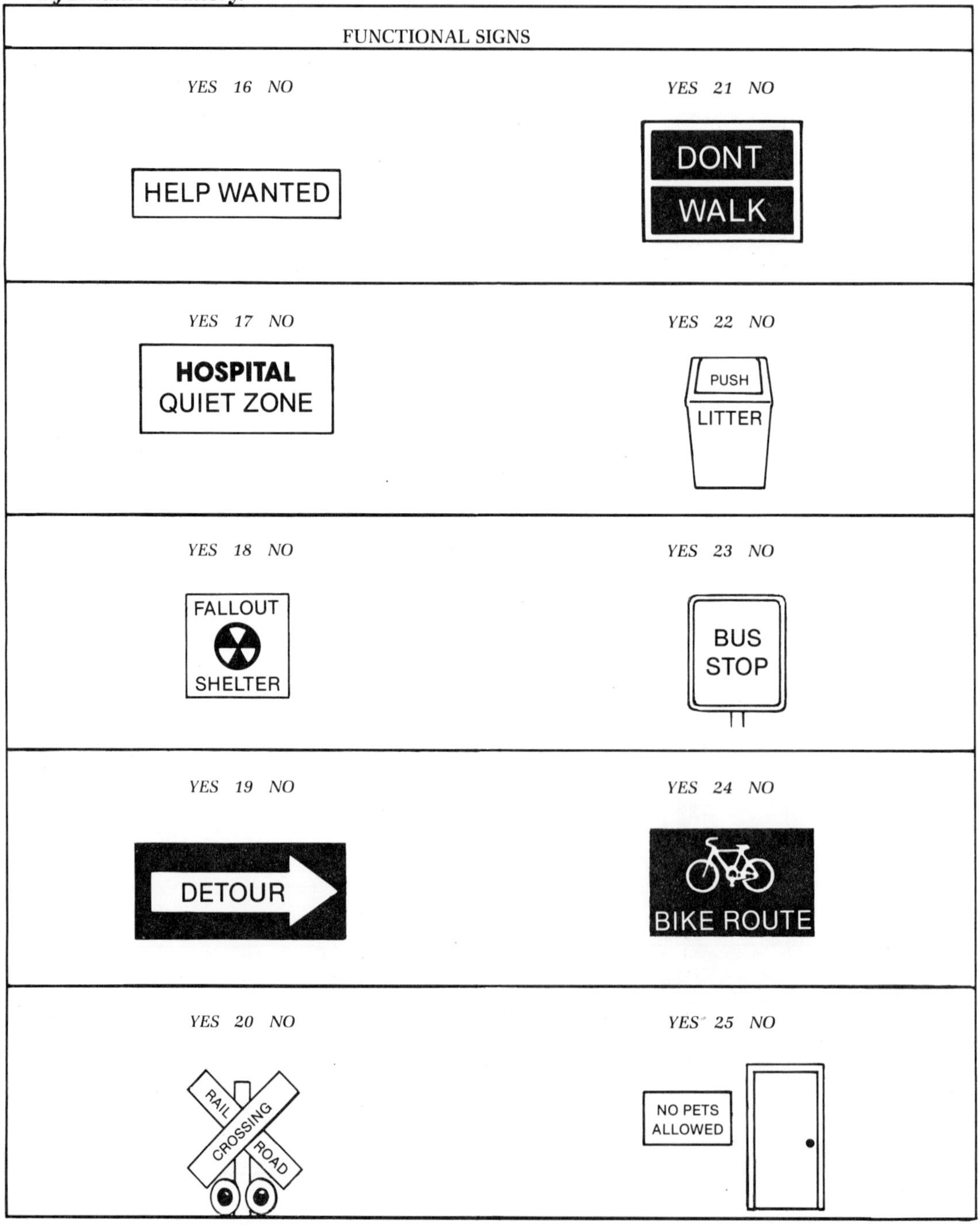

From *Social and Prevocational Inventory, Form T.* Reprinted by permission of the publisher, CTB/McGraw-Hill, 2500 Garden Road, Monterey, CA 93940.

tude are assessed. This information as well as student feedback becomes part of the career assessment data.

An example of a commercial work-sample system is the *Singer Vocational Evaluation System* (Singer Education Division). Each of the twenty work samples is self-contained and provides job tasks related to specific career areas. An audio-visual system is used to present instructions for job tasks. A few of the vocational areas represented in the work samples are electrical wiring, medical assistance, plumbing and pipe fitting, office and sales work, food preparation, engine service, and production machine operating. Other examples of commercial work samples are *Micro-TOWER* (ICD Rehabilitation and Research Center) and the *Vocational Information and Evaluation Work Sample* (Vocational Research Institute).

While the student completes tasks related to specific career areas, the work-study coordinator or occupational therapist observes the student in such areas as speed, attending skills, ability to follow directions, completion of tasks, dexterity, use of equipment, work habits, stamina, and social skills.

Since not all school systems have vocational facilities or materials necessary for comprehensive simulated experiences, the special and vocational educators may need to construct their own or arrange for a short-term shadow experience in a career area suited to the student's aptitudes and interests. In a shadow experience the student is paired with a worker to observe and participate in activities the employee performs. This type of assessment approach, which may last one or two weeks, allows the student sufficient time to perceive both those functions that are pleasant and those that the student may find disagreeable. It also allows the professional to complete formal observation of student skills and job competencies critical to success. After such an experience, the student is in a better position to make an informed decision about a career area. These experiences not only provide educational personnel with opportunities to evaluate a student's skills but also can be used to establish communication with business and industry representatives.

Assessment for career planning is complex because the content area is very broad and because educational programming based on assessment results can have long-lasting and far-reaching effects on the handicapped student (Office of Education 1977). The student's performance during assessment may determine his future community status, income, and standard of living. For career assessment to serve its purpose, professionals should encourage active participation by both parents and students in all assessment and subsequent programming decisions.

Instruction

Kokozka and Drye (1981) indicate that a major difference between special and regular educators in secondary settings is a "split between content versus methodology" (p. 23). In other words, the special educator's training tends to focus on instructional methods for remedying deficits in basic subjects, while the regular secondary educator's training emphasizes teaching specific content material. Unlike the regular teacher, who often has a wealth of instructional programs from which to choose, the secondary special educator is faced with a limited number of skill development programs appropriate for secondary handicapped students.

Another dilemma facing secondary special educators is the selection of materials. Although special educators at the secondary level may be skilled in identifying effective remedial strategies, they often are confronted with limited availability of appropriate secondary materials needed to implement remedial strategies. However, secondary specialists can minimize these instructional issues if they are skilled in modifying existing instructional materials and utilize a task analysis approach to instruction.

Modifying materials. Goodman (1978) suggests that the special teacher purchase commercial materials that address students' specific skill needs and be prepared to modify the format to fit their learning style and needs. The following are some general guidelines for modification of materials based on suggestions from the text *Mainstreaming the Learning Disabled Adolescent: A Staff Development Guide* (South Carolina Region V Educational Services Center 1977):

- Offer limited amounts of work to a student. This can be done by cutting up workbook pages so that the student sees, for example, five problems rather than twenty-five at any given time.
- Tape text material so that the student can hear and see text vocabulary simultaneously. Highlighting headings, subheadings, and the first sentences of paragraphs in a text also helps the secondary student avoid being overwhelmed by a difficult text.
- Collect various resources to supplement a material that does not provide sufficient redundancy of concepts or practice activities for mastery tasks.
- Anticipate directions that may be difficult for some students and ask them to repeat or paraphrase them.
- Rewrite the narrative of some texts to improve the format or readability or to remove apparent biases.
- Reconstruct mastery activities to allow students to respond orally or through action rather than through the typical written response.
- Develop study guides to supplement content-related texts to provide the additional structure needed by students.
- Preview vocabulary used in a text with students before they read the text.
- Develop record-keeping and reinforcement components for materials that do not provide them for students.
- If the material limits experiences to the symbolic level, gather supplemental objects to provide students with learning experiences on the concrete level.

These suggestions for adaptation of learning materials can also be implemented in the regular secondary classroom. For those teachers who are either unwilling or unable to develop these instructional modifications, it may be appropriate to have other students or parent volunteers adapt the materials for the handicapped student.

Task analysis. Task analysis can be a valuable tool to help guide special educators in developing instructional procedures, selecting materials related to career competencies, and relating career competencies to basic academic skills.

Brolin (1982) defines task analysis as "breaking down a work task into its component parts: materials, movements, and responses and then arranging or rearranging them for effectiveness and efficiency" (p. 205).

Mr. Snyder, a secondary special educator in a resource program, wished to provide Bob, one of the seniors in his program, with instruction related to the career subcompetency "planning a vacation." (Refer to Table 6–1). When talking with Bob, Mr. Snyder learned that he had a part-time job at a grocery store and wanted to celebrate his high school graduation the following spring by taking a trip to California with two friends. Their plan was to drive there in Bob's car, camping along the way. Bob needed to know how much money to budget over the next nine months to be able to take this trip. The following is a portion of the task analysis Mr. Snyder developed to help Bob prepare for his trip:

I. Determine Transportation Costs
   A. Obtain a United States road map from a travel service.
   B. Compute total miles.
      1. Locate destination on the map.
      2. Measure distance between the starting point and destination.
      3. Locate scale of miles on the map.
      4. Multiply total inches times miles per inch.
      5. Multiply one-way distance by two for round trip miles.
      6. Compute 10 percent of round trip miles (to allow for off-the-main-road-driving to find places to eat, to visit points of interest, etc.) and add it to round trip miles for total miles.
   C. Compute miles per gallon of car to be used.
      1. Record mileage after filling the gas tank.
      2. Drive until gas gauge is on empty.
      3. Fill the gas tank and record the mileage and number of gallons of gas purchased.
      4. Subtract the smaller mileage figure from the larger.
      5. Divide the mileage difference by the number of gallons purchased.
   D. Compute amount of gasoline needed, dividing total miles by miles per gallon.
   E. Compute transportation costs.
      1. Determine cost of gasoline per gallon.
      2. Multiply total gallons needed by cost per gallon.
      3. Compute 10 percent of total gasoline costs.
      4. Add 10 percent to total gasoline costs to have sufficient funds for additional transportation costs.
      5. Divide total transportation costs by number of persons sharing costs.

Next, Mr. Snyder obtained materials such as maps, camping directories, examples of traveler's checks, catalogs, and travel guides to be used in math and reading lessons with Bob.

During his senior year, Bob saved for and planned his vacation through activities that Mr. Snyder incorporated into math and reading lessons. Bob learned to interpret map symbols, chart a route, and locate items in a catalog. Further, he applied basic arithmetic operations to compute driving time and costs. In addition, he acquired valuable organizational and planning skills.

This example of instruction in career competencies illustrates that basic skills can be taught in a meaningful manner to students. As Porter (1980), encouraging special educators to approach basic academics through career education, writes:

> [S]ome advocates of "back to basics" movements are critical of career development programs and seem to assume that students who emphasize certain vocationally oriented electives during their secondary years are giving up opportunities to develop academically. This study indicates, however, that career development models do provide environments that can foster academic growth through the application of basic skills. Furthermore, many students who may have initially possessed the skills have no opportunity to apply them in a concrete way; thus the skills have remained without reinforcement (p. 464).

Consultation

The need for secondary special educators to possess consultation skills has been identified repeatedly by professionals involved with handicapped adolescents. As Zigmond, Silverman, and Laurie (1978) have pointed out:

> The plight of the student . . . is accentuated at the secondary level because curriculum in the secondary school is developed, interpreted, and presented by specialists in subject matter. These teachers often lack the psychoeducational orientation useful in designing alternative teaching and assessment strategies. There is a need for an interpreter—a liaison between the student and the content-area teacher—to help the student "make it" in the mainstream (p. 285).

The question for the secondary special educator then is, "How does one consult and with whom?" Since consultation places the special educator in the role of liaison between secondary students and content teachers, consultation must occur with the needs of both students and content teachers in mind.

In order to minimize barriers within the consultation process, the special educator may begin by giving careful attention to scheduling practices when mainstreaming handicapped students into content or vocational classes. Scheduling for handicapped students in the junior or senior high school is typically accomplished in conjunction with the guidance counselor, according to class periods that are in operation at the school. Since a typical instructional period lasts for forty-five to fifty-five minutes in most secondary schools, the special educator must arrange for instruction, mastery and review activities, plus evaluation and record keeping in a very short period of time. Further, time for consultation with regular and vocational educators must be allocated. Scheduling at this level therefore requires considerable thought and organization. The following are guidelines based on suggestions by Marsh, Gearheart, and Gearheart (1978) for helping special educators develop realistic schedules:

- The handicapped students within the secondary school should be given priority in scheduling since they have unique learning needs.

- Courses selected for the student's schedule should be those in which he or she will succeed. The student should have the prerequisite skills to complete the course, and the teacher should be empathetic to handicapped students.
- The student's course load should reflect his or her abilities. More difficult courses should be interspersed among those that are less difficult.
- If possible, handicapped students with common skill deficits should be scheduled simultaneously for special education services. For example, the first two periods within the special class could be reserved for reading instruction.
- The last two periods of the school day could be devoted to supplemental instruction and consultation. During this time handicapped students could be assigned to the special education class or a study hall and receive regular or periodic supplemental assistance.

In order to minimize problems for handicapped students in regular classes, special educators should arrange for regular written and oral communication with regular and vocational educators. For example, many special educators distribute a form on a weekly basis to general educators teaching classes in which secondary handicapped students are mainstreamed. Figure 6–2 illustrates such a form.

When special educators implement such a review process regularly, they are better able to prevent problems from becoming major issues. Consultation strategies discussed earlier should be used to solve problems identified on the form. The special educator should also make it a point to maintain oral communication with all teachers and, in particular, with regular educators who do not report problems. By visiting these teachers, the special educator may be able to anticipate problems. He or she can also use these visits as opportunities to praise the accomplishments of handicapped students in the regular classes.

☐ **FIGURE 6–2**
An Example of Written Communication with Regular Educators

Student Name ______________________ Class __________ Period ________

Attendance M T W TH F (circle if present)

Punctuality M T W TH F (circle each day student was on time for class)

Average grade for week A B C D F (please circle)

Attending skills:
Does this student need instruction in note taking or attending skills:
yes no

Does this student need help reading the text? If so, please note pages to be read for the following week. pp. ____________

Does this student need help preparing for a test or quiz? If yes, please indicate text material and topics to be included. ______________________________

Teacher's Signature ______________________________

Social Skills

In order to facilitate handicapped adolescents' integration into the mainstream of the regular classroom and peer group activities, it is important that special educators include social skill development as part of their curriculum. Within the special education classroom, teachers can provide structured activities to change students' behaviors in a variety of ecosystems. Such instruction should include recognition of the problem, identification of solutions, evaluation and monitoring of one's own behavior, and identification of realistic and appropriate social skills. An effective social skills program requires teachers to use a variety of techniques, depending upon each student's needs. Some instructional needs are best met in either informal or formal group settings. However, due to the sensitivity of some students' needs, the special educator might decide that a one-to-one approach is more appropriate. The following discussion on group meetings, values clarification, and counseling illustrates various instructional strategies and approaches for developing social skills.

Group meetings. The special educator at the secondary level might provide time for weekly **group meetings** in which small groups of students discuss topics or issues of interest to the entire group. Any personal concern or problem of an individual student should not be a weekly topic without that student's consent. Topics might include how to handle ridicule from nonimpaired peers, how to get involved in school activities, how to get parents to extend curfew for special events, or how to be more accepted by regular teachers. Using this last example, the special educator could apply task analysis to break down this skill and identify one of its subskills as developing behaviors that please teachers. The following is a description of how a group meeting might be organized to develop this subskill:

A. The special educator first attempts to increase the accuracy of students' perceptions regarding behaviors that are pleasing to teachers.
   1. Students are asked to identify the two most successful students in a regular educator's class. To identify these students, members of the group are directed to look at factors such as the frequency of the regular teacher's positive comments and smiles, and the frequency with which each student is chosen to speak, etc.
   2. Students in the group should then be given a list of questions to guide their observations of these successful students. Examples of such questions might be:
      a. What do these students wear?
      b. What do these students bring to class?
      c. Are these students on time to class?
      d. Do they smile, greet, and make eye contact with the teacher upon entering class?
      e. Do these students look at the teacher frequently?
      f. Do these students nod their heads or lean toward the teacher?
      g. Do these students ask for the teacher's help?
      h. Do these students hand in assignments?
      i. Do these students find time to talk privately with the teacher?

   j. Do these students study or begin assignments if given free time during the class period?
3. Some students in the group may place a sheet of questions such as these in their notebooks as a guide to structure their observations. They can also record their responses on the sheet immediately following their observation of the successful students.

B. After the observation period, the group meets to exchange information regarding behaviors that appear to please teachers.
   1. The special educator's role is to encourage discussion of those behaviors that each teacher finds most appealing. Rather than suggest that handicapped adolescents adopt a specific behavior, the special educator encourages them to choose one or two with which they feel comfortable.
   2. Next, students role play, portraying themselves using behaviors identified as pleasing to teachers, while one student plays the role of a specific secondary teacher. This allows adolescents in the group an opportunity to establish these behaviors as a habit. It also promotes a sense of control since they are learning coping skills to use in classes that may be threatening to their self-image. Cantor and Gelfand (1977) note that when students behave in a socially responsive manner, they are perceived by adults as more attractive and intelligent.

Silverman, Zigmond, and Sansone (1981) have developed a social skills curriculum called the *School Survival Skills Curriculum.* It is divided into three areas, each of which focuses on a set of skills with which handicapped adolescents have

In order for some handicapped adolescents to be mainstreamed into school and community life, it is necessary that educators teach appropriate social behaviors.

difficulty. Those areas are behavior control, teacher-pleasing behaviors, and study skills. A small-group instructional format is used within the program, and its authors recommend that one period per week be reserved for group instruction in survival skills.

Values clarification. Secondary special educators may use techniques associated with **values clarification,** a decision-making process, to help handicapped adolescents learn about themselves, make decisions, or understand and accept their behavior and that of others. Since the purpose of values clarification is to help students achieve personal growth, the process is more important than the outcomes of the activities used. Examples of some commercial materials for values clarification are *Values Clarification: A Handbook of Practical Strategies for Teachers and Students* (Simon, Howe, and Kirschenbaum 1972) and *Values Education Sourcebook: Conceptual Approaches, Materials Analyses, and an Annotated Bibliography* (Superka et al. 1976).

In addition, examples of values clarification activities are:

Time Capsule—Students place articles that represent major values of the present society in a time capsule.

How I Think Others See Me—Students write statements on cards about how they perceive that others in the group see them. Cards are shuffled and distributed. Members of the group guess the author of each card.

Ideal 24 Hours—Students write a description of a perfect day explaining how they would spend time, choose their activities, friends, etc. This is followed by goal setting or ranking activities according to their personal value.

Wanted: Parents—Students write "want ads" advertising for parents, describing ideal discipline, child rearing, and parent and child behaviors.

Ten Things I Love to Do—Students list ten activities they really like. Next, they place an asterisk next to those activities they do most often and a check mark next to each that meets with societal approval. This activity is followed by goal setting in the group.

Who Do You Choose?—Students choose names of group members to answer questions like, "Who would you choose to represent the group or to spend time with on a deserted island or to be your teacher?"

My Child—Students write a description of what personality traits and behaviors they might want to observe in a child their age and sex. Descriptions are shared in the group.

Success Memories—Students identify three successful experiences and share these with the group for each of four different time periods in their life.

"I" and "You" Statements—Students are given various situations involving another person. They write both "I" statements, expressing how they would feel in that situation, and "you" statements, expressing how they would feel as the other person.

Growth Mobiles—Each student makes a mobile with parts that represent his or her goals, strengths, significant people, and intended behavior changes. The mobiles are described to the group and hung in the room.

These techniques should be used in small groups of approximately four or five students. Further, the special educator should also participate in values clarification exercises to model the process as well as behavioral authenticity.

Counseling. Although many handicapped adolescents view their teachers as confidants, secondary special educators usually are not trained or certified as counselors. Many special educators in secondary schools rely on the aid of guidance counselors and psychologists to work as a counseling team. A team approach to student counseling not only helps handicapped students with their concerns but also helps special educators acquire counseling skills. While many special educators may have natural or innate counseling skills, these can always be improved through observation of and discussions with trained personnel.

POSTSECONDARY TRAINING

Just as the special educator develops and applies professional competencies on behalf of his or her students in the secondary school, the special educator's efforts should also extend to those students making the transition from the secondary school to independent living.

In order to enter the mainstream of society as adults, handicapped students must understand their needs, abilities, responsibilities, and obligations to the community at large. To that end, some type of postsecondary service or education is recommended to help handicapped youth make a smooth transition to independent living. For some handicapped young adults, postsecondary training may mean professional training at institutions of higher education. Still other handicapped adults may require further vocational training either on the job or at a training center (Boyan 1978). Regardless of the type of additional training needed, provisions for continued training that supports the diverse needs of the older adolescent or young adult should begin prior to high school graduation.

The special educator who begins to prepare the older adolescent for the transition to independent living should offer concrete assistance rather than a cursory exposure to postsecondary support systems. The first step in providing such assistance requires special educators to have a working knowledge of community and educational support systems. Familiarity with these support systems begins by visiting a variety of local agencies and educational institutions. Examples of these are the Bureau of Vocational Rehabilitation, the community mental health center, state welfare and employment offices, county court offices, banks, and local junior and technical colleges, schools, and universities.

During such visits, the special educator should obtain written information regarding the services and requirements for service of each agency and the name of a contact person within the agency. In addition, representatives from these agencies or schools might be invited to the class to explain the service they provide. In turn, the special teacher should consider arranging group or individual field trips to these agencies or institutions to minimize student hesitancy in approaching and talking with agency representatives after they have completed high school.

Another valuable strategy for preparing the older handicapped adolescent for independent living is to contact past graduates and invite them to visit the class to discuss their jobs, living arrangements, financial affairs, leisure activities, and the emotional impact of independence on their lives. Visits from past graduates should occur on a regular basis. Further, the teacher should attempt to select a group of graduates representing a variety of lifestyles. For example, some may be enrolled in postsecondary educational programs, while others may be employed full time; some may be living with their parents, while others may be living on their own.

Finally, the secondary special educator may use simulation strategies to allow older adolescents to practice some of the activities they must accomplish as young adults. Examples of such activities are locating and visiting apartments for rent, pricing furniture, cars, and insurance, and planning and purchasing food for one or two individuals.

While the secondary special educator may facilitate some of the activities designed to prepare secondary handicapped students for transition into the community, it is obvious that the teacher cannot accomplish these activities alone. Once again, the special educator is a member of a team. In this instance, the transition team may consist of the special educator, past graduates, agency and educational representatives, and school and vocational guidance counselors. The team's efforts at this stage of the adolescent's transition into adult life often will make the difference between success or failure for the young handicapped adult.

SUMMARY POINTS

- Handicapped adolescents require a wide range of programming options in order to meet their diverse needs for future independent living.
- Secondary special educators should develop an array of competencies in career education instruction, assessment and evaluation, social skills training, consultation, and postsecondary planning.
- Assessment of secondary students must be carefully planned and interpreted because of its far-reaching effects on the future lives of these students. Comprehensive assessment at the secondary level should include both academic and career assessment.
- Career education should be a component of all service delivery options for handicapped adolescents because it addresses the ecological needs of the handicapped adolescent more effectively than vocational training.
- Due to the limited number of instructional programs for handicapped secondary students, special educators must adapt existing programs and materials. The process can be facilitated by using task analysis.
- The integration of handicapped students into the mainstream of the regular education program and into society requires special educators to include social skills development as part of their curriculum.
- In order to provide the handicapped adolescent with a smooth transition into the community as a young adult, specialists must be skilled in developing and implementing postsecondary experiences prior to the handicapped student's graduation.

REVIEW QUESTIONS

1. In your community, what program options are available for secondary handicapped students, and what are the criteria for admission into each of these service delivery models?
2. What types of career and vocational programs are available in your community for handicapped students? Based upon your state's standards, what specialized training, if any, must vocational educators have to work with handicapped students? What kinds of vocational training must special educators have in order to work in a vocational setting?

SUGGESTED READINGS

Mann, L.; Goodman, L.; and Wiederholt, J.L. 1978. *Teaching the learning disabled adolescent.* Boston: Houghton Mifflin.

Payne, J. S.; Polloway, E. A.; Smith, J. E.; and Payne, R. A. 1981. *Strategies for teaching the mentally retarded.* 2d ed. Columbus, Ohio: Charles E. Merrill.

Application: Interagency Cooperation at the Secondary Level

Dana

When Dana Martin was fifteen, she entered a high school resource room program, having previously attended a self-contained program in junior high school. Dana's resource room teacher, Mr. Gold, coordinated an ongoing career and vocational assessment program for Dana. Data from this assessment program would serve as the basis for making realistic vocational decisions throughout Dana's remaining school years.

Recognizing the importance of including a vocational expert on the team, Mr. Gold contacted Ms. Place, the vocational coordinator, who arranged for Dana to spend one week at a vocational school to have her performance on a variety of work samples assessed. At the vocational school the occupational therapist, Mr. Fleck, arranged for Dana to complete work samples related to retail, medical, instructional, secretarial, and mechanical careers. He also observed and recorded Dana's work-related behaviors.

After the career and vocational assessment data had been gathered, Dana, Mr. Gold, Mr. Fleck, and Ms. Place met to discuss results. Mr. Gold indicated that the career assessment revealed the following strengths and weaknesses:

Strengths	*Weaknesses*
health care	purchasing habits
hygiene and grooming	budgeting
functional signs	banking
home-management	job search skills

Mr. Fleck reported the following interests and aptitudes:

Interests	*Aptitudes*
social service occupations	sales work
teaching	secretarial work
social work	mechanical operation
medicine	

During the group discussion, Dana indicated that she wanted to go to college and learn to be a teacher. After reviewing Dana's strengths, needs, and interests, two shadow experiences were arranged for Dana. One experience was with a legal secretary and the other with an elementary teacher.

Following these short-term shadow experiences, the group met again to discuss Dana's feelings and observations and to plan for Dana's career training needs. During this meeting Mr. Gold pointed out that Dana could successfully pursue a teaching career if she acquired better academic and study skills. Ms. Place suggested that another option for Dana would be to enroll in a secretarial course of study while in high school. Even though this was not Dana's first career choice, she demonstrated an aptitude for it and could use her secretarial skills in the future to finance her education in a teacher training program.

The team recommended that Dana spend her sophomore year in the regular high school and begin the secretarial training program, complete her basic requirements for graduation, and improve basic and study skills in the resource room.

At the end of Dana's sophomore year, she had completed basic requirements for high school graduation and all of the secretarial courses offered at the local high school. However, since her academic skills were still at a level below the demands of college, the team recommended that Dana continue in the special education resource program at the vocational high school and take additional secretarial courses. Dana agreed with all the professionals' recommendations with the exception of continued secretarial training. Instead, she selected the child care program since it more closely paralleled her interest in working with children.

During Dana's senior year, Mr. Jacob, the counselor, Dana, and the resource teacher wrote to and spoke with several colleges and universities to identify a school that would allow her to pursue her chosen career and would also be accommodating to her academic needs.

Currently Dana is continuing her education. She is enrolled in remedial classes at a local university and anticipates that it will take one more year of remedial assistance before she can participate in a regular college program. She also spends twenty hours per week in a dual role as a teacher's aide and school secretary at a children's mental health center.

Discussion Points

1. Although Dana spent her last two high school years at a vocational high school, a common option for handicapped adolescents is to remain in a traditional high school program that is augmented by tutorial services. Describe what might have happened to Dana if she had been offered this traditional service delivery option.
2. The professional team believed that the secretarial program was a realistic option for Dana despite her disagreement. Do you think that they should have pursued this option more firmly? Explain your position.

CHAPTER 7 Developing Thinking Skills

OUTLINE

INTRODUCTION

On any typical day a visitor to a classroom may encounter the following scene: The teacher has just finished a group lesson on long division and has assigned several problems for the children to complete. One child raises her hand and says, "I don't know how to do these." Teacher replies, "Now, Karen, I want you to think about what we just discussed to figure out the answers. Work for fifteen minutes and then I'll check on how you're doing." A visitor to a family dinner may observe a similar situation: The child at the table reaches for a bowl and in the process knocks over a glass of milk. Father exclaims, "Jimmy, why don't you ever think before you do something!"

The obvious common denominator of these scenarios is the emphasis on thinking, but what does this term mean? In the first example, the teacher probably wants Karen to look at examples on the board, remember the different steps, and apply the steps sequentially to the new problems. Jimmy should probably anticipate the distance between himself and the bowl, realize the obstacle, and develop a strategy (such as asking) to appropriately meet his goal. The lesson here is that when we tell a child to "think," we are being vague, and it may not be apparent to the child (or to us) what exactly it is we want the child to do.

Throughout this text the importance of observing and analyzing students' performance within the context of all facets of their environment has been emphasized. In addition, teachers must attempt to understand how handicapped learners perceive, organize, and attend to information they receive from the environment. The focus here is on what takes place in terms of thinking skills before behaviors occur. Since we cannot get inside students' minds to observe thinking activities directly, we must instead analyze observable behaviors from an information-processing perspective.

The purpose of this chapter is to present an overview of information-processing theory regarding handicapped learners and to identify related assessment and instructional approaches. The assessment and instructional strategies discussed here should be used in academic as well as nonacademic settings. Therefore, as a teacher, you should develop a student's language, social and behavioral, reading, arithmetic, and written expression skills in conjunction with his or her information-processing style.

Objectives

After reading this chapter, you will be able to

- list and tell the function of the information-processing components;
- discuss why an information-processing approach to teaching may be beneficial to educationally handicapped students;
- define the terms *attention, conceptual tempo, memory,* and *motivation* and discuss research findings related to instructing educationally handicapped students;
- discuss the importance of analyzing students' errors as well as their successes in order to implement appropriate instructional programs;

- state assessment techniques helpful in identifying students' thinking skills;
- list and discuss problems associated with an information-processing approach to teaching, including a critique of related instructional approaches.

Case Studies: Todd and Sarah

Todd

Todd, a nine-year-old, is placed in a self-contained special education class for children with learning disabilities. Casual observation indicates that he is usually working diligently on his assignments while the teacher conducts individual or small-group instruction. Although Todd is a delight in terms of self-management, his problems become apparent when examining his paperwork and reading performance.

In oral reading Todd can quickly and accurately decode words, but an analysis of his performance indicates a serious deficit in comprehension. Although his word recognition test scores are at the eighth grade level, his comprehension scores center in the second grade range. In spite of these limitations, Todd has an insatiable appetite for reading.

Todd's work sheets provide more evidence of speed and lack of understanding. Smudged handwriting, lack of attention to mathematical signs (adding instead of subtracting), and forgotten assignments are the rule. When his errors are pointed out to him, Todd seem genuinely chagrined, murmuring a hasty "I'm sorry" or "I'll do better." At times it seems that Todd is as puzzled by his performance as is his teacher.

Todd can write meaningful sentences but has difficulty with longer units of thought. His creative stories are a delight, filled with imagination but often lacking in a flow of ideas. Oral expression is also troublesome, as Todd often stammers and gives inappropriate responses. He does not seem to evaluate questions but rather responds with the first thought that occurs to him. For example, when asked to check his arithmetic problems, Todd may immediately start erasing his answers before considering whether they are right or wrong. This tendency also results in inadequate peer relationships, as Todd cannot accurately discern when his classmates are kidding him in a friendly fashion. Instead of responding with a laugh or a joke, Todd may say, "Stop it right now," leaving himself and his peers confused.

To summarize, Todd has extreme difficulty in grasping the essential elements of both academic and social activities. His most obvious strengths are his overall diligence and motivation to read; his lack of effective planning and organization appear to sabotage his intentions of producing good work. The inability to understand written passages has a parallel in the social arena, indicating a severe comprehension problem.

Sarah

Sarah Mitchell, an attractive eighth grade student, attends a junior high school in a middle-income community. She has several close girlfriends who share her interest in tennis and gymnastics, and they often spend the night at one another's homes. Sarah wants to be a teacher.

Sarah was identified in the third grade as having a mild reading disability. Through part-time placement in a resource room program, she made progress and was able to keep pace with her peers. Her parents, taking an active interest in both her academic and athletic endeavors, also enrolled her in the local university's summer reading program for two years to maintain her reading gains. Throughout the elementary years, teacher reports were satisfactory, with Sarah, her parents, and school personnel pleased with her progress in overcoming her academic difficulties. At the end of sixth grade it was decided that Sarah did not need remedial services the following year in junior high school.

Sarah's school reports during the seventh grade were lower than those received during her elementary years. Because Sarah seemed happy and active and because no negative teacher reports were sent home, her parents decided not to intervene, despite their concern over her dropping grades.

During the first grading period of eighth grade, Mr. and Mrs. Mitchell received a mid-semester teacher report indicating that Sarah was failing both science and English. The primary reason was failure to turn in written work. Mr. and Mrs. Mitchell were quite surprised, especially since Sarah had entered a science fair early in the fall and her project had been selected for regional competition.

Talking with Sarah about the problem was disastrous. She refused to acknowledge her homework responsibilities, saying that her teachers rarely assigned any work. Mr. and Mrs. Mitchell, frustrated, decided to limit Sarah's social activities until her grades improved; however, this plan failed to produce positive results.

During a conference with the science teacher, Mr. Hughes, Sarah's parents learned that he had been spending extra time with Sarah for the past two years, because he felt she had the potential to be a good student. He noted that although she participated in class, she had a difficult time getting started with assigned work, often frittering away the allotted work time. Sarah had made adequate progress the previous year, but Mr. Hughes noted a rapid decline during the present grading period. He did not feel that Sarah's previous reading problems were contributing to her failure.

Mrs. Beckwith, the English teacher, concurred with Mr. Hughes's analysis. Both teachers assigned homework on an average of three times per week. Mrs. Beckwith, however, was not as helpful as Mr. Hughes. She stated that eighth grade students should have the necessary discipline and study skills; thus, it was not her duty to "police" the students.

Mr. and Mrs. Mitchell were faced with a confusing situation. After assuming that their daughter was progressing smoothly in junior high school, they were told she was failing. One teacher refused to help, while one offered his own time but to no avail. Sarah had become obstinate concerning school work, thus upsetting the entire household. Because the individual teacher conferences did not result in a plan of action, Mr. and Mrs. Mitchell arranged to meet with the school psychologist and resource room teacher, as they had done when Sarah was in elementary school.

Points for Consideration

- *Todd's on-task behavior, indicating little frustration as he works, masks the confusion he must be encountering, given the quality of his end results.*
- *Todd's teacher needs to discover a strategy that will strengthen his comprehension skills without making the process too laborious, thereby destroying his high motivation to read.*
- *Although Todd appears not to be concerned with peer relationships, the apparent connection between academic and social difficulties points to a need for comprehensive intervention in both domains.*

- *It appears that the help Sarah received in the resource room in elementary school was not sufficient to prepare her for the additional academic burdens of junior high school.*
- *Although Sarah's teachers expressed a concern for her poor academic performance, they offered little in terms of a workable plan for intervention. Luckily her parents were familiar with the special services available and could proceed with their own investigation.*

COMMON INSTRUCTIONAL MISCONCEPTIONS

A correct answer indicates the child employed the correct process. A correct answer tells us nothing about how the student arrived at a particular decision. The child's reasoning may be based on an inefficient strategy, guessing, or a number of other possibilities. An analysis of errors provides a rich source for investigating deficiencies in content knowledge and processing abilities.

Students understand the necessity of listening closely to the teacher's instructions and can clarify any confusion they encounter. Many students do not realize the tools they have at their command to make learning easier. They may not feel that they are active participants in the educational process. Students need to learn how to identify problems as they occur and to ask appropriate questions.

Students are able to approach problems logically to arrive at a solution. Children encountering educational problems may not see any rhyme or reason to the tasks they are given. Adults are generally adept at recognizing and discarding irrelevant information in order to focus more clearly on the problem at hand. What is obvious to the teacher may represent a disturbing and confusing mass of information to the student.

Students are able to transfer skills from one content area to another. Success in one content area does not necessarily guarantee success in all subjects. A student may not realize that his or her approach to studying health can be equally effective, with some modifications, to studying biology. Other factors, such as past experiences and attitude toward any given content area might also influence a student's academic behaviors.

Problems in organization and attack strategies are confined to the academic domain. Students exhibiting problems in thinking through academic assignments and deriving successful strategies may also exhibit similar difficulties in their social relationships. Teachers need to analyze proficiency in both areas to determine if there is a possible common source.

INFORMATION PROCESSING AND EDUCATIONALLY HANDICAPPED CHILDREN

Although it may appear obvious that knowledge of how a child processes information is imperative to instruction, only recently have educational researchers begun to investigate how these processes may facilitate learning (Wittrock 1978). The reader should be aware of the cautionary tone used here in suggesting teaching interventions since the research reported in this chapter is based largely on laboratory studies unless otherwise noted. This means that the results have not been directly derived from classroom settings, limiting the ecological validity of the findings. This does not mean we should throw up our hands in despair. Rather, we need to acknowledge the limitations (which are a part of any research) and proceed intelligently with the information at hand.

Table 7–1 provides a summary of the processes believed to govern the internal flow of information. As an example of this system, imagine a child confronted with a math problem, *3 + 4*. First, the child must visually attend to the stimulus

TABLE 7–1
Information Processing

Process/Structure	*Internal Activity*	*Applied Example*
Attention	Intake of stimuli from environment, selective perception	Look at arithmetic problem, 3 + 4.
Short-Term Memory	Temporary storage of information, "working memory"	Silently repeat arithmetic sentence.
Encoding	Meaningful transformation of information, organization	Recognize stimulus as an addition problem serving as a cue to search long-term memory.
Long-Term Memory	Storage of organized information	Recall strategy to complete the problem (counting fingers, markers) or recall correct answer, 7.
Retrieval	Information taken out of long-term memory for performance, transfer, or return to short-term memory	If counting strategy is selected, return to short-term memory to apply strategy 3 + 4; if correct answer is selected, proceed to selection of response mode.
Selection of Response Mode	Method of response chosen, such as speech or muscle movement	Choose muscle movement as response mode; write 7 on paper
Feedback	When retrieval results in performance, evaluation of performance, completing information loop	Survey result. If response is considered appropriate, go to next problem. If response is not satisfactory, return to attention.

Adapted from R. M. Gagné, *The Conditions of Learning*, 3rd ed. (New York: Holt, Rinehart and Winston, 1977), 52–59.

(the problem) and not attend to other stimuli (classmates, window, desk, etc.). The learner may silently repeat the problem (rehearsal) as it is stored in short-term memory. This information serves as a cue for the learner to search long-term memory to retrieve either the answer or a strategy to solve the problem, such as counting fingers. Assuming that the new information is combined with the answer, retrieval is completed. The intervening step is selection of a response mode (speech, muscle movement) leading to performance, writing *7* on the paper. The child probably is satisfied with his work (feedback) and goes to the next problem.

The preceding illustration is a simplified view of a complex process. It is not difficult to see how our understanding of cognitive functioning or information processing is currently incomplete; yet it is important for teachers to understand that difficulty at any step in the process will influence the student's performance or product.

Before appropriate assessment and instructional strategies can be implemented, it is necessary that teachers have at least an introductory exposure to current findings regarding the information-processing system in relation to the education of handicapped students. The following is a discussion of the roles of attention, conceptual tempo, memory, and motivation in teaching handicapped pupils.

Attention

Research regarding attention focuses on two kinds of attention: **selective attention**, which is the ability to focus on the relevant features of stimuli, and **sustained attention,** or vigilance, which refers to alertness toward a task over a period of time (Douglas and Peters 1979). The tendency to attend to irrelevant stimuli is termed **distractibility.** Reviews of the literature on selective attention generally conclude that educationally handicapped children are more distractible than their peers (Douglas and Peters 1979; Ross 1976; Tarver and Hallahan 1974). Although these children are not more easily distracted by obvious laboratory impediments, such as flashing lights, problems arise when more subtle distractors, such as embedded clues, are included (Tarver and Hallahan 1974) or when essential and nonessential elements are close together (Vrana and Pihl 1980). A classroom parallel to laboratory stimuli used in the studies above would be a list of words differing only in the vowel (*pit, pat, put, pet*). If the vowels are highlighted by a different color, the differences may be more readily apparent to the child, thus making it easier to read the short vowel sounds correctly.

The possibility that educationally handicapped children experience a developmental lag in selective attention has been suggested by Ross (1976). A comparison of three age groups of learning disabled children (eight, ten, and thirteen years old) showed an increase in the ability to recall relevant information at each succeeding age level, giving some initial support for the developmental lag hypothesis (Tarver et al., 1976). Since this work is in the initial phase, further research is needed before conclusions can be drawn (Wong 1979).

Observational studies of educationally handicapped students in the regular classroom indicate they are less task oriented and more distractible than their normal peers (Bryan 1974; Feagans and McKinney 1981). This lack of attention suggests that a partial explanation for the achievement discrepancy between educationally handicapped and normal children may be found in the amount of time they spend learning. While this may appear obvious to even the most casual observer, relatively little emphasis has been given to the time dimension as a variable in evaluating children's classroom learning. Keogh and Margolis (1976) found that educationally handicapped children (third and eighth grade) differed from normal peers on tasks measuring coming to attention, decision making, and sustaining attention. The largest differences were in sustained attention. Keogh and Margolis concluded:

> It seems reasonable to infer that some of the problems of educationally handicapped pupils may have to do with inadequacy or inefficiency in defining the task, in determining salience, in organizing and evaluating the stimulus content. . . . The point to be made is that remediation for pupils with educational handicaps may well involve techniques which ensure clarity and specificity of task, which enhance pupils' abilities to organize and structure a stimulus field, and which develop analytic skills, as *well* as focusing on remedial influences more directly related to ability to sustain attention (p. 358, italics in original).

These teaching suggestions deserve further elaboration and will be discussed more fully later in this chapter.

Conceptual Tempo

A concept related to attention but involving the entire information-processing system is cognitive style. **Cognitive style** is defined as "individual variation in *modes* of perceiving, remembering, and thinking, or as distinctive ways of apprehending, storing, transforming, and utilizing information" (Kogan 1971, 242, italics in original). There are many different cognitive styles (see Kogan 1971 for review), but conceptual tempo has been the most researched dimension in relation to educational concerns.

Jerome Kagan originated the concept of **conceptual tempo** and defined it as "the child's consistent tendency to display slow or fast response times in problem situations with high response uncertainty" (Kagan 1965, 134). On the basis of test performance, reflective children respond slowly (long latency) and make fewer errors, while impulsive children are characterized by short latency and many errors (Kagan et al. 1964).

It is important not to confuse the meaning of *impulsive* in terms of conceptual tempo with its common use applied to someone who is quick to respond. For example, we may think of "impulsive spending" or "impulsive eating," which are not correct applications in terms of conceptual tempo. The reflectivity-impulsivity dimension has meaning only when classifying children according to errors and latency as measured by appropriate tests and not on the basis of classroom behavior (Moore, Haskins, and McKinney 1980).

The error dimension of conceptual tempo also has important implications for information-processing abilities. Children who are more accurate also attain higher achievement scores (Haskins and McKinney 1976) and appear to use more efficient problem-solving strategies (Block, Block, and Harrington 1974; Haskins and McKinney 1976). In their review of attention and cognitive style, Zelniker and Jeffrey (1979) note that reflective children employ an analytic problem-solving style, attending to details, while impulsive children use a global strategy, attending to the overall configuration as opposed to details. When impulsives (those attending to overall configuration rather than details) are given tasks requiring attention to contours, or object outlines, the error differences between the two groups disappears (Zelniker and Jeffrey 1976). Thus, it seems that impulsive children employ effective strategies in some situations; however, given the analytical nature of our society in general and school tasks in particular, these children may be penalized for their preference (Zelniker and Jeffrey 1979).

Memory

Our discussion of memory will include the encoding, storage, and retrieval process as outlined in Table 7-1. Memory processes are the essence of information processing, and their importance should not be overlooked by educators. As Rohwer and Dempster (1977) state:

> The fact is that educators may not appreciate the central importance of memory for attaining intellectual competence. Indeed, some give the impression that they regard memory proficiency as antithetical to academic excellence, feeling that memorization

> interferes with the operation of more laudable, higher mental processes. Such misconceptions about psychological perspectives on memory must be dispelled if work on memory development is to constitute a positive contribution to educational practice (p. 407).

Encoding processes, giving organization and meaning to stimuli, appear to be crucial in proficient memory systems as they affect both storage and retrieval of information (Rohwer and Dempster 1977). Teachers can use mnemonic devices to help students organize and memorize information. Specifically, these memory strategies or gimmicks help the learner store information and later recall it. Such strategies include rehearsal, producing images (pictures), and constructing sentence strings that emphasize what is to be remembered (ideas, rhymes, categorization, etc.). For example, one ten-year-old student had difficulty remembering how to correctly use the words *principle* and *principal* in his writings. His teacher reminded him that his principal was his pal and that the correct spelling had *pal* in it. It is thought that if learners can use such strategies, memory, and thus learning, will be enhanced (Weinstein 1978). Rigney (1978) suggests that students with high cognitive capacities but low processing resources may benefit the most from such cognitive strategies.

Torgesen (1979) studied normal children and reading disabled children with memory problems to better understand their memory processes. Questions concerned the children's plans for remembering and their strategies for finding a lost object. The good readers consistently generated more strategies and gave more planned responses, indicating an overall organization of the task. Torgesen (1979) points out that for some children with learning problems the difficulty may be one of using their capacity rather than one of having a deficient capacity. In another study Torgesen (1980) concluded that educationally handicapped students are not actively involved with learning materials and fail to use appropriate strategies, such as verbal labeling, verbal rehearsal, and categorization, to complete a task.

Motivation

A child's motivation has important implications for use of information-processing skills. Gagné (1977) uses the term *expectancies,* which is defined as "the *specific* motivation of learners to reach the goal or learning which has been set for them, or which they have set for themselves. What learners intend to accomplish can influence what they attend to, how they encode the learned information, and how they organize their responses" (p. 61, italics in original).

Motivation refers to a student's affect, or emotional response, to a problem situation, which in turn influences how that problem will be viewed and solved. The ideal emotional response includes the recognition that problems are a normal part of daily experience requiring coping strategies, that problems should be identified as they occur, and that impulsive or no-action responses are ineffective (D'Zurilla and Goldfried 1971). Helping educationally handicapped children achieve this type of problem orientation is important.

Motivation toward academic tasks is a complex phenomenon and is in part determined by learners' perceptions of causes of their successes and failures. Although there are many potential causes to which success or failure can be attributed, ability, effort, task difficulty, and luck are four general causal perceptions

(Weiner 1979). For example, a child who usually does well in school may attribute a failing grade to a lack of effort—perhaps watching television instead of studying. Because this child normally succeeds, he or she would probably not engage in self-derogation, such as "I am stupid" or "I'll never learn this" (ability attribution). In contrast, a poor student may make the above statements when a low grade is received or, may attribute a more perfect performance to blind luck. These perceptions in turn influence the child's emotional reaction the next time a similar situation arises. The first child may react positively by making a more concentrated effort to do better, while the second child may do nothing because of the expectation that failure will occur regardless of any effort.

Weiner (1979) has identified three dimensions of causal attributions that are useful in assessing a child's orientation or motivation. The first, **locus**, is described on an internal-external continuum. Generally speaking, persons with an internal locus believe they can control their environment and that outcomes are related to their own actions. An external locus is represented by the belief that outcomes are caused by forces in the environment such as luck, fate, or other persons, or, in other words, by forces outside the person. The second dimension, **control**, concerns whether or not it is within the person's power to effect a change in the attribute. For example, effort can be controlled, whereas luck cannot. It should be noted here that many writers do not separate locus and control as Weiner does but speak instead of locus of control. The last dimension, **stability**, involves whether a cause is invariant, as in ability, or changes periodically, as in effort or luck attributions. The consequences of these three dimensions—locus, control, and stability—include self-esteem, interpersonal skills, and future expectancies, respectively (Weiner 1979).

Children with a primarily internal locus of control exhibit motivational and cognitive reactions more congruent with achievement goals than do children with an external locus. Children with an internal locus display more task orientation, persistence, and efficient collection and use of relevant information (Bar-Tal and Bar-Zohar 1977). Although it would appear beneficial to teach children to be more internal than external in their perceptions of causes, it must be recognized that some situations cannot be controlled and are truly external. For a child living with an abusive parent, believing that he or she is the reason for abuse and can control the situation would be a frustrating and debilitating orientation to the problem. The lesson here is that locus of control is not fixed in each person and that both internal and external orientations are needed to appraise problem situations.

ASSESSING THINKING SKILLS

Table 7–2 presents a list of teacher probes to help identify the sources of children's errors in thinking. The complexity of information processing necessitates this type of format, as the teacher must consider a wide range of information to identify and strengthen processing skills.

Environment

A brief overview of Table 7–2 indicates that teachers must analyze their own behavior in each learning environment in addition to looking for clues in the behav-

☐ **TABLE 7–2**
Teacher Questions for The Identification of Processing Problems

Source of Error	*Teacher Probe*
Environment	1. Is type of error consistent across content areas? 2. Is type of error consistent only within a specific content area? 3. Are errors committed primarily in one setting or across settings (regular class, resource room)? 4. Are errors committed in a particular grouping pattern (individual, small group, large group)? 5. Are errors apparent primarily in timed situations?
Motivation	1. Are instructional goals implicit or explicit? 2. Does the student have goals differing from the teacher's purpose? 3. Does the student offer internal or external reasons when confronted with success or failure?
Attention	1. Is too much new information presented? 2. Does information fit with the student's past experiences? 3. Does the student scan all information before proceeding with a task? 4. Can the student differentiate important from nonimportant task features? 5. Does the student possess the prerequisite skills, concepts, vocabulary to understand the new task?
Encoding/ Memory	1. Does the student employ correct rules? 2. Can the student recognize when sufficient or insufficient information is given for problem solving? 3. Can the student apply rules sequentially?
Retrieval/ Performance	1. Is the student erratic in performance on a task, indicating forgetting of known strategies? 2. Does the student employ a cumbersome strategy at the expense of efficiency? 3. Are errors most noticeable under time constraints? 4. When asked to use a particular strategy, is the child able to do so? 5. Is the student able to verbalize the thinking process used to start and follow through with a task? 6. In a test setting, does the student perform better with some formats than with others (essay vs. multiple choice, for example)? 7. Is the student able to complete an assignment with a modality other than the one chosen by the teacher (dictating a book report as opposed to writing one)?

ior of children. We often fail to recognize that, as teachers, we contribute to the errors children make. This is not meant to condemn teachers but rather to emphasize their importance in the classroom.

It is well recognized that children's errors provide much more useful information to govern teaching strategies than do successes (Clinchy and Rosenthal 1971; Reid and Hresko 1980). Correct answers tell us only that the child attained a goal but not the path that was taken. Errors, on the other hand, provide information on what the child fails to do as well as what the child does incorrectly in the reasoning process (Clinchy and Rosenthal 1971). The teacher's task is to analyze errors systematically to devise methods of correcting the problem.

The first error source in Table 7-2 is environment. The questions listed require teacher observation over a period of time to determine if a structural or subject matter pattern can be defined. For example, when participating in a spelling bee, a student may consistently misspell words that he or she can write when tested. In such instances, teachers must investigate factors contributing to the performance. First, the teacher might determine if the student is anxious in a competitive situation. Also, the teacher should determine if the child can spell orally in an individual setting and if the child is able to execute most oral tasks. Depending on the conclusions drawn, the teacher is in the position to modify environmental factors that inhibit the child's best performance.

Motivation

A second source of errors in the reasoning process is motivation. A review of the related teacher probes indicates that it is necessary to examine the behavior of both instructor and learner to investigate motivational concerns. The first question highlights the importance of clearly stated goals. If the teacher masks the real objective of a lesson and the child does not receive the implied message, both will be frustrated. As an illustration, a student may be asked to identify adjectives (a newly acquired skill) in a story about a favorite television character; however, the teacher also has an unstated goal to measure the student's skill in using other grammatical features, such as sentence structure and punctuation. Does the child understand both goals? Sometimes it is legitimate not to make all goals explicit to assess if a skill is automatic. Many times, however, teachers are not clear about exactly what is expected of the student in an instructional setting. This lack of clarity often results in confusion and faulty performance.

The second question (Does the student have goals differing from the teacher's purpose?) is especially relevant to new teachers. It is easy to forget that students have their own purposes in mind when confronting a task. For example, one new teacher was attempting to vary a drill on short vowel sounds by using letter cubes. Although the letter cubes were an enjoyable approach, the children had never seen the materials and were more interested in rolling the cubes than in forming and reading words. This example points to the need to give children the freedom to pursue their own goals; before imposing structure, the teacher should have allowed the children to explore what they could do with the cubes themselves.

The third question (Does the student offer internal or external reasons when confronted with success or failure?) focuses on the student's success and failure attributions. Here, the teacher's best tool for assessment is observation. By attending closely to children's reactions, the teacher can determine if a child inappropriately uses external causes as justification. The child who continually makes remarks such as "I am dumb and can't do the work" needs to see a connection between effort and good results. Of course, the teacher must ensure that the work is not too difficult. The main point is to discern if there is a pattern in the child's behavior prior to employing intervention strategies. With handicapped students it is important to distinguish between source and solution attributions in intervention programs (Henker, Whalen, and Hinshaw 1980). For example, mental retardation may be appropriately named as the source of one child's academic difficulties, but it does not offer any instructional solutions. To accept the retardation as a solution, the teacher or parent in effect is saying, "It's okay that Mary can't read;

she's retarded." What is needed instead is a solution that is within Mary's control, such as learning to read pictures first or perhaps concentrating on survival words such as *stop, exit,* and *bathroom.*

Attention

Another source of errors in the reasoning process is attention. To put assessment of attention problems in proper perspective, a few introductory remarks about research data in this area are appropriate. First of all, research evidence tends to portray the educationally handicapped student as experiencing difficulties in both selecting relevant information for processing and staying with a task in an alert manner; yet, a wide range of individual differences among educationally handicapped children must be given careful consideration. For example, while hyperactive children are characterized primarily by attention problems and difficulty in inhibiting unacceptable behavior, these same characteristics may be secondary to the learning deficit for some learning disabled children or nonexistent for other students (Douglas and Peters 1979). Some learning disabled children, for example, may experience problems with sustained attention because of the difficulty of the material or a history of failure that limits their willingness to pursue an academic task (Douglas and Peters 1979).

Piontkowski and Calfee (1979) suggest two simple but important methods of assessing attentional problems: 1) observe where the child's eyes are focused and 2) ask direct questions to determine if the child is processing the relevant information. These two methods must be used in combination as we are all familiar with the phenomenon of staring intently at a page or a lecturer while covertly planning our grocery list or the following evening's activities. Teachers must become adept at observing students and asking process questions that demand more than a yes or no answer. For example, the teacher may observe a student plunging into a spelling exercise, using incorrect or misspelled words to complete the given sentences. The following questions may be helpful in determining where the problem lies:

Teacher: What are you to do on this page?

Student: Fill in all of the blanks.

Teacher: How do you know which word to use?

Student: I pick one from my list.

Teacher: Do you read the sentences first?

Student: Gee, there are so many that it takes too long to read them all.

From the above conversation, the teacher can conclude that the student has difficulty sustaining attention and, as a result, does not use an appropriate strategy to select answers. Attention is one problem, but the entire information-processing system is involved, as the student also needs to use a thinking process to uncover an approach to the task. The student most probably is also having trouble with selective attention; the student's responses indicate that the spelling lesson is a bit overwhelming in that sentences are not attended to one at a time.

Encoding and Memory

The most difficult process to assess is encoding and memory. Setting up situations that invite errors is a method that helps teachers understand the organizational mistakes children make (Bachor 1979; Clinchy and Rosenthal 1971). Putting problems in different contexts ($3 + 6$, $\begin{array}{r} 3 \\ +\underline{6} \end{array}$, $6 + 3$), adding extra or irrelevant information, and creating application questions are methods of inviting errors (Bachor 1979). It is important for both the teacher and student to understand that the goal of this process is assessment, not mastery. Errors are expected and needed for the instructor to analyze the weaknesses in the child's thinking skills. A math problem on a child's paper may resemble the following: $\begin{array}{r} 591 \\ +\,734 \\ \hline 236 \end{array}$. In examining this result, we can see that the student knows the rule for carrying but proceeds left to right instead of right to left. If only one problem is completed in this manner, it may be a fluke to be pointed out to the child for explanation. If the error is not a fluke, the teacher may explore several possibilities as to why the student made the error, including failure to apply rules in sequential order, rote application of rules lacking knowledge of place value, and failure to understand that addition results in larger, not smaller, numbers. By creating different problems with two-digit numbers and problems not needing the carrying rule and by observing the child while working, the teacher can explore different possibilities.

Retrieval and Performance

Errors in retrieval and performance are easier to assess and remediate than errors in encoding and memory, as in these cases the child knows what to do and how to organize but fails to complete some tasks consistently. Usually these children can overcome a performance difficulty through encouragement and practice (Clinchy and Rosenthal 1971). For example, in oral reading a student may guess a word based on the initial letter instead of applying a complete phonetic approach; however, the student can respond appropriately to the teacher cue "Sound it out," indicating that more practice is necessary to make the rule automatic.

Achieving proficiency in error analysis requires much practice. There are other difficulties with this approach, including demands on teacher time, lack of immediate student feedback, and lack of validation for the model (Bachor 1979). It would be misdirected, however, to ignore errors in light of the information-processing difficulties of educationally handicapped children and the number of errors these children tend to make. By becoming "error detectives," teachers can make significant strides in understanding exceptional children; analysis of students' mistakes will assist them in providing a more realistic classroom environment.

REMEDIAL TECHNIQUES

Educationally handicapped students may have difficulties with any of the information-processing skills discussed in this chapter. For example, they may have problems with selective or sustained attention or with memory processes, including encoding, storage, and retrieval; they may not be actively involved or may use inefficient strategies when approaching a task. The teaching suggestions that follow involve strategies to help children to improve and to use their information-processing capabilities.

Motivation

The first component to consider when planning remedial techniques is motivation, as it is the governing factor in information processing (Gagné 1977). Motivation refers to a student's emotional response to a problem situation and, as such, is not a skill that can be taught. However, the teacher's general classroom orientation and response to failure can significantly affect the student's perception of his or her ability to exert influence over the environment. The following suggestions reflect this principle and have been summarized from articles by Bar-Tal and Bar-Zohar (1977) and Henker, Whalen, and Hinshaw (1980):

- Failures should be treated as situation-specific instances as opposed to indications of global child deficiency. The following example illustrates this approach:

  Twelve-year-old Jason told his resource teacher that he failed another science test in the regular class and concluded with, "I'm just stupid." The resource teacher responded, " You're just stupid?" Jason proceeded to explain for one full minute how stupid he was and that no matter what he did, he was going to fail science. His teacher asked him about math and history. He said that he was doing "okay" in those areas. Then his teacher asked Jason what he did to be "okay" in math and history but not in science. They also discussed how each teacher's style was different. After fifteen minutes the resource teacher and Jason agreed that more time would be spent in the resource room on science. Also, the resource teacher would again discuss the possibility of taping the science lessons (previously the science teacher had refused to allow his lessons to be taped) since this strategy seemed to be helpful in math and history. It is important that students recognize that although there are times when they do have control of their environment, there are also times in their lives when events are beyond their control.

- Children should help identify problems and possible solutions. Their ideas should be put to use even when the teacher believes his or her solution is best. Often it is more efficient for the teacher to do a task; yet by not allowing students to participate in activities, teachers deny them opportunities to develop problem-solving skills.
- Children can learn to monitor and evaluate their own work. The goal is to encourage accurate self-perceptions to aid identification of strengths as well as areas that need further work. Often daily progress charts assist students in seeing their improvement.
- An individualized program can provide a vehicle for implementation of the strategies described above. Such a program will allow the child to be more

Because this student enjoys working at learning centers, her teacher plans individualized lessons for use at centers like the one above.

concerned with his or her individual performance since each child will be working at a different rate in a different area.

Memory

Memory is another information-processing component that merits teacher attention. While exploration of memory processes as an aid to instruction is just beginning, some evidence suggests that educationally handicapped children may not use encoding and retrieval strategies as efficiently as their normal peers. Although the evidence is meager at this point, the following instructional strategies based on Rohwer and Dempster (1977) provide a general approach to recognizing the importance of memory in the classroom:

- Providing too much information may tax the capacity of short-term memory, limiting the amount of information stored in long-term memory. Tasks need to be broken down so that a child's capacity to acquire new information is not impaired.
- Teaching specific mnemonic devices such as rehearsal, grouping, categorization, and rhymes may help students to remember. By uncovering some type of organizational structure, students may more easily recall important information. It is important to note that mnemonic devices may not help every student. By observing the student, teachers can determine if such strategies are helpful or confusing.

- Testing children under a variety of conditions to determine what they remember since some conditions may facilitate retrieval better than others. For example, some students may perform better on true-false or multiple-choice questions, while others do better under more free-form conditions, such as essays or fill-in-the-blanks.

Attention

Children with attentional deficits often miss many of the important learning concepts presented in a typical classroom. Rather than labeling an inattentive child as lazy or a day dreamer, teachers should find ways to help such a student tune in to key concepts presented through instructional activities and materials. The following teaching suggestions based on Piontkowski and Calfee (1979) are helpful for students with attentional difficulties.

Improving sustained attention. The following suggestions can help sustain student's attention:

- Vary the presentation of a task; introduce novelty. If students are usually asked to write sentences for spelling words, perhaps they can dictate a story to a peer or into a tape recorder. Use of humor is also effective in maintaining attention. A good indication of the need to vary a task is the teacher's own boredom with a particular routine.
- Help the student to attend by giving him or her time and the opportunity to prepare to respond. Rather than saying, "Name the planets in our solar system, John," prepare the student to respond with, "John, (pause) you're next. Name the planets in our solar system."
- Provide feedback to students to help them assess their progress. This strategy will help emphasize the importance of their work.
- Arrange seating assignments so that students with attention problems are in an area where the teacher most frequently makes eye contact and interacts with students. This may mean placing the most attentive students among the inattentive learners.
- Avoid overreliance on discussion, as students may become bored with drawn-out analysis of a topic. Use question and answer sessions judiciously and be aware of students' eye contact and nonverbal behavior that may indicate inattention. Also, the teacher could use a combination of convergent and divergent questions during discussion.

Improving selective attention. Suggestions for improving selective attention follow:

- Increase the salience of elements essential to learning by use of color, reduction of irrelevant features, or use of a new context. Although critical elements may be obvious to an adult, children with learning problems may not recognize the importance of understanding directions or ignoring unnecessary information in word problems.

- Consider the personal relevance of the information to the student. Can the student see a relationship between his or her experience and the task or can the teacher help to make this connection?
- Consider the amount of new information presented. It may be necessary to reduce or highlight information that is deemed important to avoid information overload.
- Use effective questioning techniques to determine if the student understands the assignment. often when a student is asked, "Do you understand the assignment?" The response is a firm yes. This is exasperating to a teacher when five minutes later this same student interrupts a lesson with, "What am I supposed to do?" To avoid these situations, give the directions and ask the student to explain in his or her own words what is to be done and also possibly do the first task in the assignment.
- Consider whether or not the child has the necessary concepts to understand the information. Using vocabulary that is not understood or building on skills that are not well developed will result in a loss of attention.
- Use reinforcement procedures with children who have much difficulty with sustained or selective attention. In essence, the teacher must draw attention to paying attention by providing specific verbal praise or allowing a child to perform a favorite activity. Praise must include what the child accomplished: "John, because you listened carefully, you could answer my questions. That's terrific!" is much more specific and direct than "Good job!"

INSTRUCTIONAL APPROACHES

There are also several instructional approaches that have been successful with some handicapped learners. These approaches, which include cognitive behavior modification and preinstructional strategies, may be applied to all content areas.

Cognitive Behavior Modification

The goal of cognitive behavior modification is to teach a child to use self-verbalizations to guide and control behavior. The underlying rationale is the developmental sequence of verbal control in children: first, adult speech controls the child's acts; then the child uses his or her own overt speech for control; this overt speech later goes "underground" as inner or private speech (Meichenbaum 1977, based on Luria 1959, 1961). As an example, think of a situation that requires your attention, perhaps maintaining a running program for exercise. As the time draws near for exercise, you may begin to prepare yourself by the following statements: "I need to run every day to see results. I didn't go yesterday, so I must go today. I'll feel so good when I'm finished." In a sense, you are convincing yourself, talking to yourself to guide your own behavior. This is the essence of **cognitive behavior modification.** Meichenbaum (1977) outlines the following sequence to train children to utilize their inner speech for their own benefit.

1. Adult models the task by talking through his or her thinking processes.
2. Child performs the task while the adult talks through the steps.
3. Child performs the task while talking out loud.
4. Child performs the task while whispering.
5. Child performs the task using private speech.

The following example of verbal self-instruction used while performing a task (copying line patterns) is given in Meichenbaum and Goodman (1971):

> Okay, what is it I have to do? You want me to copy the picture with the different lines. I have to go slowly and carefully. Okay, draw the line down, down, good; then to the right, that's it; now down some more and to the left. Good, I'm doing fine so far. Remember, go slowly, Now back up again. No, I was supposed to go down. That's okay. Just erase the line carefully . . . . Good. Even if I make an error I can go on slowly and carefully. I have to go down now. Finished. I did it! (p. 117).

The dialogue has several important features: (1) definition of the problem, (2) focusing of attention, (3) self-reinforcement, and (4) coping strategies.

The cognitive behavior modification approach has considerable appeal for use with educationally handicapped children who may not be actively involved in the learning process (Torgesen 1980). Most of the research reporting positive outcomes with this approach used hyperactive and impulsive children as subjects (Kendall 1977; Kendall and Finch 1979; Meichenbaum 1977; Meichenbaum and Asarnow 1979). Since some educationally handicapped children may be impulsive, cognitive behavioral intervention may be a viable approach. It is most appropriate for children who lack self-control—those who do not evaluate all responses and make many errors (Kendall 1977).

Using cognitive behavior modification requires a great deal of planning by the teacher. Meichenbaum (1977) recommends a "cognitive functional" approach to determine what processes are necessary to complete any given task successfully. First, the task causing the student difficulty must be carefully described. The circumstances or environmental variables present when the student exhibits problems must also be delineated. Does the child have the problem only in the regular classroom? Is it usually in the morning? In large-group work? Second, the teacher should complete the task and analyze the thought processes used. This will take some practice, as we do many things automatically without taking note of our steps. It may be helpful to ask a colleague to perform the task and report the processes used, too. An often overlooked strategy is to ask the child what he or she is thinking and feeling throughout the activity. Young children may not be adept at verbalizing their thinking, but older students may provide some useful insights. Another strategy is to ask proficient learners what they do to accomplish the task. Another way to complete the analysis is to observe the child. Perhaps the child fails to notice instructions, skips around the page, or gets distracted by fiddling with a pencil.

The next step in the cognitive functional approach is task analysis. We usually think of task analysis as the breaking down of subject matter into discrete instructional objectives. The cognitive functional approach uses the same idea, but the "task" is cognitive processes. An example is provided by Cameron (cited in Meichenbaum 1977). Cameron analyzed the problem-solving demands of a task in or-

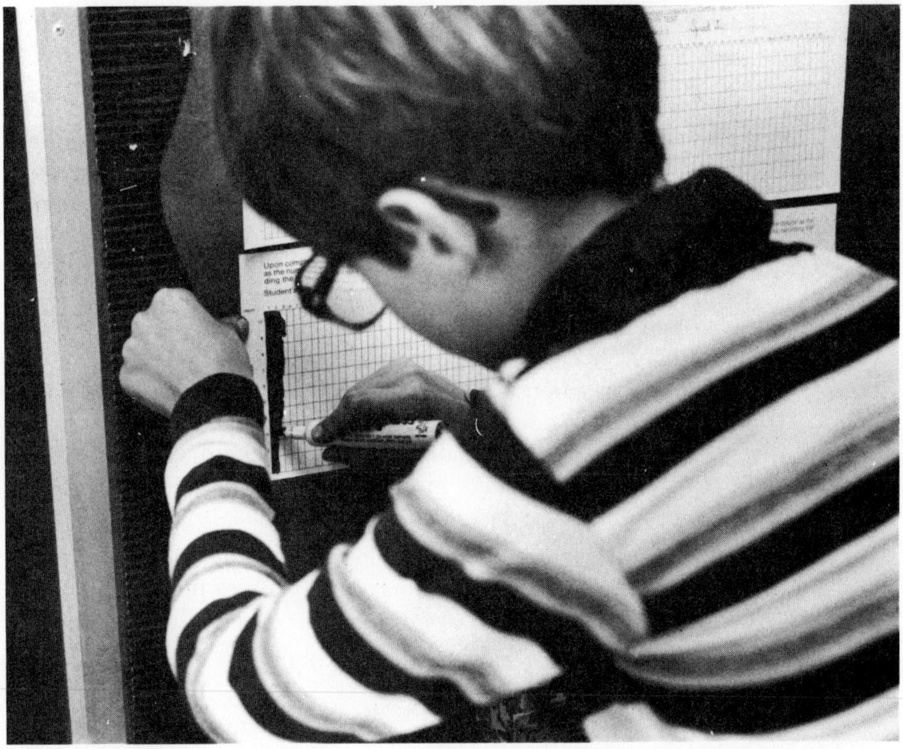

Some handicapped students must be taught how to organize their work and schedule their time. This student is charting his own progress at getting to class on time.

der to aid children with an impulsive cognitive style. The task analysis resulted in three task components: (1) comprehending instructions, (2) developing a plan of action, and (3) implementing this plan. Cameron found that impulsive children could fail to perform the problem correctly by a breakdown at any one of these three components.

After analyzing the cognitive processes, educators can manipulate variables related to the task to determine what effects modifying the task, the environment, or the instructions has on the child's performance. For example, if putting fewer math problems on a page (task manipulation) increases performance, then the teacher can surmise that the student needs to learn how to cope with many problems at once. The teacher can then develop an appropriate set of self-instructions for the student to use in order to complete longer and longer assignments.

Before employing cognitive behavior modification, educators must be aware of several limitations. First, most related research has been conducted in the laboratory, and there is no guarantee that the technique can be used effectively in the classroom (Meichenbaum and Asarnow 1979). Second, there is no strong evidence that the child will transfer newly acquired thinking strategies to other tasks and settings (Kendall and Finch 1979; Keogh and Glover 1980; McKinney and Haskins 1980; Meichenbaum and Asarnow 1979). Third, inappropriate use of the strategy may have detrimental effects; for example, it may cause interference, forcing the learner to use a strategy on a task that can already be done automatically (Hall

1980; Lloyd 1980). Also, lack of attention to relevant variables, such as motivation (Henker, Whalen, and Hinshaw 1980; Meichenbaum 1977), prerequisite knowledge (Lloyd 1980), and self-awareness (O'Leary 1980), may result in a narrow approach and doom the technique to failure before it begins. Finally, it is not clear whether the focus should be on teaching broad problem-solving techniques or instructions more specific to the task (Hall 1980; Kendall 1977).

As noted at the beginning of this chapter, there are no guarantees for success, no lock-step procedures to employ when we deal in the domain of thinking. However, there does seem to be potential in the judicious use of cognitive behavior modification. The following suggestions may assist the teacher in decision making and application:

- Self-instruction techniques should be applied directly to relevant learning tasks and not relegated to drill exercises (Meichenbaum and Asarnow 1979). There may be situations, such as lack of cognitive capacity in the educable mentally retarded, in which memorizing the steps will be a necessary condition for task application (Kendall 1977).
- Using environmental reminders, such as cartoons placed in the classroom, may aid children and make the process more like a game (Meichenbaum 1977).
- Use of operant procedures, from behavioral psychology, may be helpful (Kendall and Finch 1979).
- Consideration must be given to a child's age and maturity of cognitive and language skills, which may affect program success (Keogh and Glover 1980; Meichenbaum 1977).
- A careful appraisal of the child's existing skills is necessary. The teacher must decide whether the goal is acquisition of new material or structure and organization of existing knowledge (Keogh and Glover 1980; Lloyd 1980).
- Clear delineation of goals is necessary in view of limited transfer of skills to other areas. To judge effectiveness, the teacher must have a firm idea of what criteria will mark success (Keogh and Glover 1980).

Preinstructional Strategies

One of the functions of cognitive behavior modification is to structure and organize thinking. Preinstructional strategies can serve the same purpose but do not require self-verbalizations. Hartley and Davies (1976) reviewed the effectiveness of four such strategies: pretests, behavioral objectives, overviews, and advance organizers.

Pretests are sets of questions directly related to the material to be presented. Although they usually function as a device to determine students' existing knowledge, pretests can also alert students to important points to be made during instruction. This strategy appears to be most useful when students are of above-average intelligence and have some familiarity with the topic.

Behavioral objectives are explicit statements of what the learner is to accomplish that are made before instruction begins. Their purpose is to facilitate learning subject matter and prepare the student for the material. They are most effectively employed before long presentations that have an overall structure. Students of average ability generally profit from this strategy.

Overviews briefly present important terms, concepts, and principles before instruction. Lower-ability students profit from overviews. They are best used to acquaint students with material that may be loosely organized.

Advance organizers provide a broad conceptual framework that focuses on the processes the learner is to utilize. Because of the difficulty in preparing advance organizers and their primary utility with students possessing above-average intellectual competence and maturity, their usefulness appears limited, especially with special populations (Hartley and Davies 1976).

Attack strategies. More specific devices that have recently been employed with educationally handicapped learners are attack strategies (Lloyd 1980; Lloyd, Saltzman, and Kauffman 1981). In this approach students are taught the necessary preskills for performing a task along with a set of rules for employing the preskills.

An example of this strategy is provided by an experiment conducted by Lloyd, Saltzman, and Kauffman (1981). The task for a group of learning disabled boys was to learn to compute single-digit multiplication problems. The preskill was to learn counting sequences, such as *0, 8, 16, 24, 32, 40, 48, 56, 64.* When the specified sequences were learned, the strategy training was then taught in four steps. The child was given a multiplication problem and told: "(*a*) point to a number you can count by; (*b*) make slash marks for the other number; (*c*) count by the number you pointed to once for each slash mark; and (*d*) write in the answer space the last number you said" (Lloyd, Saltzman, and Kauffman 1981, 207). The trainer modeled the procedure by performance and verbalization, the child following suit and gradually fading overt verbalizations. To check for transfer of the new skill, the children were given paper strips with previously unlearned counting sequences to solve new problems. This was termed cue training.

The results indicated that both the preskills training and subsequent strategy training were necessary for mastery of the multiplication problems. Cue training appeared to assist in the generalization of the strategy to problems for which the specific preskills had not been taught. A second experiment illustrated that the children could be taught division using a related strategy without producing losses in previous learning (Lloyd, Saltzman, and Kauffman 1981).

Lloyd (1980) suggests that attack strategies may be more appropriate than cognitive behavior modification techniques when students lack skills. Cognitive techniques may be more useful for students who possess the skills but do not consistently apply them.

Modified behavioral-objective approach. Employing a more general approach to preinstruction, Maier (1980) used what may be termed a modified behavioral-objective approach with reading disabled elementary children. The training group was told to focus on three ideas before listening to a story: the problem, how it was solved, and the lessons of the story. Additionally, when the story was read aloud, the children were told when to look for each of the three parts. Compared with a group of reading disabled children who received no training, the trained group made fewer recall errors overall and were more proficient in answering sequence and implication questions (Maier 1980). As the author noted, these results are limited to listening and speaking skills but appear to have implications for the selective attention problems of some educationally handicapped students.

FURTHER CONSIDERATIONS

The information covered in this chapter may be new to many readers. To put the ideas into practice requires time, patience, and a commitment to understanding children's processing problems. As we have emphasized throughout, much of the research is based on laboratory studies not directly related to classroom practice, and, in some cases, the necessary research has not been conducted.

There are several reasons why teachers should not only be aware of cognitive processes, but should also understand their impact on learning. First, this approach provides another vantage point from which to view the education of handicapped children. Their problems are complex, and as practitioners we cannot afford to overlook any area that may provide insight. Second, the information-processing approach cuts across content areas and can provide an alternative or an adjunct to traditional teaching strategies in specific content areas. Third, this approach emphasizes that the learner is active in the educational process and that we need to consider the child as a total, functioning individual. It is all too easy to fragment the student, thereby losing a comprehensive approach to his or her strengths and weaknesses. It is important to remember that the instructional strategies presented are not panaceas and will not work with all students. Consultation with supervisors, school psychologists, counselors, and family members is necessary to put the process into perspective. It is the teacher's job to coordinate the educational program, to make rational decisions, and to evaluate the outcomes of any particular approach.

SURVIVAL SKILLS

Thinking, or information processing, has always been a necessary skill for survival. However, in light of the rapidly increasing complexity of our society, efficient thinking skills are more important than ever before. Effective communication and cooperation, occupational survival, and even everyday living depend on proficiency in processing information effectively.

Relating the different components of information processing (such as memory and attention) to everyday problems emphasizes the relevancy of thinking skills to educationally handicapped students. The following suggestions are appropriate ways to relate thinking skills to basic competencies needed in everyday situations:

- Have students role play real-life situations rather than rely on rote exercises to remember one's address, phone number, birth date, etc. For example, if a student is at a friend's house and would like to play an hour longer, then it is imperative to know the home telephone number. This is also an excellent opportunity to practice appropriate telephone skills.

- Use role playing to teach students how to listen for and remember important information from phone messages and other communications. Some students must learn how to focus on the purpose of a communication and their own role or responsibility in attending to it.
- Have students practice focusing on relevant features when doing comparison shopping. Activities such as going grocery shopping or having the car repaired give students opportunities to use critical thinking skills.
- Give students opportunities to weigh the pros and cons of personal issues before making decisions; for example, "Should I go out for basketball this year or not?" or "What will happen if I stay out past my curfew?" Often students fail to recognize the repercussions of their behavior. Foresight must be developed. Such opportunities also allow students to develop an awareness of those events they can control and those they cannot.
- Draw attention to positive outcomes. For example, when students who are usually ignored are invited by peers to participate in an activity, it is important that they analyze what they did to cause the invitation to be extended.
- Encourage opportunities for applying concepts such as classification to real-life situations. For example, on the next trip to the grocery store, have students make a list of food items that are part of the milk group. Another activity related to classification is to identify how the grocery aisles are labeled.
- Daily we are faced with the challenge of problem solving. Teachers can facilitate the development of appropriate problem-solving strategies in the classroom. For example, role playing can be used: "Mom wanted me to call her at work if I stayed for basketball practice after school. I lost the phone number. What should I do?"
- Often students understand how to do a task if everything goes right; however, unplanned interruptions often occur. Therefore, trouble-shooting skills need to be practiced. For example: "I've tried four times to get this lawn mower started. What could be wrong with it? What should I do now? Who could help me?"
- Appropriate planning skills are critical to effective day-to-day living. Techniques for planning out-of-school time should be encouraged in the classroom. Since every family's lifestyle is unique, it is critical that such classroom activities not conclude with just one plan of action. For example, although all students might have homework, when it should be done depends upon each student's needs; some students have jobs, whereas others have time immediately after school to do their work. Planning for home activities is also necessary. For example: "After Dad leaves, I'll need to finish painting this room by myself. Do I know exactly what he wants me to do? What additional information do I need before he leaves?"
- Handicapped students should also be encouraged to be creative. Discussions on various topics can be used to promote creative thinking and encourage other thinking skills. For example: "Every Saturday I watch TV. This is boring after a while. How can I decide on more fun things to do?"

HOME REINFORCEMENT

Parents are in a unique position to help their children apply thinking skills to problem situations in the home and community environments. Parents can capitalize on many situations that arise during the daily routine that require organization, planning, and problem solving. When a teacher is working in the classroom to develop a specific skill, it is helpful to role play home situations, thus empahsizing the relevancy of the skill. The following are additional suggestions to encourage reinforcement of skills at home:

- Encourage parents to adopt a realistic outlook on mistakes, that is, that their children's errors are necessary for learning. There is much truth to the adage "Everyone makes mistakes." When parents discuss their errors and methods of correcting them, then their children learn a variety of possible problem-solving approaches and will eventually accept mistakes as normal happenings in day-to-day living and thus feel less threatened in analyzing their own errors. For example, last night Mr. Talbot forgot to close the fence gate before he let the dog outside. As a result, he chased the dog throughout the neighborhood for two hours. Although this happened after his ten-year-old son was in bed, the next morning Mr. Talbot explained what had happened. Also included in this discussion were the father's choices—to spend time finding the dog or to let the dog roam and possibly be faced with a fine from the animal catcher.
- Provide opportunities for children to organize and plan daily and special events. For example, allow children to help with plans for a party, picnic, or meal. Younger children may assist in choosing their guests and planning a menu; older children can be responsible for thinking through the appropriate sequence of activities, such as deciding on a time, sending invitations, and determining the quantity of refreshments.
- Throughout the day emphasize attending to detail, putting events in sequence, and categorizing objects. For example, when watching television shows or reading books, ask children to guess at the ending, to discuss different characters' feelings, and to verbalize the clues that lead to their decisions.
- Provide opportunities for children to be involved in successful activities and the decision-making process. If children have assigned chores, let them plan the order and timing of completing these activities. Encourage them to discuss the implications and benefits of doing the least favored task before becoming involved in a more favored activity and also the consequences of not getting the jobs done.
- In order to help children to develop logical thinking skills, parents might think aloud through their own thought processes so that children can follow their line of reasoning. Examples include verbalizing the process of ensuring that all necessary ingredients are available before baking, deciding the best time to get the car repaired in light of family activities, and choosing a gift for a friend taking into consideration not only one's financial resources, but also the friend's hobbies, personality, likes and dislikes.

- When children encounter a problem, help them brainstorm a variety of options before choosing a particular solution. For example, a parent might say: "Hitting Timmy back is one way to let Timmy know you don't want him to hit you. What's another solution?" Comments such as these indicate respect for the child's input (even if the solution is not the best one) and also encourage the child to think of alternatives. It is important to point out the importance of giving children time to think. Often we tend to interrupt children's thoughts and thus solve the problem for them.
- It is not recommended that parents dwell on errors evident in school papers brought home. The teacher is the best person with whom to discuss these concerns.

REGULAR CLASS INVOLVEMENT

Sorting through the various elements contributing to children's errors can be difficult for teachers in regular classroom settings. As discussed earlier, it is important for teachers to maintain open minds in order to evaluate the contributions of their own behaviors to children's mistakes. By taking an ecological approach—realizing that there is more to a student's behavior than just the student—it becomes easier to identify problems and correct them. The following suggestions may be helpful to regular classroom teachers in identifying factors contributing to student errors.

- Experiment with grouping patterns. Educationally handicapped children may be more accustomed to working individually or in small groups, but some may do just as well or better in other grouping situations.
- Question students who do particularly well in content areas. Often students themselves can be a valuable source of information in terms of effective methods, processes, and tricks of the trade used in learning. Many of these are often overlooked or taken for granted by adults.
- Since special educators often are in a position to identify appropriate reinforcement procedures for a student, they can help regular teachers in selecting effective rewards.
- Set aside time for investigating errors with the class as a group. Handicapped children benefit from the realization that they are not the only ones who have difficulty. In addition, all students will realize that making mistakes is acceptable and often necessary for learning.
- Seat children who have difficulty attending and becoming involved in classwork among those students who tend to stay on task. Teachers seem to direct more attention to those who show an active interest in learning. The educationally handicapped students may be accustomed to being ignored; positive attention from the teacher may help motivation.
- Help children practice verbalizing their strategies. As seat work is being completed, move around the classroom and ask children to explain their activities. This attention should be directed toward students who consistently produce correct work as well as toward children experiencing problems.

- Ask an observer (resource room teacher, school psychologist, supervisor) to help identify environmental factors contributing to a child's failure. By focusing exclusively on a particular child or activity, trained personnel can often identify patterns that go unnoticed by others in all the activity of the regular classroom.
- Analyze successes to uncover factors that may have been slightly changed but make a difference in children's attention, motivation, and final product. Teachers often view success as what is supposed to happen, without taking credit for the unique formula they have created.

SUMMARY POINTS

- Teachers must be concerned with not only the products but also with the processes of learning. Although our understanding of cognitive processes is incomplete at this time, remedial strategies that are helpful in instructing educationally handicapped children are available.
- Analysis of breakdowns in information processing requires acute observation and questioning skills on the teacher's part. When planning a remedial program, it is necessary for teachers to assess a student's attending skills, conceptual tempo, memory, and motivation.
- An information-processing approach should be blended with ongoing classroom work. Thinking skills cannot be taught as a separate subject. Cognitive instruction is needed for academic as well as social and emotional growth.
- Errors need to be treated as data. This focus enables teachers and children to focus on *how* an answer is reached instead of exclusively on *what* the answer is.
- Advocates of cognitive behavior modification emphasize the use of self-verbalizations in developing and controlling behavior. With this approach teachers employ task analysis to look at the cognitive processes a student uses for problem solving.
- Like cognitive behavior modification, preinstructional strategies, which include pretests, behavioral objectives, overviews, and advance organizers, assist in structuring and organizing a student's thinking skills.

REVIEW QUESTIONS

1. Define the components of information processing and discuss their relevancy to teaching educationally handicapped students.
2. Identify assessment techniques related to each component of information processing.

3. Identify limitations associated with cognitive behavior modification. When might this instructional approach be most effective?
4. List and describe preinstructional strategies that can be used to help structure and organize a student's thinking skills.

SUGGESTED READINGS

Camp, B. W.; Blom, G. E.; Hebert, F.; and von Doornick, W. J. 1977. Think aloud: A program for developing self-control in young aggressive boys. *Journal of Abnormal Child Development* 5: 157–69.

Douglas, V. I. 1972. Stop, look, and listen: The problem of sustained attention and impulse control in hyperactive and normal children. *Canadian Journal of Behavioral Science* 4: 259–82.

Gagné, R. M. 1977. *The conditions of learning*. 3rd ed. New York: Holt, Rinehart and Winston.

Reid, D. K., and Hresko, W. P. 1981. *A cognitive approach to learning disabilities.* New York: McGraw-Hill.

Spivack, G., and Shure, M. B. 1974. *Social adjustment of young children.* San Francisco: Jossey Bass.

Application: Todd and Sarah

Todd

We now return to Todd, whose academic difficulties were described earlier. In order to assist Todd, the teacher assessed his problems using the set of teacher probes listed in Table 7–2.

Environment: Todd's errors were apparent across most content areas and settings. This indicated the need for a strategy with the potential to affect all of his coursework.

Motivation: The speed (indicated by illegible papers and missing work) with which Todd completed his assignments seemed to indicate that his goal was to finish them quickly regardless of the teacher's emphasis on correct answers, thorough reading, and neat handwriting. However, he was diligent and seemed to want to do the work. The teacher had to keep in mind the possibility that Todd's goals differed from her own while completing the review of teacher probes.

Attention: The teacher speculated that perhaps Todd was receiving too much seat work and that his speed was his way of coping with the workload. The teacher could have investigated this by either cutting back the number of papers or giving him one paper at a time. Todd may also have lacked appropriate organizational strategies to complete his work accurately since he tended to plunge into a task rather than attend to detail. Because of Todd's severe comprehension problems, the teacher needed to consider seriously the possibility that he did not possess the prerequisite skills. It is easy to forget about comprehension when a child has excellent word recognition skills.

After identifying several possible deficits by working through the information-processing system, the teacher's next step was to develop a remedial plan. As discussed earlier, deficits related to the environment, motivation, and attention may affect learning outcomes; so it is necessary to either correct or eliminate these factors before investigating information-processing variables as possible explanations of learning problems.

To help Todd attend to details (plus and minus signs and punctuation) his teacher had him color code them before beginning an assignment. In addition, she reduced the amount of work he received. Rather than getting three to five work assignments all at once from his work folder, the teacher restructured the task so that he could check out one assignment at a time. Before doing more arithmetic problems or reading another paragraph, Todd first had to complete the previous work assignments with 85 percent accuracy. Two weeks after beginning this program, the criterion was moved to 95 percent accuracy since Todd was readily meeting the 85 percent criterion.

Free time and teacher-made stickers were given to Todd when he completed legible and accurate assignments. A review of the daily record chart indicated these rewards were effective.

The teacher also developed a daily check list to help Todd keep track of his academic work. Before handing in each assignment, Todd was required to put a check mark on the assigned list. Although this approach appears logical and straightforward, it took several weeks before Todd was able to complete the check list without teacher prompting. For example, he would randomly check his list without carefully looking to see if he had checked the appropriate assignment. Sometimes he forgot to complete tasks that were located in other parts of the room rather than in his folder.

Encoding Memory: The problems with the check list and comprehension that still remained seemed to indicate that Todd's real trouble spot was encoding and memory. As discussed earlier, this is the most difficult area to assess and remediate. Todd's teacher decided to use a cognitive behavior modification approach. Although this process took a great deal of one-to-one instructional time, progress was made. Todd was better able to get an understanding of the comprehension process. To determine how successful the program was, after five weeks the teacher asked Todd an array of comprehension questions related to reading passages taken from several standardized tests. Although he was able to respond consistently to factual recall questions and, to a lesser degree, questions about the sequence of events in the passages, he still experienced considerable difficulty in answering more complex questions.

Although Todd made some gains in organization and comprehension, his comprehension level did not approach his word recognition skills, and many of the organizational skills did not become automatic. The entire remedial process discussed above extended over a five-month period. Obviously Todd's learning problems were severe in nature. His case was chosen to illustrate that due to the complexity of learning for many educationally handicapped students, it is critical that teachers be able to effectively implement a variety of instructional strategies.

Sarah

After consulting with Sarah's parents, present teachers, and former resource room teacher, the school psychologist and junior high school special educator concluded that the following factors contributed to Sarah's problems:

- During elementary school the resource room teacher was aware of Sarah's organizational problems and assisted in structuring Sarah's work in addition to providing reading instruction.
- Sarah's current teacher noticed that she rarely copied down assignments and never indicated the due dates.
- Sarah did not see the value of written work, believing her classroom performance during discussions proved her knowledge.
- In an individual test setting, Sarah had some difficulty reading academic texts.

In analyzing this information, it can be seen that Sarah's problems were not as severe as Todd's but nevertheless did create difficulties at school as well as at home, which is not uncommon. A major stumbling block was Sarah's motivation to complete assignments. In addition, she never made the leap from a structured elementary classroom to the junior high experience, which required more responsibility and self-discipline.

With guidance from the resource teacher, Sarah agreed to the following activities, designed to assist her in being more organized:

- Sarah would write down assignments on a note pad, indicating required reading passages and written work and related due dates. This would be done on a daily basis.
- Each teacher would review the note pad for assignments and initial the page to indicate correct understanding. If no homework were assigned, Sarah would write *N.H.,* also to be initialed by the appropriate teacher.
- Sarah was responsible for sharing this information with her parents. If the assignment sheet were not brought home, she would not earn evening privileges. (It should be noted here that after-school

activities were to be earned by Sarah rather than withheld as a punishment for not following through with her responsibilities.)

- Time in the resource room would be made available on a daily basis to assist Sarah with any reading difficulties and to keep communications between the school and home open.

Unfortunately Mrs. Beckwith, the English teacher, did not agree to participate in this plan. Her resistance led the parents to request another class for Sarah with a more receptive teacher. The resource room teacher diplomatically scheduled Sarah's remedial time during Mrs. Beckwith's class and arranged a new English class during one of Sarah's study halls.

The overall simplicity of the plan is striking. However, what is evident to outside observers is not always obvious to the participants dealing with the emotional ramifications. The plan was effective in helping Sarah recognize and take control of her responsibilities. Her parents were the key to the success. Upholding their decision to deny her telephone conversations with friends and other activities when she failed to bring her assignments home, was at times difficult. However, their consistency paid off. Although Sarah's problems may appear minor when compared with those of other educationally handicapped students, without intervention her troubles could have escalated in high school.

Discussion Points

1. Todd's case focused on the interaction between teacher and child. Which other school personnel could be consulted to assist in planning an educational program?
2. Although family background was not described, can you think of any help the family could have given to Todd by working with the teacher?
3. Sarah's English teacher was uncooperative in implementing the plan. If changing teachers were not an option, how would you, as a resource room teacher, approach this situation?
4. Sarah was not prepared for the rigors of junior high school. What activities would be useful to help children develop an organized, responsible approach to these new demands before they enter junior high?

CHAPTER 8 Developing Oral Language Skills

OUTLINE

INTRODUCTION

While most children seem to acquire language with great ease without formal training, the acquisition of language is actually a very complex process. A child must not only learn the meaning of a multitude of verbal symbols (words) but also apply a set of complicated rules each time a new utterance is heard (Battin et al. 1978).

Children's language problems can occur in one or both of the following areas: receptive language and expressive language. **Receptive language** involves listening and refers to the comprehension of oral language. **Expressive language**, on the other hand, involves speaking and refers to the production and organization of oral language.

Objectives

After reading this chapter, you should be able to

- differentiate between speech and language not only in terms of basic definitions but also in terms of specific deficits and remedial strategies;
- differentiate between receptive and expressive language and understand the relationship between these two areas of language development;
- identify specific deficits associated with both receptive and expressive language development;
- compare and contrast two theoretical models of language development and remediation;
- identify remedial strategies appropriate for specific language deficits.

Case Studies: Lisa and Aloma

Lisa

While nine-year-old Lisa currently lives in a very loving environment, her early childhood years were traumatic. Until the age of five, Lisa was exposed to considerable neglect and abuse. She was confined to a crib with a younger brother, both receiving minimal care. By age five, the only language Lisa and her brother knew was the one they created to communicate with each other.

After her fifth birthday, Lisa and her younger brother were removed by court order from their natural parents and later placed in an adoptive home. Because of the severity of Lisa's language problem, she was enrolled in a communication development program before entering kindergarten. Lisa made tremendous strides in both language and cognitive development during the one year in this special education program. The following fall Lisa entered a regular kindergarten. While she did exhibit some articulation problems, Lisa did well in the mainstreamed setting. During first grade Lisa received special help focusing on language development for one hour each day in a resource room. While Lisa was below grade level in reading at the end of first grade, neither her teacher nor her parents felt any need to be especially concerned.

After this, however, Lisa's family moved to a new area. She was then placed in a regular second grade classroom with no special education services. The next two years were difficult ones academically for Lisa. At the end of third grade, Lisa's teacher recommended retention. Her parents were upset since they had received no indications that Lisa's problems were escalating. They immediately requested a multifactored assessment. At this time Lisa was given the WISC-R, an individually administered intelligence test. Lisa obtained an IQ score of 72 on this test. On the basis of this score and the severity of her academic difficulties, Lisa was recommended for placement in a self-contained class for the educable mentally retarded.

Lisa's parents did not support the school's decision. Their reasoning, as presented to the IEP committee, was that the rate at which Lisa had progressed in language development at age five and age six indicated at least normal intellectual ability. Lisa's parents had been advised by other professionals that the WISC-R was not a valid test for a language handicapped youngster. Due to its highly verbal orientation, the test measured only Lisa's weaknesses and not her strengths or potential; for this reason, her parents objected to the EMR placement. After further testing and consultation, the team agreed that Lisa be placed in a resource room for the major part of each day but participate in the regular fourth grade activities for gym, music, and art.

Through the use of both formal language assessment tools and an analysis of spontaneous speech and language, the following strengths and weaknesses were identified:

- Lisa's concentration and attention, evident throughout testing sessions, indicated an ability to sustain auditory attention over reasonable time periods. Another strength, noted by Lisa's teacher, was that Lisa could maintain attention in the presence of extraneous stimuli.
- Lisa's performance on auditory discrimination tasks indicated some difficulty in processing certain minimally different speech sounds, such as *rat* and *ran* and *bid* and *bit*.
- Results on the *Test for Auditory Comprehension of Language* revealed that certain vocabulary items, especially prepositions, pronouns, and words with multiple meanings, were difficult for Lisa to process.
- Both test results and language samples indicated that Lisa had significant language production deficits in terms of accuracy, intonation, fluency, and speed in using common words.
- Results on sentence repetition tasks indicated that Lisa had difficulty understanding and using correct grammatical forms in both oral and written communication. Typical examples of Lisa's incorrect sentence formations included "The boys gone now," and "I jumping fast."

Aloma

Aloma's parents had been migrant workers, moving with their family from state to state harvesting seasonal crops. While Spanish was always spoken in the home, Aloma began to learn some English when she started school at the age of seven. Until she was eleven years old, Aloma's education was sporadic. Then her father found a steady factory job in Texas. While the decision was a very difficult one to make, Aloma's parents decided that she should live with her grandmother in Indiana. They not only felt the grandmother should not live alone but also thought Aloma would have better schooling opportunities in Indiana. In addition, Aloma had five brothers and sisters, and the house Aloma's parents were renting was too small for the entire family.

While Aloma was at first excited about the new vistas opening up to her with the move to her grandmother's, she was soon homesick and lonely. Her school experiences were more challenging than she had anticipated. In addition to her inadequacies in understanding and using English, Aloma found herself behind her classmates in other academic areas.

After a few months of school, Aloma's fifth grade teacher referred her for a multifactored assessment. Based on these results, Aloma was placed in a resource room for instruction in all content areas. Aloma received these special education services until the end of sixth grade. A reassessment at that time showed that while Aloma was still weak in several areas, she had made tremendous gains over the past two years. By this time Aloma was enjoying math and found that spelling was also relatively easy for her.

Aloma's major area of difficulty was language. While she was not hesitant or afraid to speak, she consistently used words incorrectly, had poor grammar, and frequently omitted word endings. Aloma's written work reflected many of the errors typical of her oral expressions—run-on sentences, frequent omission of word endings, and confusion of word meanings. In addition to this, Aloma exhibited a lack of sensitivity to the social nuances of language. Aloma had a tendency to speak in an unacceptably loud voice and frequently made inappropriate and rather rude remarks, such as "Why are you so fat?" While Aloma tried hard to improve her oral and written language skills, she had difficulty accepting corrections or criticisms. She tended to be defensive, moody, and insensitive to the rights and feelings of others.

Aloma experienced considerable isolation and misunderstanding in the junior high setting. Some of this alienation was due to her lack of social competence in interacting with others, but some of it could also be attributed to a lack of understanding on the part of her classmates as to certain behaviors and values characteristic of the Spanish-American population. For example, Spanish-American families tend to establish clear and rather rigidly defined boundaries between home and the extrafamilial world (Falicov and Karrer 1980). Families with this orientation tend to discourage interaction with friends outside of school hours. Friendships of Spanish-American children are often limited to siblings and cousins even if they are far apart in age. Aloma's lack of participation in both structured and unstructured after-school activities was perceived by classmates to reflect an aloofness or snobbishness on her part. Thus, few overtures of friendship were extended to her.

Manifestations of a learning problem exhibited by Aloma in the classroom included difficulty in putting events or ideas in a logical sequence, inability to process or carry out directions, and limited ability in abstract reasoning. These difficulties, perhaps magnified by her home environment, were attributed to innate deficits.

For the seventh grade Aloma was placed in the regular classroom for all subject areas, with one hour daily of special education tutorial instruction focusing on remediating language deficits. The following conclusions were drawn based upon formal assessment tools, informal evaluations, and observations:

- Aloma's vocabulary development was limited.
- Aloma's performance on auditory comprehension tasks indicated deficits in processing and interpreting selected word and sentence structures. This lack of understanding was especially evident in relation to words with multiple meanings and words used to express abstract or intangible ideas. Both written and oral language samples revealed similar comprehension deficits in the expressive component of language.
- Aloma's oral and written expressions indicated frequent omissions of word endings, including plurals, possessives, adjective forms (hott*er*, hott*est*), and verb tenses (writt*en*, play*ed*, look*ing*).
- Correct sentence structure was another weak area in Aloma's language development. Results on specific language production tasks indicated an inadequate grasp of basic sentence construction principles. Grammatically incorrect sentences were typical in Aloma's written and oral expressions.
- Aloma appeared to be unaware of the socially acceptable mechanics of conversation. Informal observations of Aloma's social communication skills indicated deficits in appropriate conversational tactics. Aloma not only frequently interrupted speakers but also abruptly dropped topics of conversation to introduce irrelevant and, at times, offensive remarks.
- Aloma's ability to do abstract reasoning was markedly deficient for her age.

Points for Consideration

- *The importance of considering family background and other environmental information when making placement decisions is highlighted in both of these case studies.*

In Lisa's case, formal test scores suggested below-average functioning, but her early childhood experiences and later rapid progress provided a different perspective on these findings. For Aloma, the fact that English was a second language and that she experienced inconsistent schooling had to be included in analyzing her language and learning performance. Although both students had psychoeducational deficits requiring remediation, each student's program had to be developed with consideration of past family and community experiences in addition to current environmental conditions and needs.

- *Lack of verbal stimulation in Lisa's early years resulted in language and learning deficits that impeded her progress in later academic pursuits.*

The reading and reading readiness activities introduced during kindergarten and first grade were far too difficult for Lisa to handle, as her oral language development at that time was still very immature.

- *Many tests frequently used to assess a child's intelligence or ability may discriminate against a child with language handicaps in that they focus only on weaknesses and fail to recognize strengths.*

While Lisa's computed IQ score placed her in the mildly retarded range, the tremendous gains she made after language intervention was introduced indicated at least average intelligence.

- *Data from inappropriate assessment procedures may sometimes result in improper educational placement.*

Had Lisa been placed in the EMR unit as recommended by the psychologist, her academic potential may have been severely stymied.

- *The degree of involvement of a child's parents or guardians in a language intervention program can significantly affect the child's progress in language development.*

The conscientious efforts of Lisa's adoptive parents to provide language-enriching experiences played a major role in accelerating her language development. On the other hand, because Aloma's family was unable to model and reinforce her English-speaking skills, progress in learning the English language was slow.

- *Different cultural and ethnic groups value certain social behaviors in different ways.*

While Aloma's manner of social interaction was misinterpreted by some of her peers in the junior high school, these same patterns of social behavior were generally accepted in her own cultural group. In fact, Aloma was quite popular and exhibited genuine leadership skills when interacting within the Spanish community.

COMMON INSTRUCTIONAL MISCONCEPTIONS

Speech and language are synonymous. Language is a system used to communicate ideas and meaning. It can be oral, written, tactile (Braille), or manual (sign language). Speech, on the other hand, is the physical process of transmitting language orally. In too many instances a need for language intervention is equated with a need for speech therapy.

Speech and language problems can always be detected by the way a child "talks funny" or is hard to understand. An articulation problem is only one type of communication disorder. Children may have speech or language deficits without any noticeable articulation problems. Problems communicating thoughts in an intelligible way call for an in-depth assessment by a speech or language pathologist.

If a child can't explain it, he or she doesn't know it. Perception should not be equated with production. Too often children who have poor expressive skills are not given credit for knowing or understanding a concept and are frequently labeled as slow learners. This practice results in many language handicapped students developing poor self-concepts and avoiding situations requiring them to express themselves orally.

*Test results accurately represent what a child knows.*Studies have shown that test performance, especially in the area of language, often fails to adequately represent competence (King 1975). In some cases the design of the test itself discriminates against the child by measuring only deficits and not areas of strengths or potential.

ASSESSING ORAL LANGUAGE DEVELOPMENT

Appropriate assessment of a child's oral language development necessitates an understanding of the normal language acquisition process as well as a familiarity with the basic components of language. This section focuses on the normal process through which language is acquired and also describes the basic components of language.

Normal Language Acquisition

The development of meaningful language cannot occur in isolation. Adequate language development is dependent upon a nurturing environment to give meaning and purpose to verbal interaction (Hendrick 1980). Language acquisition is also dependent upon cognitive development (Sinclair 1975); that is, a considerable amount of intellectual growth needs to occur before a young child can profit from or make use of language.

During the preverbal stage of language development, the young child is at work acquiring a basic understanding of the environment. This cognitive task is a prerequisite to using verbal symbols (words) to represent different objects or events. Johnson and Myklebust (1967) refer to the process of assimilating experiences as developing "inner language" and consider it an essential antecedent of language.

Figure 8–1 (pages 188–191) presents a sequential listing of oral language skills as they normally develop from birth through late adolescence. This check list differs from many language scope-and-sequence charts in that it includes specific linguistic skills usually acquired beyond the preschool years. While it is generally recognized that language development is far from complete by the time a child normally enters first grade, typical language development charts end with the skills expected of a child by the age of six or seven.

The purpose of Figure 8–1 is not only to develop an understanding of the hierarchical nature of language acquisition but also to provide an appropriate tool for informally assessing language development. While Figure 8–1 divides the basic language acquisition skills into the receptive and expressive areas, in actual usage and acquisition these two areas are necessarily interdependent and interactive.

Figure 8–1 was compiled from such sources as the *Receptive-Expressive Emergent Language Scale* (REEL) (Bzoch and League 1971), Bloom and Lahey's (1978) phases of language development, and Wood's (1976) stages of language acquisition. In using this scope-and-sequence chart, it should be noted that some older educationally handicapped children have language characteristics of a preschool level of development.

Components of Language

The five major components of language are (1) semantics, (2) syntax, (3) phonology, (4) morphology, and (5) pragmatics. Attention to each of these components is important in both language assessment and intervention (Schiefelbusch 1978).

Semantics. **Semantics**, as the content or function of language, refers to the meaning expressed by verbal symbols (words) as well as the meaning attached to word relationships, grammatical forms, and constructions in a language. The word *car* by itself represents a particular object in the environment; but when it is used in a phrase such as "car go," an added meaning is expressed through the relationship of the two words. "The old man's car near the water" presents additional meaning by nature of the possessive, prepositional forms and constructions used in such a phrase.

A limited vocabulary in both the receptive and expressive areas of language is characteristic of children with developmental delays in semantics. While such a limited vocabulary is sometimes more pronounced in one specific area, such as adjectives, pronouns, nouns, or adverbs, it may be noted in several of these areas. Also characteristic of children with delays in semantic development is a narrow interpretation of word meanings (Wiig and Semel 1976).

Semantic development can be informally assessed by analyzing samples of a child's spontaneous speech or by assigning various verbal tasks to the child. Such tasks may include word association activities such as the following:

Activity: Word Classification

Description: Teacher gives a word pair based on categorization according to function. The teacher then gives the first word in another similar word pair and waits for the child to supply the missing word.

☐ **FIGURE 8–1**
Scope and Sequence of Oral Language Skills

RECEPTIVE LANGUAGE	*Deficient* –	*Instruction* /	*Mastery* *
Birth to Six Months			
Startle response to loud, sudden noises			
Often focuses attention on speaker			
Begins to localize source of sound			
Six to Twelve Months			
Shows evidence of recognizing words like *Daddy, no,* and *bye-bye.*			
Begins to recognize names of family members and names of common objects (toes, coat, etc.)			
Occasionally follows simple commands like "Give me the ball."			
Appears to understand simple questions like "Where are your toes?"			
Twelve to Eighteen Months			
Can distinguish between highly dissimilar noises			
Understands names of most familiar body parts			
Understands simple questions and can carry out two consecutive commands			
Begins to associate words by categories (such as foods, animals, or clothing)			
Eighteen to Twenty-Four Months			
Begins to understand personal pronouns (*her, me, they,* etc.)			
Follows a series of two or three simple but related commands			
Recognizes the name of almost all common objects			
Understands more complex sentences such as "If you sit by the table, I'll pour some juice for you."			
Two to Three Years			
Knows names of smaller body parts			
Comprehends meaning of common action words			
Understands common adjectives (such as those relating to size or color)			
Demonstrates curiosity about how things work			
Demonstrates an understanding of simple prepositions (such as *over, near, behind,* etc.)			
Understands plurals			
Three to Six Years			
Is aware of past and present			

☐ **FIGURE 8–1—continued**
Scope and Sequence of Oral Language Skills

RECEPTIVE LANGUAGE	*Deficient* –	*Instruction* /	*Mastery* *
Carries out three-item commands consistently			
Understands simple stories			
Begins to make fine discriminations among similar speech sounds			
Understands most simple, compound, and complex sentences			
Understands likenesses and differences			
Primary Grades			
Can recognize the close relationship between making friends or being accepted by peers and the ability to communicate with people			
Can listen for particular sounds and words			
Understands the difference between commands, requests, and promises			
Can identify various emotions communicated by the voice			
Middle and Upper Elementary Grades			
Can subordinate own interests to those of the group			
Can listen for and recall a sequence of events			
Can comprehend the main idea of spoken paragraphs			
Can differentiate between fantasy and reality			
Listens for and recalls details from spoken paragraphs			
Comprehends cause-and-effect relationships			
Understands multiple meanings of words (a *broken* dish, a *broken* heart)			
Comprehends meaning of abstract words (*honest, desire, tardiness*)			
Can respect the right of others to give their opinions by being courteous and attentive			
After hearing directions once, can follow them correctly			
Can determine purpose for doing something when given an oral explanation			
Can recognize sounds that are often obscured by other sounds			
Junior and Senior High			
Can listen and visualize what is being described even though it is remote in time and space			
Can remember what is said and can report it accurately to someone else			
Can remember details of what is said and can then answer questions on the material when the speaker is finished			

☐ **FIGURE 8–1—continued**
Scope and Sequence of Oral Language Skills

RECEPTIVE LANGUAGE	*Deficient* –	*Instruction* /	*Mastery* *
Can evaluate what is said by someone else in terms of accuracy, relevancy, and consistency			
Can relate different ideas in a discussion to a main topic of conversation			
Can appreciate conversation as a social art			
Can make inferences and conclusions about what is said			
Can see a relationship between the different meanings of double-function terms (a *warm* person makes you feel *warm*) (Wood 1976)			
Begins to interpret conflict messages (such as sarcasm) where prosodic features are in disagreement with the verbal and visual features (Wood 1976)			
EXPRESSIVE LANGUAGE			
Birth to Six Months			
Begins random vocalizing other than crying			
Expresses anger or displeasure through vocalization			
Enjoys making different sounds while alone or with others			
Six to Twelve Months			
Begins to express sentencelike utterances without using true words			
Appears to be naming things in own language			
Begins to use some gestures to express meaning			
Utters first true words			
Twelve to Eighteen Months			
Attempts to manipulate others through vocalizations and gestures (trying to obtain desired objects, etc.)			
Responds to songs or rhymes by vocalizing			
Eighteen to Twenty-Four Months			
Shows a steady increase in vocabulary			
Uses some short, simple sentences			
Imitates environmental sounds			
Two to Three Years			
Begins using pronouns correctly			
Asks for help when needed			
Relates experiences from recent past			
Begins to ask questions of adults			

☐ **FIGURE 8–1—continued**
Scope and Sequence of Oral Language Skills

Three to Six Years	*Deficient* –	*Instruction* /	*Mastery* *
Gives simple account of experiences			
Begins to use plurals, prepositions, pronouns, adjectives, and adverbs correctly			
Uses compound and complex sentences			
Enjoys rhyming nonsense words and using silly exaggerations			
Asks many questions, especially questions about how and why			
Defines objects in terms of function			
Primary Grades			
Uses clear pronunication and articulation			
No longer exhibits speech-sound substitutions ("wabbit" for "rabbit")			
Uses verb tense correctly most of the time			
Uses most pronouns correctly			
Demonstrates rapid recall of common words			
Speaks without fear or embarrassment in groups or before the class			
Can retell a short story in proper sequence			
Middle and Upper Elementary Grades			
Can speak with expression and with enough volume to make self understood in the classroom			
Can dramatize events and stories effectively			
Practices social courtesies in discussion and conversation (takes turns in speaking, etc.)			
Can give information clearly			
Carries on conversations with peers			
Can tell detailed stories about favorite radio and TV programs			
Speaks in complete sentences			
Chooses appropriate words to express meaning			
Junior and Senior High			
Can formulate statements of meaning (Wood 1976)			
Uses more intricate sentence patterns			
Can strive for clarity of expression as a means to an end			
Can speak with poise before a small group of people			
Practices all social courtesies of language such as making introductions, speaking on the telephone, greeting and thanking people at social gatherings			
Can give information clearly and accurately			

Example: cottage - house
coffee - [*beverage*]

Variations: Categorizations for this activity could focus on physical descriptions (sandpaper - rough; knife - [*sharp*]), logical relationships (nephew - uncle; niece - [*aunt*]), verbal opposites (dawn - dusk; hostile - [*friendly*]), etc. The use of a check list for semantic analysis may prove helpful in using either speech samples or verbal tasks (see Figure 8–2).

Syntax. **Syntax**, as the grammar system of language, refers to the linguistic rules of word order and the function of words in sentences. A child with a syntactic language disorder may lack proficiency in ordering words correctly; for example, the child may say "No ball find" for "I can't find the ball." A deficit in this area may also cause a child to have difficulty transforming the order of words to generate a new meaning. For example, "Are we going fishing?" can be transformed to "We are going fishing." Children with delays in syntactic development tend to use shorter sentences, often omitting certain words. For "Throw the ball to me," a child may say "Throw me ball."

Tape recording and transcribing a sample of the child's spontaneous speech is one way to assess syntax informally. The recorded utterances are then compared with norms for the child's developmental age. From this a list of grammatical forms expected, but not used, can be compiled. Figure 8–3 presents an overview of the development of grammatical forms, adapted from the six stages in syntactic development outlined by Wood (1976).

Phonology. **Phonology** refers to the sound system of our language, with phonemes being units of sounds that combine with other sounds to form words. A

☐ **FIGURE 8–2**
Semantics Analysis

Date____________________

SEMANTICS ANALYSIS	*Deficient* –	*Instruction* /	*Mastery* *
Awareness of logical relationships			
Understanding of cause and—effect relationships			
Ability to identify verbal opposites			
Basic understanding of categorization			
Broad vocabulary base incorporating understanding of adjectives, pronouns, adverbs, etc.			
Ability to classify words			
Understanding of the more common double-function terms, such as *cold* weather and a *cold* person			
Understanding of basic function words, such as *and, or, but, not,* and *then*			

☐ **FIGURE 8–3**
Syntactical Analysis

Developmental Stage	*Average Chronological Age*	*Nature of Development*	*Sample Utterances*
1. Sentence-like word	one to two years	one-word utterance combined with gestures or inflections	"Mommy." "Mommy!" "Mommy?"
2. Modification	two years	modifiers joined to basic words to form four basic sentence patterns	"My ball." (statement) "Where Daddy?" (question) "No bed." (negative) "More cookie." (imperative)
3. Structure	two to three years	both subject and predicate included in sentence types	"Ball is mine." "Where Daddy is?" "I no go to bed." "I want more cookie."
4. Operational changes	three to six years	elements added to basic sentences to express more complex relationships (contractions, possessives, *ing*, plurals, etc.)	"I *don't* want to go to bed." "This is Dadd*y's* shirt." "Tim is play*ing* ball."
5. Categorization	elementary school age	word classes (nouns, verbs, and prepositions are subdivided)	"I want *some* milk." "Let's go *to* the fair."
6. Complex structures	ten years	complex structural distinctions (such as, the "promise" and "ask" structures)	"Ask him to help you." "He promised to go with her."

Adapted from Barbara S. Wood, *Children and Communication: Verbal and Nonverbal Language Development* © 1976, p. 148. Adapted by permission of Prentice-Hall Inc., Englewood Cliffs, NJ.

phoneme, as the smallest unit of speech, does not convey meaning in isolation. By age seven, most children are capable of producing all the English phonemes correctly (Weiss and Lillywhite 1976). Figure 8–4 outlines expected phonemes mastered at various levels of development.

Problems in phonology frequently show up as articulation disorders, usually involving consonants rather than vowels. Three of the most common problems in consonant acquisition are (1) omissions, (2) substitutions, and (3) distortions.

Omissions are incomplete pronunciations of words and usually involve consonants in the initial, medial, or final positions within a word. Examples of omission include "ookie" for "cookie"; "nothin" for "nothing"; and "an'er" for "answer."

In **substitution**, a child replaces a correct phoneme with an incorrect phoneme. Examples of substitutions include "toof" for "tooth" and "thilly" for "silly."

Distortions are generally represented by a muffled or slushy quality to the correct pronunciation. Distortions may be due to the complexity of the movements involved, hearing loss, or poor motor control. Two consonants that are frequently distorted are the /s/ ("snake sound") and /z/ ("buzzing bee sound"). As these

☐ **FIGURE 8–4**
Development of Phonemic Abilities

Sounds Produced	*Approximate Age*
All 14 vowel sounds and consonants *p, b, m*	3.5 years
Consonants *w, t, n, h, d, k, g*	
All dipthongs *ng* sound	4.5 years
Consonants *y, v, f,* voiced and voiceless *th* and *wh* sound	5.5 years
Consonants *j, r, s, z, ch, zh,* and *sh* sounds	6.5 years
Consonants blends such as *st, sk, sp, dr, st, sl, br, bl, pr, pl, gr, cl, gl, str,* and *thr*	7 years

Adapted from C. Weiss and H. Lillywhite, *Communication Disorders: A Handbook for Prevention and Early Intervention.* (St. Louis: C.V. Mosley, 1976), p. 51.

sounds complete many plurals and the present tense of the majority of verbs, they are encountered quite frequently in everyday conversation.

While many children with articulation problems have deficiencies in the expressive aspect of language but not in their receptive abilities, other children experience difficulties in both areas. Deficits that are confined to expressive language are generally easier to correct than problems encompassing both the expressive and receptive domains. Children who have trouble hearing the difference between /*w*/ and /*r*/, for example, will usually require more intense language therapy than those children who can make such discriminations (Wood 1976).

In assessing a child for phonological difficulties, the normal stages of phonemic development must be carefully kept in mind (refer to Figure 8–4). Some consonant substitutions are normal for young children up to certain ages. Among the more common substitutions are a /*w*/ sound for the /*l*/ and /*r*/ sounds and a /*th*/ sound for the /*s*/ sound. For example, young children up to about six years of age may say "wabbit" for "rabbit" and "thilly" for "silly."

While the diagnosis and remediation of articulation disorders are properly done by a person trained specifically in that area, it is helpful for special educators to understand the procedures generally used by such professionals. Wood (1976) offers the following three-part procedure for analyzing potential articulation problems in school-age children:

1. Listen carefully to the child's speech and record in writing the words that are misarticulated. Identify the incorrect phonemes (smallest units of sound, such as the sounds for *w, b, t,* etc.). Designate these as target phonemes (sounds to be developed).
2. Locate the target phonemes in other word positions in the child's speech. Determine if the child makes the same errors when these phonemes appear in different word positions (initial, medial, and final). For example, if the child substitutes /*w*/ for /*r*/ in "red" (saying "wed"), does he or she make a similar error with the /*r*/ in a different position, as in "so**rr**y" and "b**r**ead?" Again, record the incorrect phonemes.
3. Compare the child's articulation patterns with norms for his or her age level (Figure 8–4). A variance of more than one year from the norm may indicate a need for special help.

Morphology. **Morphology** is concerned with the smallest meaningful units of language, called morphemes. Young children's first words are free morphemes in that they can function independently and cannot be subdivided into more basic meaning units. Bound morphemes, on the other hand, must combine with at least one other morpheme and include such language units as prefixes and suffixes. The meaning of a bound morpheme is derived from its attachment to a free morpheme. The words *looked, eggs, Tony's,* and *unlock* are examples of bound morphemes (*ed, s, 's, un*) attached to free morphemes.

The bound morphemes that usually begin to emerge around five years of age include the plural and possessive word endings as well as the morphemes used to signify simple verb tense (lif*ts*, lif*ted*, lif*ting*). The more difficult tense endings (have writ*ten*) along with adjective forms (hot*ter*, hot*test*) and agentives (build*er*) tend to emerge during the child's early elementary years. Figure 8–5 presents a brief outline of stages in the child's development of morphology.

Elementary school children with deficits in morphological development tend to omit inflectional endings in their speech. Examples of this include omitting the third person *s* on verbs ("Dad work every day."), the possessive *s* on nouns ("Timmy ball."), and the *er* on adjectives ("My jacket is small than yours."). Older elementary and junior high students with deficits in morphological development may have difficulty with the irregular past verb tenses and irregular plurals ("taked" for "took" or "deers" for "deer").

To assess morphological development informally, results of specific verbal tasks presented to the child or samples of spontaneous speech can be analyzed relative to the skills expected at various ages as outlined in Figure 8–5. Specific verbal tasks may require a child to respond to specific questions. For example, the teacher may ask, "What is the child in the picture doing?" or "Where did I put the ball?" In these examples, the objective is to assess the child's use of the bound morpheme *ing* and the free morpheme *in*. The examiner records the results as either correct or incorrect on a check list of desired morphemes. Such a record then serves as a guideline for determining which morphemes need to be taught. A similar proce-

☐ **FIGURE 8–5**
Development of Morphology

Skill	*Approximate Age*
Use of first words	12–18 months
Rapid vocabulary building (free morphemes)	3+ years
Early bound morphemes plurals possessives more simple verb tenses	5+ years
Use of compound words	4–6+ years
Later bound morphemes adjective forms agentives	6+ years

Adapted from Barbara S. Wood, *Children and Communication: Verbal and Nonverbal Language Development* ©1976, p. 125. Adapted by permission of Prentice-Hall Inc., Englewood Cliffs, NJ.

dure can be used to informally measure receptive morphology. The child's task in this case is to point to a picture most clearly depicting the meaning of the teacher's sentence. For example, the teacher may say, "The car is leaving the parking lot." From a series of pictures, the child must point to the picture of the car in the process of leaving as opposed to coming into the lot or having already left the lot.

Pragmatics. **Pragmatics** deals with the use of language for communication. Bates (1976) defined pragmatics as the rules governing the use of language in context, and Schiefelbusch (1978) referred to it as the "how" of language. Pragmatics can be considered a separate process in the acquisition of language in that achievements in comprehension and production of specific linguistic elements are distinct from their rules of usage in conversation (Miller 1978).

The importance of pragmatics in language developmnt cannot be overstated. Without pragmatics, language would have no meaning and would serve no purpose. Miller (1978) has identified several specific pragmatic factors to be considered in assessing language development. These include (*a*) the child's conversational turn-taking abilities, (*b*) the child's initiation and maintenance of a conversational topic, (*c*) when and how the child changes topics, and (*d*) the nature of the child's verbal responses to adult utterances. While Miller (1978) states that these pragmatic factors ultimately become the criteria for successful language development, he recognizes that they currently lack specific operational procedures for measurement. Because of this, "one must rely on behavioral observation for their analysis" (Miller 1978, 289). Some behaviors that suggest a delay in pragmatic development include interrupting the speaker, talking at an inappropriate time, and speaking too loudly for the situation.

Research by Bryan (1978, 1977, 1976) and others indicates that many learning disabled students experience considerable difficulties in social development, interpersonal relationships, and perceiving and understanding others' affective states. Such interpersonal problems seem to be closely linked to language abilities, especially in terms of pragmatics. It seems that these students are less able than classmates to comprehend nonverbal social communications and are more likely to emit verbalizations that elicit rejection responses from others (Bryan 1976). It was found, for example, that children with learning disabilities are more likely to emit competitive statements and less likely to emit considerate statements than comparison children (Bryan et al. 1976). Thus, children with learning disabilities seem to be more vulnerable to deficits in pragmatics than the general population.

Figure 8–6 (based on information from Miller 1978; Bryan 1978, 1977, 1976) presents a check list of pragmatic skills that can be used as an informal assessment tool in the analysis of speech samples.

Language Assessment Tools

While observation, check lists, and samples of spontaneous speech have been suggested as tools in assessing a child's language developmental level and areas of difficulty, there are also a number of standardized tests that can be used for this purpose. The *Clinical Evaluation of Language Function (CELF)* (Semel and Wiig 1980) is one example of a standardized test designed to measure the various components

☐ **FIGURE 8–6**
Pragmatic Analysis

PRAGMATIC ANALYSIS	*Deficient* –	*Instruction* /	*Mastery* *
Understands the difference between requests, commands, and promises			
Is sensitive to the meaning and significance of nonverbal communication			
Uses appropriate intensity (loudness) of voice			
Requests assistance when needed			
Employs age-appropriate conversational turn-taking skills			
Can initiate a conversational topic			
Can maintain a conversational topic			
Exhibits attending behavior in the presence of a speaker			
Can give adequate directions or explanations			
Can take phone messages			
Listens for relevant information in taking directions			
Uses courtesies needed for social occasions			
Uses language to express both negative and positive feelings in socially acceptable ways			

of language. It is an individually administered test and is appropriate for children in kindergarten through twelfth grade. While the *CELF* is designed to provide a comprehensive evaluation of a child's language development, the results are not intended to serve as the sole determinant of the child's specific language-related strengths and weaknesses. The designers of the test suggest that "the results of the *CELF* should be complemented by administration of standardized measures of receptive vocabulary development and by the analysis of a spontaneous speech sample" (Semel and Wiig 1980, 2). These same authors suggest that classroom behavioral observations and evaluations of pragmatic and interpersonal communication abilities also be used to complement the results of the *CELF*. Such recommendations are generally applicable to other formal language assessment tools as well. While a number of language tests purport to be comprehensive in nature, pragmatics represents one major area that is generally omitted.

The *Test of Language Development (TOLD)* (Newcomer and Hammill 1977) is another formal language tool designed to assess different aspects of the various components of language in children ages four through eight. The five principal subtests of the *TOLD* include picture vocabulary, oral vocabulary, grammatic understanding, sentence imitation, and grammatic completion. Two supplemental tests assess the child's proficiency in word discrimination and word articulation. Although the *TOLD* subtest scores provide an indication of a child's functional level in the specific language skills assessed, such results should not be used as the sole criterion in planning an instructional program.

There are limitations associated with standardized language tools. While many tests measure a variety of language components, two areas generally not assessed are pragmatics and the receptive aspect of morphology. Also lacking are formal measures of language appropriate for upper-elementary and secondary students. Another disadvantage of standardized tests is that test performance often fails to adequately represent competence (King 1975). A study by Wilkinson and Dollaghan (1979) found that formal measures of syntactical complexity and vocabulary diversity do not give justice to children's language competencies as reflected in their spontaneous interactions.

For the purpose of program planning, assessment procedures are needed that are more specific and accurate in measuring both expressive and receptive language skills and that focus on the many aspects of language. Appropriate instructional planning requires a wide range of data pertaining to an individual's language development. Techniques that can be used to obtain such data include criterion-referenced testing, diagnostic teaching, and clinical observation.

INSTRUCTIONAL APPROACHES AND TECHNIQUES FOR LANGUAGE DEVELOPMENT AND REMEDIATION

Theoretical Approaches

Although there are many theories of language development, Reid and Hresko (1981) and Dever (1978) categorize these as either associationist or cognitive.

Associationist view. The associationist view of language development represents the behavioral school of thought and is based on the concept that language is an observable behavior that can be taught. Noticeably absent in this conceptualization of language is any type of innate mechanism for acquiring language skills (Reid and Hresko 1981).

Osgood's theory of language represents the associationist position. Osgood's model of the communication process attempts to apply mediated stimulus-response theory to the development of oral language (Osgood 1953) and forms the basis for the *Illinois Test of Psycholinguistic Abilities (ITPA)* (Kirk, McCarthy, and Kirk 1968) and related training programs employing behavioral principles for intervention (Reid and Hresko 1981). Such intervention programs include the *MWM Program for Developing Language Abilities* (Minskoff, Wiseman, and Minskoff 1972), the *GOAL* program (Karnes 1972), and *Aids to Psycholinguistic Teaching* (Bush and Giles 1969).

One of the most widely used of the language intervention programs in preschool and primary classrooms is the *Peabody Language Development Kits (PLDK)* (Dunn and Smith 1968). While the *PLDK* is another example of an Osgood-oriented language training program, attempts were made in the development of these kits to focus on global language ability as opposed to specific underlying skills (Dunn and Smith 1968). While the *PLDK* generally stimulates children to become more communicative, there is currently no evidence to support overall improvement in language ability through use of this program. In fact, as reported by Reid and Hresko (1981), doubts have been raised concerning the adequacy of the associationist view of language and the intervention programs based on this theory of language.

Cognitive view. From the cognitive perspective, language—instead of being the sum of discrete abilities—is a complex code of communication, and the acquisition of language is seen to be intrinsically related to cognitive development. According to the cognitive psycholinguistic model, language is acquired by the active child in the absence of direct language instruction (McLean and Snyder-McLean 1978; King 1975).

Intervention from the cognitive view focuses on stimulation rather than remediation. Emphasis is placed primarily on semantics and only secondarily on syntax and phonology. The child's ability to use language is also considered to be of prime importance. The need for natural language settings with appropriate opportunities for the child to extract language structure and function is, according to those espousing a cognitive view, an essential part of intervention in language development (King 1975). Intervention techniques consistent with the cognitive view include repeating, rephrasing, extending or elaborating, modifying rate, and modeling.

Halliday (1975) as well as Bloom and Lahey (1978) have proposed intervention models consistent with the cognitive psycholinguistic orientation. Halliday (1975) described the development of language as a process through which the child gradually "learns how to mean." Halliday identified seven basic functions of language, which, he said, are universally used to communicate meaning. These seven functions include (1) obtaining needs or desires; (2) controlling or influencing others; (3) establishing and maintaining contact; (4) asserting oneself (stating personal feelings or opinions); (5) exploring and learning about the world (asking questions, seeking information); (6) using language imaginatively in play and make-believe; and (7) developing interaction with others or transmitting information. From this perspective, children need experience with many kinds of language; that is, they need to hear and experiment with the whole range of language functions. Teachers intent on helping students develop many different ways of using language include language instruction as a part of the everyday classroom activities throughout the school day.

Another cognitively oriented approach to language development is one proposed by Bloom and Lahey (1978). According to this model, the form or structure of language is considered relevant only in its relationship to function. "Language intervention in a highly structured setting that is isolated from real-life experiences is not recommended unless it is impossible to get a child to attend to relevant stimuli without such isolation" (Bloom and Lahey 1978, 556), since there is no reported body of evidence to support the practice of remediation of specific language abilities.

Intervention Strategies

General considerations. Because the acquisition of language skills is not an isolated area of a child's overall development, attempts to confine language instruction to a particular time period or to certain instructional activities specifically designed to teach language skills would be inappropriate. Meaningful interactions with objects, people, and events in the environment enable students to derive the cognitive and social basis on which language competence is built (McLean and Snyder-McLean 1978). Thus, it follows that language intervention must be an all-day affair. Not only must parents and other individuals in the home environment play an active role in a language intervention program, but teachers also need to concern themselves with the quality of language and language-related experiences to which children are exposed throughout the entire school day.

The teacher's speech, language, and other communication behaviors throughout the day should serve as models for the students. If the teacher is effective in using language to ask for and receive specific information, to relate interesting experiences, to express personal feelings, and to provide relevant explanations, students will gain insights into the pragmatics of language. If the teacher can clearly express cause-and-effect relationships, can demonstrate the meaning of basic function words (*then, or, but,* etc.), can develop logical relationships, and can use a broad vocabulary, the semantic development of the students will be enhanced. If the teacher is aware of the child's developmental level and models appropriate syntactical constructions, a child is given the opportunity to experience the joy and satisfaction of success in understanding the teacher's message. If the teacher makes an effort to enunciate clearly and speak slowly, students will find it easier not only to hear the correct forms but also to process appropriate information relative to the basic sound and structure system of our language.

Another major consideration in planning an intervention program for children with language problems is reducing the influence of any factors that may be causing or contributing to the language problem. Bloom and Lahey (1978) refer to factors that inhibit language learning as "maintaining factors" since they act to maintain the language disorder. Any maintaining factors that can be eliminated or minimized are most important in planning intervention. Examples of maintaining factors include hearing loss, poor health, and unsatisfactory parent-child interaction.

Also critical to effective language intervention is the recognition of receptive communication skills as prerequisite to expressive language development (Johnson and Myklebust 1967). Wiig and Semel (1976) advocate remediation of deficits in language processing before intervention for deficits in language production since "language processing and comprehension involve recognition while language production requires recall and retrieval" (p. 131). However, as suggested by Bloom and Lahey (1978), "neither comprehension nor production should be taught apart from each other" (p. 568). These two aspects of language are interrelated and should be developed as such.

The role of the child as active constructor of his own language development should be emphatically stressed in language intervention programs. Children do not learn language by being guided through a predetermined set of hierarchical skills or by acquiring a specific amount of linguistic information. On the contrary, "children learn language as they use language, both to produce and understand messages" (Bloom and Lahey 1978, 23). Thus, it follows that the person who intervenes in (or facilitates) the language-learning process is not a teacher in the traditional sense. Rather than providing information or training for specific skills, the language facilitator arranges external events in a way that makes it easier for children to induce the rules and functions of language for themselves.

Instructional techniques. Some techniques that have proven helpful in facilitating language development include (*a*) imitation and reinforcement, (*b*) expansion, (*c*) labeling, (*d*) auditory training, (*e*) effective questioning, and (*f*) signing.

Imitation and reinforcement. **Imitation**, as a language development technique, refers to the child's repetition of words and language structures that he or she is learning. The content of such repetition may refer to all or part of the speech that the child hears. For example, the teacher may say: "Jodi, in this first picture I see that a boy is swimming. What do you see the dog in the next picture doing?" In this example, the child is learning through imitation the *ing* form of a verb. Note that imitation in this context is not an exact repetition of what the teacher says. Learning the basic form and meaning of language requires a much more complex process than exact repetition. The goal of imitation as an instructional technique for language development is to have the child assimilate such complex aspects of language as word order, formation of plurals, turn taking, and categorization. Frequent exposure to such aspects of language in meaningful contexts eventually enables the child to imitate (though not in word-for-word fashion) the words and structure of a very complex verbal communication system.

While formal imitation has received considerable criticism as a language intervention technique (Guess, Keogh, and Sailor 1978; Ruder, Hermann, and Schiefelbusch 1977), several modifications have been suggested. One such modification is to model the desired language behavior but not to formally request similar behavior from the child (Bloom and Lahey 1978). Another modification, originally suggested by Bandura and Harris (1966), is to have a third person model the expected language behavior in the child's presence. This third person (model) is rewarded by the teacher for desired language behaviors. When the child is then asked to perform the same language task, he or she is also rewarded for appropriate responses. One application of this technique would be the teacher's policy of requiring seat work to be okayed before allowing children to leave their desks for other activities. Students are to raise their hands and ask to have their work checked or request help if needed. After the language delayed child observes other children requesting help or having their work okayed, he or she may do likewise in order to earn the accompanying reward. While a reward may be to allow participation in favorite activities or obtaining preferred objects, the most natural reinforcers of appropriate language behaviors are successful communication and satisfying social interaction (McLean and Snyder-McLean 1978).

An example of a natural reinforcer of language is the child's feeling of success in managing to manipulate the environment through language. When a child says, "Help me," in attempting to do a math problem and is rewarded by receiving help from the teacher, the child's language behavior is reinforced. Similarly, if a reticent youth receives a smile and evidence of sincere interest in what he or she has to say when introducing a topic for conversation, such an individual has received positive reinforcement for efforts to communicate. While a positive response to attempts to communicate may be the only reinforcement many children need, others may also need supporting social interaction, such as praise, smiles, or hugs (Lerner, Mardell-Czudnowski, and Goldenberg 1981). Positive reinforcement for desired langauge behaviors is likely to increase the frequency with which children engage in such behaviors.

While imitation refers to what is desired on the part of the child, **modeling** represents the activity of the language facilitator. At times the child's peers may be the most effective models for language development. The peer group not only provides the motivation—and often the need—for the language impaired child's participation in the communication process but may also more clearly exemplify (or model) specific language behaviors most appropriate for that child's developmental level. Strong support exists for mainstreaming children with communication problems (Ross 1978; Ling, Ling, and Pflaster 1977) on the basis that language handicapped children will tend to imitate the desired language behaviors of their nonhandicapped peers.

Expansion. In language development, **expansion** refers to the practice of not only acknowledging and reinforcing what a child says but also expanding or extending the child's utterance. For example, when a young child says, "Crayons fall," the parent or teacher may respond by repeating the thought in a syntactically expanded form, such as "Oh, the crayons fell off the table." For the language impaired child, the expanded statement should be kept relatively short and simple to facilitate understanding and imitation (Lerner, Mardell-Czudnowski, and Goldenberg 1981).

Expansion as a language development technique can be appropriate for older children, too. Many children with language problems find it difficult to communicate specific information (giving directions, describing objects or events, etc.) and frequently overuse such phrases as "that thing" or "this one." One way to expand such utterances is to ask for clarification; for example, "When you said 'that thing,' did you mean this large map near my desk?"

Labeling. **Labeling** is a language development technique related to, but not identical to, expansion. Whereas expansion builds on what the child says, labeling requires no initial utterance on the part of the child. Through labeling the teacher provides the student with the appropriate words for actions, things, or feelings (Safford 1978). This technique can be implemented easily, often simply by commenting on what the child is experiencing. For example, a teacher might say, "Jim, I know you must be feeling angry because Jean was rude to you," or "This tool you are using is a level. The level works best on a flat surface."

Weiss and Lillywhite (1976) offer the following suggestions for labeling:

- Use labeling frequently throughout the day, but do not provide too many labels at one time.
- Bombard the child with names of key objects—those that are of greatest interest or need to the child.
- Allow hands-on experience with the objects that are referred to in labeling.
- Recognize the fact that just because a child doesn't say the label doesn't mean that he or she is not associating the label with the object. The understanding of language always exceeds and precedes the expression of language.

Another excellent instructional practice is for teachers to analyze their own language samples to determine how often they use such demonstrative pronouns as *this, that, it,* and *these* instead of appropriate labels. If a teacher overuses such words, it is certainly not surprising to find students doing the same.

Auditory training. Because of the critical role listening plays in the language acquisition process, **auditory training** is considered an important part of a language development program. Safford (1978) notes that one way to encourage listening behavior is to "model" listening when children speak. Listening to children means putting other work or activities aside, commenting on the pros and cons of their positions, and responding with interest to their questions and comments. Attending to the auditory environment of the classroom can also enhance children's ability to attend to and gain meaning from the verbal messages being presented. Teachers should be aware of and minimize extraneous noises that may distract children from attending to significant verbal stimuli.

Listening, of course, involves more than hearing. It also involves attending, discriminating, understanding, and remembering (Weiss and Lillywhite 1976). Such skills are learned behaviors and can be improved through training.

There are a wide variety of listening games and activities that can be used in both elementary and secondary classrooms to facilitate listening skills or language comprehension. Such activities include reading aloud to the class (even secondary students enjoy reading aloud if the choice of reading material is appropriate and the selection is read clearly and with enthusiasm), giving clearly stated directions only once, and playing a variety of games that require listening behavior (Simon Says, Word or Math Bingo, Mother May I, etc.). Other listening activities include working with rhyming words ("I'm thinking of a color that rhymes with *Jack*," etc.); listening for words that do not belong with others on a list ("Which word does not belong: France, Brazil, Germany, Italy?"); categorizing words ("How are these words alike: square, parallelogram, trapezoid?"); and having fun with riddles ("Which of these has an eye but cannot see: bucket, needle, or pin?").

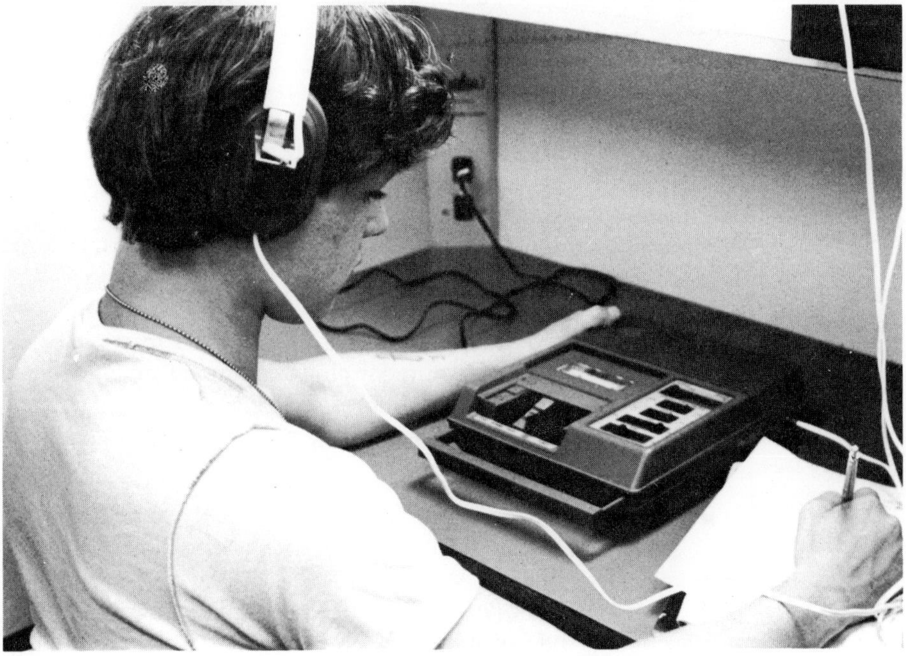

Many auditory training activities can be taped and used by students on an individual basis.

Laskey and Chapandy (1976) have suggested that the way a message is delivered can make an appreciable difference in the listener's comprehension. They suggest, for one thing, that simple syntactic constructions be used when the semantic load is more difficult. In other words, the use of simple grammar facilitates understanding, especially if the concepts being presented are either unfamiliar to the listener or of a rather complex nature. A simple, active, declarative sentence, such as "Bob rides the bus," is an example of what is meant by simple syntactical construction. The sentence becomes more complex if expressed in passive form or if expanded with conjunctions, such as *and, while,* or *but,* or with negatives. The following sentences do not represent simple syntactical form: "The bus was ridden by Bob"; "Bob rode the bus but still arrived late for school"; "Bob will not ride the bus today."

Laskey and Chapandy (1976) also suggested that context and contextual cues affect comprehension. Contextual cues include such things as pictures, word cues, and verbal redundancy. Therefore, teachers who use appropriate pictures for visual aids, repeat the same idea or message over and over, and provide many word cues to clarify a term offer their students valuable aids to comprehension.

A third suggestion for improving comprehension made by Laskey and Chapandy (1976) deals with the rate of presenting messages. They noted that a slower rate increases comprehension and offered specific ideas on how to alter the rate of presentation. "Rate of presentation can be altered by slowing the total rate of words per second presented in the message or by inserting pauses between the noun phrase and verb phrase of a sentence, within the verb phrase, or between the verb and the following noun phrase" (p. 166).

Examples: Tony and Jim (pause) are leaving.
Cindi, Jean, and Ruth (pause) will be working (pause) in this school.

In addition to modifying rate as an aid to comprehension, Bloom and Lahey (1978) also suggest modifying prosody (intonation or stress). Modification of prosody can be thought of as serving the same type of function in oral language as punctuation does for written language. The appropriate use of each facilitates the understanding of a message. Other verbal cues to comprehension can be given by repeating significant words, supplying definitions, and using exaggerations. The following sentences illustrate the use of such verbal cues:

- *Repetition*: These numerals are called mixed fractions. Mixed fractions are made up of a whole number plus a common fraction. Mixed fractions always represent a quantity of more than one.
- *Supplying Definitions*: The barge, a heavy, flat-bottomed boat, moved slowly through the canals.
- *Use of Exaggeration*: He was so determined to remain in the yard that even a bulldozer would have had trouble pushing him away.

Nonverbal cues can also be used to facilitate understanding. Nonverbal cues may include the use of pictures and other visual aids, pointing, gestures, facial expressions, and other forms of body language. Both verbal and nonverbal aids to comprehension can be especially important to handicapped students who tend to ignore messages that are difficult to understand.

Effective questioning. Throughout the school day teachers frequently ask their students questions either during a formal lesson or on an informal basis. The content of the question as well as the format used in asking the question can affect the student's ability to understand and respond appropriately. The following are general guidelines teachers can use to enhance questioning skills:

- Use questions about specific knowledge only when recall of that information is important to the student.
- Phrase questions so that students may respond verbally or nonverbally.
- Provide sufficient time for student response to questions.
- Occasionally give the student the questions before a lesson begins as an aid to organization and attending skills.
- Write questions down to assure their quality.
- Distribute questions among all of the individuals in the group.
- Ask questions that require analysis, synthesis, and evaluation skills when the student has reached mastery on a given task.
- Reinforce students for using deliberation time or giving a thoughtful response.

Some handicapped students are hesitant to speak in front of peers or may not be able to organize their thoughts in a cohesive fashion. Such students can be given opportunities to answer questions through demonstrations or written responses, after which the teacher can vocalize their actions or read their written responses. Over time the teacher can desensitize shy students so that they are able to participate in class. One advantage of allowing students to answer in writing is that it encourages a more thoughtful response if the teacher provides students with sufficient thinking and writing time.

The handicapped student with communication deficits may have a difficult time comprehending a syntactical message that deviates from a simple sentence format. According to Wiig and Semel (1980), such students profit when questions are phrased so that the traditional interrogative pronouns are deleted. For example, rather than ask, "What is the closest star to the planet Earth?" a teacher may say instead, "The star closest to Earth is called ______."

Open-ended questions generally permit students to respond correctly regardless of what factual knowledge they possess about a concept. Open-ended questions allow students to be "winners" even if they are not highly verbal or have limited knowledge about a concept. The teacher uses this type of questioning technique through such statements as "Tell me something about sets," or "What can you tell me about long vowels?" This type of questioning technique is best used after the student has received instruction related to the concept. When the student responds, the teacher is in a position to praise the student for responding if he or she is not verbal or to shape the student's response into one that is more accurate by paraphrasing it, as illustrated in the following example:

Teacher: What can you tell me about the basic food groups?

Student: Hamburgers are good for you.

Teacher: You're right! Hamburgers are one of the foods in the meat group that are good for you.

In the oftentimes hectic classroom environment, teachers may feel rushed or pressured to cover a given amount of material during a lesson. This pressure can lead teachers to ask only knowledge-type questions or reduce the amount of time given students to answer a question. Rowe (1978) indicates that the average amount of time allowed by teachers for student response to questions is only one second! This average is barely sufficient time for knowledge-type questions let alone those requiring higher-level cognitive processes. Teachers who do not allow students a reasonable amount of time to respond to questions encourage shallow responses and tend to have only a few students answering all the questions. Other students have abandoned their attempts to answer, as they cannot construct a response in the amount of time provided (Cacha 1981).

To avoid this questioning error, beginning teachers can analyze questions they plan to ask during a lesson and approximate in advance the amount of response time they will provide. Teachers can also praise students for the quality of responses reached through appropriate use of response time. In addition, by tape recording lessons, teachers can accurately assess the types of questions asked as well as the amount of time provided for student response.

To encourage effective use of response time, the teacher may make statements such as the following: "This is a question that requires a lot of thought. Take ten seconds to think about your answer." Gambrell (1980) also suggests that teachers provide additional "think time" after a student's first response; some students tend to verbalize in spurts, and the teacher should be certain that students have finished before reinforcing them or posing another question.

In order to provide sufficient response time, teachers must prepare themselves to cope with silence. According to Gambrell (1980), teachers report a sense of panic when questions are not answered immediately. Filling the silence with a restatement of the question only robs students of processing time. Allowing this time for students to reflect on their answers takes effort but often leads to higher levels of thinking and the use of more sophisticated language.

If a student responds inappropriately to a question, the teacher should analyze its syntactical format to ascertain whether it clearly conveys the intended meaning to the student. A common error made by teachers when a student fails to answer a question correctly is to ask the same question of another student who knows the answer. Since the purpose of questions is to probe for student understanding (McNamara 1981), an incorrect response by a student should result in reteaching the concept to that student. Teachers generally choose students with high rates of learning and with better language skills to respond to questions. The quick and accurate response of such students reinforces the teacher's choice. Awareness of this pattern as well as the purpose of questions can make teachers cognizant of the need to distribute questions equally to all students in the group.

Signing. Until recently, the use of signing (manual English) as a means of communication has been restricted, for the most part, to deaf or hard-of-hearing individuals. Recent studies suggest that manual communication may be beneficial to a much larger population in improving communication skills (Moores 1978; Wilbur 1976; Fristoe 1975).

At one time a strong argument against the use of signing with children who had adequate hearing was the belief that once children became successful with a signing system, they would be less motivated to express themselves verbally (Grinnell, Detamore, and Lippke 1976); but just the opposite seems to be true. Once children experience some degree of success in communicating through sign language, they seem to have a stronger inclination to express themselves verbally (Moores 1978).

One rationale for the use of signing in the development of oral communication skills is that it employs multisensory input. Through manual English, communicatively handicapped students are simultaneously exposed to visual, motor, and auditory cues. Some educationally handicapped children seem to learn better through a multisensory, rather than a unisensory, approach. Another advantage of signing is that most children can learn the system very quickly and generally enjoy doing so. In addition to this, signing as a language development technique is applicable to all ages.

Besides using signing to initiate or encourage verbal communication, it has also been suggested that signing could be utilized to develop specific expressive skills (Grinnell, Detamore, and Lippke 1976). Examples of specific objectives might be to lengthen appropriate responses; to include the correct use of such words and word parts as gerunds, plural endings, and singular and plural pronouns; and to develop use of appropriate verb agreement. Ideally, such programming would be individualized through language evaluation and analysis and the selection of specific objectives for each child.

Techniques for the bilingual child. The bilingual child often presents a unique challenge in terms of language development. This may be not only because of obvious differences in the language systems but also because of disparities in cultural values. Communication problems may be related not only to structural dissimilarities in the languages but also to differences in basic understandings and values (Hendrick 1980).

Applying a few basic considerations to the classroom situation may facilitate the language development of the bilingual child.

- *Be familiar with the home and community in which the child lives.* A teacher should know whether the bilingual child comes from a large or small community. If the child's family is the only non-English-speaking family or one of just a few, the child may be more isolated and have a greater need for group acceptance. The teacher should also know the meaning of conventions, customs, and traditions honored by the child's family. Such knowledge establishes common grounds for communication.
- *Know the child as an individual.* It is important to find out how much English the child already knows. As language comprehension precedes language production, the bilingual child's expressive language ability will not give an adequate representation of how much he or she understands. Knowing the child as an individual also means being aware of his or her background and past experiences. Knowing what objects are familiar in and around the home, what types of toys are used, and what particular needs and wants exist provides an appropriate basis for vocabulary building.
- *Provide language instruction around real situations.* Children need to interact with different objects and people in a variety of settings for new concepts and ideas to be meaningful to them. For example, children need to learn how to give directions from home to school and back so that they can relate this to

the bus driver or another teacher. Children should also be encouraged to share their own interests, hobbies, and family customs with the other children in the class.

- *Delay the use of standardized tests until the child has gained proficiency in English.* Or, administer such tests in the child's native language.

Techniques for the dialectically different child. Dialect refers to the way people speak in different parts of the country or in different social classes. Many children speak a dialect (black English or Spanish English) as opposed to standard English. The variations that become apparent in pronunciation, grammar, and vocabulary are a matter of difference rather than defect or deficit (Hendrick 1980). For example, a black child may say, "Go wif him." This form of pronunciation does not indicate a speech problem. This child is simply using the same pronunciation as the adult standard speakers in his community (Hendrick 1980). Figure 8–7 represents some of the more common phonological, syntactical, and vocabulary divergencies found between nonstandard dialects and standard English.

While nonstandard dialects are not considered language deficits, they may give rise to difficulties in many communicative efforts (Wood 1976). The best classroom recommendation seems to be that teachers should know about and respect the linguistic divergencies of the dialectally different child while also making it possible for the child to learn standard English (Hendrick 1980). Of utmost impor-

FIGURE 8–7
Common Dialectical Divergencies

Standard English	*Nonstandard English*
Phonological Differences	
head	haid
poor	po'
something	sumpin'
that	dat
get	git
other	udder
going	gon
right	rat
Syntactical Differences	
We have two dogs.	We have two dog.
He walks fast.	He walk fast.
She looked all over for you.	She look all over for you.
The books were right here.	The books was right here.
Tim is here.	Tim be here.
We are late.	We be late.
Vocabulary Differences	
They rapped (knocked) for a long time.	They rapped (talked) for a long time.
Can you dig (lift dirt) that?	Can you dig (understand) that?

tance in the communication process is the realization that content is more important than form. To children, constant correction of form may be construed as rejection. If children feel their communication efforts are being rejected, incentives to pursue verbal interaction are likely to be minimal.

SURVIVAL SKILLS

The ability to communicate effectively is perhaps the most important part of a youngster's survival kit (Wood 1976). As a survival tool, language helps children master concepts that enable them to cope with the world and with other individuals. The ability to communicate well also allows children to exert some influence over the course of their own lives.

To the educationally handicapped learner, language instruction becomes relevant and meaningful when related to basic skills needed for everyday living. The following language development activities, grouped according to receptive and expressive language behaviors, are suggestions for making language instruction relevant to real-life situations. It is important for teachers to realize that many students come to school not knowing how to perform many of these tasks and therefore need formal instruction.

Receptive Language Skills

The teacher should focus on developing skills in following directions. Depending upon the student and the task, it may be unrealistic to expect the student to memorize a task. In such instances, appropriate coping strategies, such as taking notes for phone messages or elaborate directions, should be taught. The following are examples of activities for students learning how to follow directions:

- Have the student follow directions to familiar areas; for example, tell the student, "Return this book to the library and then wait for the rest of the class outside the art room."
- Ask the student to obtain directions to unfamiliar areas; for example, the student might telephone the public transit system to find out how to get from school to the nearby mall, park, shopping center, etc.
- Help the student follow directions for assignments in other classes as well as the special classroom. Since each teacher has a different style for giving classroom and homework assignments, it is critical that the handicapped student become aware of each teacher's style.

Develop an awareness of nonverbal messages that may or may not accompany verbal messages. In order to succeed within the mainstream of the regular classroom as well as the mainstream of life, handicapped students must learn the meaning and importance of nonverbal messages. Through role playing, the following can be demonstrated:

- how people sometimes get uncomfortable if others get too close, that is, invade their personal space

- how to read both positive and negative nonverbal messages
- how to use appropriate nonverbal cues
- how to develop an awareness of social sensitivities by having the handicapped student focus on perceiving and understanding the feelings of others
- how to create classroom dramas related to social situations peculiar to the handicapped student's peer group and rehearse appropriate behavior. For example, practice how to ask someone for a date or how to ignore rude remarks.
- how to teach students to observe specific behaviors within a variety of contexts and practice appropriate skills. For example, by listening to and observing another teacher's behavior, the handicapped student can learn when and how to ask for assistance.

Expressive Language Skills

Have the handicapped student practice using language in a variety of social situations. For example, focus on the following:

- how to order from a menu
- how to use the phone for local and long-distance calls
- how to make both formal and informal introductions

When selecting classroom rewards for students, teachers should include activities, such as the game above, which involves listening and expressive language skills.

- how-to courtesies needed for specific social occasions, such as parties or school open houses

Emphasis on vocational needs should include the following:

- how to set up job interviews
- how to participate in a job interview
- how to ask for help or clarification of tasks while on the job

The importance of expressing one's feelings rather than ignoring them or handling situations in a physical manner can be demonstrated by role playing the following:

- appropriate demonstrations of positive feelings for family, friends, and acquaintances
- socially acceptable methods for expressing negative feelings
- procedures for expressing personal opinions or offering suggestions

Teaching handicapped students how to talk in a variety of social situations should focus on the following:

- giving directions, making announcements, and providing simple explanations
- reporting relevant and interesting information
- using appropriate gestures, intonations, and inflections to color meaning (loudness of voice, body language, etc.)
- sharing personal interests, hobbies, and experiences with adults and peers (in social and after-school interactions as well as in show-and-tell activities)

HOME REINFORCEMENT

Parental involvement is important in meeting the needs of the educationally handicapped child, especially in the area of language development. Bloom and Lahey (1978) state that appropriate home programs would substantially increase the chances of success in language learning. The following outline offers some suggestions for home activities that can foster language development:

- Make language experiences pleasurable. Language instruction that is charged with negative, forceful feelings is probably more detrimental to the child's language development than no instruction at all. Language instruction in the home works best if it is incorporated into the natural daily activities rather than scheduled for a set time.
- Interact with a child at his or her developmental level. Use vocabulary and syntax that are comprehensible to the child. Introduce materials and concepts that the child can easily understand.

- Provide many experiences for listening. Listening activities may include such things as carrying out instructions. This can be done in the form of a game. For example, say to the child: "Go to the kitchen. Look for a box on the table. Open the box and find a cupcake. You may eat the cupcake." Records of songs and stories can also be used to provide pleasurable listening activities in the home.
- Be a good model. Being a good model is one of the most important factors in teaching communication skills, yet it is frequently overlooked (Weiss and Lillywhite 1976). Being a good communication model means talking slowly and clearly. It also means having interesting things to talk about and using descriptive words. Good modeling involves eye contact, appropriate inflections, and natural gestures.
- Foster a need and desire to talk. Avoid letting older brothers and sisters do the talking for a younger child. Consistently reward the child's communication attempts and arrange situations in which the child needs to talk (for example, have the child ask for a desired object instead of automatically giving it to the child).
- Provide verbal stimulation throughout the day. Verbal stimulation involves a lot of talking around the child. Talk about objects, actions, and feelings. Talk about the characteristics and functions of different items. Comment on the environment and ways in which the child is experiencing it; for example, "The wind is blowing hard today. See how it blows the leaves across the street?"
- Teach receptive language. Help the child associate words with objects, actions, and experiences. This necessitates many hands-on experiences accompanied by meaningful verbalizations. "Let me pour these seeds in your hand. See how small the seeds are? You may help me plant the seeds in our garden." Demonstrating the meaning of such words as *on, under, beside,* and *between* facilitates the child's understanding of them (crawl *under* the table, stand *on* the chair, etc.). For younger children, labeling or naming objects in the home or around the yard is a good activity for increasing comprehension. For older children, using unfamiliar words many times in meaningful contexts enhances understanding. Especially for children with learning problems, demonstration and repetition are essential in teaching receptive language.
- Use questioning techniques that encourage more than one-word answers. Children should be encouraged to share their feelings and experiences. Ideally, this should be done through the child's own expressions rather than through adult interpretation. "What did you do at the park today?" will usually elicit more language than "Did you have fun at the park today?"
- Involve the child in interesting home activities such as developing a scrapbook. The pictures and mementos in such a scrapbook could reflect the child's past experiences and special events (vacations, trips, school activities, pets, infancy, etc.). Such a scrapbook represents topics familiar and interesting to the child. Not only will the process of developing the scrapbook

encourage the child to comment on the different remembered activities, but the finished product will be something to go back to again and again and something to share with grandparents, teachers, and friends.

REGULAR CLASS INVOLVEMENT

There is much that the regular classroom teacher can do to facilitate the language development of the educationally handicapped student. What must be avoided above all else is the tendency to ignore the child with language problems. Often these children contribute little in the classroom; hence, the tendency may be to overlook their special needs. Sometimes their language problems may be manifested in inappropriate and often annoying communication attempts. Inappropriate communication behaviors may include talking too loudly, exhibiting domineering and uncooperative behavior, and frequently interrupting or ignoring the speaker (Bryan 1978). Such problems do not usually go away by overlooking them.

Providing a favorable emotional atmosphere is a critical factor in developing communication skills. Children and youth need to know that they are accepted and understood. They need to know that someone is interested in them as individuals with their own special needs, likes, dislikes, backgrounds, and experiences. They need to know that someone is willing to take the time to listen to them and respond to them.

To facilitate receptive language development, the regular classroom teacher should be aware of the auditory environment and how it can influence the child's ability to function. Some children are more easily distracted than others by extraneous noises. Such noises should be minimized.

Another technique that facilitates receptive language development is requiring adequate attending behavior on the part of the child. Simply pausing after calling on a child to give him or her time to tune in for the message is one way to encourage attending behavior. This means saying the child's name first, pausing, and then asking a question or giving directions. Requesting eye contact, repetition of the teacher's message, or acknowledgment of being addressed is another technique that may enhance comprehension. Additional techniques include the use of meaningful gestures, frequent repetition, simple sentence construction, and adjustment of rate and prosody.

To facilitate expressive language development, the regular classroom teacher can involve the child or youth in a variety of language activities. To avoid intimidating a child, choices can be given as to what role to play in such activities as puppet plays, group singing, role playing, panel discussions, and show-and-tell.

Grammatical errors made by a student in conversation can be corrected in an indirect manner. Instead of saying "Don't say 'they was,' " the teacher can simply rephrase the child's comments ("So they were coming to your house."). The classroom teacher can also encourage a child to expand on what he or she is saying by asking meaningful questions, such as "What happened next?" or "How did you feel about that?" It is important for the teacher to realize that such social conversations, far from being a waste of time, can greatly enhance the child's confidence and competence in effective communication.

SUMMARY POINTS

- Language can be divided into two main areas: receptive language and expresive language. Receptive language involves listening and refers to the comprehension of language. Expressive language involves speaking and refers to the production of oral language.
- Appropriate assessment of a child's oral language development necessitates an understanding of the normal language acquisition process and a familiarity with the basic components of language.
- Language consists of five main components: (1) semantics, or meaning, (2) syntax, or grammar, (3) phonology, or speech sounds, (4) morphology, or word forms, and (5) pragmatics, or usage.
- While standardized tests can be used to assess a child's oral language development, they should not be used as the sole determinants of a child's specific language-related strengths and weaknesses. Observation, criterion-referenced testing, and analysis of spontaneous speech should also be used in determining the language development needs of an individual child.
- Techniques found to be effective for language development include imitation and reinforcement, labeling, expansion, auditory training, effective questioning, and signing.
- Language comprehension can be facilitated by repetition, simple syntax, modification of rate, modification of prosody, and attention to the auditory environment.
- Children and youth with language difficulties need understanding, acceptance, and support. Language is a form of communication that depends on a nurturing environment and good models to imitate. A nurturing environment provides encouragement and positive reinforcment.

REVIEW QUESTIONS

1. Distinguish between receptive and expressive language. Briefly explain how these two areas are interrelated. Also, identify four remedial activities for each of the two areas.
2. Define the five basic components of language. Also state instructional activities teachers can use to promote their development within the classroom and the home.

SUGGESTED READINGS

Bloom, L., and Lahey, M. 1978. *Language development and language disorders.* New York: John Wiley & Sons.

deVilliers, J. G., and deVilliers, P. A. 1978. *Language acquisition.* Cambridge, Mass.: Harvard University Press.

Newcomer, P.L., and Hammill, D. D. 1976. *Psycholinguistics in the schools.* Columbus, Ohio: Charles E. Merrill.

Weiss, C., and Lillywhite, H. 1976. *Communication disorders: A handbook for prevention and early intervention.* St. Louis, Mo.: C. V. Mosby.

Wiig, E., and Semel, E. 1976. *Language disabilities in children and adolescents.* Columbus, Ohio: Charles E. Merrill.

Application: Lisa and Aloma

Presented below are the remedial strategies implemented in the two case studies discussed earlier in this chapter. The specific language deficits for each case are first reviewed as the basis on which the remedial strategies were planned.

Lisa

In the case of nine-year-old Lisa, the following conclusions were drawn:

- Receptively, Lisa had difficulty discriminating specific phonemes and comprehending certain vocabulary items such as prepositions, pronouns, and words with multiple meanings.
- Lisa's expressive language was especially poor in correctly naming objects and pictures and in understanding and using correct grammar.

To enhance Lisa's receptive language skills, Mrs. Corin, the resource teacher, first identified the specific phonemes giving Lisa the most trouble in terms of auditory discrimination. She found these to be /*m*/, /*n*/, /*b*/, /*d*/, /*t*/, /*th*/. Working on just one of these at a time, Mrs. Corin gave Lisa the following tasks to perform in sequence to remediate the discrimination deficit (Wiig and Semel 1976):

- Identify the word with the target sound (in the example below, the *t* sound) from randomly selected words given orally by the teacher. For example:

  box - toy - desk (*toy*)
  six - five - two (*two*)

- Decide whether a word containing the target sound (*t*) is the same as or different from a word paired with it. For example:

  time - time (*same*)
  take - make (*different*)

- Identify the position (initial or final) of the target sound (*t*) in word pairs. For example:

  time - lime (*initial*)
  pin - pit (*final*)

- Decide whether a sentence containing a word with the target sound (*t*) is the same as or different from a sentence paired with it. For example:

  I will take some cookies.
  (*different*)
  I will bake some cookies.

  The new *t*oy is near the desk.
  (*same*)
  The new *t*oy is near the desk.

For each phoneme, Lisa made a notebook. For example, Lisa's *T* book contained pictures from magazines of items with the *t* sound. Mrs. Corin and Lisa then created stories based on appropriate action pictures. For example, Lisa independently cut out a picture of a train moving through the mountains. Mrs. Corin's directions to Lisa resulted in the following dialogue:

Mrs. Corin: What do you see in this picture that has the *t* sound?

Lisa: A train.

Mrs. Corin: You are right, Lisa. The train is going fast. Who is on the train?

Lisa: My family. My cat, Tinkerbell. Us visit the zoo.

Mrs. Corin: We see many animals at the zoo. Tell me the names of some animals that have the *t* sound in them.

Lisa: A scary tiger. Oh! I know. Elephant has a *t*.

While they were talking, Mrs. Corin transcribed their words onto paper and put the story in Lisa's *T* book. Each *t* sound was underlined. Lisa then took her book home and, with her parents' assistance, read her story. Although the focus of this remedial activity was on developing an awareness of a specific phoneme, note how Mrs. Corin incorporated using correct grammatical structure, also a deficit for Lisa, into the lesson.

To help Lisa understand the meaning of pronouns, Mrs. Corin provided concrete demonstrations of noun-pronoun substitutions. For example:

> This ball was on the table. *It* rolled off the table. Did you see where *it* went?

She also employed various activities requiring Lisa to decide whether or not pronouns were used correctly. For example:

> Bob already left for school. *Him* rode the bus to school. (*incorrect*)
>
> I bought these flowers for you. Now the flowers belong to *me*. (*incorrect*)

One technique Mrs. Corin found successful in helping Lisa develop expressive language skills was that of sentence completion. This technique was especially effective in improving Lisa's use of syntactic structure (grammar). Activities included the following:

- Completing sentences with a specified tense:

  Yesterday, my brother and I . . . .
  Today, the neighbor . . . .
  Tomorrow, our class . . . .

- Completing sentences with prepositional or adverbial phrases:

  The owner of the store put the money . . . .
  The pitcher threw the ball . . . .

- Completing sentences beginning with various linguistic concepts:

  After the game, they . . . .
  Before we leave, we . . . .
  If it rains, we . . . .
  When the bell rings, everyone . . . .

Another technique used both in the classroom and at home was reciting poems to help Lisa enhance her intonation and fluency. Not only did Lisa enjoy reading them with an adult, but the poems (selected from Shel Silverstein's *Where the Sidewalk Ends* 1974) also served as a stimulus to discuss a variety of feelings.

These specific techniques represent only a few of the many approaches used in the classroom to meet Lisa's language development needs. The fact that Lisa's parents were so cooperative and capable was also capitalized on in the intervention program. One area that was strongly emphasized was building a background of experiences. Because Lisa had been seriously deprived of experiential learning during her early childhood years, her adoptive parents made special efforts to introduce her to a wide variety of firsthand experiences. They took trips to the farm, the airport, and the post office. They also involved Lisa in such activities as fishing, flying kites, picking apples, and making homemade ice cream. Lisa's parents were soon in the habit of providing appropriate words for these varied experiences. Such experiences enriched both Lisa's cognitive development and her linguistic skills.

Aloma

The following conclusions about Aloma's speech and language difficulties were drawn:

- Aloma's language problems encompassed both the receptive and expressive domains.
- Semantic, syntactic, and pragmatic deficits were obvious characteristics of Aloma's speech and language problems.

- Verb tense, words with multiple meanings, and the expression of abstract ideas presented special difficulties for Aloma.
- Due to her deficits in social perception, Aloma was frequently rejected by her peers and, at times, experienced a lack of sympathy from adults.

While Aloma was pleased with the regular class placement as she entered junior high, she also found the adjustment to be academically and socially quite difficult. The daily periods of individual tutoring were a welcome respite from the overall expectations of the junior high curriculum.

In an effort to remediate Aloma's speech and language problems, the following procedures were employed:

- *The special education teacher modeled the appropriate use of verb tenses.* Using a set of pictures, the teacher commented on the social action depicted. For example: "Maria is angry with her friend"; "These boys are laughing at the girl." After a few such pictures, the teacher asked, "What's happening in this picture?" The past and future tenses were also used but not interspersed with each other or with the present tense until considerable practice had been provided with each tense individually. Because Aloma's reading and writing skills at this point, although weak, were adequate for dealing with simple sentences, some of the practice with verb tense was written as well as given orally. For example, the teacher would say, "Tell me what's happening in the picture and then write a sentence about it." Pairing written and oral expression not only provided additional reinforcement but also involved other learning modalities (visual and kinesthetic).
- *Word identification activities for comprehension and vocabulary development were also used.* Word identification activities can take many forms and can be used with synonyms, homonyms, antonyms, word classification, etc. One example in working with synonyms is to present two sentences to the student and give him or her the task of deciding whether their meaning is the same or different. For example:

  Gwen made some very rude remarks to Joel.
  Gwen's words were not very nice. (*same*)
  Sylvia took the book back to the library.
  Sylvia lost her library book. (*different*)

- *Aloma's teacher also used sentence construction activities to illustrate the multiple meanings of certain words.* For example, after identifying a multiple-meaning word (such as *broke*), the teacher constructed a set of sentences illustrating its different meanings (Heilman 1972). The same subject could be used to start each sentence, as in the following examples:

  Tom broke his arm.
  Tom said, "I'm broke."
  Tom broke the No Swimming rule.
  Tom broke his previous running record.
  Tom broke in his new shoes.

- *The tutor also helped Aloma rehearse socially appropriate verbal behavior using role playing and modeling.* Aloma was comfortable with the tutor and enjoyed discussing various experiences, concerns, and feelings with her. The tutor capitalized on this eagerness to share ideas and feelings. At times she taped and then transcribed Aloma's speech. This gave Aloma the opportunity to analyze her own oral language skills. The topics of these conversations allowed the tutor to select social situations that Aloma said she wanted to improve. For example, Alisa was a student who continually taunted Aloma. Typically Aloma would retaliate with comments such as "You bitch" or "Alisa, you and your friends are prejudiced." The special educator and Aloma discussed several alternative ways of handling these situations. They agreed that the best plan of action was to ignore Alisa's hurtful comments and decided to chart the daily effects of ignoring Alisa's behavior. Within two weeks Alisa had stopped insulting Aloma.

Other situations that they rehearsed included practicing how to ask a teacher for help in the classroom and how to invite a girlfriend to spend the night. Over a four-week period, the tutor and Aloma rehearsed choosing a friend to ask, asking the friend over, and planning appropriate activities. After some coaching, Aloma decided to ask her friend to spend the night and participate in one Mexican-American holiday activity. The tutor, recognizing that it was equally important for Aloma to retain her heritage as it was to fit into the mainstream of the dominant culture, waited for Aloma's report on this special weekend. Apparently the intensive planning and rehearsal paid off—Aloma was invited to spend the night at her friend's house the following weekend.

Discussion Points

1. Lisa's parents were very interested in playing an active role in her language development program. In addition to the suggestions outlined in the text, what other ideas would you have for actively involving Lisa's parents in the intervention program?
2. Aloma frequently experienced rejection and isolation in the junior high setting. What techniques and/or procedures might be implemented by her teachers to assist Aloma in making a more positive adjustment to this new social and academic setting?

CHAPTER 9 Developing Social and Behavioral Skills

OUTLINE

INTRODUCTION

Academic failure tends to adversely affect a student's social and emotional well-being, resulting in negative behavioral patterns that often persist even after the student becomes academically successful (Algozzine 1979). Thus, a major responsibility of special educators is the fostering of appropriate social and behavioral skills in the educationally handicapped student.

Appropriate social and behavioral skills on the part of handicapped students can make a critical difference in how successful they will be in a mainstreamed setting. Too often only the academic performance of handicapped students is evaluated to determine readiness for regular class instruction; yet research indicates that some factors, such as reflection and impulsiveness, that differentiate mildly handicapped students from their normal peers (Brent and Routh 1978; Epstein, Cullinan, and Sternberg 1977; Hallahan, Kauffman, and Ball 1973) are related to social skills and can be remediated through social skill training (Berger 1981; Brown and Conrad 1982).

Objectives

After reading this chapter you should be able to

- identify informal assessment procedures to determine a student's social and behavioral instructional needs;
- write a behavioral plan as a guide for instruction in the social domain;
- use a variety of techniques to record behaviors and behavioral change observed in students;
- apply behavioral principles to help students to strengthen or learn appropriate social and behavioral skills;
- use therapeutic techniques to help students learn more about themselves or to teach social skills;
- identify skills students need to acquire in order to survive in a variety of habitats;
- work with parents in nurturing students' social skill development;
- support the regular educator in fostering appropriate social and behavioral skills.

Case Studies: Rick and Charlotte

Rick

Ms. Chamberlin sat talking with the building principal at Pinehurst Junior High, where she would begin her new position as the special education teacher. As their conference drew to a close, Mr. Felts, the principal, said, "I don't think you'll have any problems with your students, Ms. Chamberlin, with the exception of Rick."

Later as Ms. Chamberlin was working in her classroom, Mrs. Greenburg, one of the other teachers at the junior high, introduced herself and proceeded to discuss some of the students enrolled in the special program. Her parting comments were: "You seem to have a quiet, controlled manner. I'm sure you'll have better luck with this class and, in particular, Rick Brigham. The teacher last year had a terrible time coping with him." While resting in the teachers' lounge later in the day, Ms. Chamberlin thought back to Mr. Felts's and Mrs. Greenburg's comments about Rick. Even though she hadn't met him, Ms. Chamberlin was beginning to think that it would require more than a quiet, controlled manner to help him.

On reviewing Rick's cumulative record, Ms. Chamberlin found that Rick had been placed in the special education program because of serious behavior disorders. According to anecdotal reports, he physically attacked peers, destroyed school and peer property, verbally abused authority figures, ran away from school, ate garbage from the dumpster, and was unable to attend to instruction and complete independent tasks. The *Revised Behavior Problem Checklist* (Quay and Peterson 1983) indicated that Rick exhibited poor work habits, dogmatic behavior, verbal negativism, and disturbance and restlessness. Three of Rick's teachers were asked to observe his classroom behavior and then complete the *Behavioral Academic Self-Esteem Rating Scale* (Coopersmith, 1981). As a result, all three teachers independently concluded that Rick was having difficulty working independently in the classroom and was constantly demanding inappropriate attention from his peers and teachers.

Rick's behavior on the first day of class confirmed information gathered through review of assessment data. Shortly after entering the room, Rick began pinching another student and responded to Ms. Chamberlin's command to stop the behavior with, "Why? Larry likes this." During the remainder of the morning, Rick continued to antagonize other students, slept or daydreamed, and refused to complete any assigned tasks. After observing all her students during the first week, Ms. Chamberlin realized that Rick's social and behavioral deficits were interfering not only with his own progress but also with the other students' work. She concluded that the well-being and productivity of everyone, including herself, would require changes in Rick's behavior.

Charlotte

Charlotte Adams was a small, quiet, five-year-old kindergarten student. She was the only child in a professional family; her mother was a nurse and her father a physician.

At first, the kindergarten teacher, Mrs. Phillips, was not concerned about Charlotte's quiet manner, perceiving such behavior as a typical pattern of school adjustment. One October day, however, Mrs. Phillips noticed Charlotte huddled in a corner of the building during the recess period. As Mrs. Phillips approached, Charlotte edged away, almost as if to avoid speaking with the teacher. Mrs. Phillips decided to observe Charlotte more closely.

As observations of Charlotte's behavior accumulated, Mrs. Phillips's lack of concern changed to alarm. Charlotte was not speaking to peers in the classroom or on the playground. She would not initiate conversation with adults and, when spoken to, responded with short phrases. Charlotte's nonverbal behaviors included wringing her hands, biting her fingernails, and standing with her head lowered and gaze averted. Mrs. Phillips decided to refer Charlotte for assessment.

As a part of the assessment process, the school special education supervisor, Mr. Russell, paid a visit to Charlotte's home. During this home visit, Mrs. Adams reported that Charlotte's older sister, Susan, had died from leukemia the year before. During Susan's illness, the family had been under great strain due to Susan's need for frequent hospitalization. Charlotte was often rushed off to a neighbor's or her grandparents' home during these emergencies. Mrs. Adams reported that Charlotte didn't complain or resent being left with others. In fact, she commented that Charlotte responded in a very mature fashion and tended to be quiet and cooperative during those times.

A part of the home visit was devoted to completing a social adjustment instrument, the *Behavior Rating Profile* (Brown and Hammill 1978). An analysis of this profile seemed to support Mrs. Phillips's concluding statement on the referral for assessment form: "In my opinion, Charlotte is shy to the point of being withdrawn and troubled about something."

Mrs. Phillips also completed a social adjustment instrument, the *Devereux Elementary School Behavior Rating Scale* (Spivack and Swift 1967). Analysis of items on this scale indicated that while Charlotte was self-sufficient in daily-life skills, she lacked skills in areas of self-direction, communication, and socialization.

Results of perceptual, academic, and cognitive assessment indicated that Charlotte was functioning normally, with an above-average ability for academic tasks. Results of social-emotional assessment, however, created a profile of a shy and withdrawn child.

At the placement conference for special education services, Charlotte's parents were in attendance. Based on a review of assessment results, the psychologist, Mrs. Phillips, Charlotte's mother, and the special education supervisor supported the recommendation for counseling and for part-time special education placement to help Charlotte better adjust to school. Charlotte's father, however, disagreed. He said that he could not justify her placement in a special class or counseling on the basis of shyness. He indicated that Charlotte would adjust if people would stop making such an issue of her behavior. Everyone at the meeting was shocked by the intensity of the father's response.

After further discussion and Mr. Russell's encouragement for compromise, the team recommended continued placement in the kindergarten class for Charlotte, with consultation between the regular teacher, Mrs. Phillips, and the special education teacher, Mrs. Blake, to help Charlotte adjust to the school environment and develop more positive social skills.

Points for Consideration

- *Rick's behavioral patterns aroused feelings of helplessness and anxiety in Ms. Chamberlin before she ever met him.*

Often students with behavior disorders adversely affect individuals within their environment. An ecological understanding of this phenomenon is critical to the well-being of professionals working with behavior disordered students. Just as certain variables in the environment prompt students to develop unacceptable behavioral patterns, those behavioral patterns tend to adversely affect the mental health and, at times, the behavior of adults with whom they come into contact (Curran and Algozzine 1980; George and Main 1979). Strong support exists for using a team approach to managing behavior problems such as Rick's. Through team effort, variables that prompt inappropriate behavior in each ecosystem can be altered. Additionally, team support tends to decrease the emotional strain professionals experience in their work with behavior disordered students.

■ *Students with behavior problems exhibit aggressive acting-out behaviors.*

Behavior disordered students exhibit an array of behaviors along an overcontrolled-undercontrolled continuum (Edelbrock 1979). Those behaviors range from shyness and withdrawl associated with overcontrol, as seen in Charlotte, to aggressive and impulsive behavior associated with undercontrol, as observed in Rick. Often students who are shy or withdrawn go unnoticed because their behaviors do not have the shock value of those students who are aggressive; yet without appropriate intervention, these behavioral patterns tend to become worse and finally reach a point where they can no longer be ignored (Gold and Gargiulo 1980).

COMMON INSTRUCTIONAL MISCONCEPTIONS

Children with behavior disorders respond best to various counseling techniques. While counseling, play and art therapy, and bibliotherapy are helpful procedures commonly used for students with inappropriate behavioral patterns, behavioral strategies must also be used to teach specific social skills. Simply helping students explore their feelings through counseling or therapeutic techniques without teaching them to develop improved social skills is ineffective (Kauffman 1981).

Students with behavior disorders are manipulative and can change their behavior if they really want to do so. Personal insight into one's behavioral patterns is not a sufficient condition to alter these patterns (Bandura 1973). At times, specific behavioral strategies are needed to provide structure for altering inappropriate behavioral patterns. Students identified as having behavioral problems often require the expertise of special educators trained to analyze and promote positive behavioral and social skills.

ASSESSING SOCIAL SKILLS

Appropriate intervention for students with behavior disorders begins with assessment in a wide range of environments in order to identify the origins of behaviors and to develop plans to modify those behaviors. While both formal and informal procedures are used for placement consideration, informal procedures are frequently used to measure student progress and the effectiveness of intervention strategies.

Formal Assessment Tools

The use of formal assessment instruments is critical to the complete development of an accurate profile of student strengths and weaknesses in the area of social skills. Brief descriptions of several formal assessment instruments are given below.

The *AAMD Adaptive Behavior Scale, Public School Version* (Lambert et al. 1975) measures the adaptive and social behavior of students in a school setting. Designed for use by teachers and other school personnel, scale items are clustered according to areas of maladaptive behavior, such as withdrawal, rebellious behavior, and violent and destructive behavior. This test was standardized by type of educational placement (regular classes, special classes for the mentally retarded, and resource room programs for the educationally handicapped); by sex; and by ethnic status.

The *Vineland Social Maturity Scale* (Doll 1965) is used to measure performance ability on specific skills in individuals from birth through adulthood. Items are clustered into eight categories: general self-help, eating self-help, dressing self-help, locomotion, communication, occupation, self-direction, and socialization. Through interviews with an adult, such as a parent or teacher, the individual's performance ability is established.

The *Behavior Rating Profile* (Brown and Hammill 1978) assesses students in first through twelfth grade to distinguish those students with behavior problems from those with learning disabilities. The profile encourages an ecological assessment since it utilizes information from the student being assessed, parents, teachers, and peers in a variety of settings. The profile identifies settings in which social skill deficiencies are observed as well as those in which deficiencies are not observed.

There are three different Devereux scales that can be used for assessing social skill development. The *Devereux Child Behavior Rating Scale* (Spivack and Spotts 1966) evaluates behavior of emotionally disturbed and mentally retarded children between eight and twelve years of age. Items cluster around seventeen factors such as social aggression, unethical behavior, need for adult contact, and emotional detachment. The *Devereux Elementary School Behavior Rating Scale* (Spivack and Swift 1967) assesses behavior problems of students in kindergarten through sixth grade. Items cluster around factors such as classroom disturbance, impatience, withdrawal, and inattention. Items on the *Devereux Adolescent Behavior Rating Scale* (Spivack, Spotts, and Haimes 1967) cluster around factors such as poor emotional control and peer dominance. This scale assesses students aged thirteen through eighteen, and items relate to the adolescent's behavior toward adults and peers in a school setting.

The *Behavioral Academic Self-Esteem (BASE) A Rating Scale* (Coopersmith and Gilberts 1981) is a descriptive assessment tool used by professionals to obtain an estimate of the academic self-esteem of individual students. The professional's judgments of the frequencies of several important behaviors form the basis of the student's score. These judgments are based on specific behaviors of the student in the classroom. The different areas of behaviors assessed on this rating scale are: student initiative, social attention, success/failure, social attraction, and self-confidence.

The *Tennessee Self-Concept Scale* (Fitts 1965) is used with adolescents to measure their perceptions in six areas: family self, moral-ethical self, personal self, physical self, self-criticism, and social self. Students respond through a five-point Likert scale. Analysis of student response provides information across social settings.

The *Revised Behavior Problem Checklist* (Quay and Peterson 1983) measures student behavior along four dimensions: conduct disorders, personality disorders, inadequacy/immaturity, and socialized delinquency. This instrument can be used for a student in kindergarten through eighth grade by any adult knowledgeable of the student's behavior. A forced-choice response of "not observed," "observed but mild," or "observed and severe" is recorded.

Informal Assessment Tools

Social skills training must be tailored to the needs of each student. Teachers must understand the types of skills to be assessed and subsequently determine which students require instruction over specific social skills. Informal procedures are designed to familiarize special educators with basic social skills and help them to observe and record student behavior in a variety of environments through the use of anecdotal records, behavioral charts, student interviews, check lists, and questionnaires.

Scope and sequence of social skills. Figure 9–1 presents a check list of social skills (based on information from Goldstein 1974; Silverman, Zigmond, and Sansone 1981) that may be used to guide teachers in the informal assessment of such skills.

Anecdotal reports. An **anecdotal report** is a precisely written narrative of an observation of a student's behavior. Advantages of anecdotal records are that they allow the teacher to observe environmental antecedents and responses to the student's behavior. Further, when such reports are written on a regular basis, the teacher can often substantiate specific behavioral patterns (Stephens, Hartman, and Lucas 1978).

☐ **FIGURE 9–1**
Scope and Sequence of Social Skills

Personal Skills	Deficient –	Instruction /	Mastery *
States name			
Identifies written name			
States classmates' names			
Introduces self			
Writes name			
Discriminates personal name from others			
Discriminates by sex, age, size			
States address, phone number			
Writes address, phone number			
Dials home phone number			
Classroom Skills			
Identifies classroom			
Discriminates between common and personal objects in classroom			
Demonstrates care of classroom and personal possessions			
Explains difference between borrowing and taking			
Demonstrates appropriate strategy for borrowing			
States location of specific areas of school; classroom, cafeteria, restroom, library			
Locates common areas of school: classroom, cafeteria, restroom, library			
Interpersonal Skills			
States instances when people need help: illness, injury, lost			
Recognizes need for help for basic needs, for protection			
Recognizes need for comfort			

☐ **FIGURE 9–1—continued**
Scope and Sequence of Social Skills

Interpersonal Skills—continued	Deficient –	Instruction /	Mastery *
Identifies objects and individuals who provide comfort			
Accepts and provides comfort			
Recognizes situations when help is needed			
Solicits help			
Provides help			
Explains importance of rules			
Recognizes consequences of broken rules			
Follows class rules			
Defines emotions; e.g., anxiety, fear, joy, happiness			
Defines qualities; e.g., hard working, kind, bright			
Predicts behavior based on individual's qualities			
Chooses friends based on individual's qualities			
States abilities/limitations of self and others			
Indicates understanding of individual sensitivity regarding limitations			
States consequences of attack on individual's limitations			
Recognizes nonverbal expression; sadness, fear, embarrassment, happiness, anger			
States possible causes for happiness, anger, sadness, fear, embarrassment			
Communication			
Defines communication			
Effectively gains attention of teacher, peers			
Initiates conversation appropriately with adults, peers			
Effectively listens to peers or adults			
Uses appropriate gestures when speaking or listening			
Interaction with Peers			
States supportive role of peers			
Develops guidelines for communicating respect; e.g., using person's name, recognizing others' emotions, giving assistance, sharing personal and community objects			
Describes situations in which cooperation is necessary			
Displays cooperative behavior by suggesting ideas or supporting those of others			
Uses good manners; e.g., "please", "thank you", "may I", "pardon me"			

☐ **FIGURE 9–1—continued**
Scope and Sequence of Social Skills

Interaction with Teachers	Deficient –	Instruction /	Mastery *
Makes eye contact when talking with teacher			
Maintains eye contact with teacher during instruction or when getting directions			
Uses nonverbal response that communicates interest			
Thanks teacher for help			
Takes class notes			
Follows teacher directions for use of time			
Raises hand			
School Behaviors			
Begins assignments promptly			
Completes assignments			
Arrives on time to class			
Locates information in texts			
Studies for tests			
Completes tests efficiently			
Brings appropriate materials to class			
Follows classroom rules			
Follows school rules			

There are also disadvantages to using anecdotal records. When written in a haphazard manner, they often lead to inappropriate assumptions about a student's social strengths and weaknesses and the frequency with which behaviors occur. Special educators can avoid this error by observing the following guidelines:

- Note the time, activity, location, day of week, and date when the observation occurred since these variables affect the student's behavioral response.
- Describe the behavior observed in specific, observable terms rather than global statements that call for interpretation. For example, "Matthew hits children in the rest room" is more definitive than "Matthew is aggressive."
- Observe and record student behaviors on a regular basis to document behaviors that are typical of the student's response.
- Observe students in a variety of settings, such as other classes, the lunch room, the hall, and during independent activity, since different social settings carry different expectations for behavior.

- Note and identify information received from a secondary source. Such information can provide clues as to why a student behaves in a particular manner. To maintain thorough standards of documentation, always note who the reporting source is.
- Note events that precede and follow particular student behaviors. These behavioral stimuli (events that precede) and antecedents (events that follow) provide valuable program-planning information.

Behavioral charts. When behavior patterns have been identified and documented through systematic observation, the special educator typically charts such behaviors to gain further understanding relative to their frequency and duration. Frequency refers to how often a behavior occurs within some prescribed time interval while duration refers to the length of time over which a behavior occurs.

A frequency chart can assist teachers in understanding behaviors that occur regularly. Examples of such behaviors are beginning mastery tasks, out-of-seat behavior, hand-raising behavior, or destruction of others' belongings. Duration charts may be used to record such behaviors as temper tantrums, eye contact, attending to mastery tasks, crying, or whining. Note that charting behavior should not be restricted to the inappropriate behaviors observed in students.

The type of intervention planned for the student varies with the student's behavior and its rate of occurrence. Therefore, the first step in planning intervention strategies is to establish the base line by observing and recording the frequency of the behavior prior to intervention. If the frequency of the behavior under observation is estimated to be only a few times a week or day, teachers may use paper and pencil to record its occurrence. If the behavior occurs at a high frequency, a counter or stopwatch may be used. In addition, for high-frequency behaviors, teachers may apply a time-sampling system of observation to gather base line data. For example, if Brad's teacher wants to estimate the frequency of his out-of-seat behavior, she may observe for ten-minute intervals at different times over a four-day period and average the number of times out-of-seat behavior is observed (see Figure 9–2). Later, when the teacher begins to intervene to alter this behavioral pattern, the intervention strategies are evaluated against the average number of instances of out-of-seat behavior in a ten-minute interval.

From the base line data presented in Figure 9–2, Brad's teacher could determine that prior to intervention Brad was involved in out-of-seat behavior on an average of five times per ten-minute period. After intervention, instances of out-of-seat behavior decreased markedly at first, then returned to preintervention frequency, and finally tapered off to a more acceptable level. From such data, the teacher could conclude that the intervention strategies were effective in decreasing Brad's out-of-seat behavior. The phenomenon of out-of-seat behavior returning to base line level after an initial period of intervention is a typical pattern often noted in behavior modification efforts.

Q-sort technique. The **Q-sort technique** is an assessment tool developed by Stephenson (1953) that can be used in connection with student interviews

☐ **FIGURE 9–2**
Frequency Chart Depicting Brad's Out-of-Seat Behavior

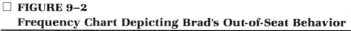

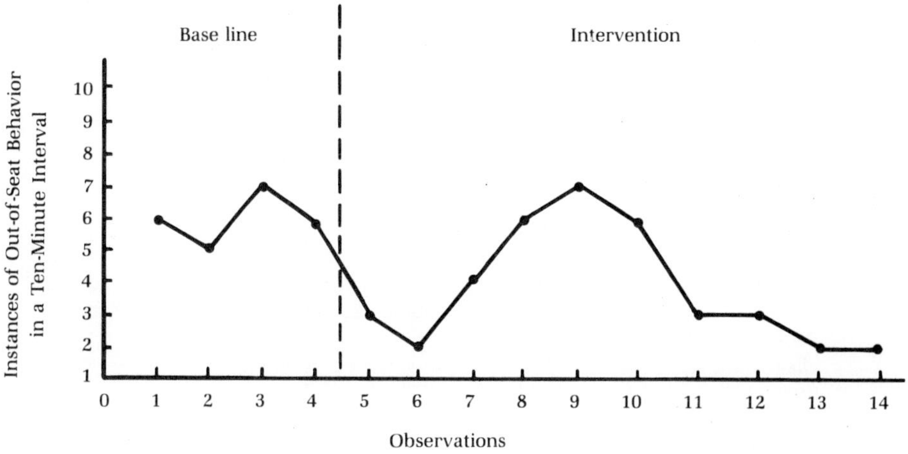

for determining targets for behavioral intervention. The Q-sort technique is based on the theory that discrepancies exist between an individual's real self and ideal self (Kroth 1975), and that identifying those discrepancies will be helpful in understanding an individual's special social development needs. When used with student interviews, this technique can be beneficial in promoting student self-determination of behavioral goals.

One way to implement the Q-sort technique is to give the student a deck of cards, each of which contains either a positive or negative descriptive statement. The student is then asked to rank each statement on a form board (as shown in Figure 9–3) along a continuum from "most like me" to "most unlike me." Listed below are examples of card items that can be used with the Q-sort technique.

Fails to hand in homework	Earns poor grades
Skips class	Has many friends
Is rude to teachers	Throws objects in class
Gets along with teachers	Finishes work
Completes work accurately	Makes noises in class

During the first time through the deck of cards, the student is instructed to rank each descriptive statement according to how he or she would most *like* to be. When the student has ordered the cards on the form board, the teacher copies the student's response. Next, the student is asked to rank the cards again on the basis of how he or she really is. The teacher copies this list next to that describing how the student wants to be (see Figure 9–4). To avoid confusing the student, it is wise to allow some time between the two sorting tasks. During a conference with the student, both teacher and student can select those behaviors valued by the student as the focus for intervention.

☐ FIGURE 9–3
Target Behavior Formboard

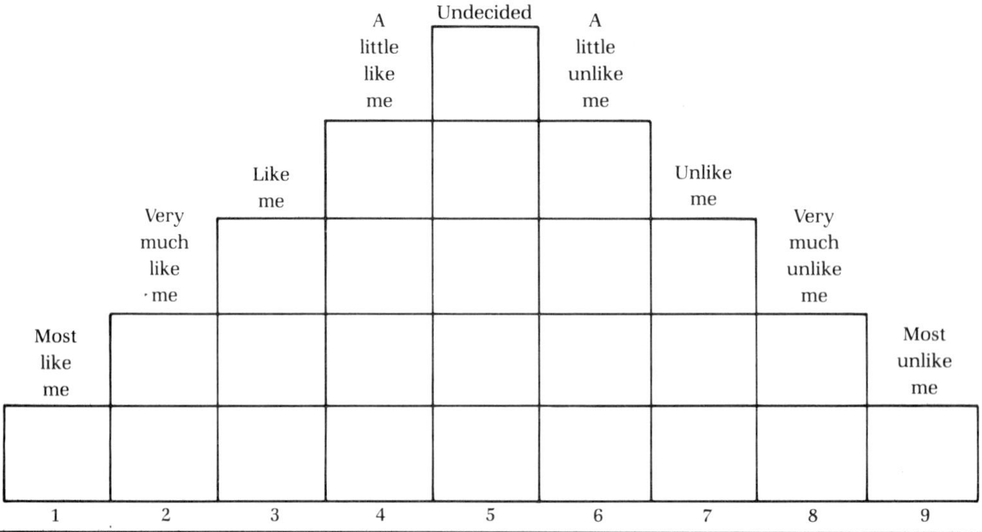

From R.L. Kroth, *Communicating with Parents of Exceptional Children: Improving Parent Teacher Relationships.* (Denver: Love Publishing Company, 1975), 44.

The Q-sort technique requires a certain amount of student maturity and is therefore recommended for students above ten years of age. Parents and teachers can also use this technique as a basis for comparison of adult perceptions of the student (Kroth 1975). For example, Ms. Lane, a special education resource room teacher, may want to find out what the parents' perception of their child in the classroom is and how this perception compares to her own and to the child's. By involving the parents in a Q-sort ranking of descriptive statements about their child's classroom behavior and comparing the results with her own and the child's ranking of such behaviors, Ms. Lane can identify those areas warranting further discussion and intervention.

Self-Report. Check lists and questionnaries completed by students provide them with opportunities to participate in the assessment process. Although self-reports are subjective and dependent on students' understanding of themselves and willingness to share information, involving students is critical to the successful implementation of any planned strategies.

With check lists, students are typically asked to indicate or describe their behaviors. For example, students may be asked to place a check mark next to each item in a list that they agree describes them, such as "gets mad easily" or "finishes homework."

A questionnaire is a variation of a check list, in which the student identifies responses to questions along a continuum. The advantage of a questionnaire is that students who can read but may not be able to express themselves verbally can be presented with a range of responses (see Figure 9–5).

Open-ended questionnaires require a written response from students. One special educator working with adolescents used information gathered through the questionnaire shown in Figure 9–6 for program-planning purposes.

FIGURE 9–4
Comparison of Real and Ideal Self

Ideal Sort	*Real Sort*
Earns good grades	Fails to hand in home work
Gets along with teachers	Earns poor grades
Completes work accurately	Skips class
Finishes work	Has many friends
Arrives on time to class	Is rude to teachers
Reads well	Reads well
Ask questions in class	Asks questions in class
Has many friends	Makes fun of others

As indicated earlier, the special educator begins planning social instruction by assessing student strengths and weaknesses. When this phase of instruction is completed, the teacher is charged with the responsibility of remediating or teaching new social behaviors. Knowledge of behavioral principles for instruction in the domain of social skills helps the teacher to meet this responsibility.

FIGURE 9–5
Behavioral Questionnaire

	Like me	*Sometimes like me*	*Not like me*
1. I have many friends.			
2. I can't get to sleep at night.			
3. I let others know I am upset when I lose.			
4. I have to solve my own problems.			
5. I have parents who are as nice as my friends' parents.			
6. I can't do many things well.			
7. I worry that bad things will happen.			
8. My parents punish me for little things.			
9. I need a lot of help.			
10. I earn good grades in school.			
11. I always get what I want.			
12. I feel tired a lot.			
13. I enjoy daydreaming.			
14. I let others decide what I will do or play.			
15. I think that most people are fair.			
16. I am often sick.			
17. I like to play by myself.			
18. I do not cry often.			
19. I am good at many things I do.			
20. I usually feel well.			

☐ **FIGURE 9–6**
Open-Ended Behavioral Questionnaire

1. I would like to be ________________
2. I would like to have ________________
3. I want my mother to ________________
4. I want my teacher to ________________
5. I do not like to ________________
6. I want my father to ________________
7. I want my friends to ________________
8. I want my sisters and brothers to ________________
9. More than anthing else, I ________________
10. Reading is ________________
11. I wish I could ________________
12. I want my family to ________________

BEHAVIORAL PRINCIPLES

Behavioral principles used in schools today are commonly attributed to the work of Skinner (1953), who postulated that since all behavior is learned through interaction with the environment, the arrangement of environmental variables can prompt the learning of new behaviors. In fact, behavioral principles have been used successfully to remediate behaviors associated with hyperactivity (Pelham 1980), distractibility (Hallahan et al. 1978), impulsiveness (Pitassi and Offenbach 1978), aggression (Switzer, Deal and Bailey 1977), withdrawal (Tarpley and Saudargas 1981), and delinquency (White and Snyder 1981).

Teacher knowledge, creativity, skill, and experience are required for successful application of the following behavioral principles. Further, success is also dependent upon teachers' willingness to modify their own behavior.

Reinforcement

A **reinforcer** is an event, desired object, or privilege that follows a behavior and results in an increase in that behavior. Reinforcers are typically clustered in two categories: tangible and social. Tangible reinforcers are such items as peanuts, candy, fruit, stickers, certificates, field trips, and free time. Social reinforcers include praise statements, hugs, smiles, and gestures.

Many teachers rely exclusively on social reinforcers to change student behavior. However, tangible reinforcers are sometimes needed with students exhibiting moderate to severe behavioral deficits or with students who, due to developmental needs, respond more favorably to them. When tangible reinforcers are used, it is critical that the teacher pair them with a social reinforcer and phase them out as soon as the student begins to respond to social reinforcement (Dorow 1980). The major goal when using any behavioral principle is to help students to shift from an external to an internal locus of control, that is, to direct themselves appropriately rather than rely on others to direct them.

Whether tangible or social reinforcers are used, appropriate selection is a critical factor for students who are learning to be self-directive. The student's age and level of maturity and the behavior targeted for intervention must be considered when selecting the type of reinforcers as well as the most appropriate schedule of reinforcement for the student. Students who are allowed to choose the type of reinforcement they will earn have a significantly higher rate of performance of the behavior being reinforced than those students whose reinforcement is chosen by others (Karraker 1977; McLaughlin 1976). Teachers can involve students in the selection of reinforcers in a variety of ways. A reinforcement menu, which is a list of possible reinforcers, can be presented for student choice. Also, individual stu-

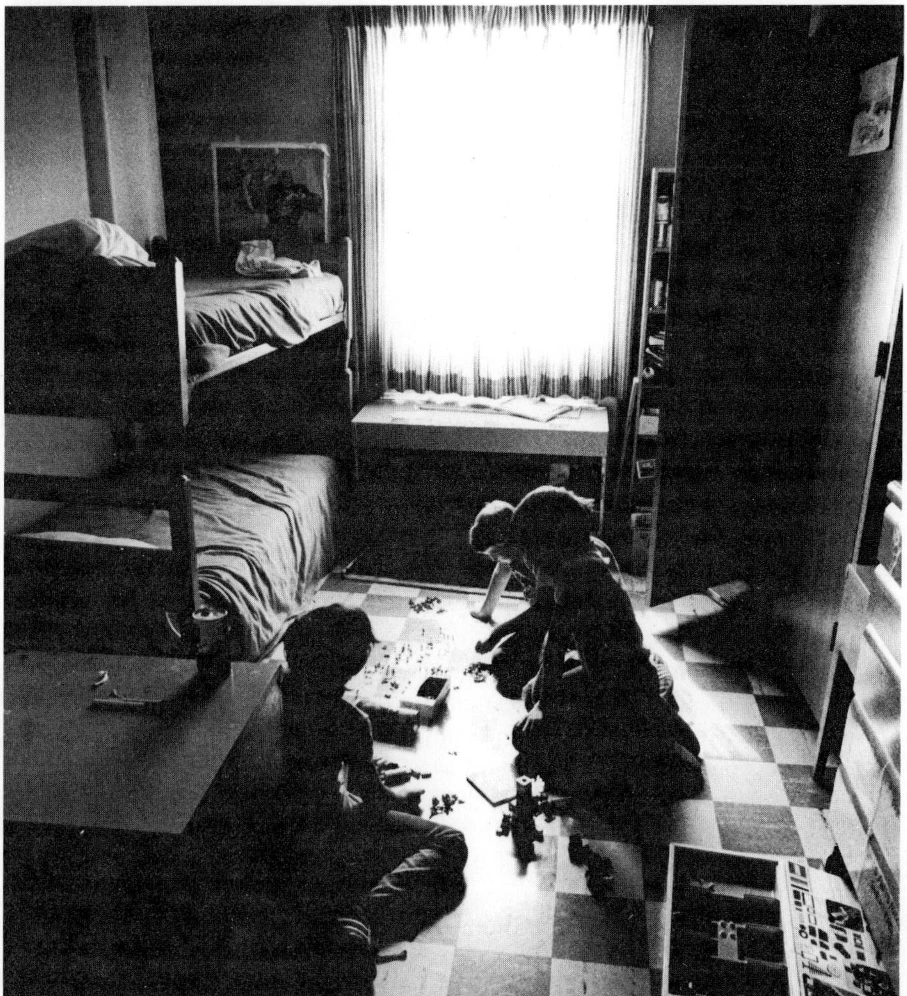

Everybody needs to feel like they are part of a group. Effective instructional programs consider a student's academic as well as affective needs.

dent conferences allow students to share ideas of what is pleasing to them. Frequently teachers observe students to ascertain the types of experiences or events they find reinforcing.

Just as students can learn social skills, so too can teachers learn to use reinforcers effectively. The following are suggestions for developing this teaching skill:

- Use quality reinforcers. Often teachers find that frequent use of praise, smiles, or gestures becomes monotonous and thus ineffective. By focusing on the behavior to be rewarded, this pitfall can be avoided. For example, continual statements like "Good job" are bound to be less effective than "John, that's a clever solution. Thanks for showing me another way to look at the problem."
- Be sure that only the desired behavior is being rewarded. Sometimes we unintentially reinforce inappropriate behaviors. If ten-year-old Mark never raises his hand before answering questions and the teacher says, "Now Mark, what do you have to do before I call on you?" it is likely that the teacher has reinforced the undesired behavior of calling out the answer. After the teacher realizes that calling attention to the undesired behavior is, in fact, reinforcing the student for such behavior, the next logical step is to ignore the undesired behavior, thereby withdrawing the reinforcer. This process of withdrawing the reinforcer is called **extinction**.

One problem related to extinction is that of ignoring many appropriate behaviors along with the inappropriate behaviors. Unfortunately, those students who are least likely to practice appropriate behavior are the students most likely to be ignored by teachers when they do practice appropriate behavior (Foster, Ysseldyke, and Reese 1975; Glidewell 1969; Lippit and Gold 1959; Taylor, Terrell, and Terrell 1981; Thurman 1977). To avoid this pattern of interaction, teachers should condition themselves to observe and attend to these children more frequently.

According to Axelrod (1977), there are several factors limiting the effectiveness of extinction. For example, if the teacher deliberately ignores specific behaviors of a student but classmates do not, the student may continue to receive sufficient reinforcement to maintain the behavior. Further, certain behaviors may be in and of themselves reinforcing. Talking to friends, daydreaming, or drawing pictures are examples of behaviors that can be inherently reinforcing to students. A third limitation is that behaviors that are ignored will initially increase in frequency. One explanation of this phenomenon is that the student can no longer accurately predict environmental responses to a behavior and so tests them by emitting the behavior more frequently. When the unknowledgeable or inexperienced teacher observes an increase in the frequency of the inappropriate behavior, that teacher may abandon the use of extinction as ineffective. In any case, the teacher certainly is not being reinforced for his or her professional efforts. However, it is advised that the teacher continue to use extinction because the increase in the inappropriate behavior is typically of short duration. After the student has repeatedly tested the environment and found that the teacher will ignore his behavior consistently, the frequency of the behavior is likely to begin to decrease.

Of course, behaviors that are clearly dangerous to the health and safety of students cannot be ignored by the teacher; yet with persistence the teacher can ignore and teach peers to ignore the majority of inappropriate behaviors observed in a school setting.

Prompting Behavior

Teachers often must deliberately arrange variables within the environment to encourage or **prompt** students to practice a new behavior. The seating arrangement, number of problems to be completed, and distance between the teacher and student are all examples of environmental variables that can be rearranged to prompt appropriate behavior.

Special educators can also facilitate desired behaviors by using appropriate cues or stimuli that require the student to focus on the teacher. For example, if a teacher determines that it is important for a student to maintain eye contact with the teacher when directions are given, the teacher may use one or all of the following environmental cues, depending upon the student's needs: eye level, a statement directing the child to look at the teacher, physical proximity to the student, or holding the student's face while giving directions.

When a desired behavior is intermittent, the strengthening of the behavior is more likely to occur when teachers use cues to prompt the behavior.

Shaping Behavior

When the teacher has arranged environmental variables to prompt occurrence of a specific behavior, the next task is to **shape** or mold that behavior until the student is able to practice it for the required amount of time without teacher intervention. One way of doing this is to use a behavioral technique called **fading,** in which the teacher gradually reduces the reinforcement as the student's skill for self-control increases. For example, if a teacher is working to help a primary student begin and finish computation of ten math facts before turning to some other activity, the teacher may initially use himself as a cue by sitting next to the student and saying, "David, find the sum of the first problem and then go on to the second problem." When David has complied, the teacher gives him a token and reinforces him by saying, "You're learning to concentrate on your work until it's finished." When behavioral charts indicate improvement, the teacher deliberately changes the prompt. Now David will be asked to concentrate on the task for the length of time it takes to compute sums of three problems, and the teacher will leave his side while he works.

Careful attention must be given to the use of fading procedures so that a student does not revert to emitting the undesired behavior. Special educators are often the most powerful environmental cues and can use a combination of voice, proximity to the student, and gestures to prompt and ultimately shape a behavior.

Punishment

Punishment is an aversive consequence that causes a decrease in a specific behavior. Typically punishments used in school can be grouped into psychological, physical, and deprivation domains. While psychological and physical punishments are not acceptable, these types of punishment are sometimes used by teachers reacting emotionally rather than professionally to student behavior. An awareness of the effects of certain behaviors on mental health as well as frequent consultation with special education supervisors and school psychologists can help teachers to avoid using psychological and physical punishment.

Punishment that falls in the category of deprivation can be effective in reducing inappropriate behavior when used judiciously. **Response-cost** and **overcorrection** are two types of deprivation punishment that have been found effective (Foxx and Azrin 1973; Gresham 1979).

When using *response-cost* as a form of punishment, the student is made to pay for certain behaviors with something of value. For example, the student may be given ten tokens that can be redeemed for regularly scheduled free time. However, if the student begins using foul language with peers, then one token is forfeited; as a result, the student loses two minutes of free time.

When using a response-cost strategy, the special educator's goal is threefold: to help the student understand that behavior has consequences; that the student has a choice about how to behave; and that the student, not the teacher, controls a behavior. Each of these points should be clearly understood by the student. The special educator using a response-cost approach gives the student a set of tangible objects, such as poker chips, to remind the student of these three goals. While such objects are redeemable for a reinforcer, they also serve to remind the student of consequences, choices, and with whom responsibility for a behavior lies.

When *overcorrection* is used as punishment, the student is required to make restitution for his or her inappropriate behavior. The student may also be required to practice a competing behavior following emittance of an inappropriate behavior. For example, the student who steals another's baseball mitt may be required to reimburse the other student for the full cost of the mitt plus an additional token sum for any inconvenience caused by the theft. Another example of the effective use of overcorrection is requiring the student who uses obscenities to apologize to all who heard them. Some teachers have misinterpreted the application of overcorrection and, as a result, have required students to practice inappropriate behaviors repeatedly. Such demands on students are ill-advised because they prompt feelings of anger and hostility and do not allow students to learn more acceptable behavioral responses.

BEHAVIORAL PLAN

After assessment and with an understanding of how to use behavioral principles in the classroom, the next step to teaching appropriate behavioral and social skills is the development of a behavioral plan. A behavioral plan not only serves as an objective means for identifying a student's behavioral needs but also facilitates the well-being of the special educator. Often handicapped students disturb the mental health and well-being of those around them just as the ecological system of these students has distorted their mental health (Curran and Algozzine 1980). As the teacher experiences the stress or anxiety that can accompany interaction with such students, the teacher's perceptions of their behavior may become distorted.

A behavior plan consists of a list of inappropriate behaviors observed in a student, related competing behaviors for each inappropriate behavior observed, possible reinforcers, and a shaping schedule. In effect, it is a lesson plan for instruction in social skills (see Figure 9–7).

To construct a behavioral plan, inappropriate behaviors are identified through assessment. These are listed in descending order of importance on the plan. Typically behaviors affecting the safety of the student or peers are given priority. Otherwise, those behaviors that occur most frequently are given priority because these behaviors are likely to have an adverse effect on others who must live and work with the student.

Step two in the construction of a behavioral plan is to write a related competing behavior for each inappropriate behavior identified. Simply defined, a com-

☐ **FIGURE 9–7**
Behavioral Plan

Student: Martha

Target Behavior: Martha will remain seated at her desk for 15-20 minutes during independent work periods.

Inappropriate Behavior	Related Competing Behavior
1. doesn't finish assignments	1. Completes all assignments
2. wanders around the room	2. remains seated at desk
3. interrupts other students	3. remains quiet during work periods

Possible Reinforcers

1. lunch with the teacher
2. praise-o-gram to parents (daily)
3. extra free time (3-5 minutes daily)
4. teacher praise at 3-5 minute intervals
5. story time with the principal

Shaping Schedule for Selected Target Behavior

1. 10:00 - 10:20; Sit near Martha and verbally remind her to stay seated—verbal praise at 3 minute intervals followed by 3 minutes free time for 12 minutes compliance.
2. 10:00 - 10:20; Sit near Martha and verbally remind her to stay seated - Praise at 4 minute intervals followed by 4 minutes of free time for 16 minutes compliance.
3. 10:00 - 10:20; Sit near Martha and remind her of the rule to stay seated. Praise at 5 minute intervals followed by 5 minutes of free time for 15 minutes compliance.
4. 10:00 - 10:20; Sit near Martha but DO NOT remind her of the rule to stay seated. Praise for compliance on random schedule. - Note to parents for 15-20 minutes compliance.
5. 10:00 - 10:20; DO NOT sit near or remind Martha of rule to stay seated. Reinforce for compliance on a random basis. Lunch with me for 18-20 minutes of compliance for one week.

☐ **FIGURE 9–8**
Examples of Inappropriate and Related Competing Behaviors

Inappropriate Behavior	*Competing Behavior*
Talks without permission	Raises hand for permission to speak
Uses foul language when angry or frustrated	Says "I feel angry because . . ." or "I feel frustrated when . . ."
Fails to complete any independent assignments	Completes all independent assignments

peting behavior is one whose performance prevents the occurrence of the corresponding inappropriate behavior. Figure 9–8 illustrates related competing behaviors for a variety of inappropriate behaviors commonly observed among students.

Following the description of competing behaviors, the teacher focuses on reinforcers that may be used to increase and maintain target behaviors. Social and tangible reinforcers to be used should be described in this section. Further, the schedules for such reinforcers should also be noted here. Later, when the teacher is ready to implement the behavioral plan, he or she should consult with the student in the final determination of reinforcers to increase the odds that the reinforcers will encourage the student to abandon the inappropriate behavior for the related competing behavior.

The final step in a behavioral plan is the shaping schedule. At this stage the special educator determines the steps that will be used to teach the first of the competing behaviors, the acceptable approximations of that behavior, and when and under what conditions the behavior will be taught. For example, social skills can be taught in an artificial environment and generalized by students to other situations (Matson et al. 1980). Optimally behaviors are taught under the conditions in which they normally should occur. For example, if Edward needs to learn to arrive on time to his seventh-period math class, the special educator should teach him that skill by accompanying him to the class. Each phase of the shaping schedule should place increasingly more responsibility for performance of the behavior on the student. Accordingly, cues and fading procedures are noted in the shaping schedule.

While several behaviors may be targeted for instruction on a behavioral plan, the teacher typically chooses only one at a time for instruction so that the student does not become confused or the teacher's efforts splintered. When the student has learned the first of those behaviors targeted for instruction, new shaping schedules are designed to teach other competing behaviors as required.

STRATEGIES FOR DEVELOPING SOCIAL SKILLS

Fenichel (1974) wrote, "We have demonstrated that the specially-trained teacher can be the most effective therapeutic agent in the life of an emotionally disturbed child and that a program of special education can result in growth in social, emotional, and behavioral as well as academic areas" (p. 73). Those special educators who are successful in helping the educationally handicapped student learn accept-

FIGURE 9–9
Contingency Contract

I, ______________________ agree to ______________________
student's name

____

from ______________ to ______________ at ______________
date date time

for which I can earn ______________________________________.

My teacher agrees to help me by ______________________________

____.

____
student's signature

____
teacher's signature

able social skills approach their task in a deliberate, methodical fashion, believing that the development of appropriate social skills is critical for independent functioning.

Many handicapped students exhibit behaviors, such as hyperactivity, impulsiveness, and distractibility, which interfere not only with learning but also with developing positive peer relations and interpersonal skills. Remediation of these deficits is contingent on the teacher's ability to choose from or combine a variety of instructional strategies. Strategies commonly used by special educators to promote social development are described below.

Contingency Contracts

A **contingency contract** is a written agreement between the teacher and student that a desirable event can be earned in exchange for performance of a less desirable behavior (Homme and Tosti 1971). An example of a contract is illustrated in Figure 9–9.

Contingency contracts are based on the work of Premack (1959), who discovered that there is an increase in the frequency of a less-preferred activity when it is followed by the opportunity to perform a more-preferred activity. Teachers who are aware of the Premack principle can often apply it through careful arrangement of the syntax of their language. For example, a senior high teacher may say, "If we can finish this discussion, there may be some time available to work on the homework assignment together." Contrast the above statement with, "If you people don't quiet down, you'll have to figure out your homework assignment on your own."

Stephens (1977) suggests that the following guidelines be used for developing contingency contracts:

- The behavior required in the contract must be specific in nature.
- Reinforcement should be stated in the contract and should be agreed upon by student and teacher. It should be available only for the required behavior.
- Through discussion the teacher and student should determine the behavior to be practiced, when and where the behavior is to be practiced, and the amount of behavior to be practiced.

When making schedules and instructional grouping decisions, teachers should consider the behavioral and social needs of their students.

- The teacher should initially prompt and watch for the behavior as agreed in the contract and then reward the behavior immediately if contract terms are met.

If the teacher plans thoroughly and has realistic expectations, contingency contracts are a viable method for helping a student or group of students develop appropriate behaviors.

Token Systems

Tokens are items such as poker chips which have no intrinsic value in and of themselves but which become valuable because they can be accumulated and redeemed for something valued by a student. Special educators have often used **token systems** with good results for a variety of target behaviors with a wide range of student populations (Alexander and Apfel 1976).

The key to successful use of a token system to teach target behaviors is thorough planning (Blackham and Silberman 1980). The following guidelines are helpful in successfully implementing a token system:

- Target behaviors should be clearly specified.
- Tokens should be given as soon as the student produces the target behavior.
- The number of tokens earned should correspond with the effort required for performance of a behavior.

- Tokens earned should be charted on a daily basis by the teacher and student as added incentive.
- Praise should always be combined with delivery of tokens so that eventually social reinforcement alone will maintain target behaviors.
- Reinforcers for which tokens may be redeemed should be obtainable only through performance of targeted behaviors or compliance with rules established through observation of student behavior.
- The token system should be functional; that is, it should not interfere with academic activities.

For beginning teachers, token economies are more likely to be successful if they are initially used for a selected time period each day. Also, it is easier to develop an effective token economy when the teacher has to concentrate on observing only one target behavior.

Life-Space Interviewing

Life-space interviewing was developed by Fritz Redl (1959) as an approach to talking with students about their behavior in a therapeutic manner. It allows the teacher to talk with a student about the events of a critical situation by focusing on what happened, why it happened, and what different options the student could use in future, similar situations. Morse (1971) suggests the following steps in using the life-space interview technique:

- Allow each student to state his or her impression of the event.
- The teacher assumes an active listening, uncritical role while asking questions to determine how accurate each student's version of the incident is.
- The teacher encourages the student to solve the problem, making suggestions only if the student cannot come to agreement.
- The student and teacher develop a plan for solving future, similar problems.

When the teacher assumes an active listening role, the students can safely release anger and frustration without fear of reprisal. It is more likely that students will solve problems in a socially acceptable manner when such a climate prevails. Alley and Deshler (1979) have suggested the following guidelines for special educators attempting to create a climate of acceptance:

- Communicate warmth, concern, and acceptance. Removing physical barriers, making frequent eye contact, and softening your voice can communicate these feelings.
- Remain aware of differences between students' values and your own. Do not judge students' values through such statements as, "I would never . . . ," "I think . . . ," "I'm shocked . . . ," "You should know better."

- Indicate limits of confidentiality. Just as most teachers would not feel obligated to report everything students tell them, it is also true that teachers should not adhere to total confidentiality. Teacher awareness of an adolescent suicide threat is an example of a situation in which teacher confidentiality could be life threatening.
- Refer students with problems beyond your competence to professionals with greater skill and training, such as guidance counselors, school psychologists, or psychiatrists.
- Be an active listener. Active listening is demonstrated by paraphrasing what your students say and by nonverbal gestures such as nodding your head and maintaining eye contact.
- Record, in written form, key factors presented by the student for recall during the solution stage of a conference.
- Give the student feedback supported by facts. For example, a teacher might say: "I don't think you feel well liked by kids at this school. You said, 'In the cafeteria, other kids' friends call them to sit by them, but no one ever asks me.' " Be specific and factual without alienating the student.
- Avoid use of judgmental terms such as "should," "right," and "wrong."
- Offer an opinion only if asked.
- End the conference with a positive comment.

Role Playing

Role playing allows the student to solve problems as well as explore and express feelings and emotions. It allows students to practice appropriate skills in a non-threatening environment or to explore feelings associated with some situation or event. In addition, work by O'Connor (1969) and, more recently, Bornstein, Bellack, and Hersen (1977) indicates that role playing is an effective approach for social skills training when an instructional component is included in the process. The teacher using this strategy to teach social skills can use the following guidelines to initiate role playing:

- Identify a problem or conflict without reference to specific individuals in the class.
- Establish roles and assign various students to these roles. If possible, allow students to volunteer for various roles.
- Allow students to role play the situation.
- Follow the role play with discussion focusing on behaviors rather than on particular students.
- Repeat the role play to encourage identification of different solutions.

For example, Ms. Patterson recently learned that one of her students was extorting money from other students. She decided to use role playing as an approach to discussion of this behavior. She began by saying: "Sometimes kids will ask for money and say that if they don't get it, they'll beat you up. I need two volunteers who can show the class how this happens." After several students had assumed the roles of victim and extortioner, Ms. Patterson asked: "What feelings did you have for the victim? How would you feel as a victim? What kinds of feelings did you have for the extortioner?" Next, Ms. Patterson asked for volunteers to play a victim who knew how to refuse the threats of an extortioner. At a later date, Ms. Patterson privately taught students she knew to be victims of extortion those responses they had seen modeled for them by peers during the class role play.

An unbiased attitude on the part of the teacher is an important component in the success of the role-play technique. Teachers should also be willing to participate in a role-play situation to motivate students and generate enthusiasm, realism, and spontaneity among students. Often students who are typically nonverbal will become actively involved and share their feelings when allowed to assume a character who is one step removed from reality.

Timeout

Timeout consists of removing a student from the immediate environment to one in which visual and auditory stimuli are markedly reduced (Sherman 1973). Because the timeout strategy deprives students of opportunities to interact with the environment, it should be used only when students signal through their behavior that they cannot respond to a situation in a nonaggressive manner. Ethical use of this approach implies that it be restricted to instances in which peers and teachers are at risk of physical injury. Timeout is not intended to be used as punishment, although if mismanaged, it can become punitive in nature (Solnick, Rincover, and Peterson 1977). The following guidelines can assist the special educator in using this strategy for the purpose for which it was developed, that is, helping students bring themselves under control:

- Remove the student to a timeout area only for acts potentially damaging to others.
- Avoid locating the timeout area in the same room where students spend most of their time to minimize humiliation.
- Allow the student who was placed in timeout to return to the group after he or she has maintained quiet for three to five minutes. This practice communicates to the student that the purpose of timeout is to help regain control over oneself rather than to punish.

Milder forms of timeout can be used for students who are distractible or impulsive. For example, a student might be encouraged to complete a task in a carrel, which limits his visual exposure to materials and activity in a classroom. If a teacher thinks a conflict is imminent, Long and Newman (1971) suggest that the student be allowed to leave the classroom on the pretext of running an errand for the teacher.

When timeout is used, teachers should take care to communicate the idea that its use is intended to aid the student. For example, the teacher might say something like: "Linda, I think you are having a hard time reading your assignment. Why don't you go to the carrel, where you'll be less distracted, to finish it."

Teachers should also encourage students to determine for themselves when to use timeout. Some students reach the point where they can monitor their behavior and move to a carrel as necessary. Teacher reinforcement of this type of self-direction encourages students to take appropriate responsibility for their behavior.

When punishment is used to reduce the occurrence of inappropriate behavior, it must be carefully planned so that it leads to increased appropriate behavior and does not humiliate or prove injurious to students. It is advisable that the decision to use punishment strategies be made and planned by a team of individuals to insure a positive behavior change. Further, punishment will not produce a permanent behavioral change when used without a method of reinforcement (Bandura 1969).

Programs for Social Skill Training

Special and general education teachers as well as parents may wish to use a commercial program to teach specific or general social skills. Generally these programs are designed to enhance self-image and provide students with opportunities to learn specific or general social skills.

On the elementary level, examples of commercial social skill programs are the *Developing Understanding of Self and Others* (DUSO) kits (Dinkmeyer 1973) and *Self-Control Curriculum* (Fagen, Long and Stevens 1975). The *DUSO* kits are divided into two levels, D-1 and D-2, for primary grades and upper primary through fourth grades respectively. The D-1 kit emphasizes concepts such as understanding self, feelings, others, independence, purposeful behavior, mastery, and competence. The D-2 kit explores themes such as self-identity, interdependence, friendship, self-reliance, and making choices. Both kits include puppets, posters, role-playing cards, stories, and songs. Typically a problem situation is presented followed by role-playing activities.

The *Self-Control Curriculum* presents eight curricular themes such as anticipating consequences, managing frustration, relaxation, inhibition, and delay. Each theme contains an introduction, rationale, goals, objectives, and suggested learning activities. Teachers can use any or all curricular areas. The curricular activities are designed to help students develop emotional and cognitive skills, reduce disruptiveness, and develop self-control skills.

The *Transition* program (Dupont and Dupont 1980) is designed for students in grades six through nine. Goals of the program are to help students cope with various social and emotional situations. Five units—communication and problem-solving skills; openness and trust; verbal and nonverbal communication of feelings; needs, goals, and expectations; and increasing awareness of values—are structured around program goals. The program includes cartoon posters, cassettes, duplicating masters, script booklets, illustrations of facial expressions, and discussion and feeling cards. Activities are designed to be used sequentially.

Examples of programs for adolescents are *School Survival Skills Curriculum* (Silverman, Zigmond, and Sansone 1981) and *Deciding for Myself: A Values-Clarification Series* (Paulson 1974). The *School Survival Skills Curriculum* focuses on three areas: behavioral control, teacher-pleasing behaviors, and study skills. Goals of the program are to provide explicit instruction in social skills to help students function responsibly and independently.

Deciding for Myself: A Values-Clarification Series (Paulson 1974) is divided into three sets: "Clarifying My Values"; "My Everyday Choices"; and "Where Do I Stand?" Students in sixth through twelfth grades as well as adults are guided to examine their values and corresponding behaviors in a variety of settings and situations. The series contains a teacher's guide and ten units within each set.

SURVIVAL SKILLS

Following are social skills students should acquire to be accepted by their peers as well as by adults within a variety of environments. Teachers can develop these skills using the techniques previously discussed. These suggestions are based on the work of Cartledge and Milburn (1978) and Stephens (1978). For primary and intermediate levels, students should learn how to

- greet peers using appropriate language;
- listen to another's comments;
- accept and reinforce ideas or suggestions of peers;
- initiate games or activities among peers;
- maintain friendships over long periods of time;
- maintain eye contact with others to communicate attention;
- ask teachers or adults for assistance when necessary;
- communicate gratitude for adult help;
- accept unpleasant events, such as assignments, without complaining;
- respond to failure through the use of problem-solving techniques;
- finish assignments;
- follow teacher directions;
- comply with teacher requests;
- volunteer to answer questions.

For junior and senior high levels, students should learn how to

- select as friends those individuals who have appropriate social skills;
- develop and maintain friendships among peers;
- resist socially inappropriate or illegal peer practices;
- detect and practice school behaviors to which secondary teachers respond positively, such as class participation;
- reinforce secondary teachers for their assistance;

- accept direction from persons in authority, such as teachers or employers;
- respond to failure or challenge by using problem-solving skills.

HOME REINFORCEMENT

If handicapped children are to acquire social skills that will allow them to build and maintain a responsive and accepting emotional climate for themselves, close cooperation between parents and special educators is necessary. Teamwork increases the likelihood that students will generalize appropriate social skills to a variety of ecosystems in their environment. Parents can guide their children in developing social and behavioral skills through the following activities:

- Provide a routine at home that includes reasonable time allocations for television, interaction among family members, homework, and maintenance activity. For example, do not allow the television to be turned on until one hour after dinner to encourage family members to participate in some constructive activity. Parents may need to put some structure on their own behavioral patterns to encourage routine and a balance of activity among their children.
- Expose the child to literature that focuses on emotional and social issues relevant to the student. Public or school librarians can help to locate such literature.
- Develop and maintain communication. Specific times for communication with the child should be set aside each day. By playing games with adolescents or regularly reading stories to younger children, parents communicate to children that they have exclusive time with their parents to talk. Also, maintaining the ritual of the evening meal as the time when the family gathers together can encourage communication.
- Model self-acceptance and reinforcement through such statements as "I really made a big mistake, but I can fix it," or "I'm glad I got that job done. It looks great!"
- Develop the habit of making praise statements to the child several times each day, typically after he or she has finished some assigned task in the home.
- Communicate respect for the child's contributions through such terms as "please" and "thank you." Adults often rely on young children to run errands. Since adults would be thanked for such activities, it is important that children be given the same respect.
- Provide exposure to various social situations through trips to restaurants, sports, and cultural events. Parents should discuss their expectations for the child's behavior prior to the event and perhaps role play these expectations with their child.
- Model the expression of positive as well as negative feelings for the child with statements such as "This makes my angry," or "I'm glad to get such good news." Such statements provide the child with appropriate examples of emotional release.

- Set the child's expectations for less desirable activity through such statements as "You will need to begin to set the table in fifteen minutes," or "We have time for one more badminton game before getting ready for bed."
- Use behavioral principles such as shaping and reinforcement to teach responsibility. For example, a ten-year-old student can first be encouraged to finish mowing one-half of the back yard; gradually parents can give more responsibility for yard work. Special educators should encourage active application of these principles in the home by teaching parents to use them and consulting regularly with them regarding the problems and success parents may encounter (Walker and Shea 1980).
- Accept arguments between siblings as normal but maintain rules against physical aggression. For example, parents may say something like "Use words," or "Why don't you handle that problem by speaking to your brother about it?"

REGULAR CLASS INVOLVEMENT

Regular and special educators should be in close communication for appropriate development of social skills among handicapped students. When such communication occurs, there is greater opportunity for students to begin to generalize these skills. Some strategies the special education teacher may suggest to the regular classroom teacher in attempting to help the handicapped student develop effective social and behavioral skills include the following:

- Ignore inappropriate behavior when possible.
- Reinforce a specific behavior on a daily basis. When the teacher provides attention to class participation, for example, the student is more likely to repeat such behavior. Small notes to oneself in a plan book will remind the teacher to attend actively to one or two behaviors that a student needs to develop.
- Seat the student among a group of students who model appropriate attending and work behavior. A student seated among better students has more opportunity to observe and practice appropriate skills.
- Include the handicapped student in the development of any plan for changing his or her behavior. Talking about misbehavior does little to help the student change. The student must see a need for change, want to change, and have a basic plan for going about making the change.
- Be realistic in expectations of behavioral change in a student. Expect and accept approximations of a desired behavior during early stages of its development.
- Use frequent verbal and nonverbal cues to prompt a new behavior in the student. For example, if a teacher wants a shy child to talk in class discussion, the teacher might tell the student that he or she will be called upon and give the student the question and its answer.

- Develop a chart with the student to record progress in acquiring a new behavior. This technique not only gives most students some motivation but also provides the teacher with opportunity to praise and encourage individual students.
- Focus on development of one behavior at a time. When the teacher and student try to alter too many behaviors at one time, both can become confused.

SUMMARY POINTS

- Assessment of a student's social skills is accomplished through direct observation, record keeping, and student involvement in addition to standardized assessment tools.
- Since student involvement is critical to the success of any intervention strategy devised by the teacher, it is prudent to initiate such involvement during the assessment stage.
- Prior to implementing any intervention strategy for social and behavioral skills, the special educator should develop a written intervention plan to maintain an accurate perception of student progress and to avoid a splintered approach to instruction in this area.
- Behavioral intervention, including reinforcement, punishment, prompting, and shaping strategies, is effective with children exhibiting aggressive and withdrawn behavioral patterns.
- Token economy and contingency contract systems are structured behavioral programs that incorporate reinforcement, shaping, and prompting strategies. Such programs require the teacher to modify his or her behavior in the process of assisting the student.
- Punishment alone does not effect a permanent behavioral change in students. In addition, psychological or physical punishment can have an adverse effect on a student's emotional and physical well-being.
- Certain types of punishment, particularly those related to deprivation, are used in combination with reinforcement to effect a behavioral change.
- Role playing and life-space interviewing are techniques used to help students acquire appropriate social skills. These techniques require the teacher to develop active listening skills and a nonjudgmental demeanor.
- Special and regular education teachers sharing responsibility for a handicapped student should maintain close communication and cooperate to focus jointly on identifying and meeting a student's social skill requirements.
- The major goal when using any behavioral principle or social skill strategy is to help the student shift from an external to an internal locus of control.

REVIEW QUESTIONS

1. One of the eight-year-old students in your class continues to disturb peers by scribbling on or tearing up their written work. After each incident, you have repeatedly explained to the student that this behavior is wrong. What action might you take to change this student's behavior?
2. A student in one of your secondary classes exhibits the following behaviors: tardiness one period per day, failure to begin homework assignments, rude remarks to teacher directions, and sleeping in class. Construct a behavior plan for this student and justify your selection of the first behavior targeted for intervention.

SUGGESTED READINGS

Kauffman, J.M. 1981. *Characteristics of children's behavior disorders.* 2d ed. Columbus, Ohio: Charles E. Merrill.

Meichenbaum, D. 1977. *Cognitive-behavior modification: An integrative approach.* New York: Plenum.

Bandura, A. 1977. *Social learning theory.* Englewood Cliffs, N.J.: Prentice-Hall.

Application: Rick and Charlotte

Rick

Based on analysis of formal and informal assessment data and observation of Rick, Ms. Chamberlin outlined the following social skill deficits:

- Rick's approach to problem solving consisted of physical and verbal confrontation.
- Rick viewed offers of teacher assistance negatively.
- Rick reacted to persons in authority with hostility.
- Rick's response to academic tasks was nonproductive.

Ms. Chamberlin developed the behavioral plan shown in Figure 9–10 by writing each of the above deficits in behavioral terms. She planned to focus first on the target behavior noted in the plan.

Ms. Chamberlin combined use of the life-space interview and role-playing strategies in the behavioral plan. For example, when Rick returned to her class following an in-school suspension for fighting with another student in the cafeteria and hitting a teacher who had tried to intervene, Ms. Chamberlin asked Rick to tell her why he had decided to fight with the student. As Rick began to talk, Ms. Chamberlin listened without interrupting or providing her

FIGURE 9–10
Rick's Behavioral Plan

Student Rick
Target Behavior ______

Inappropriate Behaviors	*Related Competing Behaviors*
1. Rick attacks students who call him names.	1. Rick will use an appropriate verbal response when students call him names.
2. Rick interrupts peers in the classroom.	2. Rick will keep his hand to himself and mouth closed unless given permission to speak.
3. Rick responds negatively to offers of teacher assistance.	3. Rick will answer yes when the teacher offers help.
4. Rick hits teachers when they attempt to control his outbursts.	4. Rick will obey teacher directions.
5. Rick does not complete independent work.	5. Rick will complete independent work.

Possible Reinforcers
1. Free time
2. Right to leave room at first dismissal
3. Praise statements: "That's realistic"; "Good job"; "I'm glad you can control your temper"—continuous schedule (reinforcing the student for each performance of the target behavior)
4. Lunch at a favorite restaurant
5. Homework exchange coupon

opinion of his conduct. Next, Ms. Chamberlin asked Rick if his decision to punch the other student for calling him a "special" had helped him avoid more problems for himself at school. Rick said that the suspension was worth it and that he was not going to let other kids get by with that. Ms. Chamberlin pointed out that the other student involved had not been given a suspension and asked Rick if there were other ways of responding that he could accept but would help him avoid trouble with school authorities. Rick said he could not think of any other approach to use. At that point, Ms. Chamberlin told Rick she had a few ideas and asked Rick to consider working privately with her.

Two days later, Ms. Chamberlin approached Rick with the idea of working on the improvement of his social skills. He said he would give it a try. She and Rick instituted several role-playing sessions that focused on alternative responses to use when students provoked him. Initially, Rick assumed the role of provoker, and Ms. Chamberlin played Rick. When Rick called her a name, she responded, "Buzz off." Gradually roles shifted, and Rick played himself until response became automatic and realistic. Ms. Chamberlin reinforced each of Rick's responses. Then Ms. Chamberlin shifted to the cafeteria, hallways, and gym for practice sessions. She also gave Rick feedback regarding the realism of his response.

Throughout the school year, Ms. Chamberlin kept a private journal in which she jotted her thoughts and personal impressions of her work. As Ms. Chamberlin reviewed journal notes, she recalled the fear and anxiety she had felt when first working with Rick. As she reread one of her latest entries, she was pleased at how her feelings had changed. The entry read: "If the truth were known, Rick is one of my favorite students. He keeps me on my toes, but at least he is reasonable if approached with respect. I think he's changed for the better, and I'd like to think I had something to do with that. At least I'm not afraid of him anymore."

Charlotte

Following the placement conference for Charlotte, Mrs. Phillips, the kindergarten teacher, and Mrs. Blake, the special teacher, met to plan intervention strategies. The focus of the intervention program was to increase Charlotte's interaction with her peers. The following strategies evolved from their discussion:

- Mrs. Phillips would use puppets in role-playing sessions depicting shy children. Emphasis would be on why some children are shy, how friends interpret shy behavior, and how shy children can become more involved.
- Several of the outgoing students in Charlotte's class would be trained to hug or greet her in the morning and to take her hand to involve her in their playground games.
- Mrs. Phillips would spend five minutes each day alone with Charlotte, holding her on her lap while reading or doing a role-playing activity.
- Mrs. Phillips would prompt and shape Charlotte's behavior to enable her to return greetings from adults and peers as well as to participate in and later initiate play with at least one peer.

To encourage Charlotte to interact with peers, Mrs. Phillips took the following actions:

- First, she selected five students from Charlotte's kindergarten class and asked them to help her make Charlotte feel happy at school. She modeled the behavior she wanted these children to use when greeting Charlotte or including her in games.
- Next, Mrs. Phillips involved these five students in role-play activities in which each student took a turn playing the role of Charlotte while the others practiced greeting

or encouraging Charlotte to join in playground games or class activities.

- When these strategies were put into effect, Mrs. Phillips began charting Charlotte's response to classmates. As indicated in Figure 9–11 and Figure 9–12, her initial response to greetings and her playground involvement were disappointing. Charlotte rarely returned classmates' greetings and ran away from children on the playground as soon as they weren't looking at her. Soon Charlotte's classmates began ignoring her again.
- Mrs. Phillips resumed role-playing activities with the five core classmates and simultaneously began role-playing activities with the whole class. She stressed the point that shy children are often very afraid and that their friends should not leave them alone if they are to overcome their fear. Charlotte's classmates began to approach Charlotte again. Mrs. Phillips verbally

☐ **FIGURE 9–11**
Charlotte's Response to Greetings

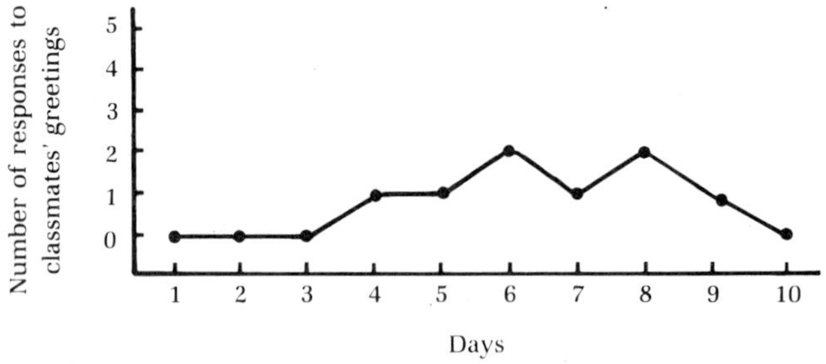

☐ **FIGURE 9–12**
Charlotte's Playground Involvement

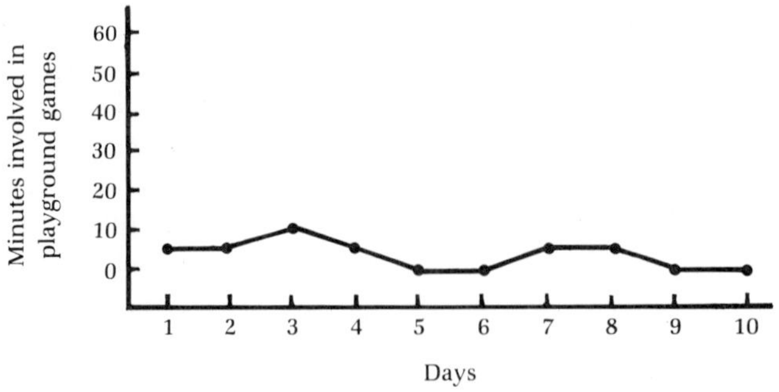

reinforced these students for trying to help Charlotte even though she would not play with them for long. Soon others in the class began to approach Charlotte.

Gradual changes in Charlotte's behavior were noticed by January. Charlotte began to respond consistently to almost all of the five childrens' greetings (see Figure 9–13) and she began to play for longer periods of time with her peers on the playground (see Figure 9–14).

Mrs. Phillips and Mrs. Blake next decided it was time to teach Charlotte to initiate play with peers.

- Mrs. Phillips used puppets in her work with Charlotte. She and Charlotte assumed the characters of the hand puppets they wore.

☐ **FIGURE 9–13**
Charlotte's Response to Greeting

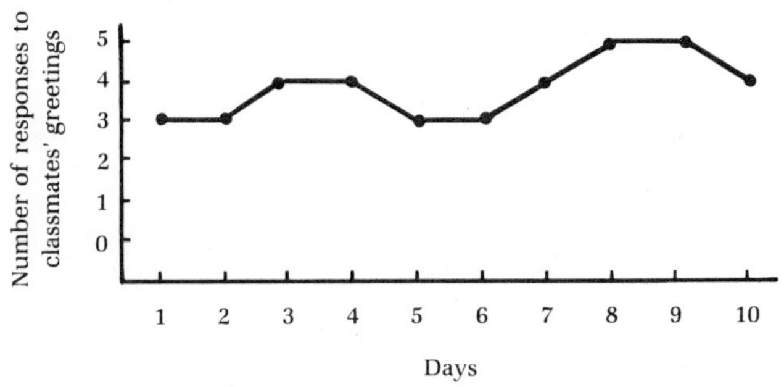

☐ **FIGURE 9–14**
Charlotte's Playground Involvement

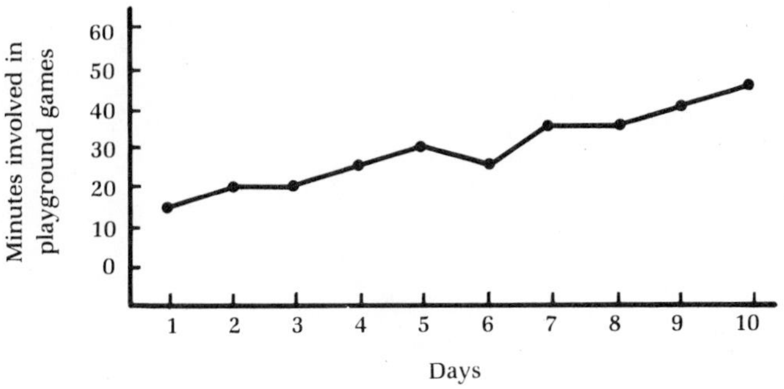

Mrs. Phillips modeled the statement "Would you like to play house with me?" Together she and Charlotte would spend their private time together playing house through the medium of puppets.

In the spring of that year, a new student was enrolled in Charlotte's class. Mrs. Phillips prepared the class for the new student and encouraged them to make her feel welcome. During free time on the new student's first day, Mrs. Phillips heard Charlotte say, "Would you like to play house with me?" With that, Charlotte took the little girl's hand and led her away.

Discussion Points

1. Ms. Chamberlin was fearful of Rick's behavior. If you were in her position, list some resource persons whom you might contact in an effort to prevent such feelings from detracting from your professional efforts with him.

2. As Charlotte's teacher, what reinforcement procedures would you use when she engaged in playground games with peers? Explain your choice.

CHAPTER 10 Developing Reading Skills

OUTLINE

I. **Introduction**
   A. Objectives

II. **Case Studies: Steve and Matt**
   A. Steve
   B. Matt
   C. Points for Consideration

III. **Common Instructional Misconceptions**

IV. **Assessing Reading Skills**
   A. Scope-and-Sequence Charts
   B. Error Analysis
   C. Word Lists
   D. Cloze Procedure
   E. Criterion Tests

V. **Reading Methods**
   A. Basal Reading Method
   B. Phonics Method
   C. Linguistic Method
   D. Language Experience Method

VI. **Remedial Instructional Methods**
   A. Multisensory Programs
   B. Behavioral Methods
   C. Neurological Impress Method
   D. High-Interest, Low-Vocabulary Methods

VII. **Techniques for Reading Instruction**

VIII. **Survival Skills**

IX. **Home Reinforcement**

X. **Regular Class Involvement**

XI. **Summary Points**

XII. **Review Questions**

XIII. **Suggested Readings**

XIV. **Application: Steve and Matt**
   A. Steve
   B. Matt
   C. Discussion Points

INTRODUCTION

Reading is a skill necessary for survival in today's society. Within the learning environment, disabled readers often feel embarrassed or humiliated and may develop behavior problems in the classroom because of their poor reading abilities. Without appropriate intervention, such students later often face limited career opportunities.

There are many explanations as to why children have reading problems. The lack of consensus regarding etiology and remediation of reading problems has resulted in many different special reading programs and instructional approaches. Since the selection of a reading program is sometimes viewed as an overwhelming task by new teachers, it is helpful to point out that there is no one right approach to the teaching of reading. Rather, due to the diversity of students' cultural backgrounds, developmental needs, motivational drives, and learning strengths and weaknesses, it is imperative that teachers utilize a variety of instructional approaches to reading.

Objectives

In this chapter, you will learn to

- use a scope-and-sequence chart of reading skills as a guide to instructional planning;
- use an error analysis procedure to identify students' skill needs;
- select basic reading methods that complement students' skill needs;
- select remedial techniques to supplement students' reading instructional programs;
- assist students in applying their reading skills to everyday situations.

Case Studies: Steve and Matt

Steve

Steve is a quiet fifteen-year-old freshman referred by his teachers for multifactored assessment because of his overall poor academic performance, withdrawn behavior, and inattentiveness observed since he entered the local high school. Steve and his nine-year-old sister, Beth, live with their divorced mother. According to Steve's mother, he spends a lot of time with his father because "he can do as he pleases."

As part of the assessment procedure, Mrs. Gifford, the resource teacher, observed Steve's classroom performance and behavior informally and administered diagnostic tests over several testing sessions. She noted that in the classroom Steve spent a great deal of time drawing and avoided eye contact with his teachers. When asked a question, he quietly replied with an "I don't know" and lowered his gaze again. He rarely completed assignments, although Mrs. Gifford noted that he would begin assignments if given class time to do so.

Mrs. Gifford first administered the *Wide Range Achievement Test* (Jastak, Bijou, and Jastak 1978) as a screening tool to obtain a general idea of Steve's overall abilities in reading, arithmetic, and spelling. Since this test focused only on word recognition, she also used the *Woodcock Reading Mastery Test* (Woodcock 1973) and other informal reading tests to gain specific diagnostic information regarding Steve's reading skills.

In each of the testing situations, Steve constantly leaned back on two legs of his chair and responded in a monotone with the correct answer if he knew it, or an "I don't know" if he did not. He made no eye contact or nonverbal gestures in response to teacher praise, although he did remain on task throughout all testing sessions. His test scores on the *Woodcock Reading Mastery Test* (Form A) were as follows:

	Easy	*Instructional*	*Failure*
Letter Identification	12.9	12.9	12.9
Word Identification	3.8	4.4	5.3
Word Attack	2.7	3.7	5.4
Word Comprehension	2.9	3.8	5.5
Passage Comprehension	3.1	4.0	5.3
Total	1.7	2.0	2.3

The *Woodcock Reading Mastery Test* yielded five subscale scores within each of three reading levels: easy, instructional, and failure. The subscale scores under the easy reading level guided Mrs. Gifford in selecting independent reading materials for Steve. The subscale scores at the instructional level provided her with a starting place for selecting appropriate reading instruction material, while the subscale scores under the failure level identified the upper limits of Steve's reading abilities.

Careful analysis of Steve's performance on both formal and informal assessment procedures helped Mrs. Gifford identify the following skills and error patterns related to Steve's performance in reading:

☐ **FIGURE 10–1**
Criterion Test of Basic Skills

Name *Matt Chamberlin* School *Crim* Date *1981* (Year) *11* (Month)

Teacher *Ken Bower* Evaluator *Carolyn Beck* Birthdate *70* (Year) *1* (Month)

Age *11* (Year) *10* (Month)

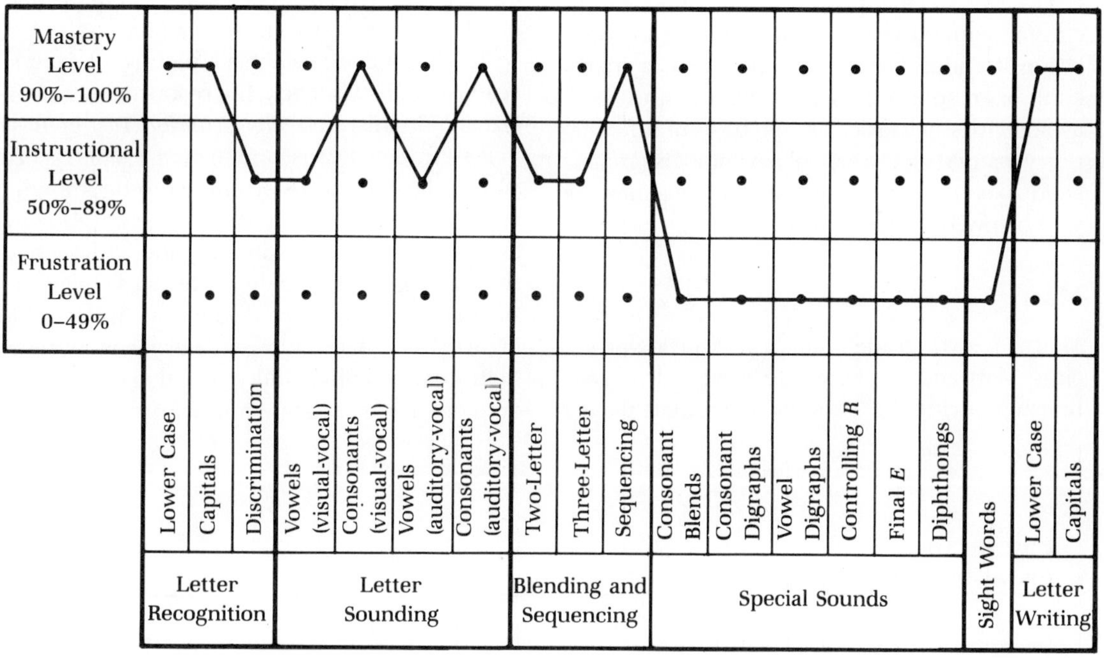

NOTES:

Source: Kurth Lundell, James Evans, and William Brown, *Criterion Test of Basic Skills: Reading.* © Copyright 1976, Academic Therapy Publications, 20 Commercial Boulevard, Novato, California 94947.

- Recognizes letters, makes sound-symbol associations for long and short vowels and initial and final consonants, and blends symbols in a CV pattern
- Reads the first two or three letters of a word and guesses at the remainder
- Is unable to identify appropriate contextual cues to decode unknown words

Overall, Steve appeared to have major difficulty in context reading with concurrent deficits in attending and social skills. He was guarded in his response to social rewards and avoided mastery tasks. On the basis of information provided by the school psychologist and vocational counselor, he appeared to be achieving well below his ability level.

Matt

Matt is a sixth grade student in Mr. Bower's class. Matt and Mr. Bower formed a close relationship during the summer when Matt played baseball on the Little League team that Mr. Bower coached.

Mr. Bower indicated some of Matt's strengths and weaknesses in comments on the referral form for multifactored assessment. Generally, Matt tries to complete assignments, participates orally in class, and is a leader among his peers. Mr. Bower also indicated that even though he has provided individual reading instruction, Matt has continued to fail at independent tasks that require reading.

To gain a comprehensive picture of Matt's reading skills, Ms. Beck, the resource room specialist, administered *The Criterion Test of Basic Skills* (Lundell, Evans, and Brown 1976). Test results indicated Matt's strengths to be knowledge of consonant sounds and blends. However, Matt's weaknesses in long and short vowel sounds, digraphs, and diphthongs as well as basic analytic skills were evident, as indicated in Figure 10–1. A teacher-made error analysis of Matt's oral reading ability revealed a variety of error patterns, as shown in Figure 10–2.

□ **FIGURE 10–2**
Error Analysis

Type of Error	
/	–hesitation
∿∿	–aided word
S.C.	–self corrected
—	–substitution
O	–unobserved punctuation

Error Analysis

Wild Things

On the/side of a hill a little pack rat is ~~hunting~~ hungry for his supper. The pack rat is hungry. And ~~while~~ will he hunts, he is afraid—very afraid—for the pack rat has many enemies.

And some of the pack rat's enemies are/these: Owl and Eagle, Fox and Bobcat, and

SNAKE.

Crawling—crawling, the snake is ~~hunting~~ hungry for his supper. S.C. super
He, too, is hungry. And/while he hunts, he is ~~afraid~~ after, for the snake has many enemies. And some of his enemies are these: Owl and Eagle, Bobcat and

FOX.

Matt told Ms. Beck that Mr. Bower tried to help him in reading, but that he was embarrassed to read in front of his friends and frustrated about being unable to read test questions or texts for social studies, science, math, and spelling. Matt's decoding skills were limiting his ability to comprehend any but the most fundamental written material. Despite support and acceptance by his general education teacher, Matt's skill deficits in reading placed him in embarrassing situations and prompted a personal sense of frustration.

Points for Consideration

- *One of the tragedies of our educational system is that as time passes, many students like Steve perceive themselves as not being capable of learning.*

Thurman (1977) speaks to the incongruity within our educational system and suggests that we place less emphasis on changing the student's behavior to fit the environment, and focus instead on modifying the environment to fit the child. Steve has a chance to become a successful reader if his teachers will try to select a procedure and set of techniques that meet his learning needs. An attempt to meet Steve on his own terms may convince him that he can be successful at learning a skill that has been extremely frustrating for him.

- *For a special reading program to be successful, all subcomponents of the reading process must be simultaneously taught according to each student's needs.*

In Matt's case, it is unlikely that he could be successful in content subjects due to the significant discrepancy between his current reading ability and that demanded by texts used for instruction in his class. The special educator is confronted with two instructional tasks. She must not only remediate basic reading deficits, but also implement alternative instructional strategies with materials related to content in Matt's regular classes.

COMMON INSTRUCTIONAL MISCONCEPTIONS

Reading instruction should not be continued beyond the elementary school level because most children have learned to read by that time and those who have not will never learn to read well. Although past educational practices tended to either ignore or give up on disabled adolescent readers, we know that many of them can be taught to read. When working with students in this age group, it is necessary to remember that they have different needs from those of young children. Also, professionals cannot ignore the possibility that a student's lack of reading skills might be attributed to inappropriate instruction.

By increasing reading instruction time, students will improve their reading skills. Not only is reading a multifaceted process, but it also requires active student participation. Children fail to learn how to read for many reasons. If reading instruction is to be successful, alternative instructional strategies must be implemented. Since there is no one effective remedial approach, the special educator must be capable of using many different approaches with each handicapped student.

ASSESSING READING SKILLS

During the initial stages of reading instruction, the special educator focuses on developing several subskills (for example, phonics, word recognition, and comprehension) simultaneously. All of these are components of the overall process we call reading.

Scope-and-Sequence Charts

As Reid (1979) and Smith (1973) have pointed out, it is erroneous to assume that the ability to read can be developed by systematically directing a student through a sequentially arranged group of skills. Rather, scope-and-sequence charts, such as the one illustrated in Figure 10–3, are designed to provide the special educator with an overview of subskills related to the reading process.

An application of the scope-and-sequence chart for one student experiencing reading problems could provide the teacher with the following information about the student's reading strengths and weaknesses:

- Has a foundation of prerequisite skills
- Needs additional instruction on vowel digraphs and blends—phonics skills
- Needs additional instruction on compound words and syllabication principles—analytic skills
- Needs assistance in using contextual clues—word recognition
- Needs to read critically for specific information—comprehension

Such information provides the teacher with a starting place for instruction. Although the teacher now knows what skills need to be taught, he or she requires assessment information from other sources to decide how to teach the needed reading skills.

☐ **FIGURE 10–3**
Scope and Sequence of Skills Associated with Reading

PREREQUISITE SKILLS	*Deficient* –	*Instruction* /	*Mastery* *
Uses meaningful vocabulary			
Sequentially relates incidents (stories, events)			
Obtains meaning from pictures			
Discriminates between similarities and differences in sounds and words			
Identifies rhyming words			
Discriminates among objects by shape, color, size			
Identifies letter names and some words such as name			
Follows one and two step directions			
Relates personal experiences with pictures or stories			
PHONIC SKILLS			
Identifies initial consonant sound in words (e.g.: cup-/*k*/ ball-/*b*/)			
Makes consonant sound-symbol association for the following: *m, g, b, h, f, d, s, t, w, n, p, c/k/, j, k, l, q, r, v, y, z, x/ks/*			
Makes short vowel sound-symbol association for the following vowels: *a/apple/, e/elephant/, i/igloo/, o/octopus/, u/umbrella/*			
Makes long vowel sound-symbol association			
Makes sound-symbol association for the following consonant			
digraphs: *ch, th, wh, sh, ph*			
Makes sound/symbol association for the following blends: *pl, sm, cr, fr, tr, gr, pr, bl, sl, st, sw, cl, dr, br, sp*			
Makes sound-symbol association for the following consonant			
variants: *y/fly/, c/certain/, g/cage/*			
Makes sound-symbol association for the following vowel digraphs: *oa/coach/, ai/pail/, ay/play, ee/flee/, ea/reach/, ie/diet/, ei/receive/, oo/balloon/*			
Makes sound-symbol association for the following blends: *str, thr, spl, spr, gl, sc/k/*			
Makes a sound-symbol association for the following diphthongs: *ow/show/, ow/cow/, oi/boil/, oy/boy/, aw/raw/, ew/blew/, ou/couch/*			
Makes sound-symbol association for consonant combinations in which the initial sound is silent (e.g., *kn, wr, gn*)			
Makes sound-symbol association for the following vowel combinations: *ar, er, ir, or, ur*			

☐ **FIGURE 10–3—continued**
Scope and Sequence of Skills Associated with Reading

ANALYTIC SKILLS	*Deficient* –	*Instruction* /	*Mastery* *
Pronounces initial consonant sounds in words			
Pronounces the following consonants when in the final position in words: *p, d, s, r, f, k, x*			
Blends sound in VC pattern (e.g., /a/ /t/ /a-t/)			
Applies vowel pronounciation principles: CVC pattern-*cat*; CCVC pattern-*that, stop*; CVCV pattern-*lake*; CVVC pattern-*boat*; CCVCV pattern-*plane, whale*; CCVVC pattern-*float, wheel*			
Identifies compound words			
States meanings of compound words			
Divides compound words			
Identifies suffixes: *ed, s, es, ing, er, est, en, ly, less, ful, ness, ous, able, y, ly*			
States meaning of suffixes			
Identifies root words			
Divides root word from suffix			
Identifies prefixes: *un, re, dis, pre, pro, ex, e*			
States meaning of prefixes			
Divides root word from prefix			
Identifies root word when spelling changed			
Divides multisyllable words according to syllabication principle:			
–divide between the prefix and root			
–divide between the suffix and root			
–divide between compound words			
–each syllable must contain a vowel; double vowels are counted as one vowel			
–divide between consonants; consonant digraphs and blends count as one consonant			
–apply vowel pronounciation principle to each syllable			
WORD RECOGNITION SKILLS			
Pronounces basic sight word vocabulary in context			
Pronounces basic sight word vocabulary in isolation			
Uses sight word vocabulary in oral sentences			
Pronounces survival word vocabulary			
Uses survival vocabulary in oral sentences			
Uses picture clues to decode unknown word			
Uses context clues to decode unknown word			

FIGURE 10–3—continued
Scope and Sequence of Skills Associated with Reading

COMPREHENSION SKILLS	*Deficient* –	*Instruction* /	*Mastery* *
Identifies main idea of a short story			
Identifies main idea of a story chapter or section			
Identifies main idea of a paragraph			
Relates sequence of events			
Answers specific who, what, when, where, how, why questions			
Locates sentences or phrases that support answer			
Identifies cause-and-effect relationships			
Uses descriptors to interpret emotional state, personality of character			
Compares story events with personal life			
Anticipates sequence of plot based on known events in the story			
Infers mood, character based on implied ideas or feelings			
Distinguishes between true and false information in plot			
Distinguishes between fact and opinion in story or book			
Distinguishes relevant information in story or book			
READING LIFE SKILLS			
Defines and can use a table of contents, glossary, index			
Uses a dictionary, index, encyclopedia, Atlas, phone book, building directory			
Can interpret frequently used abbreviations: *T., t., C., mi., ft., in., yd., K*			
Reads newspaper for information and leisure purposes and want ads, TV guide, weather map, advice column, headlines, comics, editorials, obituaries, advertisements			
Reads a road map and map legend			
Reads and follows directions on labels on drug bottles, clothing, foods, cleaning materials			
Reads magazines, books. stories for leisure			
Reads timetable charts for buses, trains, planes			
Reads and follows directions of a recipe, pattern, schematic			
Reads common community signs: road signs, names of stores, building names, street signs, public directional signs, (Watch Your Step, Exit)			

Error Analysis

In addition to knowing what reading skills need to be taught, teachers must be aware of the type of reading errors their students make. The focus here is on identifying those behaviors that inhibit reading comprehension.

Goodman (1973) outlined a process called miscue analysis to help teachers pinpoint specific types of reading errors, thus gaining direction for improving reading comprehension. The advantage of such an analysis is that it emphasizes the nature of the reading error, rather than the number of errors made. For one student, omissions and insertions in a passage may not affect understanding, but reversals and repetitions might. For another student, the opposite might occur. Each student relies to a different extent on individual reading skills for comprehension. From this perspective, it is apparent that students do not need to achieve mastery on all the skills identified on a scope-and-sequence chart. Instead, as Goodman has suggested, instructional decisions should be based on student need.

In order to analyze a student's errors in reading, the teacher should obtain both a taped reading sample of approximately 250 words, and a printed copy of the passage read by the student. The tape gives the teacher the opportunity to listen to the reading sample and the flexibility to replay and analyze before recording the type of error on the printed copy of the passage. Figure 10–4 outlines the types of errors to look for in the miscue analysis process and suggests ways of marking such errors. An analysis of reading errors is critical to selecting appropriate instructional methods and techniques that correlate with the student's reading needs.

Word Lists

Word lists such as the *Dolch Basic Word List* (Dolch 1950) or the *Hillerich Word List* (Hillerich 1974) are often used to obtain a general idea of the student's sight word skills. Unlike error analysis procedures designed to assess comprehension, word lists provide information on a student's skill in decoding words in isolation. The teacher asks the student to read each word aloud until the student mispronounces five consecutive words from a given list. Then an analysis of the student's performance on the word lists provides the teacher with information on which phonic and analytic skills need to be further developed, as indicated in the Figure 10–5 example.

When using word lists, teachers may also want to determine the speed with which the student recites each word or group of words. Even though a student may be able to decode a word, the time required to accomplish this task can distract from the student's ability to comprehend a passage in which the word appears.

Cloze Procedure

The cloze procedure (Taylor 1953) can be used for assessment as well as instructional purposes. In assessment, this procedure is used to explore a student's com-

☐ **FIGURE 10–4**
Reading Miscue Analysis

Error	*Method of Identification*	*Example*
Omission	Circle the word or word parts omitted.	The little girl jumped into the pool to save her sister.
Insertion	Use a caret to mark the place of insertion and write the added word or letter(s).	The old man sat down on the bench to watch the squirrels.
Substitution	Cross out the word and write the substitution above it.	After five minutes, I ~~recalled~~ remembered her name.
Reversal	Cross out the word and write the reversal word above it.	The boy ~~saw~~ was the train coming.
	For word pair reversals, draw a curved line going over, between, and under the reversed words.	Bill was angry and upset when he struck out at bat.
Repetition	Draw a wavy line under words that are repeated.	Beth called her father to share her good news with him.
Mispronunciation	Write the mispronunciation above the correct word.	I like spaghetti and meatballs.
Hesitation	Use a slash to indicate inappropriate hesitation.	Barbara hurried/home because she wanted/to nap.
Aided Word his car.	Underline words pronounced for the student.	The old man took fastidious care of
Unobserved Punctuation	Cross out the punctuation mark that the student ignored.	The rabbit darted across the road/ Mike said/ I wonder what's chasing him/
Self-Corrected Error	Write *sc* above the error that the student corrected without assistance.	Bill's face turned a deep shade of purple when the teacher called his name.

prehension skills. To implement the cloze procedure, the teacher obtains several paragraphs that are at, or slightly below, the student's instructional reading level. Every fifth word in each sentence except the first is omitted. The student is asked to suggest words that might fit in the incomplete sentences. The teacher continues

FIGURE 10–5
Analysis of Graded Word List

Stimulus	*Student Response*	*Skill Needed*
with	witch	|th|
home	hom	CVCV pattern, |ō|
girl	gril	|ir|
like	lick	CVCV pattern, |ī|
duck	Dick	|ŭ|

to introduce more difficult passages if the student successfully completes the easier reading passages. This procedure can be completed independently by the student, or with the teacher. In either case, the teacher should note the type of error the student makes as well as the type of word the student selects. When the cloze procedure is used for instructional purposes, many special educators combine it with a shaping procedure. Figure 10–6 illustrates this modified approach.

When the cloze procedure is used for instructional purposes, the passages chosen should be on the student's instructional reading level. The procedure can be modified by deleting specific categories or types of words, such as vocabulary words, prepositions, verbs, or adjectives. Blachowicz (1977) suggests that teachers read passages to students while leaving out certain words to encourage critical listening and comprehension. Bortnick and Lopardo (1976) have found that this procedure improves students' comprehension skills.

Criterion Tests

Teacher-made criterion tests in reading are often used to probe comprehension and phonics skills of students. Frequently special educators will use a commercial criterion test to make initial identification of a student's reading deficits and then, based upon performance on the commercial test, administer their own criterion test to gain more specific diagnostic data.

For example, one resource teacher noted that twelve-year-old Jimmy had difficulty with CVCV patterns. She obtained this information from a review of test data accumulated by another professional. At this point, all she could surmise was that a problem existed; however, the extent and detail of the problem was unknown. To gain further insight regarding this specific problem, she administered the criterion test presented in Figure 10–7 from her teacher-made test file.

An analysis of Jimmy's performance indicated that although he had an awareness of the CVCV pattern, it was not firmly established. It seemed that no specific vowel posed a problem; rather, they all were difficult for him. Also, it seemed that Jimmy had problems discriminating the letters *p* and *g*. After the testing session, the resource teacher asked him to identify the letters *p* and *g* from another word

☐ **FIGURE 10–6**
Modified Cloze Procedure

seemed grown
It was very late when the young men took her home. The night air had __________ cool, and

old young | hat coat | said told
one of the __________ men gave her his __________ to wear. She __________ the young men

street way | is was | story frame
the __________ to her home. It __________ a very old one-__________ house. The young men

watched left | they he | home the city
__________ her go into it. Then __________ started the drive for __________.

Directions: Please choose one word for each blank space in the paragraph. Circle the word chosen.

It was very late when the young men took her home. The night air had __________ cool, and

one of the __________ men gave her his __________ to wear. She __________ the young men

the __________ to her home. It __________ a very old one-__________ house. The young men

__________ her go into it. Then __________ started the drive for __________.

Directions: Choose one of the words below that best fits in each blank in the above paragraph. Write the word you chose in the space provided.

coat	young	grown	story	was
they	watched	home	way	told

It was very late when the young men took her home. The night air had __________ cool, and

one of the __________ men gave her his __________ to wear. She __________ the young men

the __________ to her home. It __________ a very old one-__________ house. The young men

__________ her go into it. Then __________ started the drive for __________.

Directions: Think of a good word which will fit in each blank in this paragraph. Write these words in the spaces provided.

Reprinted by permission of Sterling Publishing Co., Inc., Two Park Avenue, New York, New York 10016. From *Strangely Enough* by C. B. Colby © 1959 by C. B. Colby.

list. His performance confirmed her suspicion that he needed additional instruction in letter discrimination.

Due to the multifaceted nature of reading, a comprehensive assessment program is necessary to identify a student's overall reading performance. Teachers

FIGURE 10–7
Excerpt from Teacher-Made Criterion Test

Skill	a__e	i__e	o__e	u__e
	male mall	mile mill	home	huge
	cake	time	stone st/one	dupe dope
	stake stack	fine	hope hog/hoge	tune ton
	lane	gripe	cone	mule mul
	cape cage	rice rik	choke	tube

must use a combination of assessment strategies to determine a student's reading strengths and weaknesses before attempting to select a reading program.

READING METHODS

Because of the variation in student learning styles, needs, and strengths, teachers must often use or modify several methods to meet the instructional needs of each student (Gillespie-Silver 1979; Harris and Sipay 1975). To meet this wide range of instructional needs, numerous reading methods have been developed. Generally, reading methods cluster around the following approaches: *(a)* basal, *(b)* phonics, *(c)* linguistics, and *(d)* language experience.

Basal Reading Method

Most teachers use one or several basal reading series as the foundation for their instructional program in reading. Basal reading series consist of a sequential set of reading texts and related student workbooks. An accompanying detailed teacher's manual outlines goals, objectives, instructional plans, procedures, skills, and mastery activities for each lesson. In addition, supplemental materials, such as filmstrips, charts, flash cards, games, ditto work sheets, and audio cassette tapes, are often included in basal programs.

Usually basal reading programs use a sequential format of graded activities that begin at the first grade level and continue through the eighth grade. Content of a basal reading series emphasizes phonics, structural analysis, word recognition, and comprehension skills. However, the degree of emphasis on each reading skill varies among different programs. Activities in the reading text, workbook, and teacher's manual are coordinated to provide students with various experiences emphasizing specific skills.

In a typical lesson from a basal reading series the teacher uses the following format:

- Prepare the student to read a passage by teaching vocabulary and other required skills.
- Provide motivation for silent or oral reading of the passage.

- Expand the student's understanding of the passage through use of various types of comprehension questions.
- Provide instruction and mastery task(s) to reinforce skills associated with the lesson.
- Evaluate the student's understanding of skills developed in the lesson.

There are several advantages in using a basal reading method. Basal reading programs focus on the development of comprehension skills. Also, phonics, analytic skills, and word recognition skills are developed in a sequential manner, and the vocabulary is repeated throughout the text as a method of reinforcement. Further, the instructional manual provides clear and sequential instructional strategies and procedures that beginning teachers find very helpful.

There are also disadvantages associated with using a basal reading series. Student learning style and skill needs are often ignored in favor of following the directions in the teacher's manual verbatim. Teachers are not encouraged to deviate from the instructional format. An implicit assumption in the use of a basal series is that all children will profit from its use; therefore, failure to learn to read is often interpreted as deviance on the part of the student, rather than weakness in the instructional materials or procedures. Also, a shortcoming of many basal reading programs is that the content does not focus on skills for independent living.

It is possible to use basal reading materials and individualize reading instruction in your classroom. For example, the simultaneous use of several basal series permits teachers to provide varied instruction for a specific set of decoding skills until the student has attained mastery. Some teachers use only portions of a basal program to develop deficit skills identified during the assessment process.

Hall, Ribovich, and Ramig (1979) have found that a *Direct Reading Thinking Activity, (DRTA)* (Stauffer 1975) improves students' abilities to comprehend the material presented in the basal reader. Hammond (1979) has also documented increased comprehension as a result of this reading method.

DRTA procedures are designed to guide pre- and postreading discussions through a predict-read-prove cycle. The teacher encourages predictions by asking such questions as "What do you think will happen?" or "Why do you think so?" and requires the application of critical reading skills through such questions as "How can you prove it?" or "What sentence or paragraph supports your viewpoint?"

Generally, when using the *DRTA* method, open-ended questions are asked prior to reading to encourage the student to make predictions or hypotheses. Then, when the student reads a portion of the story, he or she tries to either confirm or reject the predictions rather than trying to locate specific facts. After confirming or rejecting hypotheses, students are required to apply critical reading skills to support those hypotheses that were accepted. This cycle is repeated until the reading selection is completed.

Phonics Method

Phonics instruction, sometimes referred to as decoding, has been recommended for children with reading deficits and learning disabilities (Lovitt and Hurlburt 1975; Ross 1976). Phonics instruction emphasizes grapheme-phoneme relationships. The sequence of instruction proceeds from sound-symbol associations of consonants, vowels, digraphs, and blends through analytic skills, such as root words, prefixes, suffixes, compound words, and syllabication principles.

Programs that emphasize phonics instruction can be used to supplement a basal reading series. Many include texts, workbooks, a teacher's manual, and supplemental materials. Phonics programs vary in the skills and analytic principles they teach, and in the order in which they teach the skills and principles.

As with other approaches to reading instruction, researchers have identified strengths and weaknesses in the phonics method. Rudel (1977) suggests that a phonics method may reduce the memory load for children with memory deficits. Batemen (1976) has advocated a phonics method because it provides students with a systematic approach for attending to significant grapheme-phoneme features within words. A third advantage of the phonics approach is that it eventually provides students with the ability to decode new words independently.

Kershner (1975) has indicated that a disadvantage of phonics methods is that they may hinder the development of comprehension skills in students. Students who have difficulty applying phonics skills can often lose the meaning of the material during an attempt to decode an unknown word. A phonics method may not be useful to students who have difficulty blending sounds into complete words. Some phonics programs emphasize a left-to-right blending of symbols; yet many of the words in our language cannot be decoded through sequential blending (Camp, Winbury, and Zinna 1981). A final concern is that too many phonetic rules may strain the memory capability of some students.

Phonics methods are frequently combined with other instructional approaches, such as the basal or the language experience method (Kirk, Kliebhan, and Lerner 1978). Examples of phonics programs currently used include the *Phonovisual Method* (Schoolfield and Timberlake 1974), the *SIMS Reading and Spelling Program* (Minneapolis Public Schools 1978), and the *Schmerler Phonics Program* (Schmerler 1976).

Linguistic Method

Assuming that children naturally learn the process of sound-symbol association, Bloomfield (1933, 1942) recommended that early reading instruction emphasize the following three skills: (1) letter names, (2) left-to-right tracking of symbols, and then (3) single-syllable words with a specific configuration, that is, word families. After these word families have been mastered as sight words, instruction focuses on discriminating between similar sight word families and then progresses to using them in sentences (Fries 1963). Since comprehension skills are not emphasized, they must be acquired through syntax and intonation cues (Lefevre 1969), rather than through illustrations or contextual clues. Examples of commercial materials that emphasize a linguistic approach are *Merrill Linguistic Readers* (Charles E. Merrill 1975) and *Linguistic Readers* (Harper & Row 1966).

Advocates of the linguistic approach contend that in addition to developing syntactical awareness, this approach increases vocabulary recognition because of the repetition of vocabulary words and the sequence of regularly spelled words followed by irregularly spelled words. The linguistic approach is also thought to aid students in spelling whole words rather than spelling words letter by letter (Cohen and Plaskon 1980).

Students with memory deficits may not profit from a linguistic method because of its heavy emphasis on memory skills. Also, the similarities in words encourage students to read word by word rather than in word phrases. Word-by-word reading detracts from comprehension development.

Language Experience Method

The **language experience method** usually consists of having students write or tell stories about themselves—their experiences, families, interests, likes and dislikes, dreams, and hobbies. This approach integrates oral and written expression skills with reading skills.

Typically, a language experience story is developed as follows:

- Either the teacher or student identifies a motivational topic such as an action photograph, illustration, special event, unique object, or field trip.
- The teacher and student develop a theme for the story.
- The student writes or dictates the story to the teacher.
- The teacher guides the student with reference to choice of vocabulary, sentence structure, spelling, punctuation, and sequence of ideas.
- The teacher and student read the story together.
- The student reads the story.
- The teacher uses the story to develop vocabulary for reading and spelling and to illustrate grammatical and decoding principles.
- Completed stories are placed in a special folder and are periodically reread by the teacher and student.

Advocates of the language experience method, such as Chall (1967) and Goodman (1976), emphasize that the approach naturally incorporates a student's unique interests. Further, this method encourages students to realize that written words are simply an oral language written down. As in the linguistic method, vocabulary tends to be repeated because it is based on a student's spoken language. Because the approach differs significantly from the type of reading instruction most students have received, it may reduce the anxiety and frustration of students with past failure in reading. However, inexperienced teachers may find the language experience method difficult to use because it does not provide teachers with structure or guidance in sequencing reading skills. In addition, there is a tendency for vocabulary to be limited to the student's spoken vocabulary.

REMEDIAL INSTRUCTIONAL METHODS

Many instructional methods, such as the ones just discussed, were initially designed for students in regular educational programs and then later adapted to meet the needs of handicapped students. However, there are several reading instructional methods which were developed specifically for disabled readers. Following is a discussion of several of these methods.

Multisensory Programs

By far, the most universally known multisensory method is the Fernald method, developed by Grace Fernald (1943) in the 1920s. Her method is also referred to as the Visual-Auditory-Kinesthetic-Tactile (VAKT) method. Fernald was motivated to create an alternative reading program for students who were unable to learn to read in traditional programs. The VAKT instructional process was only one aspect of a broader teaching philosophy, which Fernald called "positive reconditioning." If disabled readers were to learn to read, then changes in the environment and instructional procedures had to occur so that students could experience success and perceive themselves as capable of learning to read.

There are four stages in the Fernald program. Stage I emphasizes the use of VAKT modalities. In Stage II the tactile modality is dropped, and in Stage III the kinesthetic modality is omitted. By the time the student reaches Stage IV, he or she is able to look at a new word and decode it based on its similarity to other previously learned words.

Fernald suggested that the VAKT approach be used with children who make inversion or reversal errors, who confuse words when reading, or who exhibit socioemotional problems that can be attributed to school failure. She stated that these learning problems disappeared following treatment. In a comparison of the VAKT method with a visual method for reading instruction, Meyers, Schvaneveldt, and Ruddy (1975) did not find the VAKT method to be superior, although several researchers have found the method to be successful with mildly handicapped students (Cawley, Goodstein, and Burrow 1972; McCarthy and Oliver 1965). Myers and Hammill (1976) indicate that students with deficits in visual discrimination, memory, and sequencing may benefit more from the VAKT method than those with auditory deficits.

One variation of Fernald's original method is the modality block approach, developed by Blau and Blau (1969). Based on the premise that the visual channel interferes with information being processed through the auditory, kinesthetic, and tactile modalities during initial instructional stages, this approach does not introduce visual stimuli. Thus, the method is also referred to as the AKT, or Auditory-Kinesthetic-Tactile, method.

Based on the work of Samuel Orton, the Gillingham-Stillman (1968) remedial reading method was developed for students identified as dyslexic. *Dyslexia* has been defined by the Research Group on Developmental Dyslexia of the World Federation of Neurology (Critchley 1975) as "a disorder of children who, despite conventional classroom experience, fail to attain the language skills of reading, writing and spelling commensurate with their intellectual abilities" (p. 11). Behaviors commonly observed in dyslexic children are letter and word reversals, choppy oral reading patterns, transposition of letters in words, confusion of words with similar appearance, repetition of words or guesses during oral reading, and confusion of concepts such as over and under (Saunders 1962).

Procedures used in the Gillingham-Stillman method emphasize a multisensory approach to instruction and the simultaneous development of spelling and writing skills in students. Like Fernald, Gillingham believed that students must be motivated to attempt to read. Therefore, she suggested that students be told that they could learn to read through a new approach. Procedures associated with this method are detailed and explained in the manual to be used in implementing the method (Gillingham and Stillman 1968).

The Gillingham-Stillman method is highly structured for both teachers and students; thus, some students become bored and learn to read in a labored fashion (Klein 1977). Although this approach has been criticized because of the limited attention it gives to comprehension skills, it has been effective in helping some students learn to read (Kaluger and Kolson 1978). Because of the success attained by dyslexic students through this method, several adaptations of it are available. These include *A Multi-Sensory Approach to Language Arts for Specific Language Disability Children* (Slingerland 1974) and *Recipe for Reading* (Traub and Bloom 1970).

Behavioral Methods

DISTAR Reading: An Instructional System (Englemann & Bruner 1969) is one example of a behavioral approach to reading instruction developed for culturally different and handicapped children. It is a highly structured and sequential program of instruction for students reading on a primary level, that is, preschool through third grade. Its companion, the *Corrective Reading Program* (Englemann et al. 1975), is designed for students in upper grades who have not mastered decoding skills. According to the authors, the cause of reading errors is of no consequence to teachers. Of importance is implementing instructional strategies that will assist these students in achieving skill mastery.

The *DISTAR* program is a sequentially organized set of reading skills with applied behavior principles. Skill hierarchies are combined with immediate skill practice, teacher evaluation, and positive reinforcement. Levels I and II emphasize the acquisition of comprehension skills through materials focusing on science, social studies, and social relations. Teachers are provided with a script to follow to assure application of the appropriate behavior principles. Following is a description of procedures used in the *DISTAR* program.

- Students are grouped according to their abilities, with five or fewer children in a group.
- Students sit in a semicircle around the teacher each day for a thirty-minute reading lesson.
- Initially a set of nine phonemes that are dissimilar in sound and appearance is presented. Following mastery of twenty phonemes, students begin to read texts ranging from one to twenty-five words printed in lower-case letters.
- During group instruction, students are taught to reproduce sounds and blend them into word units. In addition to blending and sound-symbol sheets, writing sheets, workbooks, reading texts, games, records, flash cards, and wall charts are included in the program.
- When the student has demonstrated mastery of specific skills on criterion-referenced tests, he or she will be placed with a different group for

instruction. If the student does not demonstrate mastery, the skills are taught again.

The *DISTAR* program has proven successful with students in Head Start programs (Becker and Englemann 1977). However, Kirk, Kliebhan, and Lerner (1978) noted that the emphasis on auditory skills and the rigidity of instruction may have negative effects on some students.

Another program based on behavioral principles is the *Edmark Reading Program* (Bijou 1972), designed to provide a sight vocabulary to students with significant reading deficits. The 227 lessons in the program focus on sight word recognition, the ability to follow written directions, and use of illustrations as a decoding tool. Students are taught one or two vocabulary words in each lesson. This vocabulary is reinforced as the student reads sixteen stories in a storybook. Each lesson is highly structured. Vocabulary is taught in small sequential steps, and student progress is monitored through periodic pre- and posttests. Students are also reinforced throughout the lesson, and their progress in the program is charted.

The *Peabody Rebus Reading Program* (Woodcock, Clark, & Davies 1979) applies behavioral principles to prepare beginning readers to make a transition to the primer level of a traditional reading program. Students progress through this program at their own pace and are provided with immediate feedback. Skills are reinforced through repetition. The program uses a rebus, that is, a picture word, as the foundation for instruction in reading skills.

Materials for this program consist of three programmed workbooks and two reading books. In the first book, thirty-five rebus words and the use of context clues are introduced. The student is provided with immediate feedback through a color-coded system. When the student marks the correct response with a special pen, green appears and he continues to the next frame. If the student marks an incorrect response, red appears and the student must continue to search for the correct response. When the student has finished the third workbook, he will have been exposed to 120 written vocabulary words and a significant number of comprehension and decoding skills commonly found in a basal reading program.

Neurological Impress Method

The neurological impress method was developed in 1952 by Heckelman (1969) for students age ten or above with severe reading deficits and, in particular, with visual discrimination deficits. Procedures for its use are simple and require no special materials other than several books with readability levels ranging from slightly below to slightly above the student's reading level. Procedures for the use of this method are as follows:

- The teacher is seated slightly behind the student to permit the student to hear the teacher's voice.
- The teacher begins to read a passage from the text in a voice slightly louder and faster than that of the student. Initially, texts selected for oral reading should be below the student's instructional reading level to insure success. The teacher and the student do not concern themselves with mistakes. The

teacher uses a pointer such as a pencil or index finger to point to each word while reading.

- The teacher and student read together for ten minutes each day. As the student becomes familiar with the method, the teacher reads more softly and slightly increases the pace. The student may begin to point to each of the words while reading.
- No attention is given to comprehension or decoding skills. Emphasis is placed on extinguishing improper reading habits the student has developed.
- The readability level of selected materials should be adjusted every two weeks. New material of a slightly higher readability level should be selected.
- If the student has not demonstrated improved reading skills after four hours, or approximately twenty-four instructional sessions, the approach should be abandoned. If the student does demonstrate improvement, the process should be continued until the student is reading at grade level.

Lorenz and Vockell (1979) reported that they observed no significant gains in word recognition or reading comprehension among students who received instruction through this method. However, they did note that these students showed improvement in fluency, oral expression, and confidence in their ability to read. Hoskinson (1979) suggested that assisted reading could be used as an initial approach to be followed by more systematic instruction when the student had acquired more fluent reading ability.

High-Interest, Low-Vocabulary Methods

In the past, a major source of frustration for teachers and students was the limited availability of reading texts focusing on interests of the more mature student while providing instruction and mastery tasks geared to the student's reading ability. For example, adolescent students with reading ability at the 3^5 level had to read material designed for eight- or nine-year-old students because their reading skills were those of the average third grader.

Texts are available today that focus on relevant adolescent subjects, such as sports, dating, adventure, and cars, while maintaining a highly controlled vocabulary and emphasizing basic skills. Some of these high-interest, low-vocabulary materials are organized like basal readers with emphasis on phonetic, analytic, sight word, and comprehension skills. Still others are published to supplement the reading program designed by the teacher for a particular student and may focus only on comprehension and vocabulary development.

An example of a high-interest, low-readability series that is modeled after a basal reading series is *Scholastic Action* (Scholastic Book Services 1970). The series contains a teacher's manual, student workbooks, short stories, plays, records, and posters. It was designed for students in grades seven through twelve with reading skills at second through fifth grade levels. Procedures for instructional planning based on this series are the same as those described for basal reading series earlier in this chapter. A supplemental library, the *Action Libraries* (Scholastic Book Services 1970), can also be purchased to accompany the instructional program.

Reading activities for adolescents can be enjoyable if the material is appropriate.

Today there is an abundant supply of materials designed to prompt, rather than extinguish, motivation for reading among adolescents. It is suggested that special education programs for these students include three to four of these high-interest, low-readability series to meet the interests and learning needs of adolescents in the program.

TECHNIQUES FOR READING INSTRUCTION

In addition to using a variety of remedial instructional programs, special educators often use supplementary remedial techniques to develop reading skills. These reading techniques correlate with the types of reading errors described earlier in the chapter and can be helpful in correcting poor reading patterns in handicapped students.

Error: Omissions

- Print the phrase as read by the student and the phrase as printed in the text on the blackboard, and then compare the two phrases.
- Emphasize instruction focusing on building a sight word vocabulary.
- Provide choral reading experiences to help students to expand their sight vocabularies.
- Use reading guides, such as index cards or rulers, so that students do not lose their places. Also, cut passages into distinct sentences to help students keep their places.

Error: Additions

- Use choral reading strategies to encourage precision reading.
- Use a tachistoscope to help students learn to pace themselves.
- Write the phrases as read by the student and as printed in the text, and then compare the phrases.

Error: Substitutions

- Emphasize decoding skills. A syntactical approach to decoding is typically helpful.
- Print the substitution and actual word from the passage on the chalkboard and compare the two.
- Make vocabulary cards consisting of unknown words, and have students master and review these from time to time.
- Use a cloze procedure deleting only those words for which substitutions were made.

Error: Repetitions

- Build a sight vocabulary.
- Design a notched marker to prevent repeated reading.

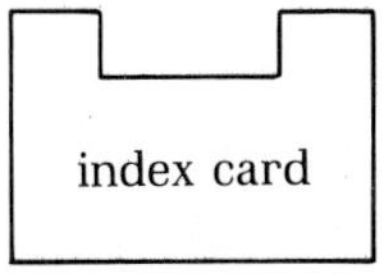

- Help the student to relax through breathing exercises.
- Use choral reading, and then have the student reread the passage alone.

Error: Reads Word by Word

- Build a sight vocabulary.
- Allow the student to hear a model of a fluent reader before reading the passage.
- Allow the student to read material below instructional level.

Error: Ignores Punctuation

- Model the error by reading passages without pauses at commas and periods.
- Highlight punctuation marks in passages student is to read.

Error: Points to Words

- Allow the student to read material below his or her instructional level.
- Emphasize sight vocabulary during reading instruction.
- Allow the student to hear a fluent model several times before reading a passage.
- Use a tachistoscope to encourage students to use their eyes for reading.

Error: Reverses Words

- Use a kinesthetic method to develop accuracy of word recognition.

- Compare words that the student reverses, emphasizing the beginning and ending sounds.
- Use a cloze procedure to encourage reliance on contextual cues for decoding unknown words.

Error: Poor Sight Vocabulary

- Use a cloze procedure to encourage reliance on contextual cues to decode unknown words.
- Develop awareness of basic word families through a synthetic phonics approach.
- Emphasize sight vocabulary through word games.

SURVIVAL SKILLS

According to Cazden (1980), an imbalance exists "between too much drill on the component skills of language and literacy and too little attention to their significant use" (p. 595). While most special educators would acknowledge that reading is an important survival skill in almost every aspect of a student's life, much remains to be done to reduce the imbalance between reading instruction and its application in daily life. In addition, reading instruction becomes more relevant for the educationally handicapped student when integrated with the student's survival needs. The following activities, grouped by grade level, present methods of applying reading to survival skills:

Primary and Intermediate:

- The teacher may want to tape information such as name, address, school and home phone numbers to the student's desk, and later have students pick their address or name from among a group.
- The teacher can prepare slides or photographs of community businesses and services, such as the drugstore, grocery store, department store, doctor, and dentist, which are useful in helping students develop a sight word vocabulary for such businesses and services.
- Teachers can prepare transparencies or dittos of a television guide or a bus schedule to help students learn how such information is organized and how to use it properly.
- Teachers can use cookbooks, simple sewing patterns, or directions for a craft item to teach sequential reading skills and help students learn to follow directions.
- Teachers can have students tape a letter, transcribe it from tape, then read the letter while listening to the tape to check for clarity and meaning.
- Teachers can schedule a daily silent reading period of ten to fifteen minutes in which everyone reads something for pleasure (Efta 1978). This activity may help students to perceive reading as a leisure alternative.

Junior and Senior High:

- Teachers can have students use the phone book to call and order a pizza for the class or a plant from the florist for the classroom. Students can plan real or imaginary trips using brochures from travel agencies to select a destination and the phone book to locate and call travel agencies and bus, train, and plane companies for price information. Students can also use the newspaper to locate recipes, available jobs, advice columns, and a variety of other specific types of information.
- Students can gather directions on medicine bottles and cleaning products to identify safety precautions and emergency procedures. Students can prepare a slide presentation of signs from around the community that correspond with vocabulary in a survival word file.
- Students can prepare food by following directions from a cookbook or create a craft project by following a set of directions.
- Students can use a road map to plot a class trip, identifying names of routes, towns, points of interest, and facilities on the route.
- Students and teachers can read for pleasure in a daily leisure reading time of ten to fifteen minutes to encourage this habit in students (Efta 1978).
- Students can read job applications, loan or credit applications, insurance brochures, or university catalogs, after which they follow directions given in the application or paraphrase the information given in brochures and catalogs.

HOME REINFORCEMENT

Parents of the educationally handicapped student can be of invaluable assistance in helping their child apply and use reading skills on a daily basis. Following is a list of activities from which parents can choose to reinforce reading skills and behavior.

- Parents can encourage reading as a leisure activity by reading for leisure in the child's presence on a daily basis.
- Parents can also read to their child on a daily basis.
- The child can prepare some special recipe for the family or read the directions and prepare the food with a parent.
- Parents can write notes for their child to read. Such notes should be positive in nature. Examples include thank-you notes for things the child did, notes of praise for accomplishments, and humorous stories or jokes.
- Parents can label common objects around the house, such as chairs, beds, doors, tables, the stove, and the sofa.
- Parents can encourage their child to locate telephone numbers, television channels, or information in the newspaper such as an item for sale or a specific article.

- Parents can play games that require reading with their children on a daily basis.
- Parents can encourage their child to plan a trip or vacation, gather information about the location, and plot the directions on a map.
- Parents and their child can take photographs of important family events. Parents can write captions dictated by the child for each photograph.
- Parents can help their child with craft activities in which the child reads or is assisted in reading directions to complete the craft.
- Parents can give their child a small portion of the grocery list that includes brand names. The child can be responsible for collecting those items at the grocery store.

These activities provide a valuable supplement to the child's reading instruction because they encourage the child to view reading as a necessary skill. Parents should approach these activities positively so that each activity is both enjoyable and reinforcing to the child.

REGULAR CLASS INVOLVEMENT

For the educationally handicapped student, reading deficits can reduce opportunities for academic success. Even though the handicapped students may understand the concepts or content of written material, the act of reading prevents the student from demonstrating his or her understanding. Through careful planning and organization, regular and special educators can provide opportunities for each student to achieve success in activities that require reading. Following are suggestions that the regular educator can use to provide successful reading experiences for the educationally handicapped student:

- Prior to introducing a unit of study, provide repeated exposure to key vocabulary included in the unit. For example, if a unit on metrics is planned for October, the regular educator could take three to five minutes daily in September to expose students to words like *kilometer, centimeter,* and *millimeter.*
- When introducing unit vocabulary, focus on word analysis, word recognition, and definition. Identify significant clues in words that aid in decoding. Provide practice exercises that encourage speed in recognition, and allow the student to use and identify each word in a sentence after its meaning has been introduced.
- Important information in texts can be highlighted and taped by a fluent reader so that the educationally handicapped student can listen to the tape while following the words in the text.
- Arrange for students to read and paraphrase questions in the study guide before reading the content in a text to encourage purposeful reading.
- Students could be provided with study sheets in which the most important facts or concepts under study are presented in outline form. A combination of basic vocabulary, such as that from the *Dolch Basic Word List* (Dolch 1950),

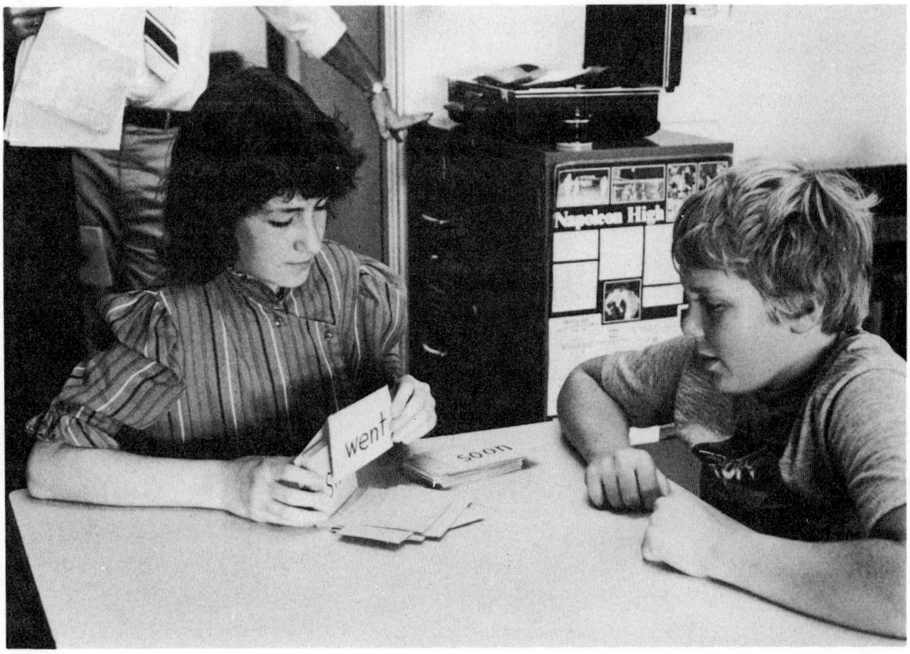

Peer tutoring can be an effective strategy for vocabulary development activities.

and vocabulary related to the unit should be used on such study sheets to insure independent reading.

- Provide some time during each lesson for independent work to encourage students to read important materials as well as to allow for individual assistance for students.
- Use a peer-tutoring model during independent study time. Pair a fluent reader with an educationally handicapped student, and provide each pair of students with a purposeful reading activity and a procedure for completing the activity.
- The regular educator can read test questions to some students and allow an oral response. A variation of this suggestion is to put test questions on tape and allow students to record or write responses according to ability.
- Use a simple sentence format for essay questions, and consider multiple-choice, short-answer, or fill-in-the-blank questions when feasible.
- Take time to read or have the student read lecture notes or assignments written on the chalkboard.

SUMMARY POINTS

- The purpose of reading instruction is to assist students in becoming literate. Reading consists of several general processes, including comprehension, decoding, and word recognition.

- Reading assessment may begin with use of formal assessment tools and progress to use of teacher-made criterion tests, miscue analysis, and graded word lists.
- A scope-and-sequence chart of reading skills provides a general idea of subskills associated with reading processes. Selection of reading subskills for instruction should be based on assessment data.
- There are four major methods for reading instruction: the basal method, the phonics method, the linguistic method, and the language experience method. Each method has specific advantages and disadvantages that should be considered with assessment data when building a reading program for a specific student.
- There are several remedial reading strategies from which teachers may select when designing instructional programs for students. While these differ from conventional reading methods, the decision to use them is also dependent upon assessment data.
- A variety of reading methods may be combined to form a specific reading program for a student. These methods may be supplemented with certain remedial reading strategies.

REVIEW QUESTIONS

1. One of the disadvantages of a basal reading series is that the arrangement of skills and concepts in such programs does not encourage assessment, daily evaluation, or record keeping. How could you compensate for this program weakness when using a basal reading series?
2. If you had determined that a phonics method should form the basis of your instructional program for one of your students, how could you assure that the student's comprehension skills would not suffer as a result?
3. You note that one of your students has developed the habit of reading word by word. What could you do to encourage reading fluency in this student?

SUGGESTED READINGS

Gillespie-Silver, P. 1979. *Teaching reading to children with special needs: An ecological approach.* Columbus, Ohio: Charles E. Merrill.

Gillingham, A., and Stillman, B. 1968. *Remedial teaching for children with specific disability in reading, spelling, and penmanship.* Cambridge, Mass.: Education Publishing Service.

Kirk, S.A.; Kliebhan, J. M.; and Lerner, J. W. 1978. *Teaching reading to slow and disabled learners.* Boston: Houghton Mifflin.

Application: Steve and Matt

Steve

The following instructional objectives were included in Steve's IEP to improve his reading skills:

- Following instruction, Steve will pronounce basic synthetic units in words with 100 percent accuracy.
- Following instruction, Steve will supply appropriate words in a passage with 90 percent accuracy.

Since Steve had attained mastery of basic phonetic skills but required additional instruction in analytical skills, Mrs. Gifford selected a synthetic phonics method and a high-interest, low-readability reading text for motivational purposes. This phonics method would prompt Steve to scan the unknown word, search for a VC, VVC, or VCV pattern, and blend this pattern with the initial consonant, digraph, or blend. In other words, this method forced Steve to temporarily ignore the first configuration in the word and skim for the vowel pattern—just the opposite of the decoding skill observed during testing.

Word rings were developed for Steve that featured short- and long-vowel units and words containing these units. For example, the phoneme */et/* was written in red with a sample of words such as *bet* and *letter* in which this VC pattern appeared. Initially, these phonemes were color coded so that Steve saw */et/* singly and in word samples in the color red. When Steve could pronounce each phoneme unit without hesitation, Mrs. Gifford deleted the color cue from the word samples.

After Steve had mastered long- and short-vowel units, blends, and digraphs, Mrs. Gifford used a closed sort strategy in which Steve was given a deck of ten to twenty word cards and asked to select those that contained specific sounds. This was followed by an open sort strategy in which Steve was to determine the criteria for membership in the set of words and deduce the rules that governed the pronunciation of particular words. These sort activities reinforced the concept that phonemes are related to some general grapheme representations.

To help Steve develop critical reading skills, Mrs. Gifford used a modified cloze procedure on passages selected in a high-interest, low-readability reader. Each day Steve read one page aloud to Mrs. Gifford. As he read, she noted any words that he added, omitted, or substituted. She then retyped the passage omitting those words that gave Steve difficulty and placing them at the bottom of the page. Steve's task was to fill in each blank in the passage by selecting an appropriate word from the group at the bottom of the page. Later Mrs. Gifford raised the level of difficulty of these cloze tasks by omitting the list of word choices at the bottom of each cloze activity.

During the annual review meeting in the spring, Mrs. Gifford recommended that Steve continue to receive reading instruction in the resource room. Her goals for Steve were to help him to *(a)* increase comprehension skills, *(b)* learn to locate information from content texts, *(c)* develop a system of cue words that would direct him in problem-solving activities, and *(d)* develop confidence in his reading ability. Steve was very fortunate that both of the professionals in his general and special educational programs saw him as a learner and were willing to take the time to assess and plan precisely to meet his need for reading instruction.

Matt

The following goals for reading were noted on Matt's IEP:

- Matt will learn long and short vowels, digraphs, diphthongs, and basic analytic skills.
- Matt will read with fluency and understanding.

Ms. Beck, Matt's resource teacher, decided to use a language experience method as a basis for reading instruction. Matt was to draft a story each week. Sometimes Ms. Beck used an action picture of a car, plane, or jet to provide a story theme; sometimes she used a "story starter," which consisted of a topic sentence such as "The day I took my first airplane ride I felt . . . " As the year progressed, Matt would often set the theme for the week's language experience story. Ms. Beck would write the story on a large chart as Matt dictated it. When finished, Ms. Beck and Matt read the story together so that Matt could develop fluency. Later in the week, the story would be cut into sentence strips which Matt would rearrange in sequential order. On Friday, Ms. Beck gave Matt a typed copy of the final version to place in his "author's notebook."

After the story was written on Monday, Matt and Ms. Beck chose five to ten vocabulary words from it to be used during the week for word study. These words were analyzed through a synthetic approach to discern the vowel patterns or other unique phonetic elements. Matt was also guided to categorize his vocabulary words according to whether they fit a compound or root-suffix pattern. At the end of the week, Matt was asked to reach each word in isolation, locate it in his story, and place the word in the appropriate category in his card file. Categories of the word file were organized according to major phonetic elements.

Ms. Beck also used a variety of learning games, mastery tasks, and rebus cards to develop and reinforce each of the phonics and analytic skills targeted in Matt's IEP. For example, Ms. Beck made rebus cards for consonant digraphs for Matt as shown in Figure 10.8.

Matt's scores on posttests at the end of the year revealed an academic gain of two years in reading. Matt's total reading instructional score on Form B of the *Woodcock Reading Mastery Test* was 4^2, indicating a reading level of four academic years and two months. An error analysis of a reading sample indicated that Matt's errors clustered around additions. Matt had become a fluent reader and had begun to decode words effectively. Matt's analytic skills indicated a need for instruction in syllabication principles, such as root-prefix combinations and multisyllable words. Therefore, Ms. Beck recommended that Matt continue to receive reading instruction in the resource room. New instructional goals for Matt were to *(a)* increase his comprehension skills through the use of high-interest, low-readability materials, *(b)* maintain phonics and analytic skills through periodic review, and *(c)* develop mastery of analytic skills with emphasis on syllabication principles.

Discussion Points

1. When reading, Steve made substitution and omission errors. As his teacher, what additional methods and strategies would you use to help him avoid these errors?
2. Matt's teacher did not use a basal reading program for instruction; yet he made a gain of two academic years in reading. Based on these results, what statements could you make about the significance of materials and methods used in reading instruction?

☐ **FIGURE 10–8**
Rebus Cards for Consonant Digraphs

Front

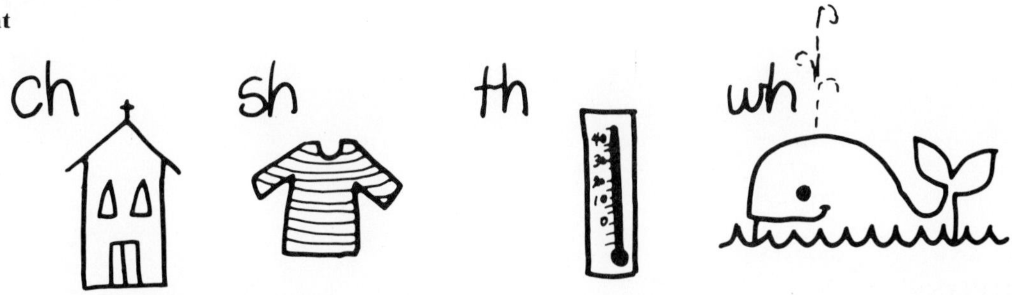

Back

ch sh th wh

church Shirt thermometer whale

CHAPTER 11 Developing Written Expression

OUTLINE

INTRODUCTION

Written expression is a complex and multidimensional process. Johnson and Myklebust (1967) refer to written expression as "one of the highest forms of language, hence, the last to be learned" (p. 193). As defined by Poteet (1980), it is "a visual representation of thoughts, feelings, and ideas using symbols of the writer's language system for the purpose of communication or recording" (p. 88).

Proficiency in written expression requires a variety of experiences and skills. Students identified as having written expression deficits may have problems in the actual writing process, the written syntax of their thoughts, spelling, grammar, and the organization of their thoughts.

The assessment and instructional strategies discussed in this chapter encourage professionals to use an ecological perspective in remediating deficit areas. A comprehensive written expression program is more likely to be successful if a student's motivational needs and other teacher's demands on the student are considered.

Objectives

After reading the chapter, you should be able to

- state a comprehensive definition for written expression;
- identify deficits associated with each area of written expression;
- choose appropriate remedial strategies for students who have written expression deficits;
- cite home intervention strategies appropriate for elementary- through high-school-aged students;
- state remedial strategies appropriate for regular classroom use.

Case Studies: Craig and Tony

Deficits in written expression are usually attributed to faulty penmanship. However, as indicated in the following two case studies, written expression is broader in scope and includes many skill areas.

Craig

Craig, a thirteen-year-old attending junior high, has a history of school failure. Although Craig experienced early difficulty in learning basic reading, spelling, and writing skills, the span between his achievement and that of his peers widened in fourth grade. At that time, Craig's academic problems became more complex, heightened by his lack of interest in school and lack of motivation.

Craig's parents became increasingly concerned over Craig's academic failure and requested that Craig be tested by the school psychologist. The results of in-depth assessment procedures indicated that Craig was performing below grade level in all subjects except math. At the IEP meeting, it was recommended that Craig be placed in a self-contained program for educationally handicapped students.

During fifth and sixth grade, Craig improved his reading, spelling, and written and verbal expression skills; yet his achievement level remained below grade-level norms. His attitude toward himself and school appeared to be much improved. In the spring of his sixth year of school, the annual review team recommended that Craig receive language arts instruction in the junior high special program. He was to be phased back into the mainstream for all other academic areas.

For Craig the adjustment from elementary school to junior high was difficult. He was confronted with an orientation to a new building, rules, peers, and teachers. In addition, he was extremely anxious about how he would perform in regular classes such as science, history, math, and health.

At the end of the first grading period, the following grade reports and comments from teachers were sent to Craig's parents:

MATH	B+	Improving!
SCIENCE	D	Seems to know material, yet test scores reflect the grade.
HISTORY	D−	Craig does not participate in class. Written assignments are habitually late, incomplete, and incorrectly executed.
HEALTH	D+	Lacks interest, poor test scores; does not follow directions; and never takes notes in class.
LANGUAGE	B−	Noticeable improvement. Craig still needs to work on written expression.

The following work sample was among those sent home by Craig's special teacher. The students had been instructed to outline information on a specific topic. Craig had chosen the topic of football.

Craig's Work Sample

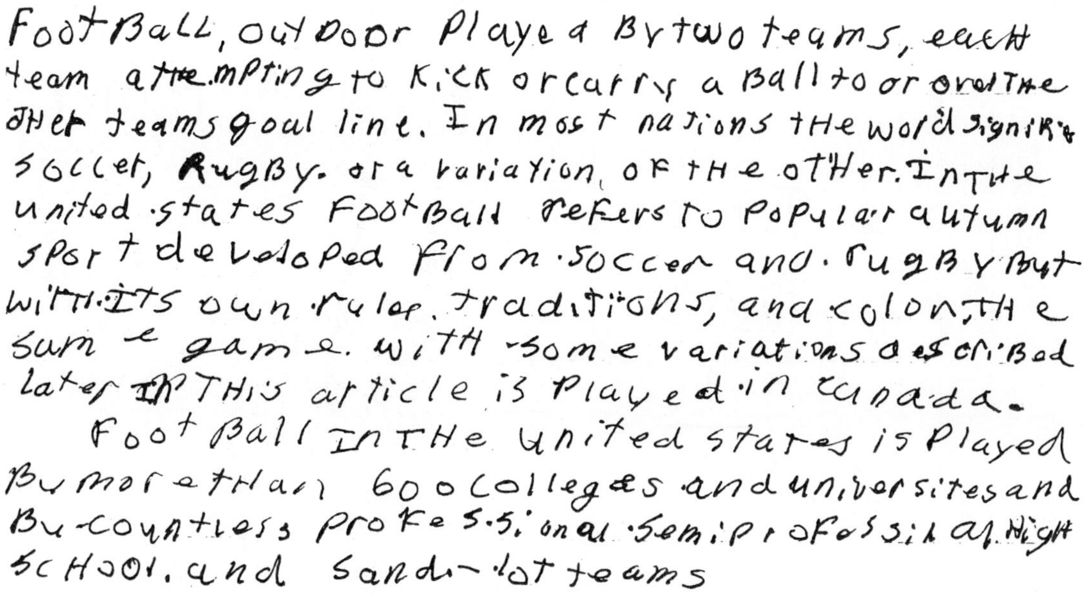

FootBall, outDoor Played By two teams, eacH team attempting to Kick or carry a Ball to or over The other teams goal line. In most nations the word signify soccer, RugBy. or a variation, of the other. In the united states FootBall refers to popular autumn sport developed from soccer and rugBy But with its own rules, traditions, and color. The same game. with some variations described later in This article is Played in Canada.

FootBall In The united states is Played By more than 600 colleges and universites and By countless professional Semiprofessinal High school, and Sand-lot teams

An analysis of the above writing sample indicated the following:

- Has difficulty sorting given information into main ideas and details
- Has difficulty structuring an outline
- Demonstrates poor penmanship due to inaccurate letter formation and spacing
- Uses both capital and lower-case letters inconsistently
- Uses both cursive and manuscript handwriting

Upon receipt of their child's grade reports, teacher comments, and work samples, Craig's parents became upset and concerned that this new adjustment was too great for their son to manage.

Tony

Eight-year-old Tony Martinez is in the third grade. His grade reports from school have reflected average academic performance and achievement in all areas except handwriting.

At the September school open house, Tony's parents expressed their concern about Tony's poor handwriting. Mrs. Ingles, the third grade teacher, explained that handwriting instruction would consist of copying daily lessons from the board, and drill practice. She reassured Mr. and Mrs. Martinez that academic grades in reading, spelling, and mathematics would be based upon Tony's knowledge. Handwriting performance would be evaluated separately. Mrs. Ingles was confident improvement would occur with maturation. She felt that worry was unnecessary due to Tony's adequate performance in other academic areas.

Throughout the year, Tony's parents collected handwriting samples of his work. Unable to detect any improvement, they requested a parent-teacher conference to restate their concern and to inquire about additional help for Tony. Discussion at the parent-teacher conference centered on the handwriting samples submitted by Tony's parents. No marked improvement was evident. Following are two of these handwriting samples:

Sample 1: Spelling Test Taken by Tony in December
(Note that the "f," bad, and sad face were made by Tony)

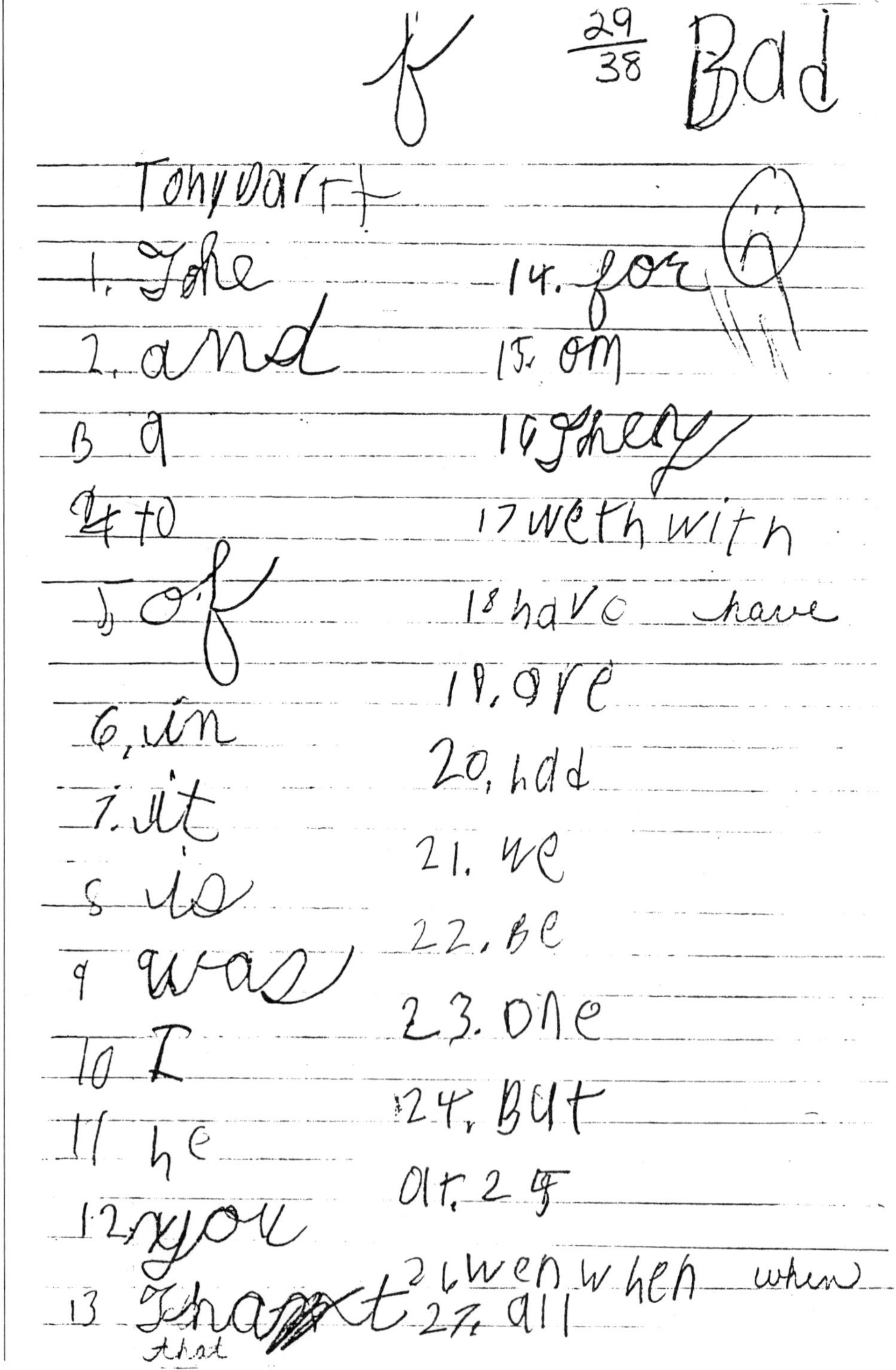

f 29/38 Bad

Tony Dart

1. Tohe
2. and
3 a
4 to
5 of
6, in
7. it
8 is
9 was
10 I
11 he
12 you
13 Thant that

14. for
15. om
16 they
17 weth with
18 havo have
19, are
20, had
21. we
22. be
23. one
24. but
or. 25
26 wen when when
27. all

Sample 2: Creative Writing Exercise Done by Tony in April

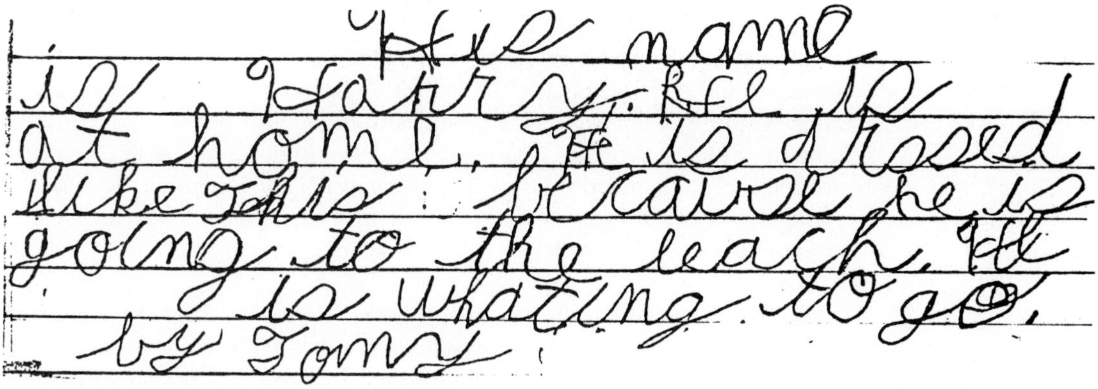

Following the conference, Tony's parents felt that they had failed to obtain help for him. In addition, they observed a progressive decline in their son's estimation of his ability to be successful at writing tasks. The third grade teacher had defended her curriculum with the argument that handwriting instruction had been delivered daily and that it had been impossible to spend individual time with one student.

Through careful error analysis of Tony's written work samples, the following conclusions were drawn:

- Tony has difficulty in letter formation both in copying and from memory.
- Spelling tests indicated the following error patterns: omissions of needed letters, reversal of consonant order, inappropriate sound-symbol association, and use of symbols with no relationship to sounds in the word.
- Tony's work samples show improper spacing between letters and words in both manuscript and cursive execution (see Sample 1).
- Letter size is improper and inconsistent throughout all work samples provided.
- Repeated failure at writing tasks had begun to have a serious negative effect on Tony's self-image.

Points for Consideration

- *Craig's difficulties in written expression were noted at a relatively early stage in his educational experience.*

His other academic lags contributed to the awareness of his written expression problems.

- *In Tony's case, the magnitude of his writing disability was camouflaged by an overall adequate academic performance.*
- *In Craig's case, the effectiveness of the intervention program provided was interrupted due to the hierarchical structure of services.*

The program change to a junior high resource room setting forced the child to confront adjustments he may not have been prepared to undertake.

- *Attempts by Tony's parents to find help for him proved futile due to the educational setting and instructor.*
- *Craig's parents were confronted with having to decide how to provide for their son's academic welfare and social adaptation within the relatively few remaining school years.*

Both sets of parents had to deal with school personnel from a subordinate position and had to let time govern their child's educational success.

COMMON INSTRUCTIONAL MISCONCEPTIONS

A disability in written expression is always accompanied by evident difficulties in other academic areas. Although some educationally handicapped students have problems related to more than one academic area or domain, this is not always the case. Some handicapped learners understand the material, but have difficulties presenting their ideas in writing. The substandard written responses of these students are too often misinterpreted by professionals as meaning that they do not understand the material. As a result, poor written expression skills can have a very serious effect on the student's sense of worth and ability (Harvey-Felder 1978).

Manuscript instruction must precede cursive instruction. Because skills acquired in manuscript instruction are thought to contribute to the development of cursive writing skills, this sequence of teaching handwriting prevails in classrooms. However, this instructional approach may not be appropriate for all students. Some students profit more from the smooth, flowing wholeness associated with cursive handwriting. In such cases, manuscript instruction need not be taught.

WRITTEN EXPRESSION SKILLS

Written language development depends on environmental variables that affect the student (Hall 1981) as well as on the acquisition of mechanical skills that permit written expression. Figure 11–1 illustrates the comprehensive nature and development of written expression skills.

From an instructional point of view, the development of written expression skills should not focus solely on developing mechanical skills. Special educators must also attend to environmental variables that affect communication.

Because written expression is so complex, it is difficult to assess student ability in a comprehensive manner. Until recently, most assessment tools in this skill area measured components of written expression such as punctuation, spelling, and grammar. As written expression became increasingly recognized as a complex form of language, serious attempts to measure student ability in a comprehensive manner evolved. Two comprehensive formal measures that enable special educators to assess students' written expression skills are the *Test of Written Language (TOWL)* (Hammill and Larsen 1978) and the *Test of Adolescent Language (TOAL)* (Hammill et al. 1980).

The *TOWL* is a norm-referenced test that may be administered individually or in groups to students aged eight and one-half through fourteen and one-half years. The seven subtests of the *TOWL* focus on the following aspects of written language: vocabulary, thematic maturity, spelling, word usage, style, thought units, and handwriting. Scores from each of these subtests are recorded on the *TOWL* Profile Chart, allowing the teacher to determine student strengths and weaknesses in these areas of written expression.

The *TOAL* allows the teacher to assess both written and oral expression in students aged eleven through eighteen and one-half. Specifically, the *TOAL* assesses listening, speaking, reading, writing, spoken language, written language, vocabulary, grammar, receptive language, and expressive language. Two of the subtests

☐ **FIGURE 11–1**
A Model of Written Language

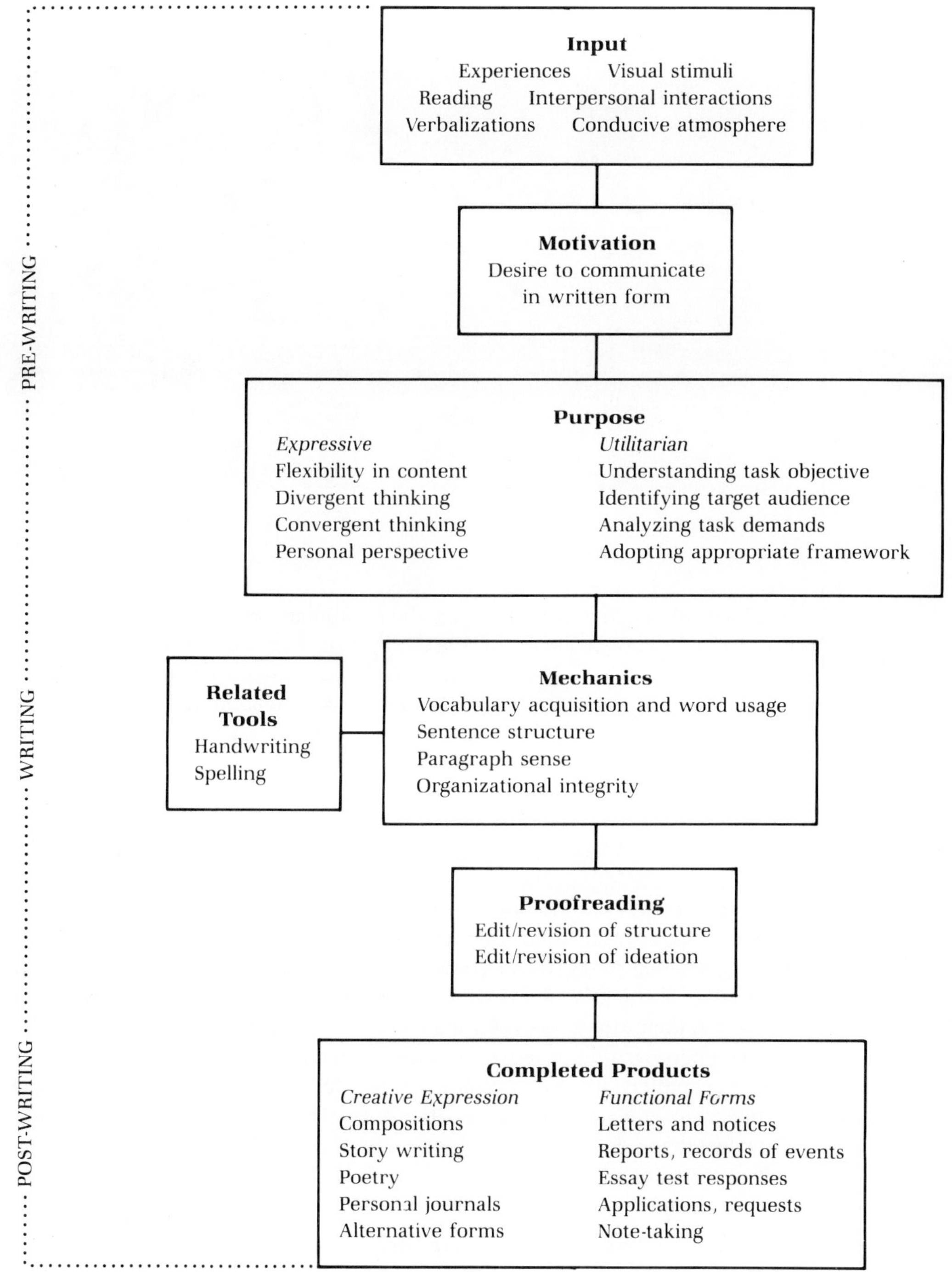

Source: From Polloway, E.A.; Patton, J.R. and Cohen, S.B. "Written Language for Mildly Handicapped Students." *Focus on Exceptional Children 14* (3):4. Used by permission of Love Publishing Company.

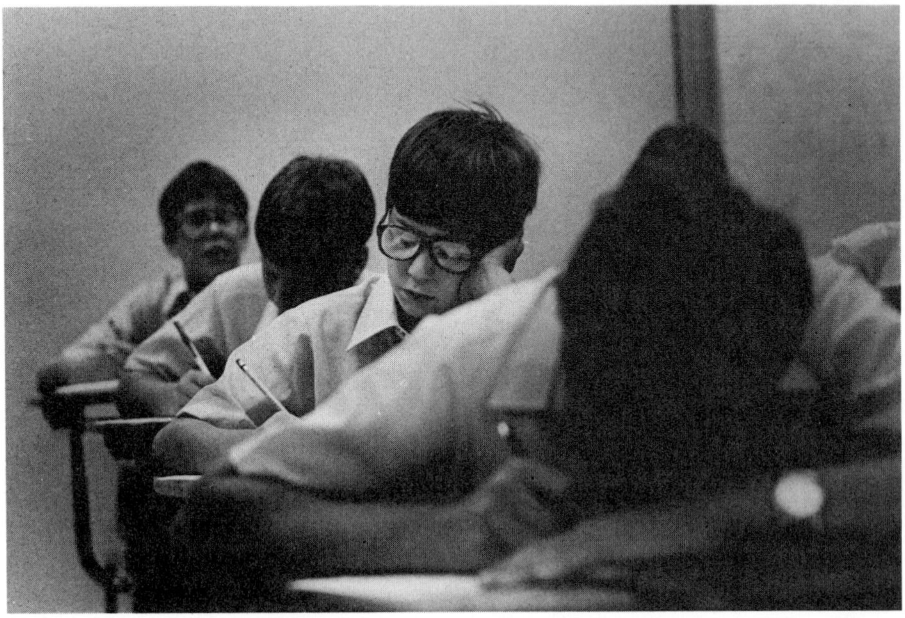

As students progress through school, the need for fluent written expression skills increases.

that focus on written expression are the vocabulary subtest and the grammar subtest. In the vocabulary subtest, the student reads a word and is asked to include that word in a meaningful sentence. In the grammar subtest, the student reads two sentences and is asked to write a sentence that combines the meaning of the original two. As is apparent, both of these subtests require reading ability to complete test tasks.

HANDWRITING

Writing disorders should not be confused with poor handwriting due to carelessness or lack of motivation. Gillingham and Stillman (1965) define students with writing disabilities as "those children whose penmanship is lagging far behind their other accomplishments in academic lines and is proving a distinct handicap to them in their attempts to express ideas in writing" (p. 289).

The handwriting process integrates visual perception, visual memory, hand-eye coordination, and motor abilities. Difficulties in writing may be due to a deficit in any one or more of these areas. An effective remedial program for handwriting disorders depends on accurate assessment of the child's problem and appropriate remedial strategies.

Assessment of Handwriting Skills

Handwriting assessment, a complex task, must evaluate written execution, syntax, grammar, punctuation, spelling, content, and organization. Thus, the special educator must know the components of written expression, the sequence for assessing these components, and the skills within each component that require scrutiny.

LeBrun and Van de Graien (1975) indicate that assessment of written expression should initially focus on manual execution of alphabet symbols. The following scope-and-sequence chart for handwriting skills (Figure 11–2) provides the special educator with knowledge of handwriting subskills. Such knowledge enables the special educator to implement instructional techniques that best facilitate the purpose and scope of target skills.

☐ **FIGURE 11–2**
Scope and Sequence of Handwriting Skills

HANDWRITING	*Deficient* –	*Instruction* /	*Mastery* *
Prewriting			
Left to right directionality			
Top, middle, bottom orientation			
Holds a writing tool			
Gross writing movements			
Fine motor writing movements			
Traces different shaped lines			
Copies different shaped straight lines			
Draws different lines from memory			
Manuscript			
Traces letters in isolation			
Traces letters in words			
Traces sentences			
Forms lower- and upper-case letters using appropriate vertical spacing			
Forms lower- and upper-case letters using appropriate horizontal spacing between letters and words			
Copies letters in isolation from a model in close proximity			
Copies letters in isolation from a model on the board			
Writes letters in isolation from short-term memory (immediate recall)			
Copies letters in words from a model in close proximity			
Copies letters in words from a model on the board			
Writes letters in words from memory			
Copies sentences from a model in close proximity			
Copies sentences from a model on the board			
Writes sentences from memory			

☐ **FIGURE 11–2—continued**
Scope and Sequence of Handwriting Skills

Cursive	*Deficient* –	*Instruction* /	*Mastery* *
Traces letters in isolation			
Traces words			
Traces sentences			
Forms lower- and upper-case letters using appropriate vertical spacing			
Forms lower- and upper-case letters using appropriate horizontal spacing between letters and words			
Copies letters in isolation from a model in close proximity			
Copies letters in isolation from a model on the board			
Writes letters in isolation from short-term memory (immediate recall)			
Writes letters from memory			
Copies connecting letters from a model in close proximity			
Copies words from a model placed at some distance			
Writes words from memory			
Copies words from a model in close proximity			
Copies words from a model placed on the board			
Writes words from memory			
Copies sentences from a model in close proximity			
Copies sentences from a model placed on the board			
Writes sentences from memory			

The scope-and-sequence chart of handwriting skills can be used as a guide for constructing teacher-made criterion tests. Such tests can effectively measure a student's ability in each subskill related to handwriting. At times, however, the special teacher may wish to use commercial instruments to assess student handwriting skills. An example of a formal test that assesses a student's handwriting ability is the *Zaner-Bloser Evaluation Scales* (1979). These scales assess manuscript writing in grades one and two and cursive writing in grades three through eight. Six elements of handwriting are evaluated by the teacher: letter formation, vertical strokes (manuscript), slant (cursive), spacing, alignment and proportion, and line quality.

Instructional Guidelines

Before discussing specific remedial strategies, it is important to identify instructional guidelines related to all facets of penmanship. The following procedural guidelines are based, in part, on suggestions made by Hofmeister (1973):

- Provide the student with adequate opportunities for practice under direct teacher supervision.
- Present students with immediate feedback so that they can compare their product with the accurate representation and thus avoid inadvertantly practicing inappropriate skills.
- Provide a good model for handwriting so that students can discriminate between the model and their product and determine necessary changes.
- Include body posture and positioning of the hands and writing paper in all handwriting instruction.
- Make necessary accommodations for left-handed and right-handed students.
- Provide standard-sized pencils and paper geared to the students' developmental needs.

Handwriting is a tool for communication consisting of skills acquired at different instructional stages. After determining a student's preferred hand for writing, instruction progresses toward developing prewriting skills. After these readiness abilities are acquired, handwriting instruction usually proceeds to manuscript and then to cursive writing.

Manuscript Versus Cursive Handwriting

In the field of special education, there is controversy over whether manuscript or cursive writing instruction should be used for handicapped children. Generally, most manuscript writing is taught during the first two school years. At some time during second or third grade, a transition is made to cursive instruction. Opinions vary as to the appropriateness of this established transition in instruction. Some argue that learning only cursive writing is much more practical and effective for the disabled (Heyman 1977; Strauss and Lehtinen 1951). Proponents of this view maintain that cursive handwriting minimizes spatial judgment problems and reversals while enhancing rhythmic continuity and the concept of wholeness.

Advocates of manuscript writing argue that the ease of manuscript letter formation makes this method better suited to the capabilities of young children (McGinnis 1977). In addition they argue that the manuscript method provides a natural foundation for later cursive development. The case for each side appears strong, and the decision remains with the educator. Careful consideration of the child's motor development, capabilities, and deficits must govern the choice of whether to use a manuscript or cursive writing program.

Remedial Strategies

Prewriting skills. Before implementing formal handwriting instruction, a teacher must determine the student's readiness for instruction. Handicapped students often have difficulty orienting themselves to the task of handwriting. Following is a list of prewriting, or readiness, errors and related remedial activities for developing the skills needed at this stage.

1. *Deficit Skill:* Difficulty in left-right orientation
   Suggested Remedial Strategies:
   (a) Provide students with age-appropriate directional cues on their papers, as shown below. Note that the first technique can also help in establishing margins.

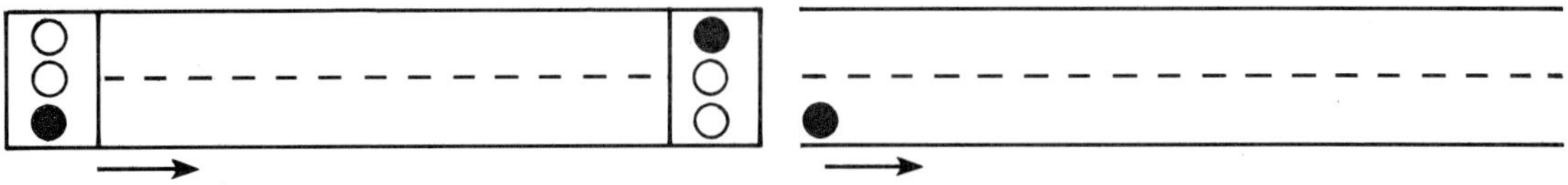

   (b) Place directional devices on the student's desk or chalkboard. In addition to the concept of left and right, these cues should subsequently address concepts such as up and down, top and bottom, vertical and horizontal, and baseline and headline (Kaminsky and Powers 1981).

2. *Deficit Skill:* Difficulty in placement of letters or numbers on the page
   Suggested Remedial Strategies: Provide students with lined paper that matches their need for spatial structure, and present concrete cues on the paper to assist in proper letter size. Concrete reference points help children who have difficulties with abstract spatial concepts.
   (a) The boy's head touches the top line; his hands are resting on his waist (the middle line); and his feet are on the ground. Directions such as "all letters rest on the ground" can be a valuable learning aid.

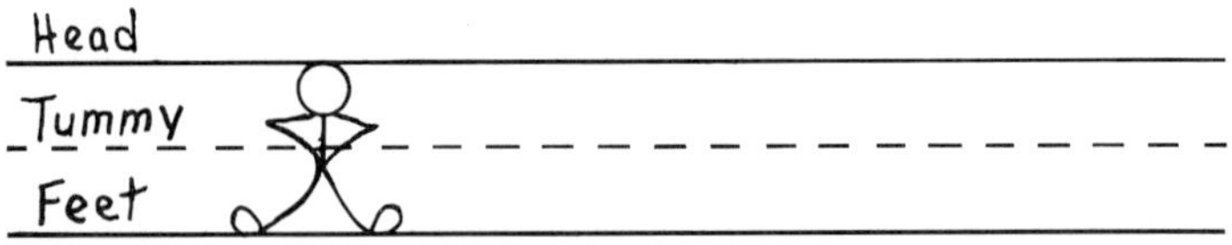

   (b) Highlight with colored markers the lines that are giving students problems.

3. *Deficit Skill:* Improper pencil grip
   Suggested Remedial Strategies: Allow the child opportunities to practice using crayons, paint brushes, chalk, magic markers, and pencils. (This allows the student to see how different writing tools affect his or her writing.) Make adjustments by:
   (a) using grippers on the utensil;
   (b) placing color-coded tape on the utensil matched with colored ink marks on the child's corresponding fingers.

4. *Deficit Skill:* Difficulty in executing smooth, rhythmic motor movements. (It is important to emphasize that merely participating in the following activities will not improve handwriting. It is necessary for the teacher to specify what the student is to do with these various media. Remember, if you want to improve handwriting, focus on handwriting activities, and not general motor tasks.)
   Suggested Remedial Strategies:
   (a) Provide the child with teacher-directed experiences in making shapes,

letters, and numbers by finger painting, using a stylus, simultaneously executing letters on the chalkboard with the teacher.

(b) Provide the child with opportunity to ease muscle tension or fatigue by teaching hand exercises, such as opening and closing hands, stretching fingers, and pressing one finger at a time on a hard surface (Kaminsky and Powers 1981). This exercise can be used during and after writing instruction.

5. *Deficit Skill:* Difficulty drawing straight and curved lines and other shapes
Suggested Remedial Strategies: Provide structured drawing activities for students. For example, have students
(a) draw a picture by connecting numbered dots;
(b) relate abstract concepts to concrete objects (by drawing mountains like  or  or the waves of the ocean like  or );
(c) trace around cardboard or wooden letters;
(d) use tracing paper to draw shapes, lines, angles, letters and/or numbers on a page (Burton 1982).

Manuscript handwriting. Once a student demonstrates readiness for formal writing, instruction should focus on developing skills in letter formation, spacing, slant, and word writing. While there are various commercial writing programs available, a teacher should plan a child's writing program according to the student's specific capabilities and limitations. Teachers have a pool of options from which to choose in structuring a program; they may adopt or adapt a commercial program or develop their own approach. Regardless of the approach a teacher chooses, it is important that students be consistently exposed to the same methodology.

Remedial strategies. Often students experiencing handwriting problems have deficits in more than one area, thus increasing the complexity of planning a remedial program. For effective instruction the choice of techniques to be used should be appropriate for the student's age as well as his or her skill level. Following are suggested instructional techniques for remediating manuscript errors.

1. *Deficit Skills*: Illegible letter forms
Suggested Remedial Strategies:
(a) Introduce letters through association with live characters, real objects or events in a story. For example:
An *s* looks like a *s*nake 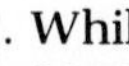 creeping through the grass.
*W*illie's mother asked him to go down 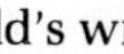 into the basement to get a bottle of *w*indow cleaner. He *w*ent down the steps and came back up 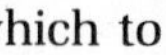 without finding it. His mother explained to *W*illie again; so he *w*ent back down 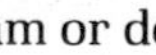 the steps and came back up 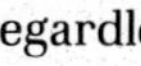 with *w*hat she *w*anted.
(b) Use transparent overlays so that the child can check his or her product with a model and trace the model if the work sample is inaccurate.
(c) Use clay or wet sand in a cookie sheet for tracing letters, lines, and angles.

2. *Deficit Skill:* Reversals (It should be noted that reversals are quite common and not necessarily a problem even in children up to about age nine.)
   Suggested Remedial Strategies:
   (a) Provide verbal and/or visual clues to guide the student in writing letters commonly reversed. For example:
   A *p* always *p*oints to the color *p*urple.
   Provide a purple colored square on the right side of the paper.

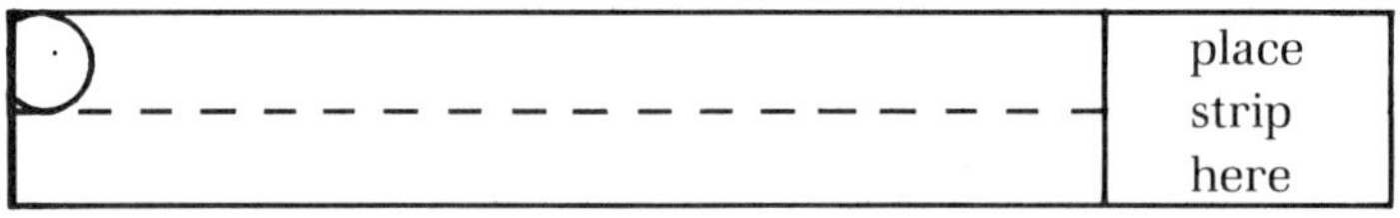

   Demonstrate visually that *v* stands for a *v*ery deep hole.
   (b) When a student reverses letters, always refer to the correct model instead of the incorrect model.
   (c) Use color to emphasize the portion of the letter that the student reproduces incorrectly, gradually withdrawing color as the student begins to form the letter appropriately and consistently.

3. *Deficit Skill:* Improper spacing between letters
   Suggested Remedial Strategies:
   (a) Provide visual cues or space holders on the paper. For example, with a colored marker, block the lined paper so that one letter fits into each block.

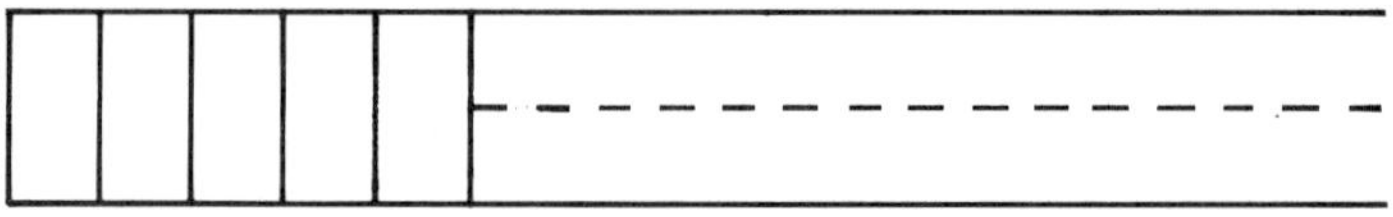

   (b) Older students may prefer to write on graph paper.

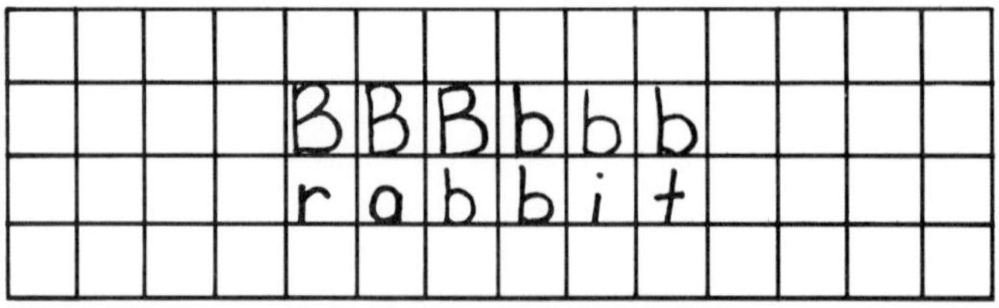

4. *Deficit Skill:* Improper spacing between words and sentences
   Suggested Remedial Strategies:
   (a) Provide the student with a visual representation of space holders between words. For example:

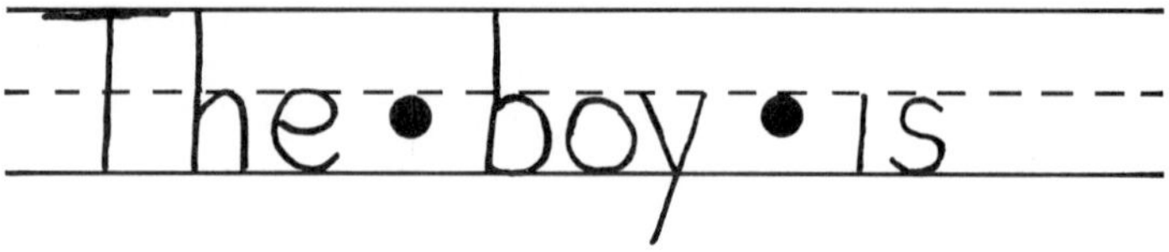

(b) Instruct students to use a finger, a pencil, a small button, or a narrow strip of stiff paper as a place holder between words.
(c) Older students writing on graph paper can be told to leave a designated number of blocks blank (two or three) depending on the size of the graphing.

5. *Deficit Skill:* Inadequate or excessive pressure on the writing tool
Suggested Remedial Strategies:
(a) Present explanations differentiating between writing pressures in story format. For example:
A mouse might write very lightly and softly because a mouse is a tiny creature. Here is an example of something written by a mouse:

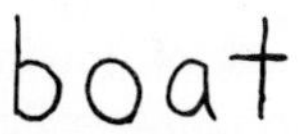

But boys and girls write darker and harder so that people can read their writing. Here is an example:

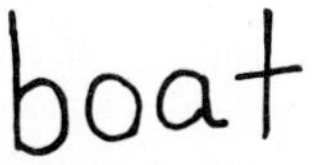

And elephants, because they are huge and heavy, might write like this:

Ask the child which example is more like his or her writing.
(b) Allow the student to practice scribbling light and heavy and bold and extremely heavy lines. Instruct the child to write using a certain scribble pressure.

6. *Deficit Skill:* Lack of motivation or lack of interest in writing
Suggested Remedial Strategies:
(a) Provide colorful action pictures or themes for writing lessons.
(b) Associate letters with objects, characters, or events in the child's life.
(c) Acknowledge or reward children's handwriting efforts with, for example, a personalized bulletin board or personal progress chart.
(d) Emphasize the practical applications of writing.
(e) Provide opportunities for students to experience the need for written communication. For example, simulate a half-hour experience when no one is allowed to speak; students must communicate their needs, ideas, and responses in writing.

Cursive handwriting. A child's readiness to transfer from manuscript to cursive style is demonstrated by manuscript proficiency; the ability to write letters from memory; initiation of cursive forms, which indicates the student's desire to advance to cursive writing; and refined muscular coordination. Because not all children attain these desired prerequisites at the same time, the teacher must carefully evaluate student readiness on an individual basis and adjust programs accordingly.

Techniques for delivering cursive writing instruction should be sequentially structured to achieve the ultimate goals of proficiency and skill maintenance. First, determine the student's capabilities; then implement the instructional program and the sequence of tasks that progress toward mastery. Refer to Figure 11–2 for a review of scope-and-sequence skills related to the development and mastery of cursive writing.

Remedial strategies. Although some errors associated with cursive writing are similar to manuscript errors, there are other errors common only to cursive writing. Following is a list of common cursive errors and suggested techniques for remedial instruction.

1. *Deficit skill:* Lack of flowing strokes (stopping and starting)
   Suggested Remedial Strategies: Provide gross motor relaxation exercises (Heyman 1977).
   (a) Teacher should draw two large circles on paper and instruct the student to trace over those circles with the palms of both hands simultaneously. The child may then trace the circles with crayon maintaining a slow, steady rhythm. The child can be taught to monitor this rhythm by listening to the crayon moving on the paper.
   (b) Similar exercises can be incorporated using letter strokes, isolated letters, connected letters, and words.

2. *Deficit Skill:* Improper letter slant
   Suggested Remedial Strategies:
   (a) Provide slant guidelines and/or cues for writing practice.
   - Structure the student's paper with colored, dotted slant lines:

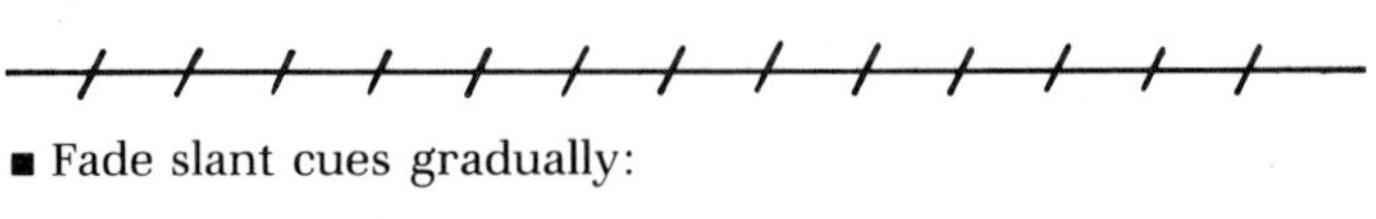

   - Next, provide subtle slant cues on the student's writing paper:

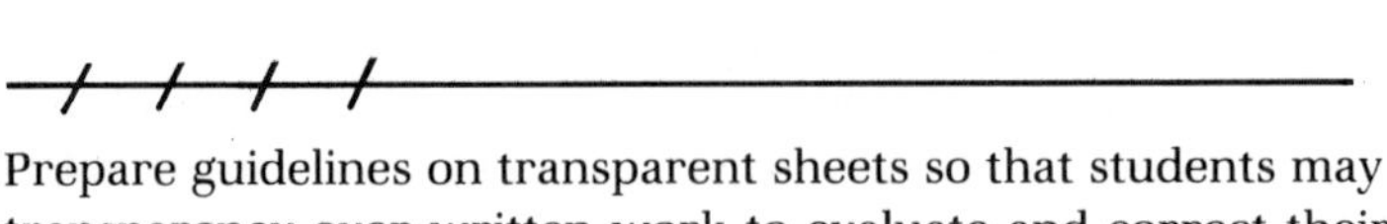

   - Fade slant cues gradually:

   (b) Prepare guidelines on transparent sheets so that students may place the transparency over written work to evaluate and correct their performance.

3. *Deficit Skill*: Improper or irregular spacing of letters
   Suggested Remedial Strategies:
   (a) Provide structural cues to assist in proper spacing.
   - Use guidelines and space holders when teaching isolated letters:

   - Use guidelines without space holders when teaching connected letters or letters in words:

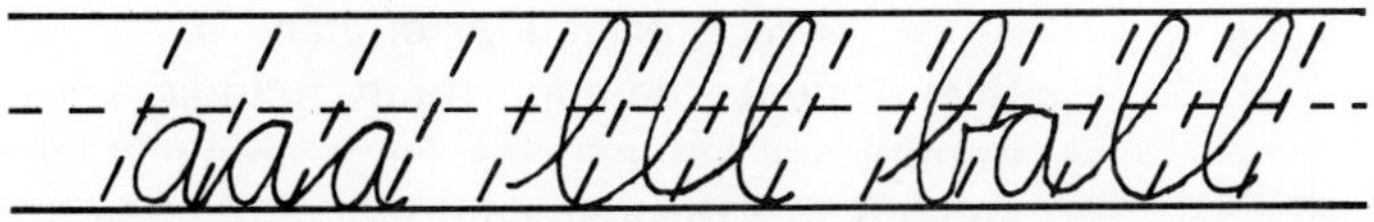

   (b) Prepare correctly written products on transparencies so that students may evaluate their work by placing the transparency on top and correct inaccuracies by tracing over the transparency.

4. *Deficit Skill:* Improper letter size
   Suggested Remedial Strategies:
   (a) Provide structural guidelines for writing properly sized letters.
   - Place glue along the writing lines to give the student a tactile reminder to make letters the proper size and shape.
   - Large-lined writing paper can be adapted to structure letter size. The teacher or students themselves can use paint or magic marker to darken the top and bottom lines on paper.
   - As students make a transition from primary to conventional lined paper, a lined guide for vertical placement of lower case letters can be drawn to help students adjust to the smaller spatial format, as illustrated:

primary | conventional lined paper | conventional lined paper—modified

   - Gradually fade the lined guide by limiting it to the first half-inch of each line, as illustrated:

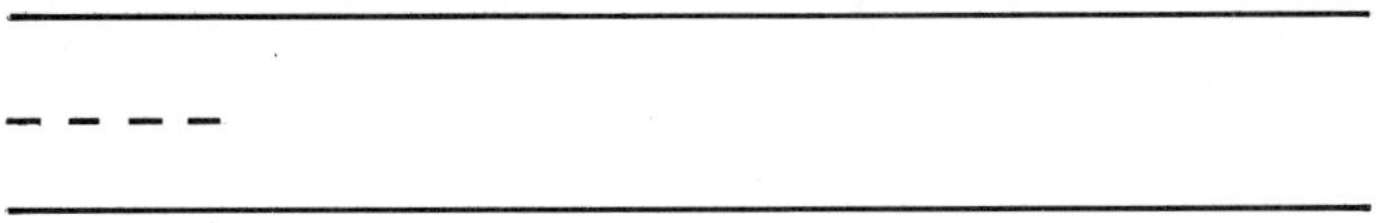

5. *Deficit Skill:* Lack of letter closings
   Suggested Remedial Strategies:
   (a) Provide stories to illustrate the necessity for completing specific letter forms by appropriately closing them. For example:
   - An alligator is a fierce animal. The word *alligator* begins with *a*. We often see alligators at the zoo in pens or cages. If the alligator's pen were left open or the cage had a hole in it, the alligator might escape. Make sure you close your *a* completely so the alligator cannot escape.

   (b) Present students with activities for evaluating letter form.
   - Provide examples of unclosed letters that are difficult to decipher, such as *a* and *o*. Explain the difficulty in identifying those letters as opposed to the correct formations of *a* and *o*.
   - Give students the opportunity to indicate their best and their worst examples of letter forms. For example: "Circle your best example of *f*, and put an *X* through your worst example. Tell me why you made your choices." It is important to recognize that the writing efforts of students naturally deteriorate due to excessive requirements for written expression. Often students will rely on the last model produced as a guide to formation of a new model. Therefore, the number of trials assigned should be closely monitored by the teacher.

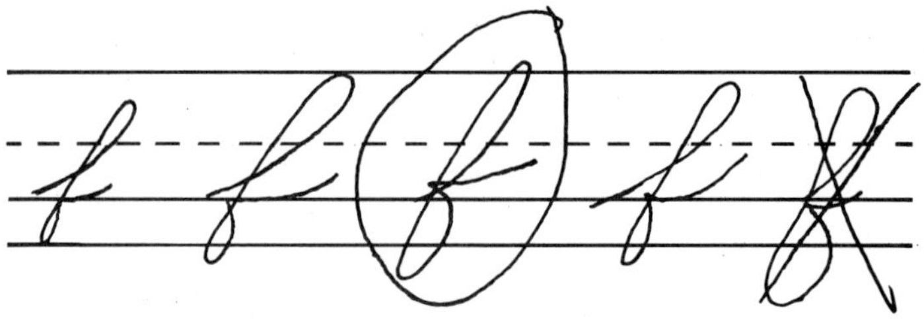

6. *Deficit Skill:* Closed top loop
   Suggested Remedial Strategies:
   (a) Provide narration to accompany illustrations of proper letter formations. For example:
   - Some children were having a race to see who could run up a hill, around a flower, and back down the hill. The rules of the game are that no one can run over the flower or run behind it. Let's try it.

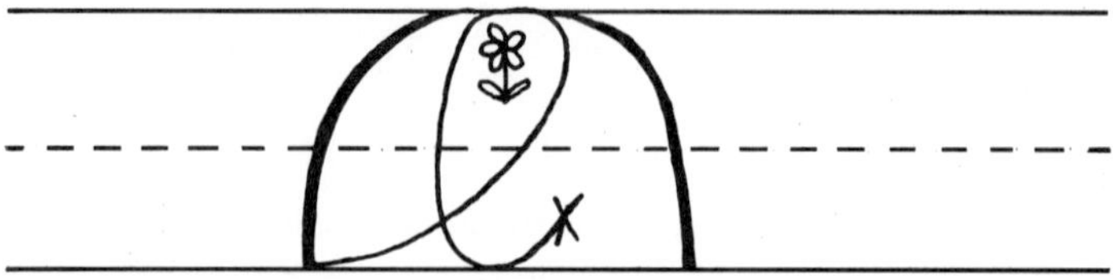

   (The teacher and the student should verbalize the route of the pencil: "Up the hill, around the flower, back down the hill.")

   (b) Previously described visual discrimination exercises and self-evaluation techniques are other methods for reinforcing the closed top loop of certain letters.

7. *Deficit Skill:* Omission of letter parts
   Suggested Remedial Strategies:
   (a) Pose hypothetical problems to students concerning what happens when a person doesn't completely finish his or her job. Relate the discussion to handwriting. Present students with activities in which they must decide how to finish or complete letters to make them correct.
   - Complete these letters:

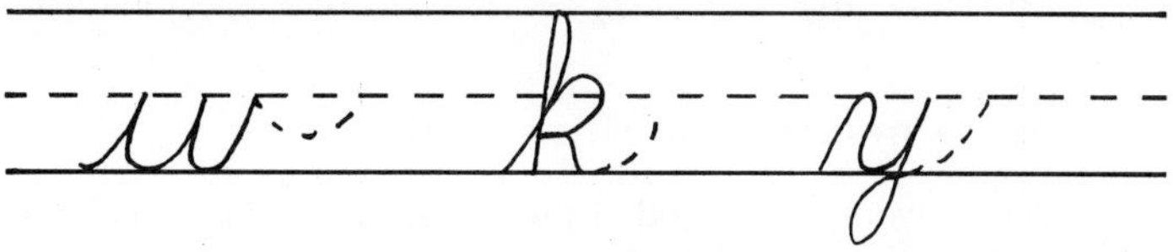

   (b) Compare letter formation to cooking, baking cookies, or making an ice cream sundae. Discuss the result of not including all the ingredients. Relate the discussion to letter ingredients. For example:
   - The dot on the *i* and *j* is the cherry on top of your ice cream sundae.
   - The cross on a *t* is one ingredient for a good letter.

   (c) Allow students the chance to evaluate teacher-made omissions.
   - The teacher may write letter examples, words, and/or sentences with intended omissions of letter parts. Students attempt to find those missing parts. Such themes as "Be a Detective," "Find the Missing Parts," and "Grade the Teacher's Paper" are just a few motivating ideas.

SPELLING

Spelling is the ability to reproduce words through sequential arrangement of letters. The alphabet provides twenty-six symbols used to express thoughts in the English language; yet there are more than forty phonemes, or speech sounds, present in its structure. Many handicapped students experience difficulty learning the sound-symbol relationship for the twenty-six symbols of the alphabet. The problem is compounded for these students when faced with the task of learning the relationship between symbol clusters and their corresponding phonemes. For example, students must learn that the grapheme [ed] relates to /t/ in *jumped* or /d/ in *sailed*; that the grapheme [ui] relates to /i/ in *built*; and that the graphemes [ei] and [ie] are related to /e/ in *receive* and *relief*.

The inherent difficulty of spelling, which evolves from the inconsistency of our language, does not protect handicapped students from unfavorable impressions created through their spelling errors. Spelling errors may give the impression that an individual is ignorant or careless when, in fact, the National Council for Research in English (Dieterich 1972) has indicated that misspelling is partially a function of teacher behavior. While there may be other factors related to spelling errors, such as physiological or motivational issues (Faigley, Daly, and Witte 1981), special educators should also evaluate instructional practices as a possible cause for spelling errors.

Many teachers place greater emphasis on teaching phonetic generalizations than on helping deficit spellers learn to recognize and reconstruct the words presented in spelling units. It is ironic that students are graded on their ability to reconstruct a group of words when their teacher has provided instruction on the *phonetic* structure of those words. While it is foolish to assume that students should learn to spell a wide variety of words from memory alone, it is also illogical to assume that students can learn to memorize and reproduce words sequentially without teacher assistance. Further, simultaneous instruction on word reproduction and phonetic structure is without merit if not accompanied by instruction on word meaning.

Assessment of Spelling Skills

Typically, handicapped students' skill in spelling is assessed initially through formal achievement and diagnostic tests (Rothschild 1982). Too often such tests provide a cursory analysis of spelling skills. Although diagnostic tests that focus on spelling are limited, some are available. Examples of diagnostic spelling tests are the *Test of Written Spelling* (Larsen and Hammill 1976) and the *Diagnostic Spelling Test* (Kottmeyer 1970).

The *Test of Written Spelling (TWS)* may be administered to groups or individuals aged five through thirteen and one-half. The *TWS* consists of two subtests, Predictable Words and Unpredictable Words. The former assesses student ability to spell words that conform to phonetic rules, while the latter assesses student ability to form words that do not follow phonetic rules. Students' raw scores on the *TWS* yield a spelling age, a spelling quotient, and grade equivalent.

The *Diagnostic Spelling Test* is a criterion-referenced test that assesses specific phonic and structural elements. One version of the test is designed for students spelling at second or third grade levels. Another version is available for students spelling at or above the fourth grade level. The test consists of thirty-two items, each of which measures a particular phonetic or structural element. A grade equivalent is derived from the student's raw score. An analysis of error patterns also directs the teacher in selecting appropriate instruction skills.

When assessing spelling ability, the special educator should determine what grapheme-phoneme relationships the student needs to acquire and what spelling behaviors are preventing successful encoding. Cohen and Abrams (1976) have identified grapheme-phoneme concepts critical to successful spelling. These concepts are listed in Figure 11–3.

In addition to knowing phonetic skills related to spelling, it is essential to investigate the pattern of errors that students make (Rothschild 1982). Knowledge of the specific nature of error patterns as well as knowledge of the skills students need to acquire, assists the teacher in developing a comprehensive instructional program. Figure 11–4 describes typical spelling errors made by students.

Although random work samples can be used to analyze spelling errors, carefully constructed tests that represent specific spelling skills can also be used. The teacher can thus analyze the student's performance of certain spelling skills to determine if error patterns exist.

As illustrated in Figure 11–5, the teacher can administer a pretest and then record and classify the types of error the student makes. After the teacher has identified skill deficits in spelling and has identified error patterns exhibited in the student's written work, an instructional approach is selected for the student. It is important to emphasize that special educators often combine a variety of spelling programs in addition to supplemental strategies in order to provide a comprehensive individualized instructional program.

Methods for Spelling Instruction

Spelling programs and supplemental procedures currently available to special educators are discussed below. Used in combination, these programs and procedures allow the teacher to broaden the traditional emphasis on phonics to include direct instruction in word recognition, reproduction, and meaning.

☐ **FIGURE 11–3**
Scope and Sequence of Spelling Skills

SPELLING	*Deficient* –	*Instruction* /	*Mastery* *
Reproduces consonants: *b, d, l, g, h, m, n, p, r, t, v, y, s, z, w, c, j, k, x, gu*			
Reproduces initial blends: *dr, gr, tr, pl, fl, sw, sp, sl, st, str, spr, spl*			
Reproduces final blends: *mp, nd, ft, lt, nt, st, lf, nk*			
Reproduces short vowels: *a, e, i, o, u*			
Reproduces diagraphs: *ch, sh, th, ng, wh, ph*			
Reproduces suffixes: *s, ing, ed, es, er, est, ly, ful, y, tion, ive, ent, en, ant, ment, ous, ness, sion, ance, ence, ible, able, fully, ally, ssion*			
Reproduces vowel combinations: *ai, ay, e__e, a__e, ee, ea, igh, i__e, y, oa, ow, o__e, u__e, __y, ie, ei, iu, io*			
Reproduces vowel diagraphs: *oo, ea*			
Reproduces vowel dipthongs: *oi, ou, ow, aw, oy, ew, au*			
Reproduces *r* and *l* controlled vowels: *ar, er, ir, ur, ear, are, ire, ore, al, el, ul*			
Reproduces prefixes: *un, re, pre, en, mis, ex, a, con, per, com*			
Reproduces vowel-consonant combinations: *et, ic, al, le, ey, us*			
Reproduces soft consonants: *c, g*			
Reproduces symbol generalizations: *ck* and *k, ch* and *tch, ge* and *dge*			
Divides words according to open (*be/come*) and closed (*sys/tem*) principles of syllabilication			
Reproduces contractions: *n't, 's, 'd, 'll, 've, 're*			
Applies the following rules: Drop final *e (raking)*			
Double final consonant (*stopping*)			
Change y to i (*friendliest*)			
Add suffix (*graciously*)			
Reproduces consonant-vowel combinations: *ti, ci, fu*			

Adapted from C. R. Cohen and R. M. Abrams. *Spellmaster, Spelling: Testing Evaluating, Book One.*

☐ **FIGURE 11–4**
Common Spelling Errors

Error	*Example*	*Explanation*
Additional Letters	Messess/messes prision/prison	Failure to check for accuracy in phoneme-grapheme relationship
Omission of Letters	litl/little cring/crying	Dependency on phonetic spelling
Reflection of Dialect	comin/coming maek/make	Dependency on phonetic spelling
Reflection of Mispronunciation	pay/pray nake/make	Dependency on phonetic spelling; speech or hearing deficit
Reversal of Whole Words	wot/tow was/saw	Inability to relate phoneme to grapheme symbol
Reversal of Consonants	tsop/stop lpan/plan	Failure to check for accuracy in phoneme-grapheme relationship
Reversal of Vowel-Consonant Order	angle/angel peracher/preacher	Failure to check for accuracy; inability to reproduce in sequence
Reversal of syllables	comein/income	Inability to reproduce in sequence; failure to check for accuracy
Phonetic Spelling of Nonphonetic Words	fotograf/photograph feecher/feature	Dependency on phonetic spelling
Inappropriate Sound-Symbol Association	gedl/cradle gagn/dragon receve/receive	Speech or hearing deficit; lack of readiness for spelling; dependency on phonetic spelling
Unrelated Letters	mircorphoner/microphone yuhnetid/united	Inability to reproduce sound-symbol association; poor motivation; perseveration

Rule-based method. The most common approach to spelling instruction in schools is rule-based instruction. Typically, students are taught a general phonetic rule, given examples of its application, and later expected to apply the rule to the spelling of unknown words. For example, when a student hears */shun/* in a word like *portion,* he or she should learn to write *tion.*

The goal of this instructional approach is to help the student associate a phoneme with a particular set of letter combinations. Through practice, the student learns to reproduce specific symbol combinations when he or she hears a particular phoneme within the word. Later, the student is taught to break up the word into recognizable elements, or syllables, and reproduce each syllable in sequence to create the whole word. Hammill, Larsen, and McNutt (1977) indicate that the most commonly used rule-based instructional programs are *Spell Correctly* (Benthul et al. 1974), *Word Book* (Rogers, Ort, and Serra 1970), and *Basic Goals in Spelling* (Kottmeyer and Claus 1968, 1972). In each of these programs, only phonetic rules that apply to accurate spelling of large numbers of words are taught.

☐ **FIGURE 11–5**
Analysis of Spelling Probe Sheet

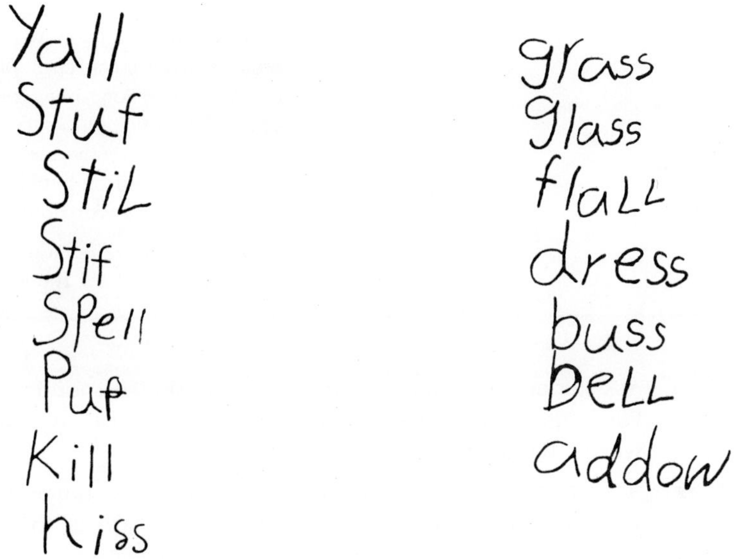

Error/Spelling Word	*Type of Error*	*Instructional Goal*
yall/yell flall/full buss/buzz	Inappropriate sound-Symbol Association	Teach encoding of short vowels and sound-symbol association for z
stuf/stuff stif/stiff puf/puff	Omission of Letters	Teach grapheme-phoneme relationship: *ff* for */f/*
flall/full	Additional Letters	Teach sequential encoding; i.e. *f-u-ll*
addow/address	Inappropriate Sound-Symbol Association	Teach grapheme-phoneme relationship

Teachers using rule-based programs should teach students to use inductive procedures to identify the principle that governs the spelling of a word (Freidman 1978). Figure 11–6 illustrates a comparison of deductive and inductive procedures used in rule-based spelling instruction.

According to Otto, McMenemy, and Smith (1973), procedures for using an inductive approach for spelling are as follows:

- Use a rebus that illustrates the word in which a specific phonetic principle is illustrated. For example,  may be drawn on the chalkboard.
- Have students pronounce the word illustrated by the rebus and then write it for them.

☐ FIGURE 11–6
Deductive and Inductive Procedures in Rule-Based Spelling Instruction

Deductive	*Inductive*
When words end in *s, x, z, ch, sh,* add *es* to make them plural. *For example*: *mass* becomes *masses* *ax* becomes *axes* *topaz* becomes *topazes* *dish* becomes *dishes* *church* becomes *churches*	Children are given the words *masses, axes, topazes, dishes, churches, plans, tents, dogs*. The teacher says: "For some words we add *s*, and for other words we add *es* to make a word plural. Your task as detectives is to figure out what rule guides us to choose between *s* and *es* when we want to make a word plural." *Anticipated Outcome*: Add *es* if the word ends in *s, x, z, ch, sh*. Add *s* if the word ends in *n, t,* or *g*.

- Ask students for examples of words with similar sounds and write them also. For example, students may give the words *buy, lie, my, sky, fry* as examples of words that sound like *eye.*
- Ask students to observe similarities in the words. Students may respond that when they observe the letters *y* or *ie* in the words, they hear */i/*.
- Have students verbalize a generalization about the similar sounds and corresponding symbols. Students should state that *y* and *ie* are used for the */i/*.
- Provide further experience with the generalization. For example, ask students, "How would the */i/* in *cry, shy,* and *die* be written?"

If rule-based instructional programs are selected, teachers should modify typical instructional procedures used with such programs to include inductive instructional strategies to teach relationships between phonics and graphic representation. Further, teachers should expand their instructional role in spelling to provide direct instruction in recognition and reproduction of spelling words.

Multisensory method. Since spelling requires students to use the visual, auditory, and motor senses, some individuals have reasoned that spelling instruction should also include these senses in order to promote learning and retention. Fernald (1943) devised an approach to spelling that included the visual, auditory, kinesthetic, and tactile (VAKT) sensory modalities. The following steps are used to implement the Fernald method for spelling instruction:

1. The teacher writes and pronounces a word while the student observes and listens.
2. The student simultaneously traces and pronounces the word, followed by copying the word while repeating it again.
3. The student writes the word from memory. If correct, the word is placed in the student's file box; if not, step two is repeated.

As the student's ability to recognize and reproduce words correctly increases, the tracing step is deleted from the method. At this stage, the student observes the teacher write and pronounce the word, and then he or she writes and pronounces the word. Finally, the student learns to spell a word by looking at it and then writing it, ultimately progressing to merely looking at the word.

The Fernald method for spelling is closely associated with her method for reading instruction. Both are based on the belief that students subconsciously deduce phoneme-symbol generalizations through repeated exposure to a variety of words within their natural vocabulary.

The Gillingham method (Gillingham and Stillman 1965) is another multisensory approach to spelling. Like the Fernald method, it is integrated with instructional strategies for reading. The following procedures are used to teach spelling through the Gillingham method.

1. The teacher pronounces a word.
2. The student repeats the word and names the letters in sequence while writing each.
3. The student reads the word he or she has written.

As soon a students can write phonetically pure three-letter words, such as *cat, sat, pin,* and *bin,* the teacher introduces sentences and story-writing activities. Drill is used to teach nonphonetic words.

Imitation training method. Stowitschek and Jobes (1977) have developed an imitation approach for spelling instruction, which has also been proven effective for handicapped students. This approach has teachers model oral and written spelling of words while students imitate them. The method is suggested as a supplement to traditional spelling programs, as it allows the teacher to help students learn to recognize and reproduce words.

Because the modeling procedures used in the imitation approach are critical to its success, teachers are encouraged to use a scripted format. The advantage of a scripted format is that it allows the teacher to present relevant organizational cues required by the student to complete the task accurately. Conversely, deviation from the script could lead students to make errors in the task presented to them. An example of the format used is given below.

- The teacher begins by saying: "We will learn to spell three new words today. The first word is *train*. A sentence using *train* is 'The train whistle blew at midnight.' *Train* is written *t-r-a-i-n*." The teacher holds up an index card on which the word is written to provide an example. While spelling the word, the teacher continues to hold the index card on which the word is written and points to each letter while stating, "*Train* is spelled *t-r-a-i-n*."
- The teacher removes the card from the student's view and says, "Spell *train*." If the student spells the word correctly, the teacher praises the student and says, "Write *train*." If the student is correct, the teacher proceeds to demonstrate the next word using the procedures outlined.
- If the student spells the word incorrectly, the teacher says, "No, let's begin again." The teacher presents the index card and says, "This is *train, t-r-a-i-n.* Spell it after me." The student spells the letters while looking at the cues on the index card. When the student spells the word correctly, the teacher

removes the card from the student's view and says, "Spell *train*." If correct, the student is asked to write the word. If not, the teacher repeats this step again.

- If the student writes the word incorrectly, the teacher presents the written word again, saying "*t-r-a-i-n*" while pointing to each letter. The student is asked to write the word with the index card in view. If the student is correct, the teacher removes the card and says, "Write *train*." If the student is not correct, the teacher repeats this cycle again until the student correctly reproduces the word.

These procedures are used to teach each spelling word on an individual basis.

Remedial Strategies

Formal spelling programs often are supplemented with remedial activities designed to correct specific spelling errors. Following are a few suggestions for such activities.

1. *Deficit Skill:* Unneeded letters
   Suggested Remedial Strategy:
   (a) The student is provided with a model of the appropriate spelling of a word and asked to correct his or her misspelled word based on comparison with the model.

2. *Deficit Skill:* Omission of letters
   Suggested Remedial Strategy:
   (a) The student is taught to recognize grapheme-phoneme relationships for which there is no direct correspondence by comparing the correct spelling of a word with both misspelled and correctly spelled models. For example:

   little litl littl little litle litte little
   crying cring crying kring krying crying

3. *Deficit Skill:* Reflection of dialect
   Suggested Remedial Strategies:
   (a) Dictate a list of spelling words that rhyme and are commonly affected by dialect, such as *picked, licked, kicked, nicked.* Additional rhyming words or word families can be found in phonetic workbooks.
   (b) A variation of this activity is to ask students to write only the letters representing the last sound heard while writing a dash to represent those letters deleted.

4. *Deficit Skill:* Reflection of mispronunciation
   Suggested Remedial Strategies:
   (a) Teachers should approach remediation of this spelling error with caution to avoid mismanagement of students with speech or hearing deficits. When spelling errors are identified that may reflect such deficits,

students should be referred to speech and hearing therapists for assessment.

(b) The student can pronounce parts of words in sequence with the teacher, as in *cl-ay*. Initially, the teacher and student speak each part slowly, later speeding up the enunciation to approximate the word more closely. Next, the student should trace letters of the word while vocalizing the sound, correlating hand and voice.

5. *Deficit Skill:* Reversal of whole words, consonants, consonant-vowel order, and syllables
Suggested Remedial Strategies: Remedial strategies for errors of mispronunciation can also be used for reversal errors. In addition, the following strategy may prove helpful:
(a) The teacher presents a rebus and dictates the letters that spell the word. Students then write each letter and pronounce the word.

6. *Deficit Skill:* Phonetic spelling of nonphonetic words
Suggested Remedial Strategies:
(a) The teacher identifies graphemes in a word that correlate with a particular sound. For example, the teacher circles those graphemes in *photograph* for which there is no one-to-one correspondence between sound and symbol. The teacher says: "*Ph* in *photograph* says */f/*. When I say */f/*, write *ph*. Now write *photograph* using *ph* to reproduce the */f/* sound."
(b) Students sort or categorize words written on cards by grouping them according to some attribute. In closed sorts, the rule that governs membership in a set of words is preestablished before the words are viewed and sorted. For example, the teacher may say, "Select a group of words in which the */e/* sound is heard." Words that contain both single vowel and digraph representation would be included in the deck of vocabulary cards as well as those words in which the symbol *e* is present but not heard. Examples might be *reach, read, receive, bed, relief, speed, lake, mike, cube, set,* and *feed*. Students would set aside those words in which */e/* is not heard in a discard pile, then invent generalizations for the grapheme-phoneme relationship for */e/*.

7. *Deficit Skill*: Inappropriate sound-symbol association
Suggested Remedial Strategy:
(a) In open sorts, words in a set are viewed and students determine common attributes of some of these words. Typically, students define an attribute based on common sounds heard in several of the vocabulary words within the deck. As in the closed sort, students construct a generalization for the grapheme-phoneme relationship they have identified.

8. *Deficit Skill:* Unrelated letters
Suggested Remedial Strategy:
(a) Students who reproduce the first two or three letters of a word correctly could be allowed to refer to a dictionary for correct spelling of the

remaining portion of the word. In addition, during spelling tests, words spelled correctly through use of a dictionary should be counted as correct.

MECHANICS OF WRITTEN EXPRESSION

Proficiency in written expression requires a student to think not only about the mechanical aspects of writing—handwriting, spelling, capitalization, and punctuation—but also about the integration and organization of his or her ideas. Hall (1981) explains that "in writing, students must translate their own inner language (which is often shorthand) into appropriate words, sentences, and paragraphs, which accurately convey an intended message" (p. 1).

As indicated in the scope-and-sequence chart presented earlier in this chapter, the written expression is complex and depends upon the integration of all skills. Mastery of written expression, leading to clear self-expression, develops gradually through the student's progressive acquisition of skills. Deficits in one or more skill area can lead to a variety of inappropriate or inaccurate representations. Figure 11–7 illustrates the wide range of possible deficits in expressive writing. Areas in which deficits may occur include capitalization, punctuation, spelling, logical sequence of thoughts and ideas, omission of words, vocabulary, sentence structure, paragraph organization, and penmanship.

Assessment of Mechanical Skills

Written expression is a highly complex process involving language (Wiig and Semel 1980), thinking (Wong 1979), and motivation (Alley and Deshler 1979) as well as a foundation in tool subjects built upon a variety of experiences and skills. The following scope-and-sequence chart (Figure 11–8) is a guide to mechanical and or-

☐ **FIGURE 11–7**
A Junior High Student's Written Explanation of How to Use the Dictionary and Encyclopedia

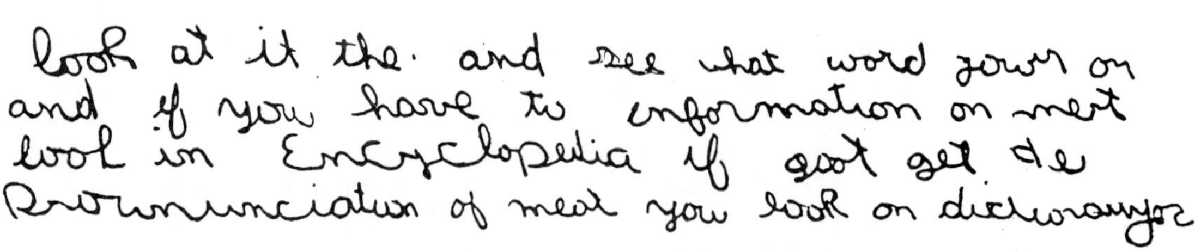

LOOK AT IT THE AND SEE WHAT WORD YOU'RE ON AND IF YOU HAVE TO INFORMATION ON NEXT LOOK IN ENCYCLOPEDIA IF GOT TO GET THE PRONUNCIATION OF NEXT YOU LOOK ON DICTIONARY

☐ **FIGURE 11–8**
Scope and Sequence of Mechanical Skills

CONTENT SKILLS	*Deficient* –	*Instruction* /	*Mastery* *
Writes about a single event, experience			
Demonstrates simple thought sequence			
Orders events logically			
Adds descriptive detail			
Expresses original ideas, humor, imagination			
Makes generalizations			
Makes judgments			
States or implies values			
Supports consistent point of view			
VOCABULARY			
Uses general nouns			
Uses general verbs			
Uses general adjectives			
Uses general adverbs			
Uses articles, prepositions, conjunctions			
Uses specific nouns			
Uses specific verbs			
Uses specific adjectives			
Uses specific adverbs			
Uses topic-imposed words			
Uses prefixes			
Uses suffixes			
Selects words deliberately			
CAPITALIZATION			
First and last names			
First words of sentences			
I			
Days of week			
Months			
Holidays			
Streets, roads			
Cities			
States			
Countries			
Specific locations			

☐ **FIGURE 11–8—continued**
Scope and Sequence of Mechanical Skills

CAPITALIZATION	*Deficient* –	*Instruction* /	*Mastery* *
Geographical names			
Abbreviations of titles			
Titles of books, plays, poems, etc.			
Titles of organizations			
Races			
Nationalities			
Religions			
First word in quoted speech			
First word in the salutation of a letter			
First word in the closing of a letter			
PUNCTUATION			
Period			
Question mark			
Exclamation point			
Period after abbreviations and initials			
Comma in dates			
Comma in addresses			
Comma after the salutation of a letter			
Comma after the closing of a letter			
Comma after an introductory clause			
Comma before a conjunction			
Quotation marks around direct quotes			
Apostrophe to show possession			
Apostrophe to show plurals of letters and numbers			
Apostrophe to show contractions			
Semicolon between two main clauses without a conjunction			
Colon to introduce a list			
Colon to show time			
Colon after business letter salutation			
SENTENCE STRUCTURE SYNTAX			
Kernal sentences (subject, verb)			
Simple sentences			
Expanded sentences			
Compound sentences			
Complex sentences			

☐ **FIGURE 11–8—continued**
Scope and Sequence of Mechanical Skills

SENTENCE STRUCTURE SYNTAX	*Deficient* –	*Instruction* /	*Mastery* *
Compound complex sentences			
(Hall 1981)			
PARAGRAPH ORGANIZATION			
Topic choice/title			
Topic statement of main idea			
Presents details and facts to develop and support main idea			
Logical sequence of events, experiences, ideas			
Concluding statement			
NOTE TAKING			
Understands purpose of note taking			
Identifies major points from lecture			
Identifies major points from written material			
OUTLINING			
Understands purpose of outlining			
Identifies major headings			
Identifies subheadings			
Identifies details			
PROOFREADING			
Checks each sentence for a basic thought			
Checks each word for correct spelling			
Checks punctuation for correct usage and inclusion			
Checks for appropriate capitalization			
Checks for use of descriptive words and phrases			
Checks for clear explanation of ideas			
Checks for precise phrasing			
Checks for integration of ideas			

Source: Burns 1980; Dankowski 1966.

ganizational skills needed for coherent written expression. Such a chart can be used to define a student's particular strengths and weaknesses as a basis for appropriate program planning.

Following is a discussion of instructional and remedial strategies for developing the skills listed on the scope-and-sequence chart. Because written expression includes both the actual act of writing as well as the organization of one's thoughts, it is critical that teachers make a distinction between these two areas. If you are teaching skills associated with the mechanics of written expression, such as punctuation or note taking, then the student's penmanship should not be the focus of evaluation. Focus on only one of these skill areas at a time to avoid confusing the student.

Remedial Strategies

In analyzing work samples of students with written expression deficits, multiple deficiencies are often noted. The greater the number of skill areas affected by weaknesses, the more complex the remedial process. Because of the wide range of possible deficit combinations, the discussion of remedial strategies below focuses on one skill area at a time. Teachers should note, however, that many remedial techniques may be integrated to develop an approach that will improve written expression.

Content. Generating ideas for written content is the initial step in expressive writing. The student must cognitively formulate thoughts, events, details, and personal feelings into a central idea before writing. According to Hall (1981), "the degree of thought development depends on the writer's ability to use, expand, and elaborate on a given stimulus" (p. 10). The following techniques may assist students in formulating ideas from given stimuli and/or internally conjuring a stimulus (idea) to prompt the expression of ideas in written form:

- Present students with a stimulus such as a picture, object, filmstrip, or list of words (Gleason 1982). The amount of stimulus provided may vary depending on the student's level of motivation and dependency upon stimuli. Examples of stimuli include:
  —A written story whose sentences are typed in random order requiring the student to organize them sequentially
  —A written story without an ending requiring one or two concluding sentences
  —A few introductory sentences that require the student to complete the story
  —An incomplete sentence that prompts the student to complete the sentence and continue to develop an entire story
- Following the oral or visual presentation of an event, prompt students to express their reactions and feelings to the situation in written form.
- Personal experiences such as field trips, classroom crises, and memorable events provide relevant stimuli for written expression.
- Present students with a stimulus situation requiring them to judge, evaluate, and draw conclusions about the situation.

Vocabulary. The following remedial strategies suggest methods for increasing the variety, appropriateness, and accuracy of students' vocabulary:

- Building students' oral vocabulary enhances their use of new vocabulary in written expression. Develop weekly vocabulary-building programs around themes such as "Wrestle With New Words," "Wipe Out Everyday Words," or

"Watch Out! We Have Word Power." Every Monday allow students to designate their new word for the week. If unable to make that decision, students may be assigned a word by drawing a new word from a "word well." Students must investigate their new word through a variety of activities (spelling, using the dictionary, using the word in sentences, defining the word, and verbally using the word daily).

- Prior to a writing activity, the teacher and student might identify vocabulary words associated with the writing theme. From this list, the teacher (and student, if appropriate) compiles a list of synonyms, more descriptive words, or alternate choices for each word. From this second list, students can choose new vocabulary words to be used in the writing exercise (Cohen and Plaskon 1980). For example:

List 1	List 2
kids boys girls	children youngsters friends, pals
glad laugh smile	happy, jolly chuckle, grin

- Sentence extension activities developed by Fennimore (1980) are also effective in enhancing students' vocabulary. To implement this strategy, students are first asked to list substitutes for nouns and verbs in kernel sentences. Next, students are asked to enhance the kernel sentences with adverbs, adjectives, and prepositional phrases. For example, the kernel sentence might be "The girl rides her bike." The teacher asks for substitutions for the noun and verb in the sentence. The students may suggest "The boy needs a bike." Next, the teacher asks for descriptors for the nouns and verb. The students may suggest "The little boy needs a blue bike." Finally, the teacher asks students for prepositional phrases, and the sentence designed by the students becomes "The little boy needs a blue bike for the race."

Capitalization. Students who make capitalization errors may do so because of inconsistency in letter formation, confusion over capitalization rules, and/or conflicting models of letter forms. A variety of activities can be used to strengthen capitalization skills. For example:

- Capitalization Campaign—The student compiles a list of words that he or she feels should be capitalized. Each student presents the list to the group with reasons why each word should be capitalized. The group votes, and words that win by a majority vote are placed on the classroom list of "Elected Capital Members." The teacher regulates appropriate selection through the power of veto on any group decision.

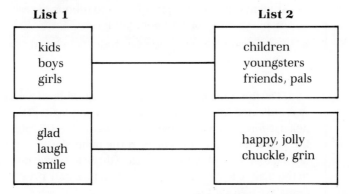

- The Clue of the Missing Capital—Present student(s) with a written passage that has no capital letters. At the end of the passage, write the number of words in the passage that should be capitalized. Students must then find and circle the words that should be capitalized. A self-checking transparency, or key, can be made available so that students can check their own work.

Punctuation. Punctuation assists the writer in communicating expression, quality of mood, and a logical, smooth progression of ideas. The following are suggested techniques for improving punctuation skills:

- Punctuation Puzzle—Present students with a written passage that has no punctuation. Instead, the passage may have circles or squares as cues to students that some type of punctuation is necessary. Cues can be omitted if inappropriate for student skill level.
- Proofreading exercises assist students in locating and correcting punctuation errors.

Written syntax. According to a number of researchers, syntactical maturity is indicated by sentence length and complexity (Hunt 1965; Loban 1963; O'Donnell, Griffin, and Norris 1967; Strickland 1961). Sentence length is determined by the average number of words in the main clause and the subordinate clauses attached to it. Complex sentences are those in which dependent clauses are attached to the main clause. The following activities may prove useful in strengthening students' written syntax:

- Present a list of simple nouns and verbs to students. Instruct students to think of and write descriptive words for each simple example. As a group, list all student ideas, and explore all possible combinations. For example:

Simple Nouns	*Student Ideas*	*Simple Verbs*	*Student Ideas*
dog	scruffy dog	barks	barks loudly
boy	little dog	runs	runs fast
	young boy	laughs	runs hard
	tall boy		

Possible Combination
the scruffy, little dog runs fast and hard

- Have students make simple sentences more detailed by using descriptive who, what, when, where, why, and how words and phrases.

Paragraph organization. Paragraph organization depends on well-developed topics; supportive facts, details, and examples; and conclusions. This component of written expression reflects the way in which students organize their ideas. Categorizing, putting ideas in logical order, stating the main idea, providing details, note taking, outlining, and eliminating hasty generalizations are all elements of paragraph organization (Hall 1981). The following techniques may increase organizational skills:

- Present the student with a grid with category labels at the top and letters down the left-hand side. Students must then think of a detail that begins with a specified letter and write it in the appropriate box. For example:

	Fruit	Animal	State
P	pear	puppy	Pennsylvania
S			
A			
C			

- Provide the students with strips of paper, each of which has a sentence written on it. The strips, when ordered correctly, form a complete story. Students must place them in the correct sequence. They can check the order of the story they create against answers coded in numbers on the reverse side of the strips.

- Allow students to practice writing in sequence the events of a specific activity such as baking cookies or starting a car.

- When instructing students on paragraph organization, provide some reference to familiar concepts. Often students can explain a concept to their peers better than the teacher can. One eleven-year-old volunteered the following: "A complete paragraph is like a sandwich. The topic sentence is like the top half of the bun. The body of the paragraph is like the meat of the sandwich, and the conclusion is the bottom half of the bun." The teacher reminded the students that if all parts of a paragraph are not included, it will fall apart as would a sandwich if not constructed properly.

Note taking. Note taking is an expressive writing tool that assists students in learning new material. Often this skill does not become necessary until the upper-elementary and junior high grades. The concepts underlying note taking are similar to those of paragraph structure in that students must possess the ability to sift through information to locate and record main ideas and details. Since oral delivery of information is new to students, the teacher should provide opportunities for students to practice note taking. Initially, this practice should be given by the teacher in the form of precise directions. Gradually, the teacher's directions should become more general as students develop increased note-taking skill.

- While lecturing on a topic, the teacher may want to use an overhead projector and transparency to demonstrate note taking of important ideas. At the same time, students should be copying the teacher's notes.
- Using a tape recorded passage or lesson, teacher and students together take notes on important ideas. The use of an overhead projector and chalkboard by the teacher facilitates guidance of student note taking.
- Instruct students to take notes on a lesson delivered orally. Following the lesson, teacher and students review the class notes.

Outlining. Outlining guides students in logical thinking, organizing details and main ideas, and learning and studying new material. Practice in outlining should be structured at first and gradually lead to student independence.

- Provide a written list of main topics, subtopics, and details. Beneath these items, structure the outline so that students are cued to the number of main topics, subtopics, and details included. Initially, the main ideas may be identified for students as a prompt to organization. Students must then fill in the outline.

Proofreading. Students who use proofreading skills are more likely to produce a better quality of written work. However, since many students perceive proofreading as an aversive activity, teachers should not assume that such skills will be used automatically (Polloway, Patton and Cohen 1981). Students must be shown how to proofread (Hillerich 1979). If the teacher provides such instruction on a gradual basis, the intrinsic reinforcement that better quality written work provides can, indeed, alter students' perceptions of this skill.

- Select one or two proofreading skills for an assignment until students practice these consistently (Polloway, Patton, and Cohen 1981).
- Students can edit their work by listening for specific types of errors as they read their compositions aloud to the teacher during editing conferences (Gleason 1982; Hansen 1978).
- To minimize student apprehension about writing and editing, initially assign topics unrelated to personal feelings, attitudes, and experiences. Faigley, Daley, and Witte (1981) have found that students do not perform as well on assignments that demand a personal reaction as they do on assignments requiring only factual information.

SURVIVAL SKILLS

According to Cohen and Plaskon (1980), American adults rely less on written correspondence today than in the past. However, written expression remains a necessary skill for everyday living, interpersonal communication, and occupational survival. The importance of good writing skills becomes apparent to the educationally handicapped learner when instruction is integrated with the individual's survival needs (Gleason 1982; Golden 1980). The following activities, grouped according to instructional level, are suggestions for developing writing as a survival tool:

Primary and Intermediate:

- Writing personal information such as name, address, phone number, name of school, and immediate family members or relatives (The teacher may want to provide information cards for this purpose; students can then carry the cards for identification.)
- Writing friendly letters to classmates, relatives, or friends in other cities
- Addressing envelopes properly
- Writing invitations to parents, grandparents, or school staff, asking them to attend a special classroom event
- Writing business letters to ask for free information or materials to be used in the class
- Writing thank-you letters following receipt of personal or classroom gifts or as a follow-up activity after a class field trip

Junior and Senior High:

- Completing personal data sheets including information one might need when completing applications
- Writing letters of inquiry for summer jobs, part-time employment, or a post-high-school career
- Writing letters of application for summer jobs, part-time employment, or a post-high-school career
- Writing thank-you letters following employer correspondence or interview
- Completing sample applications for jobs, loans, higher educational admission, insurance, etc.
- Writing a personal resume to be typed and printed if desired
- Writing personal checks
- Producing an outline of a teacher's lecture

HOME REINFORCEMENT

In order for any instructional program to be effective, the child must encounter a variety of experiences and opportunities for practice. Parental involvement in the child's written expression development can elevate the importance of writing as well as motivate and reinforce the child's efforts in this area. Such activities should be enjoyable and contribute to the child's feeling of family involvement and status as well as academic capabilities. The following list describes suggested home activities in the area of written expression:

- Encourage the child to make a card, possibly with a drawing, to send to a relative, friend, or neighbor for a variety of occasions.

- Encourage written correspondence with relatives or friends.
- Encourage the child to create lists of gift ideas that he or she might like to receive for birthdays, Christmas, etc. (This also helps to develop concepts about money.)
- Allow the child to make a list of new clothes or school supplies that he or she might like to have for a special event.
- Allow the child to make out a guest list for a party.
- Allow the child to help write party invitations and address the envelopes. (Plan ahead and space the activity so as not to present the child with too large a task at once.)
- Have high school seniors compile a list of names to whom graduation announcements will be sent and have them address announcement envelopes.
- Encourage the child to write thank-you notes for gifts received. (Remember that lined stationery helps the young child in written execution.)
- Allow the child to help in writing the family shopping list.
- Allow the youth to compile a menu for party snacks, a special birthday celebration, or a graduation open house.
- Allow the youth to devise shopping lists for the family's weekly meals.
- Encourage the child to write a message when leaving the household to play, indicating where he or she will be and a phone number.
- Ask the child to write down phone messages taken for other family members.
- Have the child make a list of emergency phone numbers to post near the family telephone(s).
- Ask the child to make a list of the names and phone numbers of relatives and friends frequently called.
- Allow students to write their own absence excuse notes to be signed by the parent(s).
- Encourage the child to write and send postcards while away on vacation.
- Encourage the youngster to maintain a daily journal of events and places visited during the family's vacation.
- Encourage the youth to keep a personal diary or journal.
- Suggest that the youth use old family and personal photos to compile a family scrapbook with captions or stories about the events depicted.

It is critical to remember that the purpose of each activity is to provide practice and that parents should assume a motivational role rather than an evaluative one. These experiences should be short, enjoyable, and undemanding tasks.

REGULAR CLASS INVOLVEMENT

For the educationally handicapped student in mainstreamed regular education classes, difficulties in written expression may create barriers to academic success.

More seriously, such failure experiences may create long-term apprehension about writing tasks (Lerner 1981; Golden 1980). These barriers confronting the mainstreamed educationally handicapped student can be alleviated through cooperative efforts of special and regular educators. The following section presents suggestions that may be implemented by regular and special educators:

- Provide the student with a handwriting model (manuscript or cursive) that can be referred to easily. The model can be taped to the desk, laminated on a large 8½"-by-11" piece of paper, or laminated on a wallet-sized card.
- Provide students with plastic templates that complement the handwriting system being used. Typically, these templates are available from the company that supplies other materials used in the handwriting program.
- Move the child's seat close to the model if copying from the chalkboard is routine, or provide an individual model of the same information to be used at the individual's desk.
- Modify testing situations to suit the individual. For example,
  —provide matching, multiple-choice and true-false items instead of fill-in-the-blanks, short-answer, or lengthy essay questions;
  —allow the student to take tests orally;
  —permit the student to answer test questions by tape recording responses; or
  —allow the student to dictate test answers to a personal secretary (peer tutor, regular educator, or special educator).
- Adapt written assignments such as reports or compositions. For example,
  —provide the student with a structured outline indicating the scope and sequence of content;
  —assist the student in proofreading and editing rough drafts;
  —allow the student to have someone with good penmanship write the final copy, or encourage the student to type the final copy;
  —encourage use of the dictionary to check spelling of the final copy.
- Provide structured guidelines if note taking is an element of instruction in the regular class. For example,
  —organize the lecture according to a given outline of important information presented on an overhead projector or chalkboard;
  —present the student with a personal outline of the lecture on which he or she may record additional comments;
  —permit the student to check or copy the notes of a responsible classmate.
- Modify the task for the individual when outlining written material is a requirement in the regular class. For example,
  —provide a skeleton outline indicating content clues and the number of important details, subheadings, and main headings to be included;
  —allow the student to highlight the content's important information and to receive teacher feedback prior to constructing the outline.
- Evaluate the logic of the content and ideas expressed in student's work when assigning personal themes, stories, or journals (Tiedt 1975).

SUMMARY POINTS

- The ability to express one's thoughts in writing is a highly complex act that encompasses more than handwriting.
- When determining whether to teach manuscript or cursive writing, a teacher should assess the students' skills individually. For example, some children's writing is more legible in cursive.
- Beyond the elementary level, students are required to rely more on their written expression skills. Frequently, alternative instructional strategies and modes of output for handicapped students can be agreed upon with regular teachers.
- Because of the complexity of written expression, it is important for teachers to remember the purpose of each assignment in judging a student's work. For example, if the assignment is creative writing, then grading should not be based on punctuation, spelling, paragraph structure, or letter formation.
- When using rule-based spelling methods, teachers should expand their instructional role to include helping students learn to reproduce spelling words. Thus, students are more likely to learn phonetic generalizations as well as appropriate spelling of words.
- Use of an inductive approach may allow students to acquire and retain phonetic generalizations emphasized in spelling instruction more efficiently.

REVIEW QUESTIONS

1. Provide a comprehensive definition of written expression. Which, if any, of the components of written expression is most frequently emphasized? Why?
2. What criteria would you use to determine whether a student should use manuscript or cursive writing?
3. You are invited to give a talk to regular teachers and parents on remediating written expression deficits. For each component of written expression, outline suggestions and activities you would give to this diverse audience.

SUGGESTED READINGS

Cramer, R. L. 1978. *Writing, reading, and language growth.* Columbus, Ohio: Charles E. Merrill.

Hillerich, R. A. 1978. *Writing vocabulary of elementary school children.* Springfield, Ill.: Charles C. Thomas.

Application: Craig and Tony

Based on the diagnostic and background information presented in the case studies, the following remedial strategies were developed for Craig and Tony.

Craig

Assessment of thirteen-year-old Craig's written expression skills indicated the following:

- A lack of knowledge in structuring an outline
- Difficulty in sorting given information into main ideas and details
- Poor penmanship due to inaccurate letter formation and spacing
- Poor academic grades, reflective of the effect poor written expression has had on content area performance

To develop skills in outlining, Craig's resource teacher, Mrs. Simms, took the following steps:

- First, Mrs. Simms presented a skeleton outline and defined each component. In addition, she completed part of the outline as shown below, to help Craig get started.

Football	(Title/Topic)
I. The team players	(Main Heading or Idea)
A. Offensive Players	(Subheading)
1. ______	
2. ______	(Details)
3. ______	
B. Defensive players	(Subheading)
1. ______	
2. ______	(Details)
3. ______	
II. History of football	(Main Heading or Idea)
A. ______	(Subheading)
1. ______	
2. ______	(Details)
3. ______	
B. ______	(Subheading)
C. ______	(Subheading)

To assist Craig in sorting main ideas, subheadings, and details, the following remedial techniques were used:

- Mrs. Simms began developing the concept of main ideas and details through categorizing exercises. These activities required Craig to categorize lists of objects and ideas such as baseball, football, soccer, sports, volleyball, and tennis.
- Next, she gave Craig a small body of information in which the information for an outline was already underlined. Mrs. Simms used different colors of highlighters to distinguish main ideas from subheadings. Later she added a third color to differentiate details.
- Next, Craig was asked to read a small body of information and underline or highlight the main ideas. Once the main topics were identified and written on a rough outline, he reread the information to identify subheadings, which he then highlighted and wrote on the outline. Finally, Craig had to read the information again in order to pick out any details of importance, highlight or underline these details, and transfer them to the outline. For a posttest, Craig had to select a topic to research and outline independently.
- Since outlining is an important skill at the junior high level, Mrs. Simms taped lectures in Craig's other classes. Then he was required to outline the information he heard on the tape.

Craig demonstrated poor written execution of letter forms and poor spacing. In an attempt to strengthen his penmanship, his teacher was faced with the difficulty of devising strategies that were age-appropriate as well as skill-specific. The following is a list of several strategies Mrs. Simms used:

- First, after a discussion with Craig, she determined which method of writing he preferred—manuscript or cursive.
- Next she provided lined paper sized according to Craig's needs. Thin-lined paper required Craig to write smaller, giving the appearance of congestion; however, he refused to use the wide-lined paper, which he called "babyish."
- For Craig, using a typewriter for classroom assignments was an alternative. However, in the resource room, he practiced improving his cursive spacing and letter formation.

The comments of Craig's regular education teachers on his grade reports were investigated to determine how his poor written expression skills were affecting his academic functioning. Often students experience note taking, report writing, and written essay tests for the first time in junior high school. For students like Craig who have deficits in written expression, the adjustment to these new instructional methods is difficult. The special educator should determine if this is the problem and cooperate with regular educators to alleviate these barriers. Craig's regular teachers agreed on the following adaptations:

- Taping class lectures in addition to having students take notes
- Using an overhead projector to present main ideas for note-taking purposes
- Outlining the most important lecture points on the chalkboard
- Modifying test procedures so that Craig could take oral exams, tape record answers, or take tests in the resource room, dictating answers to someone who could write legibly
- Providing Craig with a structured outline of information to be included in research or report assignments
- Giving Craig the option of presenting research or report assignments to the instructor or to the class

Tony

In the case of eight-year-old Tony, the following conclusions were drawn:

- Demonstrates poor letter formation but has better execution when presented with a model in close proximity
- Has difficulty with proper spacing between letters and words
- Uses improper and inconsistent letter size and has difficulty monitoring letter slant without a model
- Executes cursive writing better than manuscript but is not yet completely accurate and consistent
- Exhibits the following error patterns in spelling: reversal of vowel-consonant order, inappropriate sound-symbol association, unneeded letters, and omissions of letters

In order to strengthen Tony's skills in letter formation, consistent models were provided, and activities were designed to gradually decrease his dependence on the models. Ms. Scanlon, Tony's resource teacher, took the following steps:

- She provided drill work sheets on letter formation that presented a model letter and required Tony to write examples of the letter.
- She taped a model of all upper- and lower-case letters to Tony's desk for easy reference.
- Ms. Scanlon also provided written cues on work sheets to remind Tony to use the models. For example: "See" if your letters match your model; 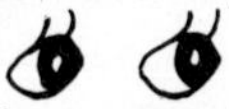
- The teacher made it a game for Tony to cover the model during an assignment, execute the written performance, and then check and evaluate his own performance against the model.
- When Tony demonstrated no further need for an individual model, Ms. Scanlon removed it but allowed him to refer to the classroom model alphabet.
- Ms. Scanlon developed a cursive notebook for Tony to record each letter he successfully mastered. This proved to be an aid in motivation and also allowed Tony to monitor his own progress.

Tony's cursive writing samples showed improper spacing between words and sentences. The following techniques were implemented to correct this problem:

- Prior to a copying assignment, Tony's teacher marked space holders on Tony's paper to allow spaces between words and sentences. For example:

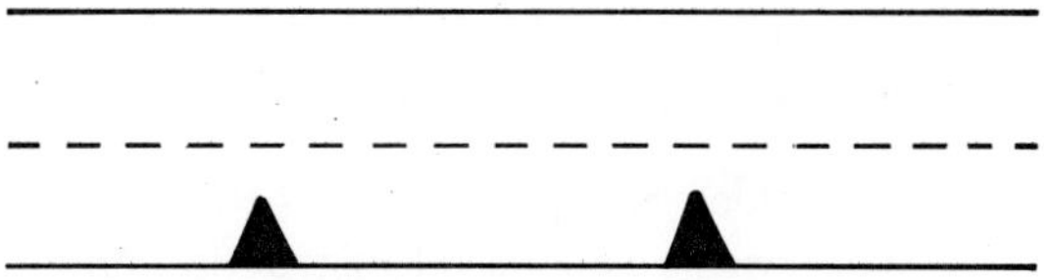

- Tony and Ms. Scanlon agreed that he would place a small sticker between words and sentences. If executed correctly, the stickers would not touch any of the words.
- Ms. Scanlon allowed time for joint evaluation sessions with Tony to decide whether his spacing was too great, too close, or just right.

Tony's cursive letters were often too large and extended beyond the limits established by lined paper. The following remedial strategies were tried by Ms. Scanlon to diminish this problem:

- She presented Tony with larger lined writing paper. The size of the lined paper was gradually reduced.
- Ms. Scanlon darkened the bottom line with red ink to remind Tony that all letters had to sit on this line. After Tony mastered placing his letters on the bottom line, Ms. Scanlon made the top line red. Then she color-coded the middle line. If she had asked Tony to focus on the

bottom, top, and middle all at once, he would have been overwhelmed.

Ms. Scanlon thought Tony's difficulty with letter slant was due to improper paper positioning as well as an inability to monitor consistent slant. The following techniques were used to improve proper letter slant:

- She taped Tony's work paper in the proper position on his desk.
- Later, she placed strips of tape on his desk to indicate the proper placement of paper.

Tony's spelling errors included reversals, omissions, unneeded letters, and inappropriate sound-symbol association. Most of his spelling errors were attributed to inappropriate sound-symbol association, so Ms. Scanlon designed the following strategies to correct this pattern:

- She selected a spelling series that emphasized rule-based instruction and taught phonetic generalizations through an inductive approach.
- A closed sort procedure was used to supplement the inductive approach for spelling. Each week, Ms. Scanlon wrote the words from Tony's spelling unit on index cards, and together they sorted these words according to phonetic principles emphasized in the unit that week.
- Following the word sort, Ms. Scanlon pronounced the phonemes emphasized in the unit while Tony reproduced them.
- Ms. Scanlon developed a chart on which Tony's spelling scores were recorded as a visual indication of his progress.
- Weekly "success-o-grams" written by Tony were sent through the mail to his parents to build and reinforce Tony's image of his spelling ability.
- Ms. Scanlon used continuous verbal reinforcement with Tony during spelling practice sessions. Following his oral and written spelling of each word, she made it a point to say something positive to him.

Discussion Points

1. Often educationally handicapped adolescents lack motivation in the classroom. List five motivating activities or themes a junior high resource teacher might use to promote handwriting skills.
2. Identify self-evaluation procedures that Tony and Craig could use to monitor their progress in written expression tasks completed in class.

CHAPTER 12 Teaching Arithmetic Skills

OUTLINE

INTRODUCTION

Because of rapidly developing technological advances occurring in our society, today's handicapped students are faced with additional demands for using their arithmetic skills. Traditional daily living tasks demanding arithmetic proficiency include telling time, cooking, and planning trips. However, today's students must also be skilled in performing emerging tasks that require further arithmetic fluency. Examples of these new tasks include using money cards and calculators as well as understanding and using computers.

In the past, many handicapped students with primarily math-oriented learning problems were overlooked. Certainly an outcome of the increased need for using arithmetic-related skills is that greater attention is being given to arithmetic deficits. This chapter focuses on assessment and instructional procedures that teachers can use to assist handicapped students in attaining greater arithmetic independence.

Objectives

After reading this chapter, you should be able to

- identify students' arithmetic skill deficits by using formal and informal assessment procedures;
- provide a sequential instructional program in arithmetic for handicapped students;
- select a student's developmental instructional level based on informal test data and observation;
- prepare students to apply arithmetic skills to everyday problems;
- discuss the purpose and limitations of popular commercial arithmetic instructional programs;
- use instructional procedures that prevent or remediate common arithmetic problems among handicapped students.

Case Studies: Larry and Theresa

Larry

Fifteen-year-old Larry Erikson is the youngest member of his family, who lives in a middle-class neighborhood of a small city. In January of Larry's freshman year, Ms. Simpson, the math teacher, sent home a note with the following comments: "Larry is not turning in homework. Further, his study habits are weak; he makes inefficient use of class time, is acting up in class, is inconsistent in his performance, and does not know how to add or subtract, let alone multiply or divide. Larry is at risk of failing this course."

After receiving permission from the Eriksons for a multifactored assessment, the special education teacher, Mr. Russell, first reviewed Larry's past records. It seemed that arithmetic had never been his strong subject; however, performance in all other academic areas was above average. Mr. Russell then decided to outline an assessment plan. First, he would administer the *Criterion Test of Basic Skills: Arithmetic* (Brown, Lundell, and Evans 1976) and the *Key Math Diagnostic Arithmetic Test* (Connolly, Nachtman, and Pritchett 1976). Then he would observe Larry's performance and have him complete other informal assessment activities to determine his developmental instructional level.

According to formal test performance, Larry needed instruction in all basic operations, money, time, arithmetic symbols, fractions, and decimals. Data gathered from informal assessment sources revealed similar deficits. Observation findings confirmed that Larry did have specific learning problems in arithmetic, and that he was capable of performing math problems at the symbolic or abstract level.

On the basis of all reported assessment information, the following strengths and weaknesses were noted:

Strengths

Recognizes coins and currency equivalencies

Measures to the half-inch

Identifies 1, 1/2

Tells time

Understands months and days and can use calendar correctly

Reads and writes numerals

Counts numbers

Weaknesses

Cannot perform basic operations

Has difficulty making change

Cannot write a check or identify its value

Does not identify measurement values

Does not compute percentages

As a result, the placement team recommended that Larry receive arithmetic instruction from the resource room teacher for one period each day.

Theresa

Currently, seven-year-old Theresa Nichols is completing the second grade in a large urban area school. Although Theresa was described by her teacher as a "hard worker," she was unable to grasp arithmetic concepts and perform basic arithmetic operations.

The special education consultant administered the *Key Math Diagnostic Arithmetic Test* (Connolly, Nachtman, and Pritchett 1976) and the *Brigance Diagnostic Inventory of Essential Skills* (Brigance 1980) to Theresa. Tests in reading, perceptual and social skills, and in vocational areas were also administered.

Assessment results indicated that Theresa had good learning potential. She was socially astute, had good problem-solving skills, and had reading skills above grade-level expectations; yet arithmetic was a problem area. Specifically, the following strengths and weaknesses were identified:

Strengths

Identifies 1, 1/2

Counts to 100

Counts objects to 10

Computes sums for addends 3 through 10

Identifies coins

Measures to the inch

Identifies clock, calendar

Tells time to the hour

Weaknesses

Cannot compute differences for 3 through 10

Cannot identify cues for subtraction in word problems

Cannot construct coin equivalencies for $.05, $.10, $.25, $.50, $1.00

Cannot tell time to the quarter-hour, half-hour, five-minute interval

Cannot convert date to day or day to date on calendar

After arithmetic strengths and weaknesses were identified through formal assessment, the special education consultant administered an informal math inventory (IMI) to identify specific instructional needs. Each portion of the IMI allowed the consultant to focus exclusively on a specific math skill and observe Theresa's efforts over many trials. Theresa's responses on a part of the money section are presented in Figure 12–1. It should be noted that in the actual testing session, Theresa was allowed to use real coins to formulate her answers. As indicated by Theresa's performance, this task proved to be too difficult for her. However, during this informal testing time, Theresa consistently knew which coins had greater value.

At the placement meeting, the psychologist commented that Theresa had good problem-solving ability on a concrete level and had basic arithmetic readiness skills. He noted that Theresa appeared to be apprehensive and needed to use objects or her fingers to complete computations. The team recommended special educational support in arithmetic for Theresa from a tutor for one academic year, after which her arithmetic skills would be reevaluated.

Points for Consideration

- *In both cases, academic deficits were limited to mathematics.*

It is apparent that the arithmetic skill deficits that Larry exhibited developed over a long time; yet, since his skill deficits were limited to arithmetic, Larry's previous teachers apparently did not perceive him as needing special services. If Larry had been referred and assessed earlier in his school program, perhaps skill deficits in arithmetic could have been remediated in the regular classroom.

- *In our culture arithmetic skills are critical to independent functioning.*

The most basic decisions confronting the average person are governed by the ability to interpret or manipulate numbers and related concepts. Deciding what time to get up in the morning, the temperature at which to set the oven, how much to tip the waitress, the speed to drive at, and which coins to put in the electronic game are but a few examples of our reliance on number concepts. The implications for students with arithmetic deficits in our culture are serious. For example, how must Larry feel when someone asks him for the time or when he must decide if he has enough money for a pizza with friends? Obviously such events are threatening and can have a negative effect on a student's self-image. Because of the need for arithmetic skills in all of a student's ecosystems and the negative effects skill deficits can have on a student, early identification and remediation of arithmetic deficits are critical.

☐ **FIGURE 12–1**
A Portion of Theresa's Performance on an Informal Math Inventory

1 dime = __8__ pennies
1 nickel = __5__ pennies
1 quarter = __20__ pennies
1 quarter = __dk*__ dimes and __dk__ nickels
1 dime = __dk__ nickels
1 quarter = __dk__ nickels

Here is a dime. Count the number of pennies that equal it.
Response: __7__

Here is a nickel. Count the number of pennies that equal it.
Response: __5__

Here is a quarter. Count the number of pennies that equal it.
Response: __dk__

Here is a dime. Count the number of nickels that equal it.
Response: __2__

Here is a quarter. Count the number of nickels that equal it.
Response: __3__

Here is a quarter. Count the number of dimes and nickels that equal it.
Response: __dk__

*dk means that Theresa did not know the answer.

COMMON INSTRUCTIONAL MISCONCEPTIONS

Students with arithmetic deficits are likely to have problems in other subject areas as well. Although some students may have learning disabilities related to several content areas, there are many identified handicapped learners whose difficulties are limited to mathematics (McLeod and Armstrong 1982). Proficiency in arithmetic requires students to understand concepts different from those associated with other content areas such as reading or spelling. These differences can be seen in the vocabulary, language sets, procedures, and mastery tasks related to arithmetic instruction.

Once students learn basic arithmetic facts, they will not have difficulties with other arithmetic operations. There are hundreds of facts associated with each basic operation students are required to recall. While recall or memorization is a low-level cognitive skill, it is important to note that many arithmetic problems require students to use memorization as well as more sophisticated abstract skills. Thus, to determine a student's instructional needs, the teacher must analyze the cognitive skills necessary to complete an arithmetic task. Some students might, for example, be able to recite basic facts with 100 percent accuracy, but have difficulty applying this information to higher-level cognitive problems.

Students will use their arithmetic skills to solve everyday problems that occur outside the classroom. Teachers cannot rely on incidental learning if students are to apply their arithmetic skills to everyday problems. They must systemtically plan instructional activities that require students to use arithmetic skills in everyday situations. In fact, students are more likely to be motivated to increase their arithmetic skills when aware of the relationship the skills have to daily living.

ASSESSING ARITHMETIC SKILLS

As in other academic skill areas, a comprehensive arithmetic assessment battery should include both informal and formal procedures. Frequently formal tests are initially used to identify global problem areas; however, informal procedures permit teachers to identify a student's specific skill deficits and learning style, both of which are necessary for effective instructional programming.

Informal Assessment Techniques

To determine if an informal arithmetic assessment program is thorough, teachers might ask themselves the following:

- First, have the subskills associated with each arithmetic skill area been identified?
- Next, are assessment tools available to identify a student's performance in these skill areas?
- Finally, how does a student perform these arithmetic tasks?

By using scope-and-sequence charts, criterion-referenced tests, and observation techniques, teachers will be able to answer these questions and thus plan an effective individualized instructional program.

Scope and sequence of arithmetic skills. A scope-and-sequence chart such as the one in Figure 12–2 hierarchically identifies skills within each arithmetic area. This hierarchical sequence of arithmetic skills can be a valuable tool in planning instruction to remediate arithmetic deficits since the teacher can specifically identify which skills have been mastered as well as which areas need additional instructional time.

☐ **FIGURE 12–2**
Scope and Sequence of Arithmetic Skills

READINESS SKILLS	*Deficient* –	*Instruction* /	*Mastery* *
Discriminates by size, shape, quantity			
Counts from 1 to 10			
Counts a group of objects from 1 to 10			
Associates a number with a set of objects			
Writes digits 1 to 10			
Demonstrates one-to-one correspondence			
BASIC OPERATIONS: ADDITION			
Defines the plus sign (+)			
Computes from memory sums less than 10			
Computes from memory sums from 10 through 18			
Computes sums for the following number statements without regrouping: 2 digits + 1 digit			
2 digits + 2 digits			
Computes sums for the following number statements with regrouping: 2 digits + 1 digit			
2 digits + 2 digits			
Groups three-digit numerals by ones, tens, and hundreds			
Computes sums for the following number statement without regrouping: 3 digits + 3 digits			
Computes sums for the following number statement with regrouping: 3 digits + 3 digits			
Computes sums for the following number statement with regrouping: 4 or more digits + 4 or more digits			
Solves addition word problems			
BASIC OPERATIONS: SUBTRACTION			
Defines minus sign (–)			
Computes missing addend			
Defines subtraction as opposite of addition			

☐ **FIGURE 12–2—continued**
Scope and Sequence of Arithmetic Skills

BASIC OPERATIONS: SUBTRACTION	*Deficient* –	*Instruction* /	*Mastery* *
Computes from memory differences for minuends and subtrahends less than 10			
Groups two-digit numerals by ones and tens			
Computes from memory differences for minuends and subtrahends less than 19			
Computes differences for the following number statements without regrouping: 2 digits – 1 digit			
2 digits – 2 digits			
3 digits – 2 digits			
Computes differences for the following number statements with regrouping from tens to ones: 2 digits – 1 digit			
2 digits – 2 digits			
3 digits – 2 digits			
Computes differences for the following number statements with regrouping from hundreds to tens to ones: 3 digits – 2 digits			
3 digits – 3 digits			
Computes differences for number statements in which zero appears in the minuend in the hundreds', tens', or ones' place			
Computes differences for the following number statements with regrouping from thousands to hundreds to tens to ones: 4 digits – 2 digits			
4 digits – 4 digits			
4 digits – 3 digits			
Solves subtraction word problems			
BASIC OPERATIONS: MULTIPLICATION			
Defines multiplication sign (×)			
Defines *factor* and *product*			
Computes from memory products for factors less than 10			
Demonstrates understanding of relationship between 1 × 5 and 10 × 5; 3 × 6 and 3 × 60			
Computes product for 2 digits × 1 digit without regrouping			
Regroups by ones and tens			
Computes product for 2 digits × 1 digit with regrouping			
Regroups by ones, tens, and hundreds			

☐ **FIGURE 12–2—continued**
Scope and Sequence of Arithmetic Skills

BASIC OPERATIONS: MULTIPLICATION	*Deficient* –	*Instruction* /	*Mastery* *
Computes the products for the following number statements with regrouping: 2 digits × 1 digit			
2 digits × 2 digits			
3 digits × 1 digit			
3 digits × 2 digits			
3 digits × 3 digits			
3 digits × 4 digits			
4 digits × 4 digits			
Solves multiplication word problems			
BASIC OPERATIONS: DIVISION			
Defines division signs (÷,/,a/b)			
Defines *divisor, dividend, quotient*			
Defines division as opposite of multiplication			
Computes quotients for dividends and divisors less than 10			
Computes quotients for the following number statements without a remainder: 2 digits ÷ 1 digit			
3 digits ÷ 1 digit			
Computes quotients for the following number statements with a remainder:			
1 digit ÷ 1 digit			
2 digits ÷ 1 digit			
3 digits ÷ 1 digit			
Demonstrates understanding of relationship between $8 \div 2$, $80 \div 2$, $800 \div 2$			
Rounds two- and three-digit numerals to the nearest ten: $32 = 30$, $47 = 50$, $423 = 420$			
Estimates quotient after rounding to the nearest ten for the following statements:			
2 digits ÷ 2 digits			
3 digits ÷ 2 digits			
Computes quotient for the following number statements:			
5 digits ÷ 3 digits			
5 digits ÷ 4 digits			
Solves division word problems			

☐ **FIGURE 12–2—continued**
Scope and Sequence of Arithmetic Skills

FRACTIONS: READINESS	*Deficient* –	*Instruction* /	*Mastery* *
Identifies representation of fraction			
Defines *fraction* as a portion of one			
Defines terms *numerator* and *denominator*			
States fraction name when shown 1/2, 1/3, 1/4, 2/3, 3/4			
Divides object and identifies 1/2, 1/4, 3/4, 1/3, 2/3			
Compares fractions indicating larger, smaller, equal			
Reduces fraction to simplest terms			
Writes a mixed numeral from improper fraction			
Writes an improper fraction from mixed numeral			
Computes least common denominator based on largest common multiple			
FRACTIONS: ADDITION			
Computes sum for fractions with like denominators: 1/3 + 1/3			
Computes sum for mixed numbers with like denominators: 2-1/3 + 3-1/3			
Computes sum with regrouping for fractions with like denominators: 4/5 + 3/5			
Computes sum with regrouping for mixed and simple fractions: 2-1/6 + 5/6			
Computes sum with regrouping for two mixed fractions: 2-1/3 + 2-2/3			
Computes sum for fractions with different denominators: 1/3 + 2/6			
Computes sum for mixed fractions with different denominators: 2-1/3 + 2-2/6			
Computes sum with regrouping for mixed fractions with different denominators: 2-1/3 + 2-5/6			
Computes sum of three fractions with different denominators: 1/3 + 1/5 + 1/4			
Solves addition word problems that include fractions			
FRACTIONS: SUBTRACTION			
Computes difference between fractions without regrouping: 3-2/3 − 2-1/3			
Computes difference between fractions with regrouping: 3-1/3 − 2-2/3			
Computes difference between fractions with different denominators without regrouping: 4-5/6 − 2-1/3			

☐ **FIGURE 12–2—continued**
Scope and Sequence of Arithmetic Skills

FRACTIONS: SUBTRACTION	*Deficient* –	*Instruction* /	*Mastery* *
Computes difference between fractions with different denominators with regrouping: 4-1/3 − 2-5/6			
Solves subtraction word problems that include fractions			
FRACTION: MULTIPLICATION			
Computes product of whole number and fraction: 3 × 1/2			
Renames 1 as fraction: 6/6, 7/7, 2/2			
Computes product of two fractions: 1/5 × 1/3			
Computes product of mixed fraction and whole number: 5 × 3-1/5			
Computes product of fraction and mixed fractions: 1/5 x 3-1/5			
Computes product of two mixed fractions: 3-1/5 × 2-7/8			
Solves multiplication word problems that include fractions			
FRACTIONS: DIVISION			
Computes quotient for whole number divided by fraction: 2 ÷ 4/5			
Computes quotient for fraction divided by fraction: 4/5 ÷ 1/2			
Computes quotient for mixed fraction divided by mixed fraction: 4-4/5 ÷ 2-1/2			
Solves division word problems that include fractions			
MONEY			
Identifies coins			
States coin names			
States coin values			
States coin equivalencies:			
nickel = 5 cents			
dime = 2 nickels or 10 cents			
quarter = 2 dimes and 1 nickel			
= 2 dimes and 5 cents			
= 5 nickels			
= 25 cents			
= 3 nickels and 1 dime			
Makes change to one dollar			
Recognizes currency: one-dollar, five-dollar, ten-dollar, twenty-dollar bills			

☐ **FIGURE 12–2—continued**
Scope and Sequence of Arithmetic Skills

MONEY	*Deficient* –	*Instruction* /	*Mastery* *
Recognizes written money notation: 5¢, $.05, $1.05, $20.00			
Makes change to five, ten, twenty dollars			
TIME			
Identifies a clock, minute hand, hour hand			
Tells time to hour, half-hour, quarter-hour, 1-minute interval, 5-minute interval, before and after hour			
States days of week in sequence			
States day in terms of yesterday and tomorrow: yesterday was Monday; tomorrow is Wednesday			
States months of year in sequence			
Reads calendar: month, day of week, date			
MEASUREMENT			
Identifies ruler, yardstick, meter stick, measuring cup, pint, quart, gallon, liter			
Measures to inch, foot, yard, centimeter, decimeter, millimeter			
Measures to half-inch, quarter-inch			
States measurement equivalencies: 1 foot = 12 inches			
1 yard = 3 feet			
2 cups = 1 pint			
2 pints = 1 quart			
2 quarts = 1/2 gallon			
4 quarts = 1 gallon			
8 pints = 1 gallon			
Estimates height and length in appropriate units of measure			
Estimates volume in appropriate units of measure			
Defines *ounce, pound, ton*			
Identifies abbreviation for *ounce, pound, ton*			
Compares weights using a balance or scale			
Weighs to nearest pound, ounce			
Estimates weight of object in pounds			
LIFE SKILLS: MONEY			
Budgets money			
Saves money			
Chooses best buy through unit price, taste, quality			
Estimates money needed for activity: e.g., lunch at a restaurant			

□ **FIGURE 12–2—continued**
Scope and Sequence of Arithmetic Skills

LIFE SKILLS: MONEY	*Deficient* –	*Instruction* /	*Mastery* *
Defines *credit card*			
Defines banking terms: *checking account, check, deposit, deposit slip, withdrawal, withdrawal slip, savings account, passbook, bank card*			
Writes a check			
Computes checkbook balance			
Makes a deposit to checking account, savings account			
Makes a withdrawal from checking account, savings account			
Uses a bank card			
Defines types of insurance: life, whole life, term, home, car			
States reasons for insurance			
Defines types of expenses such as: utilities, leisure, home, miscellaneous, loan payment, credit charges			
Creates budget for family			
LIFE SKILLS: MEASUREMENT			
Measures 1/2, 1/4, 3/4, 1/3, 2/3 cup; 1, 1/2, 1/4, 1/8 teaspoon, tablespoon			
Uses appropriate measure in recipe or for medicine			
Reads Fahrenheit and centigrade thermometers			
States relationship between very cold, cold, warm, very warm, hot and the current outside/inside temperature			
Reads medical thermometer			
Sets oven and stove temperature			
Computes area and perimeter			
Converts square feet to square yards			
Computes cost of various yard goods			
LIFE SKILLS: TIME			
Associates holidays with season and month			
States time equivalencies: 7 days = 1 week, 4 weeks = 1 month, 30 days = 1 month, 12 months = 1 year, 60 minutes = 1 hour, 24 hours = 1 day			
Associates activity with time of day: e.g., 12:00 = lunch, 8:00 = favorite TV show			
Estimates preparation time: e.g., getting ready for school, driving to a location			
Subtracts preparation time from arrival time to compute starting time			

□ **FIGURE 12–2—continued**
Scope and Sequence of Arithmetic Skills

LIFE SKILLS: TIME	*Deficient* –	*Instruction* /	*Mastery* *
Estimates travel time			
Uses various time schedules for planning: TV guide, bus and plane timetables, calendar			

Criterion tests. Often developed in conjunction with skills listed on scope-and-sequence charts, criterion-referenced tests are designed to measure a student's performance in specific skill areas. Such information permits teachers to determine whether a student's skill performance is consistent or whether it is occurring by chance. Teachers are able to make such determinations with criterion tests since the student must complete a group of related problems rather than just one representative problem, as in norm-referenced tests.

While special educators can construct informal arithmetic tests that include a variety of arithmetic skills, it is suggested that teachers limit the number of skills in any given testing session. By focusing on one specific skill, teachers are better able to analyze performance in a more comprehensive manner. The following are examples of items on two informal arithmetic criterion-referenced tests. The first test is on time, and the second test is on fractions.

1. Show the student clocks with the following times displayed on them. Ask the student to orally state the correct time. Circle correct responses.

2:00	4:30	12:45	11:15	9:00	8:30
1:10	1:30	12:00	1:15	3:50	6:15

2. Name and write the fraction that is shown by the shaded area in each figure.

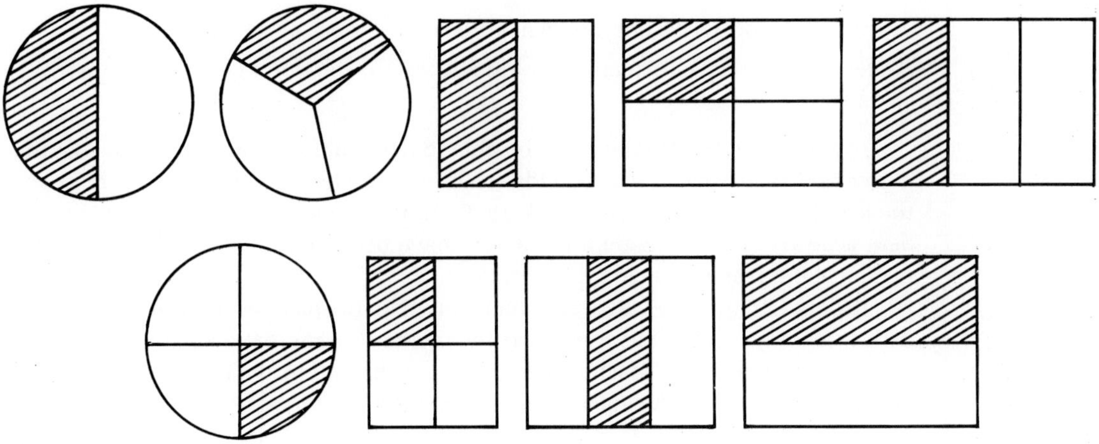

It is apparent that a student's performance on these tasks is more informative for planning an instructional program than a percentile or grade-equivalent score.

Observation techniques. Through observation special educators can gather significant information about how a student approaches or processes an arithmetic problem. For example, Ms. Curtis asked one of her young students the following question from the *Key Math Diagnostic Arithmetic Test* (Connolly, Nachtman, and Pritchett 1976): "How many inches are in a foot?" After counting the ridges on the sole of his shoe, the student exclaimed: "Thirty-one inches! You know, Ms. Curtis, I'm glad I wore these shoes today. Otherwise, I never would have figured that out." Obviously, this student is operating at a concrete level of conceptualization and is reducing a problem to its simplest elements as well. Not all approaches to problem solving are as apparent to even a trained observer. However, there are certain steps professionals can take to improve their observation skills.

One observation technique is the observation interview, in which the teacher asks the student to describe orally the process used to solve the problem. Typically, the teacher prepares a work sheet of three to five problems of the type on which the student makes errors and asks the student to describe the steps used to solve the problems. Such work sheets are called probe sheets because they focus on a specific skill, tentatively identified as one with which the student is having difficulty. The following is an example of an observation interview based on a student's performance on three multiplication problems:

$$\begin{array}{r} 31 \\ \times\ \underline{16} \\ 186 \\ \underline{31} \\ 217 \end{array} \qquad \begin{array}{r} 27 \\ \times\ \underline{23} \\ 81 \\ \underline{54} \\ 135 \end{array} \qquad \begin{array}{r} 49 \\ \times\ \underline{82} \\ 98 \\ \underline{392} \\ 490 \end{array}$$

Teacher: Paul, please tell me what you do to get the answer for these multiplication problems.

Student: First I multiply six times one and write the answer. Then six times three and write the answer. Next, I go to the one and multiply one times one, then write the answer.

Teacher: Do you write one underneath six?

Student: Yeah, I have to keep my columns straight so I don't get mixed up when I add.

Even though the teacher may be able to deduce the error pattern by looking at the student's work, it's a good idea to interview the student as well to discover the logic behind the error (Ashlock 1976). In this example, it's likely that the student is aware of place value but may not have been taught or retained the information about place value in multiplication.

Radatz (1979), who views arithmetic error patterns as correlating with a student's cognitive skills, has identified five general error patterns, which are described in Figure 12–3. Teachers can use this information as a basis for identifying questions to be asked during an observation interview.

Formal Assessment Tools

Formal arithmetic tests cluster into two general types, achievement and diagnostic. Achievement tests address numerous arithmetic subskills and yield information about a student's general arithmetic ability. Such tests typically yield a raw

FIGURE 12–3
Error Patterns in Mathematics

Error Pattern	*Rationale for Error*
Errors due to language difficulties	Student misunderstands the semantics of a mathematical statement such as "How many are there altogether?"
Difficulty in obtaining spatial information	Mathematics materials are used that limit an illustration of a concept to the semiconcrete or symbolic level.
Insufficient mastery of prerequisite skills	Students are given problems in division before mastery of multiplication and subtraction.
Incorrect associations	The student is not taught relevant cues for applying the appropriate algorithm or process.
Use of irrelevant rules or strategies	Student repeats algorithm which worked in the past.

(Adapted from Radatz, H. "Error Analysis in Mathematics Education." *Journal for Research in Mathematics Education*, 1979, pp. 163–172.)

score that is converted to approximate grade-level ability. Often achievement tests are most appropriately used as screening instruments. Diagnostic tests focus on fewer arithmetic subskills but tend to probe these subskills in greater depth.

Achievement tests. The *Peabody Individual Achievement Test* (*PIAT*) (Dunn and Markwardt 1970) is norm referenced for students in kindergarten through twelfth grade. The mathematics subtest focuses on skills such as matching, recognizing and discriminating numerals, solving word problems involving basic operations, time, money, measurement, mathematics vocabulary and symbols, algebra, geometry, and trigonometry. This subtest requires ten to fifteen minutes of demonstration time and does not require reading. Students may respond orally or through gesture. The *PIAT* is recommended for screening purposes rather than educational decision making (Salvia and Ysseldyke 1981).

The *California Achievement Tests* (*CAT*) (CTB/McGraw-Hill 1977, 1978) are both norm and criterion referenced for students in kindergarten through twelfth grade. The mathematics subtests assess students' abilities in areas such as number readiness skills, word problems involving basic operations, whole numbers, fractions, mixed numbers, decimals, and algebraic expressions. The reference subtest also assesses such mathematically related skills as interpretation of tables and diagrams and the use of banking and tax forms.

The *SRA Achievement Series* (Naslund, Thorpe, and Lefever 1978) is a norm- and criterion-referenced test battery administered to groups of students in kindergarten through twelfth grade. Concepts in the eight levels of the mathematics subtest include number and numeral identification, sets, counting, place value, geometric shapes, time, money, problem solving, whole numbers, fractions, decimals, measurement, basic operations, statistics, and probability. A user's guide with instructional suggestions accompanies the test.

The *Stanford Achievement Test* (*SAT*) (Madden et al. 1973) is a widely used and highly recommended test because standardization, reliability, and validity are quite good (Salvia and Ysseldyke 1981). The mathematics subtests measure student skill in a variety of concepts such as number meaning, reading and writing numerals, mathematical symbols, basic operations, geometry, measurement, logical thinking, fractions, time, percentages, probability, decimals, statistics, and problem solving.

Diagnostic tests. The *Key Math Diagnostic Test* (Connolly, Nachtman, and Pritchett 1976) is used to measure a variety of arithmetic skills for students in kindergarten through ninth grade. The fourteen subtests are grouped into three areas: content, operations, and applications. The three content subtests assess skills in numeration, fractions, and geometry and symbols, all of which are necessary for performing basic operations and for applying these skills in problem-solving situations. Operations subtests include addition, subtraction, multiplication, division, mental computation, and numerical reasoning. The five application subtests analyze a student's skill in solving word problems and finding missing elements as well as performance in using money, measurement, and time concepts. This test, individually administered in thirty to forty-five minutes, requires no reading on the part of the student; however, some items related to basic operations do require a written response. Also included are instructional objectives for each test item.

The Brigance diagnostic inventories are designed to assess an individual's functional and academic development in the range from developmental age 0 to grade twelve. The Brigance diagnostic tests are comprised of three batteries: *The Diagnostic Inventory of Early Development* (Brigance 1978) for children who function developmentally at ages less than seven years, *The Diagnostic Inventory of Basic Skills* (Brigance 1977) for use with students in kindergarten through sixth grade, and the *Diagnostic Inventory of Essential Skills* (Brigance 1980) for secondary students. No special training is required to use any of the batteries, although adherence to suggested testing procedures is recommended. The arithmetic subtests cover such skills as basic numeric concepts, basic operations, geometry, time, and money. Instructional objectives are provided, as is a record-keeping system to monitor student progress.

The *Diagnostic Mathematics Inventory* (*DMI*) (Gennell 1977) is a criterion-referenced test that measures mastery of 325 mathematics objectives for students in grades 1.5 to 8.5. The test allows special educators to design IEPs, evaluate student progress, group students, and locate instructional programs and materials. Each test item correlates with an instructional objective, which is paired with learning activities. A *Guide to Ancillary Materials*, which also correlates with test objectives, allows the teacher to select both mathematics texts and supplemental materials that teach and reinforce specific objectives.

REMEDIATING ARITHMETIC DEFICITS

Poor arithmetic performance has been attributed to many factors. Guerin and Maier (1983) have stated that, in addition to overall general intelligence, the following variables could be related to a student's arithmetic problems:

- Difficulty in recognizing and recalling computational words, symbols, and numerals, such as ×, +, *27*, and *eight*.
- Lack of opportunites to use a new skill repeatedly so that it can eventually be performed automatically.
- A poor foundation in basic arithmetic skills.
- Reading comprehension skills that are inadequate for completion of arithmetic word problems.
- Poor use of checking skills, especially difficulty in estimating the reasonableness of one's answers.

Certainly, the impact of these variables on a handicapped student's arithmetic performance cannot be minimized. The development of a successful instructional program requires their consideration.

For the beginning special educator, pulling all of this information together to determine a student's instructional needs is indeed a challenge. Such instructional decisions can be facilitated by identifying a student's developmental instructional level, by having students develop problem-solving strategies regardless of their skill level, and by being aware of various commercial programs available for disabled math students.

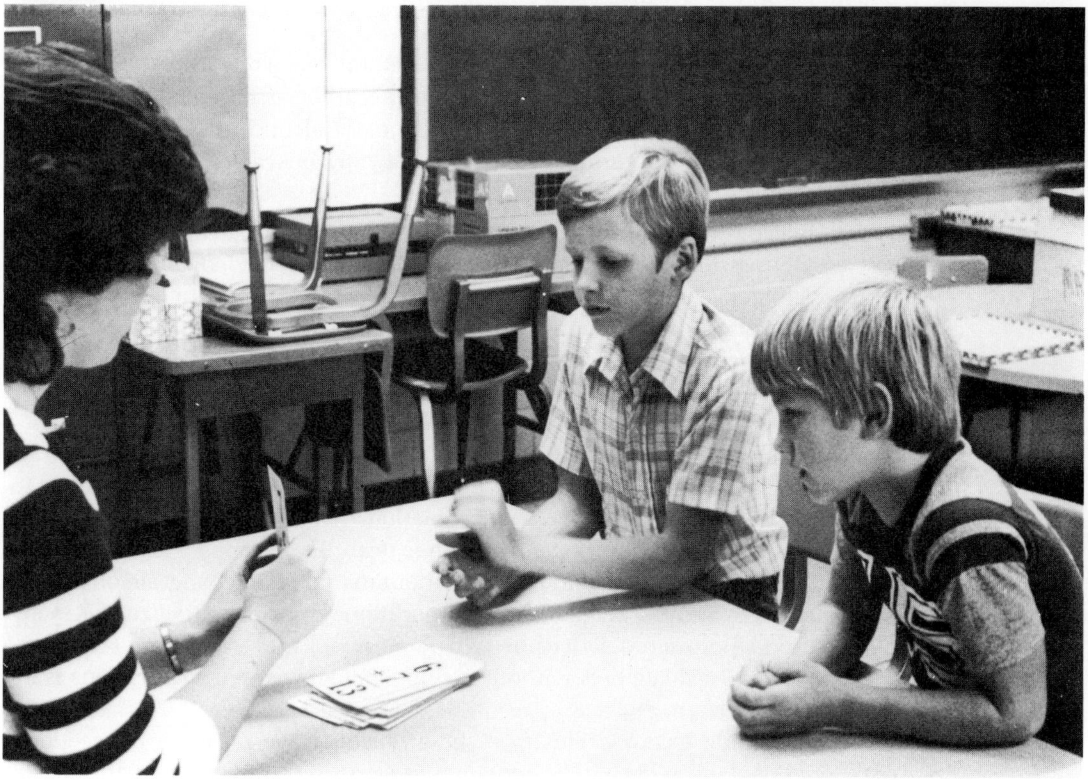

In order to perform more complex arithmetic tasks, students must have a firm understanding of the basic operations.

Instructional Level

The first consideration in developing an individualized instructional program is to identify the student's level of conceptual understanding. A child's ability to understand and solve problems depends on how these learning problems are presented, that is, what materials are used and how the student is involved in the learning task. Some students can learn on a symbolic or abstract level, while others need a semiconcrete instructional approach; other students require an even more defined, concrete, instructional setting. The focus here is on how, not what, a student will best learn. For example, although a teacher may be faced with teaching five students how to identify fractional parts, it may be that three students are functioning at a concrete level, one at a semiconcrete level, and one at an abstract instructional level.

According to Piaget (1953), instruction at a concrete level implies use of manipulatives to assist students who are functioning at the preoperational and concrete stages of development. Such students are generally perceptually oriented and are more likely to grasp spatial and numerical concepts when they are presented three-dimensionally. Commercial products designed to supplement arithmetic instruction at the concrete level include the following:

- Developmental Learning Materials, an educational publisher in Illinois, offers such items as number lines, scales, cubes, learning games, puzzles, clock stamps, and metric materials. Such materials may be used to teach arithmetic skills on a concrete or semiconcrete level.
- Montessori materials are based on the methods developed by Maria Montessori. They are self-correcting and useful for arithmetic instruction at a concrete level. Examples of Montessori materials include counting boxes, bead frames, metric number rods, and learning boards with pegs for basic operations.
- Cuisenaire rods (Davidson 1969) are aids to teaching basic operational skills typically used in grades kindergarten through six. They consist of 291 wooden blocks of different colors and lengths. Colors are white, red, green, purple, yellow, dark green, black, brown, blue, and orange. Each color represents a numeral. The rods are manipulated according to digits in a number sentence to arrive at the sum, product, difference, or quotient.

Learners at the semiconcrete level can solve arithmetic problems with the assistance of two-dimensional materials. Such students rely on these illustrations to recall past experiences or to make extrapolations from available data. Since students at this developmental stage can form logical relationships, illustrations are sufficient to help them construct reality without manipulating concrete objects.

Students beyond the stage of formal operations can conceptualize abstractly without the use of manipulatives or two-dimensional representation. For them, the use of numerical symbols without manipulative devices or illustrations is instructionally effective.

The following example illustrates how teaching the meaning of fractional parts could be done at each developmental level. At the concrete level, the special educator may use three-dimensional objects such as fruit or clay cut according to various fractional denominators. Using an apple to illustrate the concept of one-fourth, the teacher would divide it into four equal parts, count each with the student, and pick up one saying, "I have one of four parts. I have one-fourth of the apple."

At a semiconcrete level, the teacher may use similar instructional procedures; however, the materials used to illustrate the concept of fractional parts would be two-dimensional, such as work sheets with illustrations of objects like pies or circles.

At a symbolic level, the teacher may use numerals to communicate the concept of fractional parts, without relying on two- or three-dimensional examples and illustrations. For example, at the symbolic level, the teacher may write one-fourth (1/4) on the chalkboard and, pointing first to the four and then to the one, say, "Four means that any object is divided into four equal parts, and one means that one of these parts is present."

When teaching arithmetic concepts at the concrete, semiconcrete, and symbolic levels, the procedures followed may be similar, but the materials used should be selected according to the student's developmental needs. It is possible that special educators may have several students with similar instructional needs but different developmental abilities. In such cases, the special educator should carefully consider the grouping arrangements for such students in order to focus simultaneously on the skill level and developmental needs of each student.

Problem Solving

Certain components of the arithmetic curriculum are sequential; for example, readiness is a prerequisite for mastery of arithmetic operations (Hendrickson 1979; Good 1979). Problem-solving strategies, however, should be taught to students regardless of their age or skill level.

In order to complete arithmetic tasks successfully, handicapped students must be skilled in recognizing the essential cues in any given problem; that is, they must be able to identify what their role is in the problem situation. To assist students in developing effective problem-solving strategies, LeBlanc (1977) recommends that teachers deliberately arrange the instructional setting. Specifically, instruction on how to use problem-solving strategies should be presented to students in the following sequence:

1. Understanding the problem
2. Planning the solution
3. Solving the problem
4. Comparing the solution in the context of the problem.

Certainly not all students need instruction in all four steps. However, most handicapped students do need structured learning activities in order to increase at least one of these problem-solving skills.

To help students develop problem-solving skills, Earp (1970) recommends that students adopt the following process:

1. Read the problem to visualize the situation. (Some students could also have the problem read to them.)
2. Reread for essential facts.
3. Identify technical or difficult concepts.
4. Reread to plan steps for solution.
5. Reread a third time to compare understanding of the nature of the problem with the planned solution.

In addition, Vos (1976) has suggested that problem situations can be best understood through visual representation. By having students draw or concretely manipulate materials, they are more likely to understand and solve the problem. Such techniques are appropriate in remedial instructional settings as well as beneficial when new mathematical concepts are introduced.

Commercial Programs

When faced with selecting a remedial approach for students with learning problems in arithmetic, teachers have several choices. They may

- develop and use teacher-made materials,
- use a specialized commercial program and materials,
- select the program and textbook used in the regular mathematics program,
- adapt the regular program and text.

According to McLeod and Armstrong (1982), many special educators use all four remedial approaches; however, it seems that commercial materials are most frequently used. Several commercial arithmetic programs designed for use by handicapped students are discussed below.

DISTAR Arithmetic Kits. DISTAR Arithmetic Kits, developed by Englemann and Carnine (1972, 1975, 1976), stress direct instruction and the application of behavioral principles to instruction. DISTAR offers three levels of instruction: DISTAR I focuses on ordinal counting, simple addition and subtraction facts, signs, and story problems; DISTAR II focuses on more advanced addition and subtraction facts, place value, multiplication facts, fractions, and money, time, and measurement skills; and DISTAR III addresses advanced instruction in the four basic operations, place value, and word problems. The DISTAR kits contain a teacher's guide, presentation books, work sheets, and workbooks. Some kits contain geometric cards, form boards, fact cards, and a card stand.

Procedures used in the DISTAR arithmetic program are similar to the DISTAR reading program. Students are taught in small groups, and teachers follow a script for instruction. Lessons are fast paced, and students respond orally, although written work is provided. DISTAR kits have been used successfully with economically disadvantaged students (Becker and Englemann 1976; Stallings and Kaskowitz 1974).

Structural Arithmetic. Structural Arithmetic (Stern 1965), designed for students in kindergarten through third grade, is organized around four kits, each of which contains an instructional manual, student workbooks, and various manipulatives. The purpose of the manipulatives is to guide students in the discovery of number facts. Lessons are designed around experiments in which students use manipulatives to make discoveries and generalize what they have learned. These experiments progress from number concepts to problem solving. Arithmetic skills are organized sequentially, and workbooks provide opportunity for skill practice. Concepts included in the program consist of readiness concepts, basic operations, and problem solving. Pretests, interim tests, and posttests are included to assess student progress. Since mathematical concepts are introduced on a concrete and semiconcrete level, this program has been helpful to handicapped students (Bartel 1978).

Project MATH. Project MATH (Cawley et al. 1976) was developed for students in kindergarten through sixth grade, but has also been used for older students with math deficits. Project MATH consists of four kits, each of which spans one and one-half grade levels and includes learning activities designed to provide students with a variety of response choices to demonstrate mastery. Thus, the program can be used by students with limited reading skills. Further, the program is designed to include a variety of "input and output modes" to allow both the student and teacher various options for communication. The concepts included in the program focus on readiness skills, basic operations, geometry, fractions, and measurement. An important component of this program is the *Mathematical Concepts Inventory*, designed to determine student mathematical needs. Finally, special units called *LABS*, which focus on topics such as calculator use, telephone skills, and social and emotional development, are included.

Real-life Math. Real-Life Math, offered by Hubbard Scientific Company, a publisher in Illinois, is used for adolescents aged thirteen through eighteen and provides instruction on basic life skills in arithmetic. While basic arithmetic skills are not taught in this program, their application to real-life situations is emphasized. Students learn these applications through simulation activities and are provided with realistic materials for banking and business. Students use program manipulatives to establish and operate their own businesses. The program contains posters, audio cassettes, skill books, spirit masters, a mailbox, expendables for ten students, desk signs, and a teacher's manual. The program lends itself to instruction on a concrete level because of its use of manipulatives and simulation activities.

SURVIVAL SKILLS

Educationally handicapped students have two basic needs relative to arithmetic instruction. Each student needs to perform basic arithmetic operations and, subsequently, to apply arithmetic skills to everyday problems as a survival tool. Too often instructional programs emphasize the first of these two arithmetic needs at the expense of the second. Classroom instruction in basic operations and problem solving should be associated with real-life skills, which can be divided into three categories: money, time, and measurement.

The following are several suggestions for assisting students in applying arithmetic skills to these everyday problems.

- When possible, use realistic materials. For example, when teaching coin recognition, use real money if students' instructional level requires manipulatives.
- Classroom activities should reflect real-life events. For example, since banking is an important part of our lives, teachers can help students learn banking procedures and vocabulary by creating a classroom banking system in which students receive privileges through checks. Students can deposit their privilege checks in a savings account to earn extra privileges or cash them for tokens, which can be used to purchase privileges.
- Students can be exposed to comparative shopping. They learn to select the best buy for a given item through classroom simulation. For example, a student could select a purchase card and three choice cards, as illustrated below.

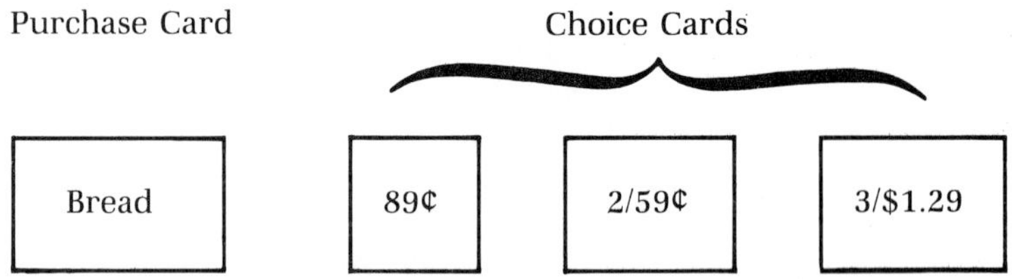

The student must compute the unit price on each choice card and select the best buy. Older students can be taught to select the best buy based on other factors, such as quality, personal taste, and durability.

- Teachers can help students develop an understanding of the calendar by asking routine questions, such as "What month is it?" and "What is today's date?" However, to further motivate students, more personal questions, such as "How many days until payday?" or "What day is your birthday?" would be appropriate.
- Students should be given practical experiences with liquid measurement. For example, younger students can practice with water and sand, while older students can participate in cooking activities that require measuring.
- The use of credit cards can also be simulated in the classroom. For example, students are given simulations of credit cards and allowed to charge limited amounts of free time on a daily basis. Students receive a weekly "bill" with interest and may repay the time by studying at home or completing extra learning activities.

- Students can be taught to construct a family or personal budget through simulation. To play a budget game, for example, students select a family profile card. Students take turns moving around a game board, based on a roll of the dice, selecting event cards at every stop. Students carry out the directions on the event cards, some of which call for mandatory purchases

Activities depicting real life experiences often increase a student's motivation to learn in the classroom.

and others for optional purchases, as indicated in the game cards shown below. Included on the game cards are unexpected bills as well as windfall incomes. Teachers can develop different card decks to correlate with specific skills being taught in the classroom. The individual who reaches the end of the maze with the most money left in the savings account wins.

Examples of Budget Game Cards

Family Profile Card

Jones Family: Mary, Bill,
Susan, Alica
Income: $300 weekly, net pay
Budget: $450 rent, $200 food
$150 utilities,
$100 savings,
$150 incidental,
$150 car
Savings: $500 in the bank

Event Card

The car needs new tires ($200) and a muffler ($100). Purchase these items.

Event Card

Your family wants to purchase a pet. Besides the actual price of the pet, what other costs must be considered?

Event Card

Your daughter wants an electronic game ($69) for her birthday. What are you going to do?

- Students can apply linear measurement skills by computing the amount of paint, floor covering, or curtain fabric needed for a project. Teachers can supply pictures or photographs of rooms and the necessary dimensions.
- Students can compute mileage, transportation costs, and accommodation costs for a real class trip or simulated trip.
- Students can set alarm clocks to coincide with school bells or special events.
- Cooking activities in the classroom provide opportunities for students to use measuring skills. Recipes used can be halved or doubled on occasion.

HOME REINFORCEMENT

There are many opportunities for handicapped students to use arithmetic skills in the home and community. Often the special educator can only simulate experiences that occur naturally outside of the school environment. Parents, however, can support their child's development of arithmetic skills in a natural setting. The following are some suggestions that parents may consider for reinforcing their child's arithmetic skills:

- Provide an allowance for the child and help him or her to budget the money; for example, establish a certain percentage for spending and for savings.

- Pay your child by check to help him or her become familiar with banking terms and practices. If possible, have the child open a savings account at a nearby bank to encourage regular savings.
- Use specific time and number concepts when giving directions to the child; for example, "Please get four forks, knives, and spoons," or "Be home for dinner at 5:30," or "Put the blue socks in the middle drawer."
- Provide your child with a wrist watch and alarm clock as he or she learns to tell time. Be sure to ask him or her to tell the time and correlate this information with daily events. For example: "You're right; it is 11:30. It is still morning and almost time for lunch. What time do we eat lunch?"
- Plan shopping trips to grocery or clothing stores, for example, which require the child to select the best buy. The emphasis should be on comparison shopping. Sometimes the cheapest isn't always the best selection.
- Provide regular opportunities for cooking experiences to help the child use measurement skills taught in the classroom.
- Involve the child in planning for trips by having him or her compute distance, travel, and accommodation costs.
- Help the child anticipate planning time through modeling or questioning. For example: "The amusement park opens at 10:00 A.M. If we want to arrive at 10:00, we need to allow two hours for travel and one hour to get ready. That means we should set the alarm for 7:00 A.M."; or "Your dentist appointment is at 9:30 A.M. For what time should you set your alarm?"

REGULAR CLASS INVOLVEMENT

Cawley and Vitello (1972) developed an approach to arithmetic instruction for handicapped students involving a learning set, an interactive component, verbal information processing, and conceptual processing. One aspect of this program, the interactive component, provides an excellent framework for teaching arithmetic to handicapped students in the regular classroom. The framework illustrates teacher input and student output. The following examples from the interactive component may be useful for regular educators in planning arithmetic instruction for the educationally handicapped student (see Figure 12–4).

In addition, the following suggestions would benefit mainstreamed students who have arithmetic learning problems:

- Make sure that students have the necessary prerequisite skills for new arithmetic tasks.
- Try to use concrete or semiconcrete, rather than abstract, examples as much as possible.
- Provide lots of review practice, limiting the number of skill problems and expanding the number of practice sessions.
- When students make mathematical errors, ask them to explain what they did to solve the problem.

☐ **FIGURE 12–4**
The Interactive Unit of Cawley's Arithmetic Program

	Do	See	Say
Input			
Output			

Examples of each of the nine possible combinations:

Mode combination			
Input	Output	Teacher Behavior Illustrated	Student Behavior Illustrated
Do	Do	The teacher has three toy cars and three balls. She says, "Watch me." She groups the three toy cars into a set and the three balls into another set. She says, "Now you do what I did."	The child has the same kind and number of toy cars and balls. He is expected to group the objects into two sets similar to his teacher's groups.
Do	See	The teacher lays seven pieces of string on a table. All of the pieces are of the same color and texture, three are five inches shorter than the other four, all of which are the same size. She separates the three short ones from the four longer ones––making two sets.	The child is shown four pictures, only one of which contains two sets. The remaining three pictures contain more than two sets. The child is asked to point to the picture that is like the display which the teacher constructed.
Do	Say	The teacher combines three sets of blocks, each of which contains two blocks.	The child is asked to write the algorithm that describes what was done and to solve the problem.
See	Do	The teacher presents the following stimulus to the child: $8 - \square = 6$	With a group of blocks, the child is asked to solve the problems by stacking the number of blocks that belong in the box.
See	See	The teacher presents the following problem: $3 + 2 - 1 =$	The child is asked to point to the correct response among the following alternatives: 5 1 2 4 6 0
See	Say	The child is presented with the following stimulus and asked to tell what time it is: 	The child is expected to say, "Three o'clock."

From "Model for Arithmetic Programming for Handicapped Children" by J. F. Cawley and S. J. Vitello, *Exceptional Children, 39*, 1972, 103. Copyright 1972 by The Council for Exceptional Children. Reprinted by permission.

- Organize study sessions using peer tutoring to aid in recall of facts and application of skills.
- Provide visual cues to help students apply an algorithm.

SUMMARY POINTS

- It is important to learn why a student fails at arithmetic tasks. Analysis of error patterns, observation, interviews, and teacher-made tests are used to determine reasons for failure.
- The educator uses a combination of assessment tools to determine a student's arithmetic skills and needs. Achievement and diagnostic tests, scope-and-sequence charts, and observation techniques all provide valuable information to the special education diagnostician.
- When planning arithmetic instruction, the special educator focuses on remediation of skill deficits, followed by instruction in new arithmetic skills. A knowledge of the sequence of arithmetic skills helps the teacher to determine which new skills will be taught.
- There are a variety of explanations for why a student may be experiencing learning problems in arithmetic. In fact, the number of "reasons why" tends to increase as the student gets older. To help identify a realistic instructional program, teachers can develop instructional activities related to a student's interests as well as to everyday activities needed for survival.
- Teachers working with handicapped students must provide deliberate instruction on how to solve problems. Too often students' difficulties in arithmetic are related to faulty problem-solving skills.
- Special education teachers often use a combination of commercial and teacher-made programs when developing an individualized arithmetic instructional program. Program selection can be facilitated by reviewing the age level, reading level, etc., of each program and comparing this information with each student's needs.
- Instructional planning should address the application of arithmetic skills to everyday problems. Parents can be very effective in helping the special educator meet this need since daily living requires the constant use of arithmetic expertise.
- Special educators should present concepts and algorithms on various levels of conceptualization. The materials used to teach an arithmetic skill as well as the algorithm greatly affect student learning.

REVIEW QUESTIONS

1. Do your state standards require the use of specific diagnostic tests for identifying students with learning disabilities in arithmetic? If yes, list them.

2. Discuss the purpose and limitations of the three types of informal assessment techniques described in this chapter.

SUGGESTED READINGS

Reisman, F. K., and Kauffman, S. 1980. *Teaching mathematics to children with special needs*. Columbus, Ohio: Charles E. Merrill.

Undershill, R. G.; Uprichard, A. E.; and Heddens, J. W. 1980. *Diagnosing mathematical difficulties*. Columbus, Ohio: Charles E. Merrill.

Howell, D.; Davis, W.; and Underhill, L. 1974. *Activities for teaching mathematics to low achievers*. Jackson, Miss.: University Press of Mississippi.

Application: Larry and Theresa

Larry

Since the IEP team recommended that Larry spend time daily in the resource room, Mr. Russell was faced with the challenging task of developing an individualized arithmetic instructional program. To plan Larry's program, Mr. Russell used results and past observations; in addition, he involved Larry in daily diagnostic teaching sessions for one week to learn more about how Larry approached various arithmetic learning tasks and how he solved them.

At the end of the week, Mr. Russell decided that although Larry had problems in several areas, instruction would initially focus on developing skills in basic operations, beginning with addition, since these skills are critical to successfully completing more complex arithmetic problems. Based on the speed with which Larry learned new tasks when they were presented sequentially in small doses, Mr. Russell also hypothesized that some of Larry's difficulties could be attributed to insufficient mastery of prerequisite skills. For example, before Larry had mastered basic addition skills, he had been involved with subtraction tasks, then multiplication, and later division problems. As a result, Larry's deficits were compounded.

Since Larry seemed to be functioning at a symbolic level, Mr. Russell used the following strategies to teach basic addition facts. Each week, Larry worked with one specific number family, spending time each day constructing subsets for the number family on an addition grid and writing number sentences to correspond with the sets he had made. Following this phase of his arithmetic lesson, Mr. Russell gave him a timed test based on facts related to the number family under study. The accuracy with which Larry completed this test was recorded on a graph (see Figure 12–5). When Larry could complete these tests with 95 percent accuracy in one minute or less, a new set of facts was introduced.

Later, to teach subtraction facts, Mr. Russell regrouped similar addition and subtraction facts to convey the idea that subtraction is the inverse of addition. Larry simultaneously reviewed addition facts, such as $9 + 8 = 17$, which were paired with their inverse subtraction facts, $17 - 8 = 9$ and $17 - 9 = 8$.

FIGURE 12–5
Graph for Monitoring Arithmetic Achievement

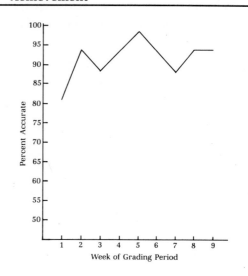

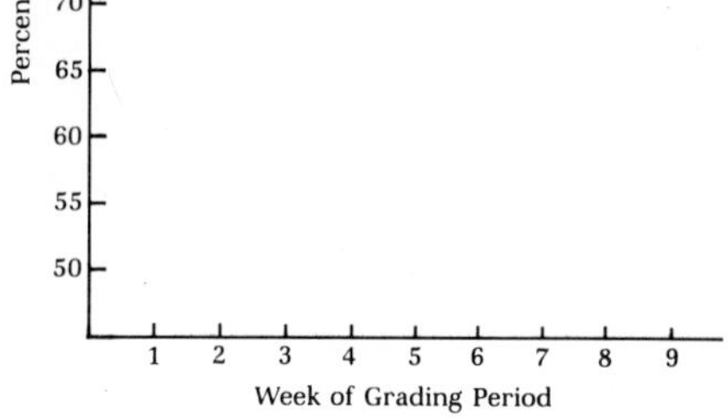

Larry's resource room time was divided into two periods. Thirty minutes was spent on activities designed to develop basic operations; the remaining ten minutes was devoted to updating Larry's personal budget. Mr. Russell knew that Larry worked twenty hours a week as a delivery boy in his uncle's dry cleaning business and that Larry wanted to buy an electric guitar. He knew that he could use this information about Larry's out-of-school life to help Larry develop real-life problem-solving skills involving basic addition and subtraction.

Together, Mr. Russell and Larry did the following:

- First, they analyzed Larry's paycheck to see how it was divided (social security, taxes, net pay, etc.). This information was then converted to percentages (a skill being worked on in the regular classroom).
- Mr. Russell then helped Larry to develop a realistic budget and related time line to reach his goal of buying the guitar. This activity required Larry to log his spending habits for two weeks prior to developing his personal budget.
- Next, Larry opened savings and checking accounts. Prior to Larry's first trip to the bank, Mr. Russell developed instructional objectives and activities that focused on banking vocabulary and how to complete the different forms.
- Together Mr. Russell and Larry charted Larry's progress toward reaching his goal.

It is important to point out that these activities required skills that Larry did not have. The purpose of this ten-minute instruction time was for Larry to develop a more positive attitude toward arithmetic and to illustrate its application in daily living. The budgeting and banking activities motivated Larry to complete his basic skills activities. An additional benefit of this time was that Mr. Russell got to know Larry better.

Theresa

After reviewing Theresa's folder, Mrs. Place, the tutor, discussed Theresa's instructional needs with the resource teacher. In summary, it seemed that problem areas included understanding basic subtraction facts and related algorithms, telling time, and using money. It was evident that Theresa relied on concrete objects for conceptualization.

The resource teacher, tutor, and regular teacher all agreed that the intervention should focus on developing an understanding of basic subtraction skills.

Mrs. Place initiated instruction on basic subtraction facts with activities that demonstrated the relationship between addition and subtraction.

- First, basic addition and subtraction vocabularies were presented. The regular teacher as well as the tutor deliberately overused these vocabulary words on a routine basis. Next, a teacher-made game designed to reinforce the concepts of addition and subtraction was used in the regular classroom.
- To emphasize that subtraction is the inverse of addition, the following instructional sequence was used:

$$6 - 1 = \underline{\quad}$$
$$\underline{\quad} + 1 = 6$$

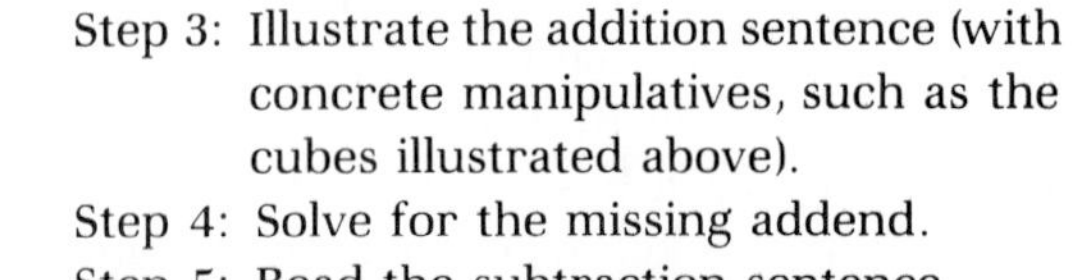

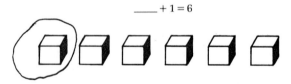

Step 1: Read the subtraction statement.
Step 2: Write the corresponding addition sentence.
Step 3: Illustrate the addition sentence (with concrete manipulatives, such as the cubes illustrated above).
Step 4: Solve for the missing addend.
Step 5: Read the subtraction sentence.

- Mrs. Place also gave Theresa repeated practice over time in changing subtraction statements to addition statements, as shown here:

$9 - 5 =$ ___	$9 -$ ___ $= 3$	___ $- 2 = 7$
___ $+ 5 = 9$	$3 +$ ___ $= 9$	$7 + 2 =$ ___

- In addition, she used the communicative and associative properties and number families to teach the relationship between basic facts.

Number Family	*Basic Facts*
3 4 7	$3 + 4 = 7$; $4 + 3 = 7$; $7 - 3 = 4$; $7 - 4 = 3$

- Mrs. Place made a fact ring for Theresa to use at home when her parents expressed an interest in helping her. As Theresa was introduced to various number families, they were recorded on tag boards and placed on the number ring. Theresa's mother agreed to spend at least five minutes, but no more than ten minutes, each evening reviewing the number families being taught in the tutoring sessions.

Although the majority of the tutoring sessions focused on basic operations, activities designed to improve deficits in other arithmetic skills were used in the regular class and at home. They included the following:

- Before beginning instruction at a semiconcrete level on time, money, or measurement, the educational team agreed that Theresa needed more of a basic conceptual understanding of part-whole relationships. The following activities were used to develop this understanding:
- Theresa made a series of books illustrating the following concepts: whole, one-half, and one-fourth. The first book consisted of magazine pictures showing whole objects. For the second book, Theresa used pictures of whole objects but used a marker to divide each object in half. In the third book, Theresa divided pictures of whole objects into fourths. Thus, Theresa was actively involved in developing a concrete product illustrating the meaning of part-whole relationships.
- Every Monday and Wednesday, Theresa used a cassette recorder in the regular class to describe her activities for each part (morning, afternoon, and evening) of the previous day.
- In addition, nursery rhymes and songs about time, days of the week, and months of the year were learned at home. These served as mnemonic aids to help Theresa remember, for example, which month comes next.

As Theresa's understanding of part-whole relationships improved, Mrs. Place spent the last six to seven minutes of each tutoring session introducing basic time and money concepts.

In the spring, Mrs. Place, the Nicholses, the third grade teacher, and the resource teacher met to discuss Theresa's progress and her school program for the following year. Mrs. Place indicated that Theresa had made substantial gains. She had mastered basic facts, responded on an automatic level, and relied less on tangible objects for understanding. Also, end-of-year test performance indicated improvement in telling time and using money, still at a concrete level. It was decided that Theresa continue in the tutoring during the summer and first grading period of third grade. If improvement continued, the tutoring would be phased out during the second grading period.

Discussion Points

1. If Larry continues to receive arithmetic instruction in the resource room, what additional skills should the special teacher plan for instruction?
2. If Larry were to be placed in a regular mathematics class, what variables should a placement team consider when making the decision?
3. The special tutor did not focus on a life-skill curriculum for Theresa. What justification could you cite for this decision? Would you have included life-skill arithmetic concepts? Explain your decision.

References

Action libraries. 1970. Englewood Cliffs, N.J.: Scholastic Book Services.

Affleck, J. Q.; Lowenbaum, S.; and Archer, A. 1980. *Teaching the mildly handicapped in the regular classroom.* 2d ed. Columbus, Ohio: Charles E. Merrill.

Alexander, R., and Apfel, C. 1976. Altering schedules of reinforcement for improved classroom behavior. *Exceptional Children* 43(2):413–19.

Algozzine, B. 1979. Social-emotional problems. In *Children and adolescents with learning disabilities,* ed. C. D. Mercer. Columbus, Ohio: Charles E. Merrill.

Algozzine, R.; Schmid, R.; and Conners, R. 1978. Toward an acceptable definition of emotional disturbance. *Behavioral Disorders* 4(1):48–52.

Alley, G., and Deshler, D. 1979. *Teaching the learning disabled adolescent: Strategies and methods.* Denver, Colo.: Love.

Anastasi, A. 1976. *Psychological testing.* 4th ed. New York: Macmillan.

Archer, A., and Edgar, E. 1976. *Teaching academic skills to mildly handicapped children.* In *Teaching the mildly handicapped in the regular classroom.* eds. J. Q. Affleck, S. Lowenbaum, and A. Archer. Columbus, Ohio: Charles E. Merrill.

Ashlock, R. B. 1976. *Error patterns in computation: A semi-programmed approach.* 2d ed. Columbus, Ohio: Charles E. Merrill.

Ausubel, D. P. 1978. In defense of advance organizers: A reply to critics. *Review of Educational Research* 48:215–58.

Axelrod, S. 1977. *Behavior modification for the classroom teacher.* New York: McGraw-Hill.

Bachor, D. G. 1979. Using work samples as diagnostic information. *Learning Disability Quarterly* 2(1):45–52.

Bandura, A. 1969. *Principles of behavior modification.* New York: Holt, Rinehart and Winston.

Bandura, A. 1973. *Aggression: A social learning analysis.* Englewood Cliffs, N.J.: Prentice-Hall.

Bandura, A., and Harris, M. 1966. Modification of syntactic style. *Journal of Experimental Child Psychology* 4:341–52.

Baratta-Lorton, M. 1976. *Mathematics their way.* Menlo Park, Calif.: Addison-Wesley Publishing.

Barksdale, M. W. 1970. Mentally retarded and culturally deprived children: Some parallels. *Phylon* 31:48–53.

Bar-Tal, D., and Bar-Zohar, Y. 1977. The relationship between perception of locus of control and academic achievement. *Contemporary Educational Psychology* 2:181–99.

Bartel, N. R. 1978. Problems in mathematics achievement. In *Teaching children with learning and behavior problems,* eds. D. D. Hammil and N. Bartel. 2d ed. Boston: Allyn & Bacon.

Barth, R. 1979. Home-based reinforcement of school behavior: A review and analysis. *Review of Educational Research* 49:436–58.

Bateman, B. 1976. Teaching reading to learning disabled children. Paper presented at the Reading Conference sponsored by the National Institute of Education, April, May, June, University of Pittsburg, Pittsburg, Pa.

Bates, E. 1976. *Language and context: The acquisition of pragmatics.* New York: Academic Press.

Battin, R.; Haug, C.; Blair, C.; and Miller, S. 1978. *Speech and language delay.* Springfield, Ill.: Charles C. Thomas.

Bauer, H. 1975. The resource teacher—A teacher consultant. *Academic Therapy* 10:299–304.

Becker, L. D. 1978. Learning characteristics of educationally handicapped and retarded children. *Exceptional Children* 44:502–11.

Becker, W. C., and Englemann, S. 1977. *The Oregon direct instruction model: Comparative results in Project Follow Through: A summary of nine years of work.* Eugene, Oreg.: University of Oregon Follow Through Project.

Becker, W. C., and Engelmann, S. E. 1976. *Technical report, 1976-1*. Eugene, Oreg.: University of Oregon.

Belch, P. 1979. Toward noncategorical teacher certification in special education—Myth or reality? *Exceptional Children* 46(2):129–31.

Bell, J. P. 1979. Our needs and other ecological concerns: A teacher's personal view of working with "secondary school-aged seriously emotionally disturbed children." *Behavior Disorders* 4(3):168–72.

Bensky, J.; Shaw, S.; Gouse, A.; Bates, H.; Dixon, B.; and Beane, W. 1980. Public Law 94–142 and stress: A problem for educators. *Exceptional Children* 47:24–29.

Benthul, H. F.; Anderson, E. A.; Utech, A. M.; Biggy, M. U.; and Bailey, B. H. 1974. *Spell correctly*. Morristown, N.J.: Silver Burdett.

Berger, M. 1981. Remediating hyperkinetic behavior with impulse control procedures. *School Psychology Review* 10:405–7.

Bijou, S. W. 1972. *The Edmark reading program*. Seattle, Wash.: Edmark Associates.

Bingham, G. 1978. Career attitudes among boys with and without specific learning disabilities. *Exceptional Children* 44:341–42.

Blachowicz, C. 1977. Cloze activities for primary readers. *The Reading Teacher* 31(3):300–2.

Blackham, G. J., and Silberman, A. 1980. *Modification of child and adolescent behavior*. 3d ed. Belmont, Calif.: Wadsworth.

Blake, K. A. 1974. *Teaching the retarded*. Englewood Cliffs, N.J.: Prentice-Hall.

Blake, K. A. 1975. Amount of practice in retarded and normal pupils' learning. *Journal of Research and Development in Education* 8:128–36.

Blake, K. A. 1976. *The mentally retarded: An educational psychology*. Englewood Cliffs, N.J.: Prentice-Hall.

Blau, H., and Blau, H. 1969. A theory of learning to read by "modality blocking." In *Successful programming: Many points of view*, ed. J. Arena. Pittsburg, Pa.: Association for Children with Learning Disabilities.

Block, J.; Block, J. H.; and Harrington, D. M. 1974. Some misgivings about the Matching Familiar Figures Test as a measure of reflection impulsivity. *Developmental Psychology* 10:611–32.

Bloom L., and Lahey, M. 1978. *Language development and language disorders*. New York: Wiley.

Bloomfield, L., ed. 1933. *Why a linguistic society? In language*. New York: Holt, Rinehart, and Winston.

Bloomfield, L. 1942. Linguistics and reading. *Elementary English Review* 19:125–30, 183–186.

Bornstein, M. R.; Bellack, A. S.; and Hersen, M. 1977. Social-skills training for unassertive children: A multiple baseline analysis. *Journal of Applied Behavior Analysis* 10:183–95.

Bortnick, R., and Lopardo, G. S. 1976. The cloze procedure: A multi-purpose classroom tool. *Reading Improvement* 13(2):113–17.

Boyan, C. 1978. A flexible approach to career development: Balancing vocational training and training for independent living. *Habilitation* 13:209–13.

Brent, D. E., and Routh, D. K. 1978. Response cost and impulsive word recognition errors in reading disabled children. *Journal of Abnormal Child Psychology* 6:211—19.

Brigance, A. 1977. *Brigance diagnostic inventory of basic skills*. North Billerica, Mass.: Curriculum Associates.

Brigance, A. 1978. *Brigance diagnostic inventory of early development*. North Billerica, Mass.: Curriculum Associates.

Brigance, A. 1980. *Brigance diagnostic inventory of essential skills*. North Billerica, Mass.: Curriculum Associates.

Brolin, D. E. 1982. *Vocational preparation of persons with handicaps*. 2d ed. Columbus, Ohio: Charles E. Merrill.

Brolin, D. E., and D' Alonzo, B. J. 1979. Critical issues in career education for handicapped students. *Exceptional Children* 45:246–53.

Brown, K., and Conrad, K. 1982. Impulse control or selective attention: Remedial program for hyperactivity. *Psychology in the School* 19(1):92–97.

Brown, L. L., and Hammill, D. D. 1978. *Behavior rating profile*. Austin, Tex.: Pro-Ed.

Brown, W.; Lundell, K.; and Evans, J. 1976. *Criterion test of basic skills: Arithmetic*. San Rafael, Calif.: Academic Therapy Publications.

Bryan, T. 1976. Peer popularity of learning disabled children: A replication. *Journal of Learning Disabilities* 9:307–11.

Bryan, T. 1977. Learning disabled children's comprehension of nonverbal communication. *Journal of Learning Disabilities* 10:501–6.

Bryan, T. 1978. Social relationships and verbal interactions of learning disabled children. *Journal of Learning Disabilities* 11:107–15.

Bryan, T. S. 1974. An observational analysis of classroom behaviors of children with learning disabilities. *Journal of Learning Disabilities* 7:26–34.

Bryan, T.; Wheeler, R.; Felcan, J.; and Henek, T. 1976. "Come on, dummy": An observational study of children's communications. *Journal of Learning Disabilities* 9(10):53–61.

Burns, P. C. 1980. *Assessment and correction of language arts difficulties*. Columbus, Ohio: Charles E. Merrill.

Burton, G. M. 1982. Writing numerals: Suggestions for helping children. *Academic Therapy* 17(4):417–23.

Bush, W., and Giles, M. 1969. *Aids to psycholinguistic teaching*. Columbus, Ohio: Charles E. Merrill.

Butler, A. S., and Maher, C. A. 1981. Conflict and special service teams: Perspectives and suggestions for school psychologists. *Journal of School Psychology* 19:62–70.

Bzoch, K., and League, R. 1971. *Receptive-expressive emergent language scale*. Gainesville, Fla.: Tree of Life Press.

Cacha, F. B. 1981. Managing questions for student participation. *The Clearing House* 54(6):263–64.

Camp, L. W.; Winbury, N. E.; and Zinna, D. R. 1981. Strategies for initial reading instruction. *Bulletin of the Orton Society* 31:175–88.

Campbell, D. P. 1974. *Strong-Campbell interest inventory*. Stanford, Calif.: University of Stanford Press.

Cansler, D. P.; Martin, G. H.; and Voland, M. C. 1975. *Working with families*. Winston-Salem, N.C.: Kaplan.

Cantor, N. L., and Gelfand, D. M. 1977. Effects of responsiveness and sex of children on adults' behavior. *Child Development* 48:232–38.

Carlson, N. A. 1980. General principles of learning and motivation. *Teaching Exceptional Children* 12(2):60–62.

Carnine, D., and Silbert, J. 1979. *Direct instruction reading*. Columbus, Ohio: Charles E. Merrill.

Carroll, A. W. 1974. The classroom as an ecosystem. *Focus on Exceptional Children* 6:1–11.

Cartledge, G., and Milburn, J. F. 1978. The case for teaching social skills in the classroom: A review. *Review of Educational Research* 1:133–56.

Cawley, J. F.; Fitzmaurice, A. M.; Goodstein, H. A.; Lepore, A. U.; Sedlack, R.; and Althaus, V. 1976. *Project MATH*. Tulsa, Okla.: Educational Development Cooperation.

Cawley, J. F.; Goodstein, H. A.; and Burrow, W. H. 1972. *The slow learner and the reading problem*. Springfield, Ill.: Charles C. Thomas.

Cawley, J. F., and Vitello, S. J. 1972. Model for arithmetic programming for handicapped children. *Exceptional Children* 39:101–10.

Cazden, C. B. 1980. What we don't know about teaching the language arts. *Phi Delta Kappan* 61(9):595–96.

Chall, J. 1967. *Learning to read: The great debate*. New York: McGraw-Hill.

Clinchy, B., and Rosenthal, K. 1971. Analysis of children's errors. In ed., G. S. Lesser, *Psychology and educational practices*. Glenview, Il.: Scott Foresman, 1971.

Cohen, C. R., and Abrams, R. M. 1976. *Spellmaster, spelling: Testing, evaluating, book one*. Exeter, N.H.: Learnco.

Cohen, S. B.; Alberto, P. A.; and Troutman, A. 1979. Selecting and developing educational materials: An inquiry model. *Teaching Exceptional Children* 12(1):7–11.

Cohen, S. B., and Plaskon, S. P. 1980. *Language arts for the mildly handicapped*. Columbus, Ohio: Charles E. Merrill.

Colby, C. B. 1959. *Strangely enough*. New York: Sterling.

Connolly, A. J.; Nachtman, W.; and Pritchett, E. M. 1976. *Key math diagnostic arithmetic test*. Circle Pines, Minn.: American Guidance Service.

Coopersmith, S. 1967. The antecedents of self-esteem. San Francisco: W. H. Freeman.

Coopersmith, S., and Gilberts, R. 1981. *Behavioral Academic Self-Esteem (BASE), A rating scale*. Palo Alto, Calif.: Consulting Psychologists Press, Inc.

Cramer, W. 1978. *How to conduct an effective parent-teacher conference*. Portland, Maine: J. Weston Walsch.

Criscuolo, N. P. 1974. *100 individualized activities for reading*. Belmont, Calif.: Fearon Publishers.

Critchley, M. 1975. Developmental Dyslexia: Its history, nature, and prospects. In *Reading perception and language: Papers from the World Congress on Dyslexia*, eds. D. D. Duane and M. B. Rawson. Sponsored by the Orton Society in cooperation with the Mayo Clinic. Baltimore: York Press.

Croft, D. J. 1979. *Parents and teachers: A resource book for home, school, and community relations*. Belmont, Calif.: Wadsworth.

CTB/McGraw-Hill. 1977, 1978. *The California achievement tests*. Monterey, Calif.: CTB/McGraw-Hill.

Curran, T. J., and Algozzine, B. 1980. Ecological disturbance: A test of the matching hypothesis. *Behavioral Disorders* 5:169–74.

Dankowski, C. E. 1966. Each pupil has his own editor. *Elementary School Journal* 66:249–53.

Davidson, J. 1969. *Using the cuisenaire rods*. New Rochelle, N.Y.: Cuisenaire.

Deshler, D. D.; Lowrey, N.; & Alley, G. R. 1979. Programming alternatives for LD adolescents: A nation-wide survey. *Academic Therapy* 14:389–97.

Dever, R. B. 1978. *TALK: Teaching American language to kids*. Columbus, Ohio: Charles E. Merrill.

Dieterich, D. J. 1972. Diserroneosospellingitis or the fine (language) art of spelling. *Elementary English* 49:245–53.

Dinkmeyer, D. 1973. *Developing understanding of self and others*. Circle Pines, Minn.: American Guidance Service.

Dinkmeyer, D., and Carlson, J. 1975. *Consultation: A book of readings*. New York: John Wiley.

Dolch, E. W. 1950. *Teaching primary reading*. 2d ed. Champaign, Ill.: Garrard Press.

Doll, E. A. 1965. *The Vineland social maturity scale: Condensed manual of directions*. Circle Pines, Minn.: American Guidance Service.

Dorow, L. G. 1980. Generalization effects of newly conditioned reinforcers. *Education and Training of the Mentally Retarded* 15(1):8–14.

Douglas, U. I., & Peters, K. G. 1979. Toward a clearer definition of the attentional deficit of hyperactive children. In *Attention and cognitive development*, eds. G. A. Hale and M. Lewis. New York: Plenum Press.

Doyle, W. 1979. Classroom tasks and students' abilities. In *Research on teaching: Concepts, findings and implications*, eds. P. L. Peterson and H. J. Walberg. Berkeley, Calif.: McCutchan.

Dunn, L., and Smith, J. 1968. *The Peabody language development kits*. Circle Pines, Minn.: American Guidance Service.

Dunn, L. M., and Markwardt, F. C. 1970. *Peabody individual achievement test*. Circle Pines, Minn.: American Guidance Service.

Dupont, H., and Dupont, C. 1980. *Transition*. Circle Pines, Minn.: American Guidance Service.

D'Zurilla, T. J., and Goldfried, M. R. 1971. Problem solving and behavior modification. *Journal of Abnormal Psychology* 78:107–26.

Earp, N. W. 1970. Procedures for teaching reading in mathematics. *Arithmetic Teacher* 17:575–79.

Easley, J. A., and Zwoyer, R. E. 1975. Teaching by listening—towards a new day in math classes. *Contemporary Education* 47:19–25.

Edelbrock, C. 1979. Empirical classification of children's behavior disorders: Progress based on parent and teacher ratings. *School Psychology Digest* 8:355–69.

Efta, M. 1978. Reading in silence: A chance to read. *Teaching Exceptional Children* 11(1):12–14.

Elman, N. M.; and Ginsberg, J. 1981. *The resource room primer*. Englewood Cliffs, N.J.: Prentice-Hall.

Englemann, S., and Carnine, D. 1972. *DISTAR arithmetic level III*. Chicago: Science Research Associates.

Englemann, S., and Carnine, D. 1975. *DISTAR arithmetic level I*. Chicago: Science Research Associates.

Englemann, S., and Carnine, D. 1976. *DISTAR arithmetic level II*. Chicago: Science Research Associates.

Englemann, S.; Becker, W.; Carnie, L.; Meyers, L.; Becker, J.; and Johnson, G. 1975. *Corrective reading program: Teacher's management and skills manual*. Chicago, Ill.: Science Research Associates.

Englemann, S., and Bruner, E. 1969. *DISTAR: An instructional system*. Chicago: Science Research Associates.

Epstein, M. H.; Cullinan, D.; and Sternberg, L. 1977. Impulsive cognitive tempo in severe and mild learning disabled children. *Psychology in the Schools* 14:290–94.

Fagen, S. A.; Long, N. J.; and Stevens, D. J. 1975. *Teaching children self-control: Preventing emotional and learning problems in the elementary school*. Columbus, Ohio: Charles E. Merrill.

Faigley, L.; Daly, J. A.; and Witte, S. P. 1981. The role of writing apprehension in writing performance and competence. *Journal of Educational Research* 75(1):16–21.

Falicov, C. J. and Karrer, B. M., 1980. Cultural variations in the family life cycle: the Mexican-American family. In *The family life cycle: A framework for family therapy*, eds. E. A. Carter and M. McGoldrick. New York: Gardner Press, Inc.

Feagans, L., and McKinney, J. D. 1981. The pattern of exceptionality across domains in learning disabled children. *Journal of Applied Developmental Psychology* 1:313–28.

Federal Register 42(163). 23 August 1977.

Fenichel, C. 1974. Carl Fenichel. In *Teaching children with behavior disorders: Personal perspectives*, eds. J. M. Kauffman and C. D. Lewis. Columbus, Ohio: Charles E. Merrill.

Fennimore, F. 1980. Attaining sentence verve with sentence extension. In *Dealing with Differences*, ed. G. Stanford. Urbana, Ill.: National Council of Teachers of English.

Fenton, K. 1977. *Role expectations: Implications for multidisciplinary pupil programming*. Washington, D.C.: Bureau of Education for the Handicapped, Division of Innovation and Development.

Fenton, K. S.; Yoshida, R. K.; Maxwell, J. P.; and Kaufman, M. J. 1979. Recognition of team goals: An essential step toward rational decision making. *Exceptional Children* 45:638–44.

Fernald, G. 1943. *Remedial techniques in basic school subjects*. New York: McGraw-Hill.

Fitts, W. 1965. *Manual: Tennessee self-concept scale*. Nashville: Counselor Recordings and Tests.

Forness, S. R. 1981. Concepts of learning and behavior disorders: Implications for research and practice. *Exceptional Children* 48:56–64.

Forte, I.; Frank, K. M.; and MacKenzie, J. 1973. *Kids' stuff: Reading and language experiences, intermediate-junior high*. Nashville, Tenn.: Incentive Publications.

Forte, I.; Pangle, M. A.; and Tupa, R. 1973. *Center stuff for nooks, crannies, and corners*. Nashville, Tenn.: Incentive Publications.

Foster, G. G.; Ysseldyke, J. E.; and Reese, J. N. 1975. I wouldn't have seen it if I hadn't believed it. *Exceptional Children* 41:469–73.

Foxx, R. M., and Azrin, N. H. 1973. The elimination of autistic self-stimulatory behavior by overcorrection. *Journal of Applied Behavioral Analysis* 6:1–14.

Freidman, P. G. 1978. *Interpersonal communication innovations in instruction*. Washington, D.C.: National Education Association.

Fries, C. C. 1963. *Linguistics and reading*. New York: Holt, Rinehart and Winston.

Fristoe, M. 1975. *Language intervention systems of the retarded*. Decatur, Ala: Lurleen B. Wallace Development Center.

Frith, G. H. 1981. "Advocate" vs. "professional employee": A question of priorities for special educators. *Exceptional Children* 47(7):486–93.

Gagné, R. M. 1977. *The conditions of learning*. 3d ed. New York: Holt, Rinehart and Winston.

Gallagher, J. J. 1979. The interdisciplinary sharing of knowledge. *Journal of Special Education* 14:41–43.

Gallagher, P. A. 1979. *Teaching students with behavior disorders: Techniques for classroom instruction*. Denver: Love.

Gambrell, L. B. Nov. 1980. Extending think-time for better reading instruction. *The Reading Teacher* 34:143–46.

Gath, A. July 1974. Sibling reactions to mental handicaps: A comparison of the brothers and sisters of mongol children. *Journal of Child Psychology and Psychiatry* 15:187–98.

Gennell, J. K. 1977. *Diagnostic mathematics inventory*. Monterey, Calif.: CTB/McGraw-Hill.

George, C., and Main, M. 1979. Social interactions of young abused children: Approach, avoidance, and aggression. *Child Development* 50:306–18.

Gickling, E. E., and Theobald, J. T. 1975. Mainstreaming: Affect or effect? *Journal of Special Education* 9(3):317–28.

Gillespie-Silver, P. 1979. *Teaching reading to children with special needs*. Columbus, Ohio: Charles E. Merrill.

Gillingham, A., and Stillman, B. 1968. *Remedial teaching for children with specific disability in reading, spelling, and penmanship*, 7th edition. Cambridge, Mass.: Educators Publishing Service.

Gillingham, A., and Stillman, W. 1965. *Remedial training for children with specific disability in reading, spelling, and penmanship*, 7th ed. Cambridge, Mass.: Educators Publishing Service.

Gleason, B. 1982. Writing a way out of the LD dilemma. *Academic Therapy* 17(5):573–79.

Glenn, H. W. 1975. The myth of the label "learning disabled child." *Elementary School Journal* 75:357–61.

Glidewell, H. C. 1969. The child at school. In *Modern perspectives in international child psychiatry*, ed. J. G. Howells. New York: Brunner/Mazel.

Gold, V., and Gargiulo, R. Dec. 1978. An ounce of prevention is worth a pound of cure. *The Ohio Elementary Principal*, November 1980, pp. 23–24.

Golden, J. M. 1980. The writer's side: Writing for a purpose and an audience. *Language Arts* 57:756–62.

Goldstein, H. 1974. *Social learning curriculum*. Columbus, Ohio: Charles E. Merrill.

Good, R. 1979. Children's abilities with four basic arithmetic operations in grades K-2. *School Science and Mathematics* 79:93–98.

Goodman, L. 1978. Meeting children's needs through materials modification. *Teaching Exceptional Children* 10(3):92–94.

Goodman, K. S. 1976. *Acquiring literacy is natural: Who killed Cock Robin?* Paper presented at the Sixth World Reading Congress, August, Singapore.

Goodman, K. S., ed. 1973. *Miscue analysis: Application to reading instruction*. Urbana, Ill.: ERIC Clearinghouse on Reading and Communication Skills.

Gray, L. J. April 1979. Slow down: You move too fast. *Teacher* 96:52–53.

Gresham, F. M. 1979. Comparison of response cost and time out in a special education setting. *Journal of Special Education* 13:418–23.

Grinnell, M.; Detamore, K.; and Lippke, B. 1976. Sign it successful—manual English encourages expressive communication. *Teaching Exceptional Children* 8:123–24.

Gronlund, N. E. 1973. *Preparing criterion-referenced tests for classroom instruction*. New York: Macmillan.

Grossman, H. J., ed. 1973. *Manual on terminology and classification in mental retardation.* Washington, D.C.: American Association of Mental Deficiency.

Guerin, G. R., and Maier, A. S. 1983. *Informal assessment in education.* Palo Alto, Calif.: Mayfield.

Guess, D.; Keogh, W.; and Sailor, W. 1978. Generalization of speech and language behavior. In *Bases of language intervention,* ed. R. Schiefelbusch. Baltimore: University Park Press.

Hall, J. K. 1981. *Evaluating and improving written expression.* Boston: Allyn & Bacon.

Hall, M.; Ribovich, J.; and Ramig, C. 1979. *Reading and the elementary school child.* 2d ed. New York: Van Nostrand.

Hall, R. J. 1980. Cognitive behavior modification and information-processing skills of exceptional children. *Exceptional Education Quarterly* 1(1):9–15.

Hallahan, D. P.; Kauffman, J. M.; and Ball, D. W. 1973. Selective attention and cognitive tempo of low achieving and high achieving sixth grade marks. *Perceptual and Motor Skills* 36:579–83.

Hallahan, D. P.; Tarver, S. G.; Kauffman, J.; and Graybeal, N. L. 1978. A comparison of the effects of reinforcement and response cost on the selective attention of learning disabled children. *Journal of Learning Disabilities* 11:39–47.

Halliday, M. 1975. Learning how to mean. In *Foundations of language development,* eds. E. H. Lenneberg and E. Lenneberg, vol. 1. New York: Academic Press.

Halpern, A.; Raffeld, P.; Irvin, L. K.; and Link, R. 1975. *Social and prevocational information battery.* Monterey, Calif.: CTB/McGraw-Hill.

Hammill, D. D.; Brown, V. L.; Larsen, S. C.; and Wiederholt, J. L. 1980. *Test of adolescent language.* Austin, Tex.: Pro-Ed.

Hammill, D. D., and Larsen, S. C. 1978. *Test of written language.* Austin, Tex.: Pro-Ed.

Hammill, D. D.; Larsen, S. C.; and McNutt, G. 1977. The effects of spelling instruction: A preliminary study. *The Elementary School Journal* 78:67–72.

Hammond, W. D. 1979. *The effects of reader predictions on prequestions in the recall of relevant and incidental information found in expository material.* Paper presented at the annual meeting of the International Reading Association, April, Atlanta.

Hansen, C. L. 1978. Writing skills. In *The fourth R: Research in the classroom.* eds. N. G. Haring, T. C. Lovitt, M. D. Eaton, and C. L. Hansen. Columbus, Ohio: Charles E. Merrill.

Hardin, V. B. 1978. Ecological assessment and intervention for learning disabled students. *Learning Disability Quarterly* 1(2):15–20.

Haring, N., ed. 1978. *Behavior of exceptional children.* 2d ed. Columbus, Ohio: Charles E. Merrill.

Haring, N. G., and Schiefelbusch, R. L., eds. 1976. *Teaching special children.* New York: McGraw-Hill.

Harris, A. J., and Sipay, E. R. 1975. *How to increase reading ability.* 6th ed. New York: David McKay.

Harris, L. P.; and Wolf, S. R. 1979. Validity and reliability of criterion-referenced measures: Issues and procedures for special educators. *Learning Disability Quarterly* 2(2):84–88.

Hartley, J., and Davies, I. K. 1976. Preinstructional strategies: The role of pretests, behavioral objectives, overviews, and advance organizers. *Review of Educational Research* 46:239–65.

Harvey-Felder, Z. C. 1978. *Some factors relating to writing apprehension: An exploratory study.* Unpublished doctoral dissertation, University of North Carolina.

Harwell, J. 1979. The LD syndrome: How to recognize and deal with it. *Instructor* 89:72–76.

Haskins, R., and McKinney J. D. 1976. Relative effects of response tempo and accuracy on problem solving and academic achievement. *Child Development* 47:690–96.

Hawisher, M. F., and Calhoun, M. L. 1978. *The resource room: An educational asset for children with special needs.* Columbus, Ohio: Charles E. Merrill.

Hayden, A. H.; Smith, R. K.; von Hippel, C. S.; and Baer, S. A. 1978. *Mainstreaming preschoolers: Children with learning disabilities.* Washington, D.C.: U.S. Government Printing Office.

Heckelman, R. G. 1969. The neurological impress method of remedial reading instruction. *Academic Therapy* 4:277–82.

Heller, H. W. 1972. The resource room: A mere change or real opportunity for the handicapped? *Journal of Special Education* 6:369–75.

Heller, H. W. 1981. Secondary education for handicapped students: In search of a solution. *Exceptional Children* 47(8):582–83.

Helsel, E. D. 1978. IEP: Impatient expectations of parents. In *Periscope: Views of the individualized education program,* ed. B. B. Weiner. Reston, Va.: Council for Exceptional Children.

Hendrick, J. 1980. *The whole child.* St. Louis, Mo.: C. V. Mosby.

Hendrickson, A. D. 1979. An inventory of mathematical thinking done by incoming first-grade children. *Journal for Research in Mathematics Education* 79:7–23.

Henker, B.; Whalen, C. K.; and Hinshaw, S. P. The attributional contexts of cognitive intervention strategies. *Exceptional Education Quarterly* 1(1):17–30.

Heron, T. E., and Catera, R. 1980. Teacher consultation: A functional approach. *School Psychology Review* 9:283–89.

Heward, W. L.; Dardig, J. C.; and Rossett, A. 1979. *Working with parents of handicapped children*. Columbus, Ohio: Charles E. Merrill.

Heyman, E. 1977. Cursive writing begins with chalk. *Teaching Exceptional Children* 9(4):106–9.

Hill, W. F. 1977. *Learning through discussion*. Beverly Hills, Calif.: Sage.

Hillerich, R. L. 1974. Word lists—getting it all together. *The Reading Teacher* 27:353–60.

Hillerich, R. L. 1979. Developing written expression: How to raise—not raze—writers. *Language Arts* 56:769–77.

Hobbs, N. 1966. Helping disturbed children: Psychological and ecological strategies. *American Psychologist* 21(12):1105–15.

Hofmeister, A., and LeFevre, D. Spring 1977. Time is of the essence. *Teaching Exceptional Children*, 9:82–83.

Hofmeister, A. M. 1973. Let's get it write. *Teaching Exceptional Children* 6:30–33.

Holland, R. 1980. An analysis of the decision-making process in special education. *Exceptional Children* 46(7):551–54.

Homme, L., and Tosti, P. 1971. *Behavior technology: Motivation and contingency management*. San Rafael, Calif.: Individual Learning Systems.

Honig, A. S. 1979. *Parent involvement in early childhood education*. rev. ed. Washington, D.C.: National Association for the Education of Young Children.

Hoskinson, K. 1978. A response to "A critique of teaching reading as a whole task venture." *The Reading Teacher* 32:652–59.

Howell, K. W., and Kaplan, J. S. 1978. Monitoring peer tutor behavior. *Exceptional Children* 45:135–37.

Howell, K. W., and Kaplan, J. S. 1980. *Diagnosing basic skills: A handbook for deciding what to teach*. Columbus, Ohio: Charles E. Merrill.

Howell, K. W.; Kaplan, J. S.; and O'Connell, C. Y. 1979. *Evaluating exceptional children: A task analysis approach*. Columbus, Ohio: Charles E. Merrill.

Hoyt, K. B. 1977. *A primer for career education*. Washington, D.C.: U.S. Government Printing Office.

Hunt, K. 1965. *Grammatical structures written at three grade levels*. Urbana, Ill.: National Council of Teachers of English.

Hutt, M. L., and Gibby, R. G. 1979. *The mentally retarded child: Development, training, and education*. 4th ed. Boston: Allyn & Bacon.

Jastak, J. F.; Bijou, S. W.; and Jastak, S. R. 1978. *Wide range achievement test*. Wilmington, Del.: Jastak Associates.

Jenkins, J. R., and Pany, D. 1978. Standardized achievement tests: How useful for special education? *Exceptional Children* 44:448–53.

Johnson, A. B.; Gold, V.; and Vickers, L. L. 1982. Stress and teachers of the learning disabled, behavior disordered, and educable mentally retarded. *Psychology in the Schools* 19:552–57.

Johnson, C. A., and Katz, R. C. 1973. Using parents as change agents for their children. *Journal of Child Psychology and Psychiatry* 14:181–200.

Johnson, D. J., and Myklebust, H. R. 1967. *Learning disabilities: Educational principles and practices*. New York: Grune & Stratton.

Kagan, J. 1965. Impulsive and reflective children: Significance of conceptual tempo. In *Learning and the educational process*, ed. J. Krumboltz. Chicago: Rand McNally.

Kagan, J.; Rosman, B. L.; Day, D.; Albert, J.; and Phillips, W. 1964. Information processing in the child: Significance of analytic and reflective attitudes. *Psychological Monographs* 78(1, Whole No. 578).

Kaluger, G., and Kolson, C. J. 1978. *Reading and learning disabilities*. 2d ed. Columbus, Ohio: Charles E. Merrill.

Kaminsky, S., and Powers, R. 1981. Remediation of handwriting difficulties: A practical approach. *Academic Therapy* 17(1):19–25.

Karnes, M. B. 1972. *Goal program: Language development*. Springfield, Mass.: Milton Bradley.

Karraker, R. J. 1977. Self versus teacher selected reinforcers in a token economy. *Exceptional Children* 43(7):454–55.

Kass, C. E., and Johnson, M. 1972. Paradoxical values in learning disabilities. *Journal of Learning Disabilities* 5:463–66.

Kauffman, J. M. 1981. *Characteristics of children's behavior disorders*. 2d ed. Columbus, Ohio: Charles E. Merrill.

Kendall, P. C. 1977. On the efficacious use of verbal self-instructional procedures with children. *Cognitive Therapy and Research* 1:331–41.

Kendall, P. C., and Finch, A. J. 1979. Developing nonimpulsive behavior in children: Cognition-behavioral strategies for self-control. In *Cognitive-behavioral interventions*, eds. P. C. Kendall and S. D. Hallan. New York: Academic Press.

Keogh, B., and Levitt, M. 1976. Special education in the mainstream: A confrontation of limitations? *Focus on Exceptional Children* 8(1):1–11.

Keogh, B. K., and Glover, A. T. 1980. The generality and durability of cognitive training effects. *Exceptional Education Quarterly* 1(1):75–82.

Keogh, B. K., and Margolis, J. S. 1976. A component analysis of attentional problems of educationally handicapped boys. *Journal of Abnormal Child Psychology* 4:349–59.

Kershner, J. R. 1975. Visual-spatial organization and reading: Support for a cognitive developmental interpretation. *Journal of Learning Disabilities* 8:30–36.

King, M. 1975. Language: Insights from acquisition. *Theory into Practice* 14(5):293–98.

Kirk, S.; McCarthy, J.; and Kirk, W. 1968. *Illinois test of psycholinguistic abilities*. Urbana, Ill.: University of Illinois Press.

Kirk, S. A. 1962. *Educating exceptional children*. Boston: Houghton Mifflin.

Kirk, S. A.; Kliebhan, J. M.; and Lerner, J. W. 1978. *Teaching reading to slow and disabled learners*. Boston: Houghton Mifflin.

Klasen, E. 1972. *The syndrome of specific dyslexia*. Baltimore: University Park Press.

Klein, C. L. 1977. Orton-Gillingham methodology: Where have all the researchers gone? *Bulletin of the Orton Society* 27:82–87.

Kogan, N. 1971. Educational implications of cognitive style. In *Psychology and educational practices*, ed. G. S. Lesser. Glenview, Ill.: Scott Foresman.

Kokozka, R., and Drye, J. 1981. Toward the least restrictive environment: High school LD students. *Journal of Learning Disabilities* 14(1):22–23.

Kottmeyer, W. 1970. *Teacher's guide for remedial reading*. New York: McGraw-Hill.

Kottmeyer, W., and Claus, A. 1968, 1972. *Basic goals in spelling*. New York: McGraw-Hill.

Kroth, R. 1978. Parents—Powerful and necessary allies. *Teaching Exceptional Children* 10(3):88–90.

Kroth, R. L. 1975. *Communicating with parents of exceptional children*. Denver: Love.

Kroth, R. L., and Scholl, G. T. 1978. *Getting schools involved with parents*. Reston, Va.: Council for Exceptional Children.

Lambert, N.; Windmiller, M.; Cole, L.; and Figueroa, R. 1975. *AAMD Adaptive Behavior Scale, Public School Version (1974) Revision*. Washington, D.C.: American Association on Mental Deficiency.

Larsen, S. C., and Hammill, D. D. 1976. *Test of written spelling*. Austin, Tex.: Empiric Press.

Laskey, E., and Chapandy, A. 1976. Factors affecting language comprehension. *Language, speech, and hearing services in schools* 7:159–68.

Laurie, T. E.; Buchwach, L.; Silverman, R.; and Zigmond, N. 1978. Teaching secondary learning disabled students in the mainstream. *Learning Disability Quarterly* 1:62–72.

LeBlanc, J. F. 1977. You can teach problem solving. *Arithmetic Teacher* 25:16–20.

LeBrun, Y., and Van de Graien, P. 1975. Developmental writing disorders and their prevention. *Journal of Special Education* 9:201–7.

Lefevre, C. A. 1969. A comprehensive linguistic approach to reading. In *Readings on reading*, eds. A. Binter, J. Daebel, and L. Kise. Scranton, Pa.: International Textbook.

Lerner, J.; Mardell-Czudnowski, C.; and Goldenberg, D. 1981. *Special education for the early childhood years*. Englewood Cliffs, N.J.: Prentice-Hall.

Lerner, J. W. 1981. *Learning disabilities: Theories, diagnosis, and teaching strategies*. 3d ed. Boston: Houghton Mifflin.

Ling, D.; Ling, A.; and Pflaster, G. May 1977. Individualized educational programming for hearing-impaired children. *The Volta Review*, 79(4) pp. 204–30.

Linguistic readers. 1966. New York: Harper & Row.

Lippit, R., and Gold, M. 1959. Classroom social structure as a mental health problem. *Journal of Social Issues* 15:40–58.

Lloyd, J. 1980. Academic instruction and cognitive behavior modification: The need for attack strategy training. *Exceptional Education Quarterly* 1(1):53–63.

Lloyd, J.; Saltzman, N.; and Kauffman, J. 1981. Predictable generalization in academic learning as a result of preskills and strategy training. *Learning Disability Quarterly* 4(2):203–16.

Loban, W. D. 1963. *The language of elementary school children*. Champaign, Ill.: National Council of Teachers.

Long, N. J.; Morse, W. C.; and Newman, R. G. 1980. *Conflict in the classroom: The education of emotionally disturbed children*. 4th ed. Belmont, Calif.: Wadsworth.

Long, N. J., and Newman, R. G. 1971. Managing surface behavior of children in schools. In *Conflict in the classroom: The education of emotionally disturbed children*, eds. N. J. Long, W. C. Morse, and R. G. Newman. 2d ed. Belmont, Calif.: Wadsworth Publishing.

Lorenz, L., and Vockell, E. 1979. Using the neurological impress method with learning disabled readers. *Journal of Learning Disabilities* 12:420–22.

Losen, S. M., and Diament, B. 1978. *Parent conferences in the schools*. Boston: Allyn & Bacon.

Lott, L. A.; Hudak, B. J.; and Scheetz, J. A. 1975. *Strategies and techniques for mainstreaming: A resource room handbook*. Monroe, Mich.: Monroe County Intermediate School District.

Lovitt, T., and Hurlburt, M. 1975. Using behavioral analysis techniques. *Journal of Special Education* 8:57–72.

Lundell, K.; Evans, J.; and Brown, W. 1976. *Criterion test of basic skills*. Novato, Calif.: Academic Therapy.

Lundell, K.; Evans, J.; and Brown, W. 1976. *Criterion test of basic skills: Reading*. Novato, Calif.: Academic Therapy Publications.

Luria, A. 1959. The direction function of speech in development. *Word* 18:341–52.

Luria, A. 1961. *The role of speech in the regulation of normal and abnormal behaviors*. New York: Liveright.

MacMillan, D. L.; Jones, R. L.; and Meyers, C. E. 1978. Mainstreaming the mildly retarded: Some questions, cautions, and guidelines. In *Readings in Mainstreaming*. Guilford, Conn.: Special Learning.

Madden, R.; Gardner, E. F.; Rudman, H. C.; Karlsen, B.; and Merwin, J. C. 1973. *Stanford achievement test*. New York: Harcourt Brace Jovanovich.

Mager, R. F. 1962. *Preparing instructional objectives*. Belmont, Calif.: Fearon Publishers.

Maier, A. S. 1980. The effect of focusing on the cognitive processes of learning disabled children. *Journal of Learning Disabilities* 13:34–38.

Malouf, D. M., and Halpern, A. 1976. A review of secondary level special education. *Thresholds in Secondary Education* 2:6–7, 25–29.

Mandell, C., and Fiscus, E. 1981. *Understanding exceptional people*. St. Paul, Minn.: West.

Marsh, G. E.; Gearheart, C. K.; and Gearheart, B. R. 1978. *The learning disabled adolescent: Program alternatives in the secondary school*. St. Louis, Mo.: C. V. Mosby.

Matson, J. L.; Esveldt-Dawson, K.; Andrasik, F.; Ollendick, T. H.; Petti, T.; and Hersen, M. 1980. Direct, observational, and generalization effects of social skills training with emotionally disturbed children. *Behavior Therapy* 11:522–31.

McCarthy, W., and Oliver, J. 1965. Some tactile-kinesthetic procedures for teaching reading to slow learning children. *Exceptional Children* 31:419–21.

McDowell, R. L. 1982. President's page. *Behavior Disorders* 7:135.

McGinnis, P. J. 1977. *The McGinnis Hammondsport Plan*. New York: Walker Publications.

McKinney, J. D., and Haskins, R. 1980. Cognitive training and the development of problem-solving strategies. *Exceptional Education Quarterly* 1(1):41–51.

McLaughlin, T. 1976. Self-control procedures in the management of classroom behavior problems. *Education* 96(4):379–82.

McLean, J., and Synder-McLean, L. 1978. *A transactional approach to early language training*. Columbus, Ohio: Charles E. Merrill.

McLeod, T. M., and Armstrong, S. W. 1982. Learning disabilities in mathematics—Skill deficits and remedial approaches at the intermediate and secondary level. *Learning Disability Quarterly* 5(3):305–11.

McLoughlin, J. A., and Lewis, R. B. 1981. *Assessing special students*. Columbus, Ohio: Charles E. Merrill.

McNamara, D. R. 1981. Teaching skill: The question of questioning. *Educational Research* 23(2):104-9.

Meichenbaum, D. 1977. *Cognitive-behavior modification: An integrative approach*. New York: Plenum Press.

Meichenbaum, D., and Asarnow, J. 1979. Cognitive-behavioral modification and metacognitive development: Implications for the classroom. In *Cognitive-behavioral interventions*, eds. P. C. Kendall and S. D. Hallan. New York: Academic Press.

Meichenbaum, D., and Goodman, J. 1971. Training impulsive children to talk to themselves: A means of developing self-control. *Journal of Abnormal Psychology* 77:115–26.

Mercer, C. D. 1979. *Children and adolescents with learning disabilities*. Columbus, Ohio: Charles E. Merrill.

Merrill linguistic reading program. 1975. Columbus, Ohio: Charles E. Merrill.

Meyers, D. E.; Schvaneveldt, R. W.; and Ruddy, M. G. 1975. Loci of contextual effects on visual word recognition. In *Attention and performance V*. eds. P. M. A. Rabbit and S. Dornic. New York: Academic Press.

MICRO-TOWER. n.d. New York: MICRO-TOWER Institutional Services, ICD Rehabilitation and Research Center.

Miller, J. 1978. Assessing children's language behavior. In *Bases of language intervention*, ed. R. Schiefelbusch. Baltimore: University Park Press.

Minskoff, E.; Wiseman, D.; and Minskoff, J. 1972. *The MWM program for developing language abilities*. Ridgefield, N.J.: Educational Performance Associates.

Montessori, M. 1965. *The Montessori elementary material.* Cambridge, Mass.: Robert Bentley.

Moore, M. G.; Haskins, R.; and McKinney, J. D. 1980. Classroom behavior of reflective and impulsive children. *Journal of Applied Developmental Psychology* 1:59–75.

Moores, D. 1978. The utilization of nonvocal communication with handicapped children. *School Psychology Digest* 7:44–54.

Morgan, W. G. and Bray, N. M. 1978. Establishing and maintaining the IEP team. In *Periscope: Views of the individualized education program,* ed. B. B. Weiner. Reston, Va.: Council for Exceptional Children.

Morse, W. 1976. The helping teacher/crisis teacher concept. *Focus on Exceptional Children* 8(4):1–11.

Morse, W. C. 1971. Worksheet on life-space interviewing for teachers. In *Conflict in the classroom: The education of emotionally disturbed children,* eds. N. J. Long, W. C. Morse, and R. G. Newman. 2d ed. Belmont, Calif.: Wadsworth.

Morse, W. C. 1977. Special pupils in regular classes: Problems in accommodation. In *Exceptional children in regular classrooms,* eds. M. C. Reynolds and M. D. Davis. Minneapolis: Department of Audio-Visual Extension, University of Minnesota.

Myers, P., and Hammill, D. 1976. *Methods of learning disorders.* 2d ed. New York: Wiley.

Naslund, R. A.; Thorpe, L. P.; and Lefevre, D. W. 1978. *SRA achievement series.* Chicago: Science Research Associates.

Neisworth, J. T., and Smith, R. M. 1978. *Retardation, issues, assessment, intervention.* New York: McGraw-Hill.

Newcomer, P. 1977. Special education services for the mildly handicapped: Beyond a diagnostic and remedial model. *Journal of Special Education* 11:153–165.

Newcomer, P., and Hammill, D. 1977. *The test of language development.* Austin, Tex.: Pro-Ed.

O'Connor, R. D. 1969. Modification of social withdrawal through symbolic modeling. *Journal of Applied Behavior Analysis* 2:15–22.

O'Donnell, R. C.; Griffin, W. J.; and Norris, R. C. 1967. *Syntax of kindergarten and elementary school children, Research Report 8.* Urbana, Ill.: National Council of Teachers of English.

Office of Education, Department of Health, Education, and Welfare. 1977. *Training educators for the handicapped: A need to redirect federal programs.* Washington, D.C.: U.S. Government Printing Office.

O'Leary, S. G. 1980. A response to cognitive training. *Exceptional Education Quarterly* 1(1):89–94.

Osgood, C. E. 1953. *Method and theory in experimental psychology.* New York: Oxford University Press.

Otto, W.; McMenemy, R. A.; and Smith, R. J. 1973. *Corrective and remedial teaching.* Boston: Houghton Mifflin.

Parker, C. A., ed. 1975. *Psychological consultation: Helping teachers meet special needs.* Reston, Va.: Council for Exceptional Children.

Parson, L. R., and Heward, W. L. 1979. Training peers to tutor: Evaluation of a tutor training package for primary learning disabled students. *Journal of Applied Behavior Analysis* 12:309–10.

Paulson, T. 1974. *Deciding for myself: A values-clarification series.* Minneapolis: Winston Press.

Pelham, W. E. 1980. Behavioral and stimulant treatment of hyperactive children: A therapy study with methylphenidate probes in a within subject design. *Journal of Applied Behavioral Analysis* 13:221–36.

Phelps, L. A. 1978. Vocational education for special needs learners: Past, present, and future. *School Psychology Digest* 7:18–34.

Piaget, J. 1953. How children form mathematical concepts. *Scientific American* 189:2–6.

Piontkowski, D., and Calfee, R. 1979. Attention in the classroom. In *Attention and cognitive development,* eds. G. A. Hale and M. Lewis. New York: Plenum Press.

Pitassi, T. D., and Offenbach, S. I. 1978. Delay of reinforcement effects with reflective and impulsive children. *Journal of Genetic Psychology* 133(1):3–8.

Polloway, E. A.; Patton, J. R.; and Cohen, S. B. 1981. Written language for mildly handicapped students. *Focus on Exceptional Children* 14(3):1–16.

Poplin, M. S. 1979. Science of curriculum development applied to special education and the IEP. *Focus on Exceptional Children* 12:1–16.

Porter, M. E. 1980. Effect of vocational instruction on academic achievement. *Exceptional Child* 46:463–64.

Poteet, J. A. 1980. Informal assessment of written expression. *Learning Disability Quarterly* 3(4):88–98.

Premack, D. 1959. Toward empirical behavior laws: I. Positive reinforcement. *Psychological Review* 66:219–33.

Prieto, A. G., and Rutherford, R. B. 1977. An ecological assessment technique for behaviorally disordered and learning disabled children. In *Behavior*

Disorders, ed. A. H. Fink. Lancaster, Penn.: Lancaster Press.

Public Law 94–142. *Education for all handicapped children act*. 29 November 1975.

Quay, H. C. 1978. Behavior disorders in the classroom. *Journal of Research and Development in Education* 11:8–17.

Quay, H. C., and Peterson, D. R. 1983. *Revised manual for the behavior problem checklist*. Champaign, Ill.: Children's Research Center.

Radatz, H. 1979. Error analysis in mathematics education. *Journal for Research in Mathematics Education* 79:163–72.

Razeghi, J. A., and Davis, S. 1979. Federal mandates for the handicapped: Vocational education opportunity and employment. *Exceptional Children* 45:353–59.

Redl, F. 1959. The concept of the life-space interview. *American Journal of Orthopsychiatry* 29:1–18.

Reger, R. 1972. Resource rooms: Change agents or guardians of the status quo? *The Journal of Special Education* 6:355–59.

Reger, R. 1979. Learning disabilities: Futile attempts at a simplistic definition. *Journal of Learning Disabilities* 12:529–32.

Reid, D. K. 1979. Some suggested strategies for teaching children with memory deficits. *Special Education '79*. Ontario, Canada: York University Press.

Reid, D., and Hresko, W. 1981. *A cognitive approach to learning disabilities*. New York: McGraw-Hill.

Reid, D. K., and Hresko, W. P. 1980. Thinking about thinking about it that way: Test data and instruction. *Exceptional Education Quarterly* 1(3):47–57.

Rhodes, W. C. 1967. The disturbing child: A problem of ecological management. *Exceptional Children* 33:449–55.

Rhodes, W. C. 1970. Community participation analysis of emotional disturbance. *Exceptional Children* 36:309–14.

Rigney, J. 1978. Learning strategies: A theoretical perspective. In *Learning strategies*, ed. H. F. O'Neil, Jr. New York: Academic Press.

Robinson, N. M., and Robinson, H. B. 1976. *The mentally retarded child*. 2d ed. New York: McGraw-Hill.

Rogers, D. C.; Ort, L. L.; and Serra, M. C. 1970. *Word book*. Chicago: Lyons Y. Carhahan.

Rohwer, W. D., and Dempster, F. N. 1977. Memory development and educational processes. In *Perspectives on the development of memory and cognition*, eds. R. V. Kail and J. W. Hagan. Hillsdale, N.J.: Lawrence Erlbaum Associates.

Roper, D. 1977. Parents as the natural enemy of the school system. *Phi Delta Kappan* 59(4):239–42.

Ross, A. O. 1976. *Psychological aspects of learning disabilities and reading disorders*. New York: McGraw-Hill.

Ross, M. 1978. Mainstreaming: Some social considerations. *The Volta Review*, 80(1):21–30.

Rothschild, I. N. 1982. Spelling instruction for the dyslexic child. *Academic Therapy* 17:395–400.

Rowe, M. B. 1978. *Teaching science as continuous inquiry: A basic*. New York: McGraw-Hill.

Ruben, R., and Balow, B. 1971. Learning and behavior disorders: A longitudinal study. *Exceptional Children* 38:293–99.

Rucker, C. N., and Vautour, J. A. 1978. Don't forget the regular classroom teacher. In *Periscope: Views of the individualized education program*, ed. B. B. Weiner. Reston, Va.: Council for Exceptional Children.

Rudel, R. 1977. Neuropsychology and reading. Televised discussion on *Sunrise Semester: Teaching the Learning Disabled*. CBS-TV, February.

Ruder, K.; Hermann, P.; and Schiefelbusch, R. 1977. Effects of verbal imitation and comprehension training on verbal production. *Journal of Psycholinguistic Research* 6(1):59–72.

Ryor, J. 1978. 94–142: The perspective of regular education. *Learning Disability Quarterly* 1(2):6–14.

Safford, P. 1978. *Teaching young children with special needs*. St. Louis, Mo.: C. V. Mosby.

Salvia, J., and Ysseldyke, J. E. 1981. *Assessment in special and remedial education*. 2d ed. Boston: Houghton Mifflin.

Samuels, J. S. 1979. An outside view of the neuropsychological testing. *Journal of Special Education* 13:56–60.

Saunders, R. E. 1962. Dyslexia: Its phenomenology. In *Reading disability: Progress and research needs in dyslexia*, ed. J. Money. Baltimore: Johns Hopkins Press.

Schiefelbusch, R., ed. 1978. *Basis of language intervention*. Baltimore: Univeristy Park Press.

Schmerler, F. M. 1976. *Schmerler reading program*. St. Paul, Minn.: EMC.

Scholastic action. 1970. New York: Scholastic Book Services.

Schoolfield, L. D., and Timberlake, J. B. 1974. *The phonovisual method*. rev. ed. Rockville, Md.: Phonovisual Products.

Semel, E., and Wiig, E. 1980. *Clinical evaluation of language functions*. Columbus, Ohio: Charles E. Merrill.

Sherman, A. R. 1973. *Behavior modification: Theory and practice*. Belmont, Calif.: Wadsworth Publishing.

Silberman, C. E. 1970. *Crisis in the classroom*. New York: Random House.

Silverman, R.; Zigmond, N.; and Sansone, J. 1981. Teaching coping skills to adolescents with learning problems. *Focus on Exceptional Children* 13(6):1–20.

Silverstein, S. 1974. *Where the sidewalk ends: The poems and drawings of Shel Silverstein*. New York: Harper & Row.

Simon, S. B.; Howe, L. W.; and Kirschenbaum, H. 1972. *Values clarification: A handbook of practical strategies for teachers and students*. New York: Hart.

SIMS reading and spelling program. 1978. 3d ed. Minneapolis: Minneapolis Public Schools.

Sinclair, H. 1975. The role of cognitive structures in language acquisition. In *Foundations of language development*, eds. E. H. Lenneberg and E. Lenneberg. New York: Academic Press.

Singer vocational evaluation. n.d. Rochester, N.Y.: Singer Education Division/Career Systems.

Sitlington, P. L. 1979. Vocational assessment and training of the handicapped. *Focus on Exceptional Children* 12(4):1–11.

Skinner, B. F. 1953. *Science and human behavior*. New York: Free Press.

Slingerland, B. H. 1974. *A multi-sensory approach to language arts for specific language disability children*. Cambridge, Mass.: Educators Publishing Service.

Smith, F. 1973. *Psycholinguistics and reading*. New York: Holt, Rinehart and Winston.

Smith, M. J. 1975. *When I say no I feel guilty*. New York: Dial Press.

Smith, R. M. 1974. *Clinical teaching methods of instruction for the retarded*. 2d ed. New York: McGraw-Hill.

Solnick, J. V.; Rincover, A.; and Peterson, C. R. 1977. Some determinants of reinforcement and punishing effects of timeout. *Journal of Applied Behavior Analysis* 70(3):415–24.

South Carolina Region V Educational Services Center, 1977. *Mainstreaming the learning disabled adolescent: A staff guide*. Lancaster, SC.

Speece, D. L., and Mandell, C. J. 1980. An analysis of resource room support services for regular teachers. *Learning Disability Quarterly* 3:49–53.

Spivack, G., and Spotts, J. 1966. *Devereux child behavior rating scale*. Devon, Pa.: Devereux Foundation.

Spivack, G.; Spotts, J.; and Haimes, P. E. 1967. *Devereux adolescent behavior rating scale*. Devon, Pa.: Devereux Foundation.

Spivack, G., and Swift, M. 1967. *Devereux elementary school behavior rating scale*. Devon, Pa.: Devereux Foundation.

Stainback, S., and Stainback, W. 1980. Some trends in the education of children labelled behaviorally disordered. *Behavioral Disorders* 5(4):240–49.

Stallings, J. A., and Kaskowitz, D. H. 1974. *Follow-through classroom observation evaluation*. Menlo Park, Calif.: Stanford Research Institute.

Stauffer, R. G. 1975. *Directing the reading thinking process*. New York: Harper & Row.

Stephens, T. M. 1977. *Teaching skills to children with learning and behavior disorders*. Columbus, Ohio: Charles E. Merrill.

Stephens, T. M. 1978. *Social skills in the classroom*. Columbus, Ohio: Cedars Press.

Stephens, T. M.; Hartman, A. C.; and Lucas, V. H. 1978. *Teaching children basic skills: A curriculum handbook*. Columbus, Ohio: Charles E. Merrill.

Stephenson, W. 1953. *The study of behavior: Q-Technique and its methodology*. Chicago, Ill.: University of Chicago Press.

Stern, C. 1965. *Structural arithmetic*. Boston: Houghton Mifflin.

Stewart, J. C. 1978. *Counseling parents of exceptional children*. Columbus, Ohio: Charles E. Merrill.

Stowitschek, C. E., and Jobes, N. K. 1977. Getting the bugs out of spelling—or an alternative to the spelling bee. *Teaching Exceptional Children* 9(3):1974–76.

Strauss, A. A., and Lehtinen, L. E. 1951. *Psychopathology and education of the brain-injured child*. New York: Grune & Stratton.

Strickland, R. 1961. Evaluating children's compositions. In *Children's writing: Research in composition and related skills*, ed. A. Burrows. Champaign, Ill.: National Council of Teachers of English.

Superka, D. P.; Ahrens, C.; Hedstrom, J. E.; Ford, L. J.; and Johnson, P. L. 1976. *Values education sourcebook: Conceptual approaches, materials analyses, and an annotated bibliography*. Boulder, Colo.: Social Science Education Consortium.

Switzer, E. B.; Deal, T. E.; and Bailey, J. S. 1977. The reduction of stealing in second graders using group contingency. *Journal of Applied Behavior Analysis* 2:267–72.

Tarpley, B. S., and Saudargas, R. A. 1981. An intervention for a withdrawn child based on teacher recorded levels of social interaction. *School Psychology Review* 10:409–12.

Tarver, S. G., and Hallahan, D. P. 1974. Attention deficits in children with learning disabilities: A review. *Journal of Learning Disabilities* 9:560–69.

Tarver, S. G.; Hallahan, D. P.; Kauffman, J. M.; and Ball, D. W. 1976. Verbal rehearsal and selective attention in children with learning disabilities: A developmental log. *Journal of Experimental Child Psychology* 22:375–85.

Taylor, J.; Terrell, F.; and Terrell, S. 1981. Effects of type of reinforcement on the intelligence test performance of black children. *Psychology in the Schools* 18:225–27.

Taylor, W. 1953. Cloze procedure: A new tool for measuring readability. *Journalism Quarterly* 30:415–33.

Thomas, E. D., and Marshall, M. L. 1977. Clinical evaluation and coordination of services: An ecological model. *Exceptional Children* 44(1):16–22.

Thurman, S. K. 1977. Congruence of behavioral ecologies: A model for special education programming. *Journal of Special Education* 11:329–33.

Tiedt, I. M. 1975. Input. *Elementary English* 52:163–64.

Torgesen, J. K. 1979. Factors related to poor performance on memory tasks in reading disabled children. *Learning Disability Quarterly* 2:17–23.

Torgesen, J. K. 1980. Conceptual and educational implications of the use of efficient task strategies by learning disabled children. *Journal of Learning Disabilities* 7:364–71.

Traub, N., and Bloom, F. 1970. *Recipe for reading.* Cambridge, Mass.: Educators Publishing Serivce.

U.S. Department of Labor. 1970. *Manual for the USES nonreading aptitude test battery.* Washington, D.C.: U.S. Government Printing Office.

Van der Veen, F., and Novak, A. C. 1974. The family concept of the disturbed child. *American Journal of Orthopsychiatry.* 44:763–72.

Vocational information and evaluation work sample (VIEWS). n.d. Philadelphia, Pa.: Vocational Research Institute.

Von Isser, A.; Quay, H. C.; and Love, C. T. 1980. Interrelationships among three measures of deviant behavior. *Exceptional Children* 46:272–76.

Vos, K. E. 1976. The effects of three instructional strategies on problem-solving behavior in secondary school mathematics. *Journal for Research in Mathematics Education* 7:265–75.

Vrana, F., and Pihl, R. O. 1980. Selective attention deficit in learning disabled children: A cognitive interpretation. *Journal of Learning Disabilities* 13:387–91.

Walker, F. E., and Shea, T. M. 1980. *Behavior modification: A practical approach for educators.* St. Louis, Mo.: C. V. Mosby Co.

Wallace, G., and Larsen, S. C. 1978. *Educational assessment of learning problems: Testing for teaching.* Boston: Allyn & Bacon.

Wehman, P., and McLaughlin, P. J. 1980. *Vocational curriculum for developmentally disabled persons.* Baltimore: University Park Press.

Wehman, P.; Schutz, R.; Bates, P.; Renzaglia, A.; and Karan, O. 1978. Self-reinforcement programs for mentally retarded workers: Implications for developing independent vocational behavior. *British Journal of Social and Clinical Psychology* 17:183–97.

Weiner, B. 1979. A theory of motivation for some classroom experiences. *Journal of Educational Psychology* 71:3–25.

Weinstein, C. E. 1978. Elaboration skills as a learning strategy. In *Learning strategies,* ed. H. F. O'Neil, Jr. New York: Academic Press.

Weisenstein, G. R. 1977. Vocational education's contribution in the career development of retarded individuals. *Education and Training of the Mentally Retarded* 12:158–60.

Weiss, C., and Lillywhite, H. 1976. *Communication disorders: A handbook for prevention and early intervention.* St. Louis, Mo.: C. V. Mosby.

Westling, D. L.; Koorland, M. A.; and Rose, T. L. 1981. Characteristics of superior and average special education teachers. *Exceptional Children* 47(5):357–63.

White, M. J., and Snyder, J. J. 1981. Covert self-instruction among delinquent adolescents: Getting them to stop and think before they act. *Resources in Education* 9:127–34.

Wiederholt, J. L. 1974. Planning resource rooms for the mildly handicapped. *Focus on Exceptional Children* 5:1–10.

Wiederholt, J. L. 1978. Adolescents with learning disabilities: The problem in perspective. In *Teaching the learning disabled adolescent,* eds. L. Mann, L. Goodman, and J. L. Wiederholt. Boston: Houghton Mifflin.

Wiederholt, J. L.; Hammill, D. D.; and Brown, V. L. 1978. *The resource teacher.* Boston: Allyn & Bacon.

Wiig, E., and Semel, E. 1976. *Language disabilities in children and adolescents.* Columbus, Ohio: Charles E. Merrill.

Wiig, E. H., and Semel, E. M. 1980. *Language assessment and intervention for the learning disabled.* Columbus, Ohio: Charles E. Merrill.

Wilbur, R. 1976. The linguistics of manual systems and manual sign languages. In *Communication assessment and intervention strategies,* ed. L. Lloyd. Baltimore: University Park Press.

Wilkinson, L., and Dollaghan, C. 1979. Peer communication in first grade reading groups. *Theory into Practice* 18(4)267–74.

Williams, E. P. 1977. Steps toward an ecobehavioral technology. In *Ecological perspective in behavior analysis,* eds. A. Rogers-Warren and S. F. Warren. Baltimore: University Park Press.

Wittrock, M. C. 1978. The cognitive movement in instruction. *Educational Psychologist* 13:15–29.

Wong, B. 1979. Research and educational implications of some recent conceptualizations in learning disabilities. *Learning Disability Quarterly* 2:63–68.

Wood, B. 1976. *Children and communication: Verbal and nonverbal language development.* Englewood Cliffs, N.J.: Prentice-Hall.

Woodcock, R. W. 1973. *Woodcock reading mastery tests.* Circle Pines, Minn.: American Guidance Service.

Woodcock, R. W.; Clark, C. R.; and Davies, C. O. 1979. *Peabody rebus reading program.* Circle Pines, Minn.: American Guidance Service.

Youngs, B. B. 1978. Anxiety and stress—How they affect teachers' teaching. *NASSP Bulletin* 62(42):78–83.

Ysseldyke, J. E.; Regan, R.; Thurlow, M.; and Schwartz, S. 1981. Current assessment practices: The "cattle dip" approach. *Diagnostique* 7(2):16–27.

Zaner-Bloser Evaluation Scales. 1979. Columbus, Ohio: Zaner-Bloser.

Zelniker, T., and Jeffrey, W. E. 1976. Reflective and impulsive children: Strategies of information processing underlying differences in problem solving. *Monographs of the Society for Research in Child Development* 41(5, Serial No. 168).

Zelniker, T., and Jeffrey, W. E. 1979. Attention and cognitive style in children. In *Attention and cognitive development,* eds. G. A. Hale and M. Lewis. New York: Plenum Press.

Zigmond, N.; Silverman, R.; and Laurie, T. 1978. Competencies for teachers. In *Teaching the learning disabled adolescent,* eds. L. Mann, L. Goodman, and J. L. Wiederholt. Boston: Houghton Mifflin.

Zigmond, N.; Vallecorsa, A.; and Silverman, R. 1983. *Assessment for instructional planning in special education.* Englewood Cliffs, N.J.: Prentice-Hall.

Glossary Terms

Adaptive behavior A concept that refers to a person's ability to adjust to the environment by displaying adequate levels of independence and responsibility in daily life. Along with intelligence, adaptive behavior is now considered to be a major criterion for defining mental retardation.

Advance organizers A teaching strategy designed to help students organize and structure their learning. The focus of this technique is on the processes the learner is to use.

Anecdotal report A precisely written narrative of an observation of a student's behavior.

Assessment Educationally, the process used by professionals to obtain information about students' instructional needs.

Behavior disordered Behavior deviates from a normal range, occurs over an extended period of time, and is extreme in terms of intensity and frequency.

Behavioral objectives Precise measurable statements of what a student is expected to achieve, including the conditions under which the student will achieve, and the criteria for measuring the achievement.

Broken record A communication strategy in which an individual states and restates his or her goal without tones of anger or frustration as many times as necessary to attain the goal.

Career training Training in areas related to successful performance in finding and maintaining a satisfactory career. Career training is broader in concept than vocational training and includes such areas as job exploration, decision making, job seeking, good work habits, and training for a specific type of employment.

Child-centered pathology model An approach to understanding and remediating learning and behavior problems that attributes such problems to some type of dysfunction within the student. Intervention efforts based on this approach tend to overlook the possible influence of environmental variables.

Cognitive behavior modification An instructional approach to modifying a child's behavior through the use of self-verbalizations.

Cognitive style Individual variation in ways of perceiving, remembering, and thinking.

Conceptual tempo A consistent tendency to display slow or fast response times in stressful situations with high response uncertainty.

Conduct disorders Behaviors that differ from expectations set by the school or other social institutions, and are clearly aversive to others.

Consultant model An approach to meeting the special instructional needs of handicapped students in which the special educator provides diagnostic and other support services to the regular educator.

Contingency contract An instructional technique involving a written agreement between the teacher and student which implies that a desirable event can be earned in exchange for performance of a less desirable behavior.

Control Refers to the act or power of controlling. As a causal attribution dimension, control concerns whether or not it is within the person's power to effect change.

Criterion-referenced tests Tests designed to compare an individual's performance or skill level with material to be mastered.

Distortions An articulation disorder represented by a muffled or slushy quality to the correct pronunciation.

Distractibility Tendency to attend to irrelevant instead of relevant features of stimuli.

Dyslexia Full or partial inability to read. Pupils with this problem are often classified under the broader category of learning disabilities.

Ecological theory An approach to psychology and education that perceives a child's academic and social behavior to be influenced by all the factors in the environment; this approach emphasizes factors external to the child rather than internal.

Ecosystem A system of relationships affecting the experience and behavior of an individual. An individual's ecosystem is a composite of physical and social habitats in which that person lives.

Educable mentally retarded The term used by educators to refer to pupils with a mild level of intellectual retardation (usually defined as functioning within an IQ range of 50–75 with concurrent below normal adaptive behavior).

Educationally handicapped students Children and youth who have consistently experienced failure in the traditional learning environment. Such students are often labeled as learning disabled (LD), behavior disordered (BD), or educable mentally retarded (EMR).

Elaboration errors Mistakes made in the process of working through a problem.

Emotionally disturbed As defined in P.L. 94–142, it refers to a condition exhibiting one or more of the following characteristics over a long period of time and to a marked degree, which adversely affects educational performance: (a) an inability to learn which cannot be explained by intellectual, sensory or health factors; (b) an inability to build or maintain satisfactory interpersonal relationships; (c) inappropriate types of behavior or feelings under normal circumstances; (d) a general pervasive mood of unhappiness or depression; or (e) a tendency to develop physical symptoms or fears associated with personal or school problems. The term does not include children who are schizophrenic or autistic.

Encoding Giving organization and meaning to stimuli.

Error analysis A series of steps to follow in identifying the student's errors, including scoring the assignments, categorizing the error, searching for a pattern, summarizing the types of errors, and hypothesizing why the errors were made.

Expansion A language development technique in which new words and concepts are added to what a child says.

Expressive language The ability to encode language and present it in an oral, written, or gestural form.

Fading A behavioral technique involving a gradual reduction of reinforcement, appropriate in situations where the student's skill for self-control has increased.

Fogging The ability to agree in principle with the truth or logical criticism while still maintaining a seemingly contradictory position.

Free information A communication strategy designed to encourage further conversation by introducing new information.

Group meetings Meetings designed to provide participants the opportunity for discussing topics or issues of interest to the entire group.

Imitation A language-development technique in which children repeat words and language structures they are presently learning. Imitation, as a language-development technique, does not mean that a child repeats exactly what someone else says.

Inadequacy-immaturity Consists of behaviors that are developmentally unexpected, including short attention span, excessive giggling, and clumsiness.

Individualized Educational Plan (IEP) A major requirement of P.L. 94–142; requires a plan of instruction to be written by an educational team to include the following information: (1) statement of the child's current level of educational achievement; (2) annual goals; (3) short-term objectives; (4) specific services required for the child to be educated; (5) dates when the services will begin; and (6) methods for evaluating the effectiveness of the planned services.

Informal assessment Identifying an individual's strengths and weaknesses in relation to mastery of content. Informal assessment procedures compare a student's performance with material or content to be mastered instead of comparing a student's performance with a norm group. Teachers generally use informal, versus formal, assessment procedures for planning instruction.

Input errors Errors that occur when a student does not scan or attend to all the critical details of the content, or when a student is receiving too much information at a time.

Instructional objectives Precise statements describing expected student behaviors following instruction.

Labeling A language development technique involving the use of names for actions, things, or feelings.

Language experience method An approach to reading instruction that integrates the use of oral and written expression skills with reading skills. This method usually consists of having students write or tell stories about themselves and their personal experiences.

Learning centers A set of activities or games which allows students to explore a particular skill area.

Learning disabled Refers to (a) children whose learning problems are not due to mental retardation or to environmental, cultural, or economic disadvantage; (b) children who have difficulty in understanding or using spoken or written language; and (c) children demonstrating a significant discrepancy between their learning potential and actual achievement.

Learning disabilities A disorder in one or more of the basic psychological processes involved in understanding or using spoken or written language. Such a disability may manifest itself in an imperfect ability to listen, think, speak, read, write, spell, or do mathematical calculations.

Life-space interviewing An approach to talking with students about their behavior in a therapeutic manner for the purpose of promoting personal and social development. The teacher using this approach assumes an active listening, uncritical role and encourages the student to find an acceptable solution to the problem.

Locus An individual's perceptions of the extent to which they can control their own environment. Persons with an *internal* locus believe that outcomes are related to their own actions. Persons with an *external* locus believe that outcomes are caused by events in the environment.

Mastery learning Learning that has occurred when a student has reached a specified performance criteria determined acceptable by the teacher.

Modeling A language development technique in which individuals interacting with the child demonstrate appropriate language behaviors.

Morphology That aspect of language dealing with the smallest meaningful units of language, called morphemes. Examples of morphemes include: *un*, *ing*, and *come*.

Motivation A student's affect or emotional response to a problem situation which in turn influences how that problem will be viewed and solved.

Negative inquiry A communication technique in which one inquires about implied or direct criticism.

Nonfunctional group role A style or posture assumed by a group member, either consciously or subconsciously, that serves as a barrier to effective team functioning.

Observation An assessment technique used to analyze a student's academic and social behaviors. This technique is often used to determine not only the frequency of a particular problem, but also to identify a possible pattern or cause for the problem behavior. Observation can also be used to measure change in behavior over time.

Omissions As an articulation disorder, refers to an incomplete pronunciation of words (e.g. "ookie" for "cookie").

Output errors Errors that occur when a student is expressing the answer.

Overcorrection A type of punishment sometimes used to reduce inappropriate behaviors. With overcorrection, students are required to make restitution for their unacceptable behaviors. Overcorrection may also mean that a student is required to practice a competing behavior following emittance of an inappropriate behavior.

Overlearning Practicing a skill beyond the point of mastery so that a student will retain it.

Overviews A teaching strategy in which important terms, concepts, and principles are presented in an outline-type format before instruction.

Personality disorders As defined in the field of education, refers to a condition characterized by social withdrawal, sensitivity, an inability to have fun, chronic sadness, and other behavior having a negative impact on the child.

Phonology The system of sounds used in a language.

Pragmatics Linguistically, the component of language dealing with the rules governing its use in meaningful context.

Pretest A set of questions that are directly related to instructional material to be presented. Pretests can be used to determine students' preknowledge and to alert students to important points that will be made during instruction.

Prompting Deliberately arranging variables within the environment to encourage or prompt students to practice a new behavior.

Punishment As related to behavioral principles, an aversive consequence which follows and causes a decrease in the frequency of a specific behavior.

Q-Sort technique An assessment technique designed to help individuals identify discrepancies between themselves as they really are and themselves as they would like to be. Special educators sometimes use this technique to determine targets for behavioral intervention.

Receptive language The ability to receive and understand transmitted language.

Reinforcer As related to behavioral principles, an event which follows a behavior and increases the frequency of that behavior.

Resource model An approach to special education in which handicapped students receive part of their instruction from a special teacher in a resource room, with the remainder of the students' needs being met in a regular class setting.

Response-cost A form of punishment requiring individuals to pay for certain unacceptable behaviors with something of value. Tokens, which can be redeemed for desired objects or activities, are often used by special educators using a response-cost strategy. Students are required to forfeit such tokens if they engage in certain unacceptable behaviors, such as fighting or using foul language.

Role playing An instructional strategy sometimes used for developing desired social skills. With this strategy, students act out real-life situations, then discuss and study them.

Selective attention The ability to focus on the relevant features of stimuli; or the ability to sort out relevant from irrelevant stimuli.

Self-disclosure A communication technique that involves offering an opinion.

Semantics One of the major components of language that deals with the underlying meanings expressed by verbal symbols (words) as well as the meanings attached to word relationships, grammatical forms, and constructions in a language.

Shaping An instructional technique involving reinforcement of successive approximations of the target behavior.

Socialized delinquency A condition associated with the behaviors found in delinquent subcultures, including involvement in gang activities, cooperative stealing, and truancy.

Standardized tests Tests designed to compare an individual's performance to a group of individuals with similar characteristics.

Substitutions As an articulation disorder, refers to the replacing of a correct phoneme with an incorrect phoneme (e.g. "tookie" for "cookie").

Sustained attention An educational term referring to alertness toward a task over a period of time.

Syntax That aspect of language dealing with the linguistic rules of word order and the function of words in a sentence.

Task analysis The breaking down of a task into its smallest elements in the proper sequence.

Timeout A technique used by some educators for dealing with unacceptable student behavior. With this technique, students are removed from the immediate environment to one in which visual and auditory stimuli are markedly reduced.

Token system A reward system sometimes used in instructional programs to teach target behaviors. In this system, tokens (items of no intrinsic value) can be accumulated and redeemed for something valued by a student.

Tokens Items having no intrinsic value, but which become valuable in that they can be accumulated and redeemed for something valued by the individual. Poker chips have often been used as tokens which, in an instructional setting, can be redeemed for certain desirable objects or activities such as stickers or a specified amount of free time.

Values clarification A decision-making process designed to help participants understand and accept their behavior and that of others. This technique is sometimes used by secondary special educators to help their students develop social skills necessary for successful integration into the mainstream of regular classroom environment and peer group activities.

Vocational training Educational experiences designed to provide students with an employment skill.

Workable compromise A communication strategy that can be used to resolve issues involving differences of opinion. Use of this strategy avoids infringing on the self respect of either party involved in the discussion.

Work sample analysis An informal assessment technique that seeks to identify a student's procedural errors when attempting a task. The focus of a work sample analysis is on a student's thinking process in attempting the task rather than on the outcome of the student's efforts.

Work-study programs Educational programs for mildly handicapped secondary students in which participants work part-time under the school's supervision and go to school part-time.

Author Index

Subject Index

†